LABORATORY Manual

CHEMISTRY

CBSE Class XII

Author
Saleha Pervez

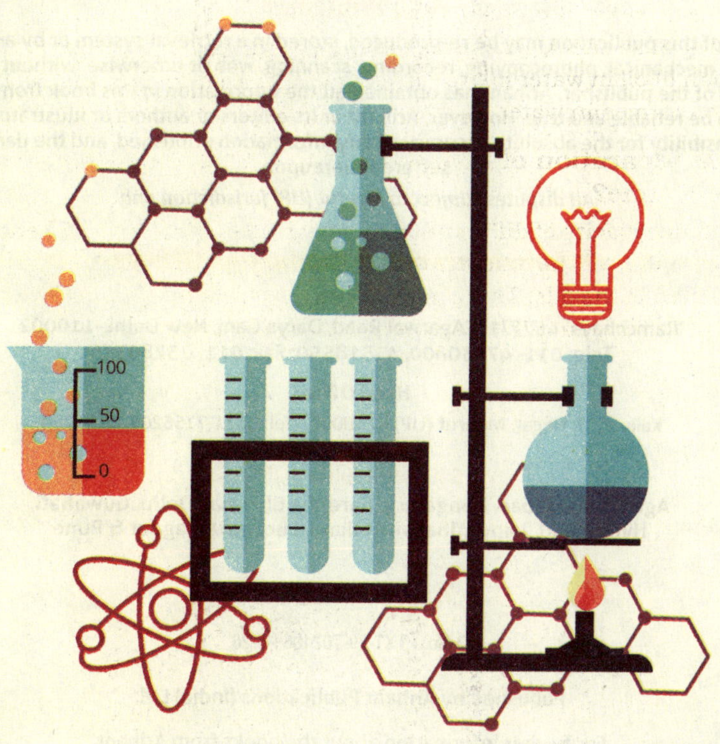

Name...

Class........................ **Section**........................**Roll No**........................

School..

Arihant Prakashan (School Division Series)

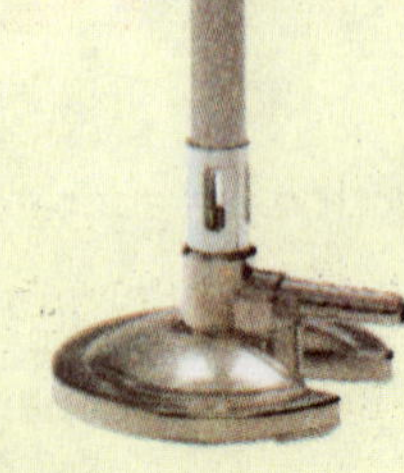

Arihant Prakashan (School Division Series)

卐 Administrative & Production Offices

Regd. Office
'Ramchhaya' 4577/15, Agarwal Road, Darya Ganj, New Delhi -110002
Tele: 011- 47630600, 43518550; Fax: 011- 23280316

Head Office
Kalindi, TP Nagar, Meerut (UP) - 250002, Tel: 0121-7156203, 7156204

卐 Sales & Support Offices
Agra, Ahmedabad, Bengaluru, Bareilly, Chennai, Delhi, Guwahati, Hyderabad, Jaipur, Jhansi, Kolkata, Lucknow, Nagpur & Pune

卐 Price : ₹ 350.00

卐 **PO No.** : TXT-29-T071061-5-26

Published by Arihant Publications (India) Ltd.

For further information about the books from Arihant, log on to **www.arihantbooks.com** or email to **info@arihantbooks.com**

Follow us on   

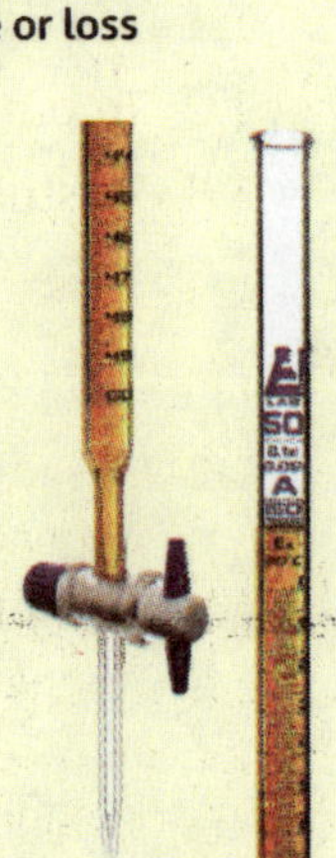

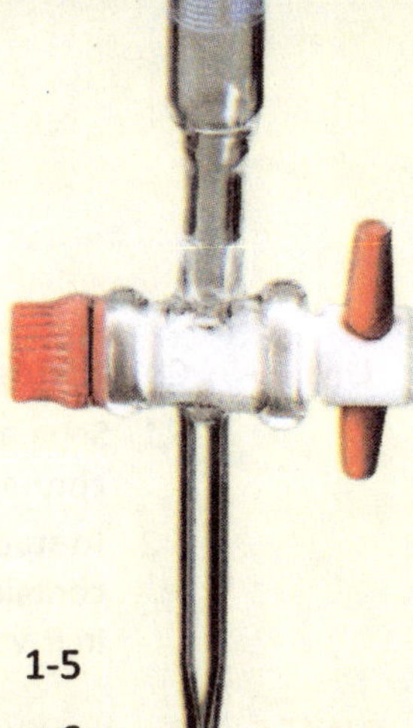

Contents

List of Experiments

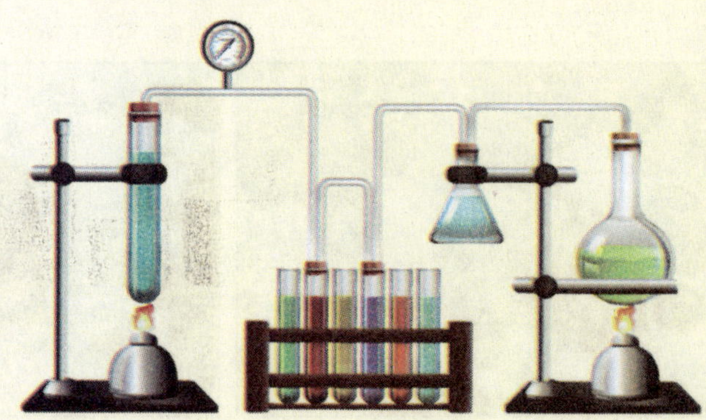

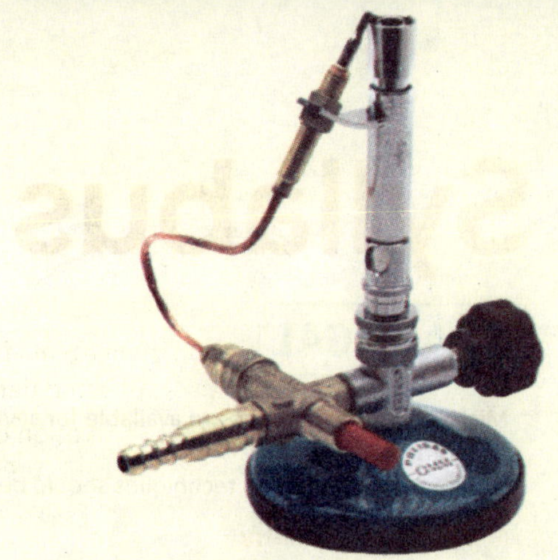

INVESTIGATORY PROJECTS

Syllabus

PRACTICAL

Micro-chemical methods are available for several of the practical experiments.
Wherever possible such techniques should be used.

A. Surface Chemistry

1. Preparation of one lyophilic and one lyophobic sol.
   Lyophilic sol - starch, egg albumin and gum Lyophobic sol - aluminium hydroxide, ferric hydroxide, arsenous sulphide.
2. Dialysis of sol-prepared in *(a)* above.
3. Study of the role of emulsifying agents in stabilising the emulsions of different oils.

B. Chemical Kinetics

1. Effect of concentration and temperature on the rate of reaction between sodium thiosulphate and hydrochloric acid.
2. Study of reaction rates of anyone of the following:
   (i) Reaction of iodide ion with hydrogen peroxide at room temperature using different concentration of iodide ions.
   (ii) Reaction between potassium iodate (KIO_3) and sodium sulphite (Na_2SO_3) using starch solution as indicator (clock reaction).

C. Thermochemistry

Anyone of the following experiments

1. Enthalpy of dissolution of copper sulphate or potassium nitrate.
2. Enthalpy of neutralisation of strong acid (HCl) and strong base (NaOH).
3. Determination of enthalpy change during interaction (hydrogen bond formation) between acetone and chloroform.

D. Electrochemistry

Variation of cell potential of the cell Zn I Zn^{2+} II Cu^{2+} I Cu with change in concentration of electrolytes ($CuSO_4$ or $ZnSO_4$) at room temperature.

E. Chromatography

1. Separation of pigments from extracts of leaves and flowers by paper chromatography and determination of R_f values.
2. Separation of constituents present in an inorganic mixture containing two cations only (constituents having large difference in R_f values to be provided).

F. Preparation of Inorganic Compounds

1. Preparation of double salt of ferrous ammonium sulphate or potash alum.
2. Preparation of potassium ferric oxalate.

G. Preparation of Organic Compounds

Preparation of anyone of the following compounds

1. Acetanilide
2. Dibenzalacetone
3. *p*-nitroacetanilide
4. Aniline yellow or 2-naphthol aniline dye.

H. Tests for the Functional Groups Present in Organic Compounds:

Unsaturation, alcoholic, phenolic, aldehydic, ketonic, carboxylic and amino (primary) groups.

I. Characteristic Tests of Carbohydrates, Fats and Proteins in Pure Samples and their Detection in Given Food Stuffs.

J. Determination of Concentration/ Molarity of $KMnO_4$ Solution by Titrating it Against a Standard Solution of:

1. Oxalic acid,
2. Ferrous ammonium sulphate (Students will be required to prepare standard solutions by weighing themselves).

K. Qualitative Analysis

Determination of one cation and one anion in a given salt.

Anions CO_3^{2-}, S^{2-}, SO_3^{2-}, SO_4^{2-}, NO_2^-, NO_3^-, Cl^-, Br^-, I^-, PO_4^{3-}, $C_2O_4^{2-}$, CH_3COO^- (Insoluble salts excluded)

Cations

Pb^{2+}, Cu^{2+}, As^{3+}, Al^{3+}, Fe^{3+}, Mn^{2+}, Ni^{2+}, Zn^{2+}, Co^{2+}, Ca^{2+}, Sr^{2+}, Ba^{2+}, Mg^{2+}, NH_4^+

PROJECTS

- Study of the presence of oxalate ions in guava fruit at different stages of ripening.
- Study of quantity of casein present in different samples of milk.
- Preparation of soyabean milk and its comparison with the natural milk with respect to curd formation, effect of temperature, etc.
- To study the effect of potassium bisulphate as food preservative under various conditions (temperature, concentration, time, etc.)
- To study of digestion of starch by salivary amylase and effect of pH and temperature on it.
- A comparative study of the rate of fermentation of following materials: wheat flour, gram flour, potato juice, carrot juice, etc.
- Extraction of essential oils present in saunf (aniseed), ajwain (carum), illaichi (cardamom).
- To study the common food adulterants in fat, oil, butter, sugar, turmeric powder, chilli powder and pepper.

Note: Any other investigatory project, which involves about 10 periods of work, can be chosen with the approval of the teacher.

INDEX

S.No.	Name of the Experiments	Page No.	Date	Remarks

INDEX

S.No.	Name of the Experiments	Page No.	Date	Remarks

LABORATORY Manual

CHEMISTRY

CERTIFICATE

This is to certify that Activities &
Projects recorded in this Practical Notebook
have been performed by ____________________
(Student's name)

of __________ of ______________________________
(class/section) (school name)

during academic session ____________________

....

Examiner Signature

....

Principal Signature
(with school stamp)

....

Teacher Signature

Introduction to Laboratory Equipments

Within the laboratory, the students learn about the various techniques used for the identification, preparation, purification and estimation of chemical compounds. In order to start a work in the laboratory, a student must know about the apparatus and chemicals. A student must also know the proper use of each equipment to be used and the precautions to be taken while working in the laboratory and the place from where he/she will get them. A **chemistry laboratory** is provided with the following elements with which the student must become familiar.

1. Demonstration Table

This table is meant for the teacher to give instructions and to demonstrates any part of the experiment to be carried out by the students. The teacher explains the correct procedure which is to be followed and precautions to be taken while performing the experiments.

The students stand around the demonstration table and note the instructions given to them by their teacher.

2. Student's Working Table

A number of concrete or wooden table are provided for the working of students. Each seat is complete in itself and is provided with

(i) **Gas Taps** These are fitted on the working table for supply of LPG to the burners for heating purposes. These must be used carefully and kept tightly closed when not in use.

(ii) **Water Taps and Sinks** For supply of water, a water tap is fixed on each seat and waste liquids are thrown in the sink. Never throw any insoluble solid materials like filter papers, broken glass apparatus, etc., into the sink as these can block the drain.

(iii) **Reagent Shelves** Reagents or chemicals to be used very frequently are kept on these shelves. e.g. HCl, H_2SO_4, HNO_3, NaOH, NH_4OH, etc.

(iv) **Dustbin** It is meant for disposing waste materials like used filter papers, broken apparatus, etc.

3. Side Shelves

Mostly, there are big shelves fitted on the walls of the laboratory. Chemicals and reagents, which are less frequently used are kept in these shelves. e.g. Nessler's reagent, potassium ferricyanide, starch solution, silver nitrate, dimethylglyoxime, etc.

4. Fume Closet or Cupboard

There is atleast one fume closet in the corner of the laboratory. It is a small chamber having a sliding glass wall and a chimney fitted with an exhaust fan at the top. All experiments giving out poisonous gases or vapours are performed in this closet.

5. Balance Room

It is a small room attached to the laboratory. In this, a number of chemical balances are kept for weighing the substances.

6. Exhaust Fans

The exhaust fans are fitted on the upper portion of the wall opposite to the doors. This facilitates the removal of harmful fumes and circulation of fresh air in the laboratory.

Basic Laboratory Equipments used for Different Procedures

Procedures like heating, filtration, decantation, weighing liquids and solids, measuring volumes are used very frequently while doing the experiments in laboratory. To perform these procedures, a student must be aware of the glass apparatus and equipments and should understand the techniques to handle them properly.

The basic laboratory apparatus and their utility in experimentations are listed below :

Name of the Apparatus	Use	Figures
Boiling tube It is similar to the test tube but is of large diameter.	It is used when large volume of solution is required to be heated.	
Beakers These are the cylindrical vessels with a large diameter and are usually made up of pyrex or corning glass. These are available in various sizes, ranging from 5 mL to 2000 mL.	These are used for keeping liquid solution during experimental work and to pour solution from one beaker to another.	250 mL 500 mL
Conical flask It is a hollow glass vessel which is of conical shape and is available in various sizes ranging from 5 mL to 2000 mL, also referred as Erlenmeyer flask.	It is usually used for carrying out volumetric titrations and hence, also called titration flask.	50 mL 250 mL
Round bottom flask It is round glass bottle flask and cannot be placed on the table directly due to its round bottom.	It is used where heating is necessary and in the preparation of organic compounds and gases.	500 mL
Flat bottom flask It is a glass bottle having a flat bottom with a long narrow neck. It can be kept on the table without falling.	It is used for carrying out chemical reactions and distillation processes.	
Measuring flask It is usually made up of borosil/pyrex/corning glass and is of different sizes and volumes like 50 mL, 100 mL, 250 mL or 500 mL. They have long and narrow neck with a flat bottom. At the upper part of the long neck, a mark is engraved upto which the liquid is to be filled.	They are used for making definite volumes of standard solutions.	100 mL 500 mL

Name of the Apparatus	Use	Figures
Distilling flask It is a round bottom flask containing a tube at the cylindrical neck.	It is used in the distillation process.	
Buchner funnel The upper portion of Buchner funnel is cylindrical and lower base has conical shape with a stem pipe like structure. It is made up of porcelain or ceramic.	It is used for filtration.	
Separating funnels These are made up of glass having oval shape at mid. The mouth is wide and has a glass cap stopper. The other end is having a tube fitted with a stopcork. They are of various sizes and shapes.	It is used to separate two immiscible liquids.	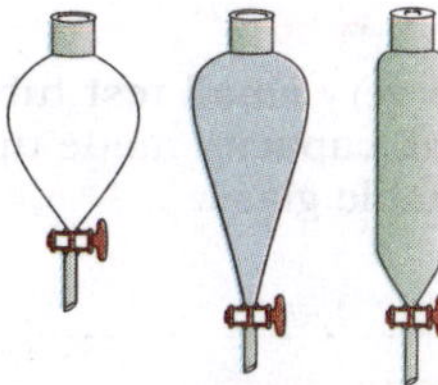
Measuring cylinder It is a cylindrical shaped apparatus with graduated marks. It is made up of glass or plastic and is available in various volumes.	It is used for measuring different volumes of liquids.	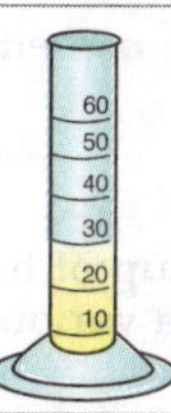
Air condenser It is a long tube having a slightly wide mouth at the end. It is connected to a flask during a reaction where the hot vapour rises up and condenses in colder regions of the tube. The length and diameter of the glass tube vary. There is a rapid transfer of heat from hot vapour to the surrounding air and vapour condenses.	It is used for refluxing and distillation of solutions or liquids with high boiling points.	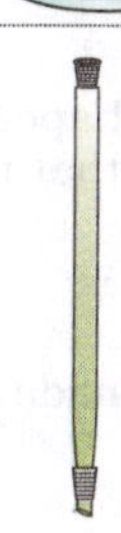
Water condenser It is made up of glass tubes with an inner tube surrounded by an outer jacket with an inlet and an outlet for circulating water. Inlet is connected to the tap. Heat is transferred from hot vapour to the surrounding water.	It is used for refluxing and distillation of solutions of low boiling point.	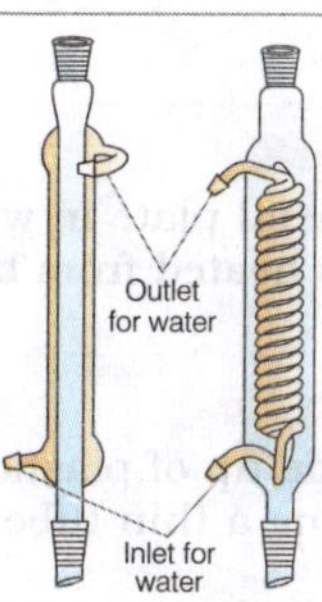
Desiccator It is made up of glass and has two compartments. The lower portion contains a ground tile which is used for placing dehydrating agent such as $CaCl_2$. The substance to be dried is kept at the upper portion of the desiccator.	It is used to remove moisture from a substance.	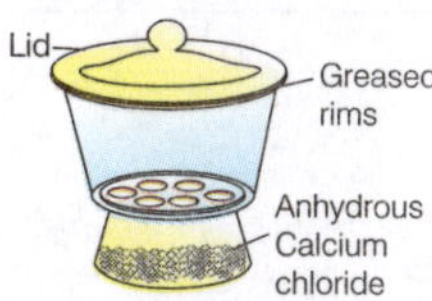

Name of the Apparatus	Use	Figures
Mortar-pestle It is a thick walled vessel with a hemispherical shape with a base. It is made up of porcelain.	It is used for grinding the salts and other substances with the help of pestle.	
Gas jar It is a cylindrical vessel having one side opened.	It is used to collect a gas during their preparation.	
Fusion tube It is a very small test tube of about 1-2 mL capacity made up of easily breakable glass.	It is used for preparing Lassaigne's extract required to test extra elements present in an organic compound.	
Platinum wire A platinum coated wire fitted with a glass rod.	It is used for performing flame test.	
Triangular file It is made up of hard cast iron and are available in various shapes and sizes.	It is used to mark scratch while cutting a glass rod or tube.	
Watch glass It is a curve shaped transparent glass apparatus so that the substance do not fall off.	It is used for crystallisation and mixture analysis.	
Water bath It is a vessel made up of brass having oval shape.	It is used for heating water. Inflammable substance cannot be warmed on a direct flame, thus, heated in a vessel kept on the water bath. Electric water baths are also available in laboratories.	
Sand bath It is a metal plate in which sand is kept and it is heated from below.	Any apparatus that requires uniform heating is kept on a sand bath.	
Wash bottle It is made up of plastic, polythene containing a thin tube.	It is used for washing and rinsing glass apparatus.	

Heating Devices

Heating work in laboratories can be done with the help of a gas burner, spirit lamp or a kerosene lamp.

Bunsen Burner

In chemistry laboratories where gas supply is available, Bunsen burners are used. This burner was devised by Robert Bunsen in 1855.

Various parts of Bunsen burner are described as

- **The Base** The burner rests on a cast iron base. It keeps the burner in a stable upright position. The base has a side tube connected to a gas tap called gas tube.

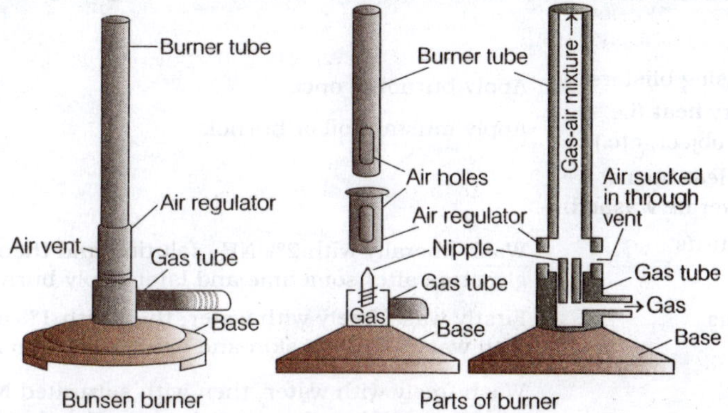

- **The Burner Tube** It is a long metallic tube which has two holes diametrically opposite to each other near the lower end which form the air vent. The tube can be screwed at the base. The gas coming from the nozzle gets mixed with the air coming through the air vent and burns at its upper end.
- **The Air Regulator** It is a short metallic cylindrical sleeve with two holes diametrically opposite to each other. When it is fitted to the burner tube, it surrounds the air vent of the burner tube. In order to control the flow of air through the air vent, size of its hole is adjusted by rotating the sleeve.

Working of Burner

When the burner is connected to the gas supply, the gas escapes through the nozzle and there is a fall of pressure due to which air is sucked through the air holes. The mixture of air and gas burns at the upper end of the burner, producing a flame. The flame can be luminous or non-luminous depending upon the quantity of air mixed. The hottest zone is oxidising flame, called non-luminous zone and is used for heating purposes.

Probable Accidents and their First Aid Treatment

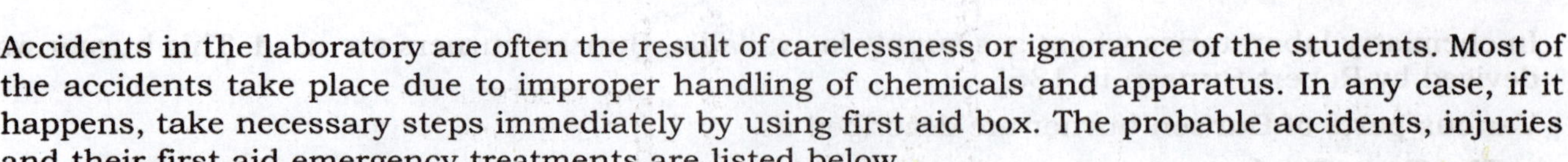

Accidents in the laboratory are often the result of carelessness or ignorance of the students. Most of the accidents take place due to improper handling of chemicals and apparatus. In any case, if it happens, take necessary steps immediately by using first aid box. The probable accidents, injuries and their first aid emergency treatments are listed below

S.No.	Type of accident	First aid emergency treatment
1.	**Burns**	
	(i) Burns causing blisters	Apply burnol at once.
	(ii) Burn by dry heat (i.e. flame, hot object, etc.) **Caution** Heat burns should never be washed.	Apply mustard oil or burnol.
	(iii) Bromine burns	Wash liberally with 2% NH_3 solution and then rub glycerine. Wipe off glycerine after sometime and later apply burnol.
	(iv) Alkali burns	Firstly wash freely with water, then with 1% acetic acid and, then again with water. Dry the skin and apply burnol to it.
	(v) Acid burns	Wash freely with water, then with saturated $NaHCO_3$ solution and again with water. If burning persists, wipe the skin (dry) and apply burnol to it.
2.	**Eye accidents**	
	(i) Alkali in eye	Wash thoroughly with water and then with 1% boric acid solution.
	(ii) Acid in eye	Wash thoroughly with water, afterwards with 1% sodium bicarbonate solution and then with water again.
3.	**Cuts**	
	(i) Minor cuts	Allow to bleed for a few seconds. Remove the glass piece if any. Apply methylated spirit and cover it with a piece of cotton or you can apply $FeCl_3$ solution to stop bleeding.
	(ii) Major cuts	Apply pressure above the cut to stop bleeding. Call the doctor immediately.
4.	**Poisons**	
	(i) Poisons not swallowed	Spit out immediately. Wash mouth with plenty of water.
	(ii) Inhalation of gases like Cl_2, SO_2, Br_2, etc., causing suffocation	Loosen the clothes at the neck. At once go in the open air. Inhale dilute vapours of ammonia or gargle with sodium bicarbonate solution.
	(iii) Acid swallowed	Drink lot of water. Drink lime water. No emetic [a substance causing vomiting] should be taken.
	(iv) Caustic alkalies swallowed	Drink plenty of water. Drink a glass of lemon or orange juice. No emetic should be taken.
5.	**Fire**	
	(i) Beaker containing inflammable liquid catches fire	Immediately cover the beaker with duster or damp cloth.
	(ii) Clothes catch fire	Do not run in hustle. Wrap with a blanket, then lie down on the floor and roll.

Go to the doctor after getting first aid.

HOW TO RECORD AN EXPERIMENT?

A neat and systematic recording of the experiment in the laboratory notebook is very important for keeping an upto date record of the work which has been done in the laboratory.

Infact, a proper record of the experimental results and conclusions is an indispensable part of scientific work. The laboratory notebook must be well maintained and protected from mechanical and chemical damage. It should be made checked regularly by the teacher.

The experiment should be recorded in the laboratory notebook under the following heads as

Date......	Experiment No.	Page No. ......

Aim or Objective of the Experiment *State clearly and precisely the objective of the experiment to be performed.*

Materials Required *Mention the name of the apparatus and chemicals to be used in the experiment clearly.*

Theory or Principle *Mention the concept on which the experiment is based in a very brief manner. Also, write the formula used, clearly explaining the symbols involved.*

Procedure *Mention various steps in the experiment followed with precautions.*

Chemical Reactions *The chemical reactions that takes place in the experiment should be written on the left hand side of the notebook.*

Diagrams *Wherever required, draw the diagrams on the left hand side of the notebook.*

Observations *Record the observations or data in a tabular form as far as possible, neatly and without any overwriting.*

Calculations *[wherever desirable] For writing the calculations, substitute the observed value in the formula and do the computations systematically and neatly.*

Result *State the conclusions drawn from the experimental observations. If the result depends upon the conditions of temperature and pressure, mention these conditions also along with the result.*

Precautions *Mention the precautions observed during the course of setting an apparatus and the steps followed while performing the experiment.*

Discussion *Under this heading mention any special inferences or special difficulties faced during the experimentation.*

These may include points for making the experiment more accurate and for better understanding of the basic principle involved.

Unit 1

Surface Chemistry

Surface chemistry deals with the phenomenon that occurs at the surfaces or interfaces, i.e. at the boundary separating two bulk phases. Some areas of study under surface chemistry are adsorption, catalysis and colloids including emulsions and gels.

Colloidal State of Matter

The term **colloid** refer to that state of matter whose solute particle size lies between 1 to 1000 nm. Thus, colloid is not a substance but is a particular state of the substance which depends upon the size of its particles.

On the other hand, if the size of solute particles is less than 1 nm, then the state of substance refer to **true solutions**.

In a true solution, solute particles mix homogeneously with the molecules of the solvent and thus, form a single phase. However, a colloidal solution is a heterogeneous system in which very fine particles of one substance called **dispersed phase** disperse into another substance called **dispersion medium**.

Colloidal particles are larger in size than simple molecules but small enough to remain suspended in the dispersion medium.

Classification of Colloids

Depending upon whether the dispersed phase and the dispersion medium are solids, liquids or gases, eight types of colloidal systems are known. Out of these, three are most common which are sols (solid dispersed in a liquid), gels (liquids dispersed in a solid) and emulsions (liquid dispersed in a liquid).

Types of Sols

Depending upon the nature of interaction between the dispersed phase and the dispersion medium, colloidal sols are of two types:

Lyophilic Sols (Solvent attracting)

In this type of sols, the particles of dispersed phase have great affinity for the particles of dispersion medium. e.g. egg albumin, starch and gum. In such sols, the dispersed phase does not get precipitated easily.

Therefore, lyophilic sols are highly stable. These sols are directly formed by mixing substances like gum, gelatin, starch, rubber and egg albumin with suitable liquid like water which acts as dispersion medium.

If the dispersion medium of lyophilic sols is separated from the dispersed phase by evaporation, the sol can be reconstituted by simply remixing with the dispersion medium. Hence, lyophilic sols are also called **reversible sols.** If water is dispersion medium, these are called **hydrophilic sols**.

Lyophobic Sols (Solvent repelling)

In this type of sols, the dispersed phase has either a very little or no affinity for the dispersion medium. e.g. freshly prepared ferric hydroxide, aluminium hydroxide and arsenic sulphide sols. These sols are not very much stable. These are readily precipitated (or coagulated) on the addition of small amount of electrolytes by heating or shaking.

Further, once precipitated, they do not give back the colloidal sol by simple addition of (or shaking with) the dispersion medium. Hence, lyophobic sols are called **irreversible sols.** If water is dispersion medium, these are called **hydrophobic sols**. Hence, due to their less stability, these sols are prepared only by special methods (discussed later).

Factors Responsible for the Stability of Sols

Two factors responsible for the stability of sols are charge and the solvation of the colloidal particles by the solvent. Stability of lyophilic sols is primarily due to the solvation of colloidal particles by the solvent whereas lyophobic sols are stabilised by the charge on the colloidal particles.

Due to their charges, colloidal particles remain suspended in the solution and coagulation does not take place. These charges may be positive or negative. Some examples of negatively charged sols are starch and arsenious sulphide. Positively charged sol of hydrated ferric oxide is formed when $FeCl_3$ is added to the excess of hot water and a negatively charged sol of hydrated ferric oxide is formed when ferric chloride is added to NaOH solution.

Purification Of Colloidal Solutions

Colloidal solutions when prepared, generally contain excessive amount of electrolytes and some other soluble impurities. Although the presence of electrolyte is essential for the stability of the colloidal solution but large quantities of electrolytes may coagulate the solution. It is therefore necessary to reduce the concentration of these electrolytes to a requisite amount.

The process used for reducing the amount of impurities to a minimum requisite amount is known as **purification** of colloidal solution.

The purification is carried out by the following methods : dialysis, electrodialysis, etc.

Dialysis

The process of removing electrolytes (ions or molecules) from a colloidal solution by means of diffusion through a suitable semi-permeable membrane is known as dialysis.

Note *The membrane which allows only the molecules of electrolyte to pass through it and not the colloidal particles is called 'semipermeable membrane'.*

This apparatus used for this purpose is called **dialyser**. When a solution containing colloidal particles and molecules of the electrolyte is taken in a parchment or cellophane paper (or membrane) and suspended in a vessel through which fresh water is continuously flowing, the molecules and ions of electrolyte diffuse through membrane into the outer water leaving behind the pure colloidal solution.

Electrodialysis

This process of dialysis is quite slow. It can be made faster by applying an electric field. If the dissolved substance in the impure colloidal solution is only an electrolyte which is removed by applying an electric field around the membrane, then the process is termed as **electrodialysis**.

Emulsions

An emulsion is a type of colloidal solution in which both the dispersed phase and the dispersion medium are liquids and both mediums are distinguished by their relative amounts. The one which is present in smaller proportion is called dispersed phase while the other which is present in relatively large quantity is known as dispersion medium.

Emulsions are of two types:

- **Oil in water emulsion** Here oil acts as dispersed phase and water acts as dispersion medium. e.g. Milk and vanishing cream, etc.
- **Water in oil emulsion** Here, water acts as dispersed phase and oil acts as dispersion medium. e.g. Butter and cream, etc.

The process of making an emulsion is known as **emulsification**. These are obtained by simply vigorously agitating the mixture of both the liquids.

To get a stable emulsion, small quantities of certain other substances are added during their preparation. The substances added to stabilise the emulsions are called **emulsifier** or **emulsifying agents**. For example, long chain compounds with polar groups like soap and detergents, act as emulsifiers. Other example of emulsifiers are agar-agar, egg albumin, gelatin and gum.

Soaps are the sodium or potassium salts of higher fatty acids, like sodium palmitate ($C_{15}H_{31}COONa$), sodium stearate ($C_{17}H_{35}COONa$), etc.

A molecule of soap consists of two parts, the long aliphatic chain ($C_{15}H_{31}$—, $C_{17}H_{35}$ —, etc.) which being non-polar, is soluble in oil and the polar carboxyl group (COO^-Na^+) which is soluble in water.

R	:	COO^-Na^+
Hydrophobic part (Soluble in oil)		Hydrophilic part (Soluble in water)

The droplets of oil are surrounded by soap solution, the *R*-part (hydrocarbon part) of the soap remains in the oil and COO^-Na^+ polar part remains in water.

In this way, the soap molecules concentrate at the oil-water interface and thus, decreases the interfacial surface tension between oil and water.

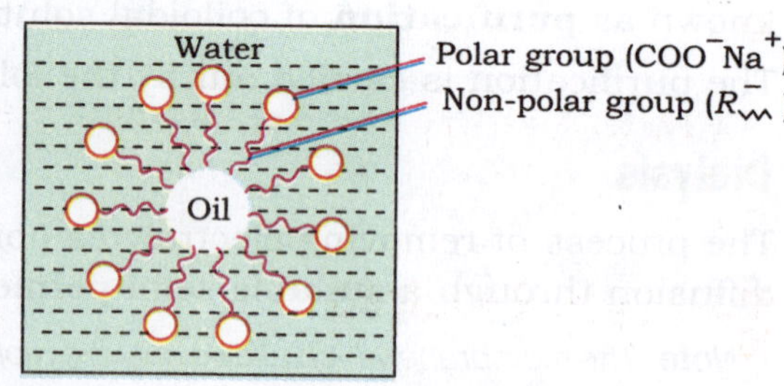

Due to reduced interfacial tension, the tiny droplets of oil do not come together and thus, oil mixes with water. Hence, the emulsions become stable and emulsification takes place. Different emulsifying agents lower the interfacial tension to different extent, so they have different capacities for emulsifying a given oil.

The process of separating the emulsion into its constituent layers is called **demulsification**. The relative stabilities of emulsions can be studied by noting the time taken for the separation of the two liquids.

Experiment 1.1

AIM

To prepare (a) lyophilic sol and (b) lyophobic sol.

Theory/Principle

Preparation of Sols

Lyophilic Sols Starch, gum and egg albumin being lyophilic sols can be easily prepared by simply mixing and shaking the substance with a suitable liquid. These sols are quite stable and are not affected by the presence of electrolytes or other impurities.

Lyophobic Sols Aluminium hydroxide, ferric hydroxide and arsenious sulphide sols being lyophobic sols and cannot be prepared by direct mixing and shaking. Therefore, some special methods are employed to prepare these sols.

Aluminium hydroxide sol is prepared by hydrolysis of aluminium chloride.

$$AlCl_3(aq) + 3H_2O(l) \longrightarrow \underset{\text{Colourless sol}}{Al(OH)_3(s)} + 3HCl(aq)$$

Ferric hydroxide sol is prepared by the hydrolysis of ferric chloride with boiling distilled water.

$$FeCl_3(aq) + 3H_2O(l) \xrightarrow{\text{Boil}} \underset{\text{Red sol}}{Fe(OH)_3(s)} + 3HCl(aq)$$

This hydrolysis reaction produces insoluble ferric hydroxide particles which undergo agglomerisation to yield bigger particles of colloidal dimensions. These particles adsorb Fe^{3+} ions preferentially from the solution to give positive charge to the sol particles. Stability of the sol is due to the charge on the sol particles. Hydrochloric acid which is produced during hydrolysis tends to destabilise the sol and hence, it must be removed from the sol by dialysis.

- Arsenious sulphide, As_2S_3 is obtained by the hydrolysis of arsenious oxide (As_2O_3) with boiling distilled water, followed by passing H_2S gas through the solution obtained.

$$As_2O_3 + 3H_2O \xrightarrow{\text{Boil}} 2As(OH)_3$$

$$2As(OH)_3 + 3H_2S \longrightarrow \underset{\text{Yellow sol}}{As_2S_3} + 6H_2O$$

- In the colloidal solution of arsenious sulphide, each particle is surrounded by HS^- ions produced by the dissociation of H_2S. This sulphide ion layer is further surrounded by the counter ion layer of H^+ ions.

Materials Required

Item		Qty	Item		Qty
Beaker (250 mL)	:	1	Distilled water	:	As per requirement
Watch glass	:	1	Egg	:	1
Porcelain dish	:	1	Sodium chloride (NaCl)	:	5 g
Measuring cylinder (100 mL)	:	1	Ferric chloride ($FeCl_3$)	:	2 g
Pipette (10 mL)	:	1	Aluminium chloride ($AlCl_3$)	:	2 g
Graduated pipette (20 mL)	:	1	Starch/gum	:	500 mg
Tripod stand	:	1	Arsenious oxide	:	0.2 g
Conical Flask (100 mL)	:	1	Glass rod	:	1
Kipp's Apparatus	:	1	Filter paper	:	1
Bunsen Burner	:	1			

Procedure

Lyophilic Sol

A. Egg Albumin Sol

1. Prepare 100 mL of 5% $\left(\frac{w}{V}\right)$ solution of NaCl in water in a beaker of capacity 250 mL.

2. Break one egg in a porcelain dish with the help of glass rod and collect its colourless liquid called **albumin** (yellow yolk is decant off into another beaker of 50 mL) or pour directly egg albumin in sodium chloride solution [Fig. 1.1]. Stir well to ensure that the sol is well prepared.

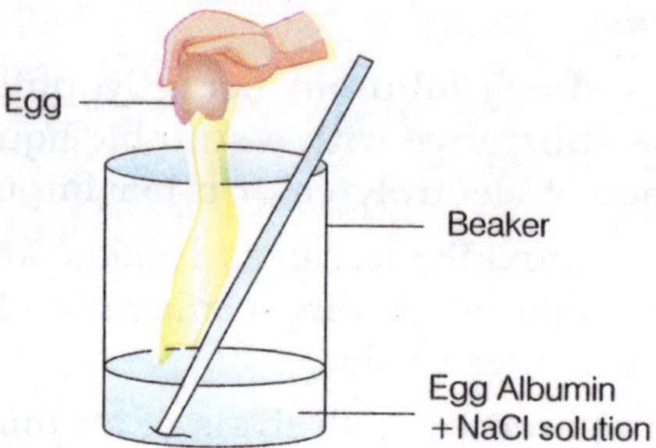

Fig. 1.1 *Dissolving egg albumin in sodium chloride solution.*

B. Starch/Gum Sol

1. Measure 100 mL of distilled water with the help of a measuring cylinder and transfer it to a 250 mL beaker and heat the beaker to boil the water.
2. Make a thin paste of 500 mg starch or gum in hot water [Fig 1.2 (i)] and transfer this paste to 100 mL of boiling water with constant stirring. Continue to keep the water boiling and stirring for 10 min after the addition of paste. [Fig 1.2 (ii)]

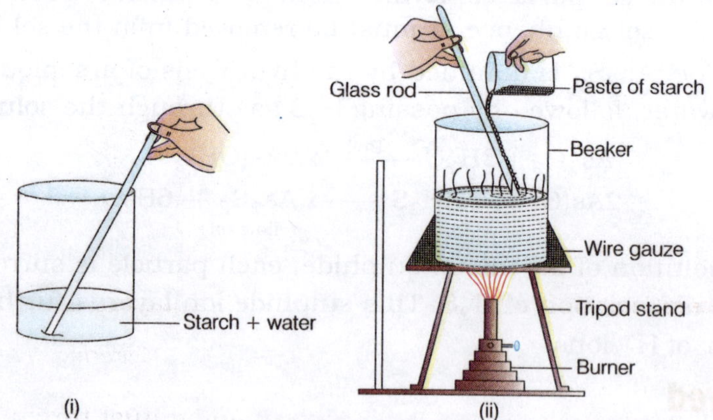

Fig. 1.2 (i) *Dissolving starch in distilled water* (ii) *Preparation of starch solution*

Lyophobic Sol

A. Ferric Hydroxide Sol/Aluminium Hydroxide Sol

1. Take a 250 mL beaker and clean it by steaming out process as shown in Fig 1.3.
2. Take 100 mL of distilled water in a 250 mL beaker and boil it.

> **⚠ ALERT**
>
> *Aluminium chloride is highly corrosive while arsenic compounds are highly toxic, hence, dangerous. Thus, handle these chemicals with great care.*

3. Add 2 g of ferric chloride powder to the boiling water and stir it well with the help of glass rod.
4. Take 100 mL of distilled water in another 250 mL beaker and boil it.
5. Add drop by drop 10 mL of ferric chloride solution, which is already prepared in step (3), into the boiling water with constant stirring. Keep the water boiling till brown sol is obtained.

Note *In the same manner (as detailed in above steps), aluminium hydroxide sol can be prepared by the hydrolysis of aluminium chloride. The colour of aluminium chloride sol is white.*

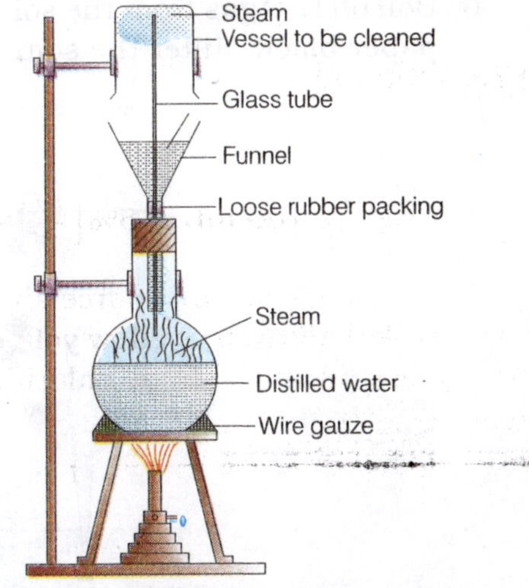

Fig. 1.3 *Steaming out process for cleaning a beaker*

B. Arsenious Sulphide Sol

1. Clean a 250 mL beaker by steaming out process. (as shown in Fig. 1.3)
2. Take 100 mL of distilled water in a 250 mL beaker.
3. Now, add 0.2 g of arsenious oxide (As_2O_3) to it and boil the contents of the beaker [Fig. 1.4]
4. Cool the above solution and filter it through fluted filter paper [Fig. 1.5].

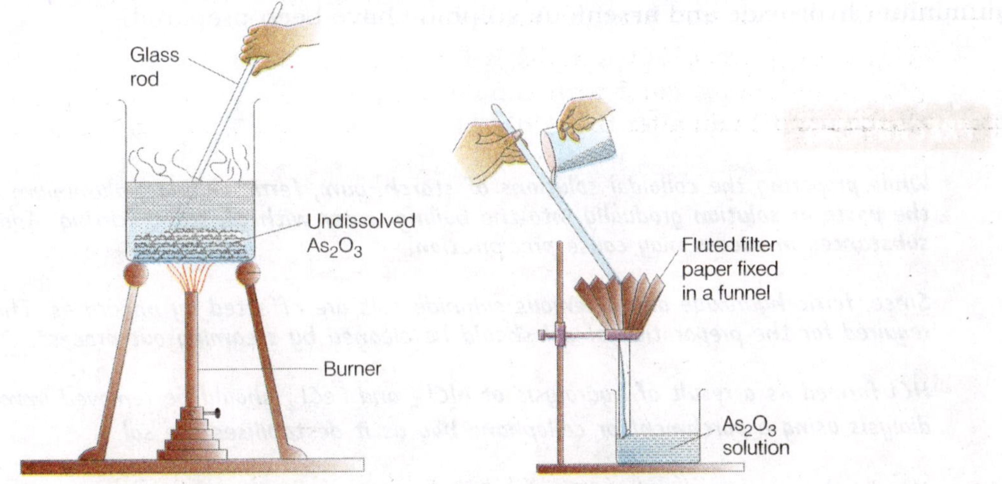

Fig. 1.4 *Dissolving As_2O_3 in boiling water*

Fig. 1.5 *Filtering of As_2O_3 solution*

5. Pass hydrogen sulphide (H_2S) gas (using Kipp's apparatus) through the filtered solution, till it smells of H_2S [Fig 1.6]. A yellow coloured solution is formed due to the formation of arsenious sulphide (As_2S_3) and continue till the intensity of colour does not change further.

6. Boil off H_2S gas from the sol by slow heating till the escaping gas does not turn lead acetate paper black. Filter the solution.

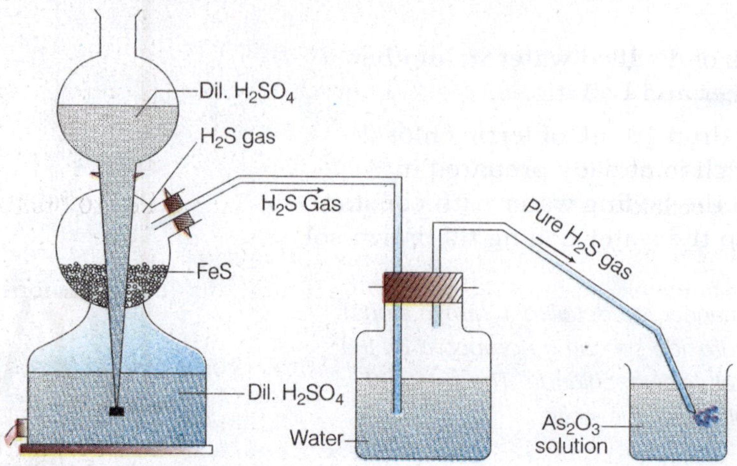

Fig. 1.6 *Preparation of* As_2S_3 *sol*

7. Collect the bright yellow filtrate in a dry conical flask and closed it by a cork. The collected filtrate is arsenious sulphide sol.

Observations

Lyophilic sols of egg albumin and starch or gum, while lyophobic sols of ferric hydroxide or aluminium hydroxide and arsenious sulphide have been prepared.

PRECAUTIONS

- *While preparing the colloidal solutions of starch, gum, ferric chloride, aluminium chloride, etc pour the paste or solution gradually into the boiling water with constant stirring. Addition of these substances in excess may cause precipitation.*
- *Since, ferric hydroxide and arsenious sulphide sols are affected by impurities. The apparatus required for the preparation of sol should be cleaned by steaming out process.*
- *HCl formed as a result of hydrolysis of $AlCl_3$ and $FeCl_3$ should be removed immediately by dialysis using a parchment or cellophane bag as it destabilises the sol.*
- *Handle the arsenious oxide with care since, it is highly poisonous. Wash your hands immediately every time after handling this chemical.*
- *Only diluted solution of arsenious oxide should be used.*
- *Use freshly prepared reagents for better sol formation and use only distilled water to prepare the solution.*
- *While doing the experiment, do not eat, drink or smoke.*

Viva-Voce

Q.1 What is meant by the term colloidal solution?

Ans. A colloidal solution is a solution in which the size of dispersed particles ranges between 1 nm to 1000 nm.

Q.2 What is the diameter of colloidal particles?

Ans. The diameter of colloidal particles varies between (1-1000 nm) i.e., 10^{-9} to 10^{-6} m.

Q.3 Is it possible for gases to form colloidal solutions?

Ans. No, it is not possible for gases to form colloidal solutions because gases form only homogeneous mixture and colloids are heterogeneous in nature.

Q.4 Which sols are more stable — lyophilic or lyophobic?

Ans. Lyophilic sols are more stable.

Q.5 Name one positively charged sol and one negatively charged sol.

Ans. $Fe(OH)_3$ solution is a positively charged sol and As_2S_3 is a negatively charged sol.

Q.6 Why is it advised to use a clean apparatus to prepare colloidal solutions?

Ans. Apparatus when used unclean, they may contain impurities like acidic or basic, which may cause coagulation of the colloidal particles.

Q.7 Why are lyophilic colloidal sols more stable than lyophobic colloidal sols?

Ans. The lyophilic colloidal sols are more stable due to greater force of attraction between the particles of dispersed phase and that of dispersion medium.

Q.8 Why does a colloidal solution coagulate when an electrolyte is added?

Ans. When a colloidal sol is mixed with excess electrolyte particles the ions of opposite charge are attracted to the colloidal particles and the charge on it gets neutralized leading to their coagulation.

Q.9 What happens when a freshly prepared precipitate of $Fe(OH)_3$ is shaken with a small amount of $FeCl_3$ solution?

Ans. Positively charged sol formation takes place due to the preferential adsorption of Fe^{3+} of $FeCl_3$ over $Fe(OH)_3$.

Q.10 Which gas is passed to prepare arsenious sulphide sol?

Ans. Hydrogen sulphide (H_2S) gas.

Q.11 What happens when a positively charged sol like $Fe(OH)_3$ is mixed with As_2S_3?

Ans. As_2S_3 is a negatively charged sol. Thus, on mixing with $Fe(OH)_3$ coagulation takes place.

Q.12 Why should substances be added slowly into boiling water during sol preparation?

Ans. To avoid precipitation, substances should be poured gradually into boiling water with constant stirring.

Q.13 Why is constant stirring necessary while preparing sols?

Ans. The constant stirring prevents precipitation and helps in uniform dispersion.

Q.14 Why should solute not be added all at once during sol preparation?

Ans. Solute should be added slowly with stirring to ensure proper dispersion and avoid precipitation, which can occur if added all at once.

Q.15 Why is it important to wash hands after handling arsenious oxide?

Ans. It is important to wash hands after handling arsenious oxide because it is poisonous and any residue left on the skin can be harmful if accidentally ingested or absorbed.

Questions From NCERT Lab Manual

Q.1 How will you differentiate between a true solution and a colloidal dispersion?

Ans. **True solution** In a true solution, solute particles mix homogeneously with the molecules of the solvent and thus, form a single phase.

Colloidal dispersion A colloidal solution is a heterogeneous system in which very fine particles of one substance called (dispersed phase) disperse in another substance called dispersion medium.

Q.2 Differentiate between a sol and a gel.

Ans. In the sol, solid is dispersed phase and liquid is dispersion medium whereas, in a gel, liquid is dispersed phase and solid is dispersion medium.

Q.3 Out of lyophilic and lyophobic sols, which can be easily converted into gel and why?

Ans. Lyophilic sols can be more easily converted into gel because in them, there is great affinity between dispersed phase and dispersion medium.

Q.4 What is coagulation? How is coagulation different from peptization?

Ans. The process of aggregating the colloidal particles together so as to change them into large sized particles which ultimately settle as a precipitate is called coagulation. The particles settle down under the force of gravity. In contrast, peptization is a process of converting a fresh precipitate into colloidal particles by shaking it with the dispersion medium in the presence of small amount of suitable electrolyte. The electrolyte added is called peptizing agent.

Q.5 What are the applications of colloids in the field of medicine, defense and in rocket technology?

Ans.

- **In medicines** Most of the medicines are prepared in the form of colloids.
  (i) Milk of magnesia, an emulsion is used for stomach disorders.
  (ii) Colloidal gold is used for intramuscular injection.
  (iii) Alum and $FeCl_3$ solution stop bleeding due to coagulation.
- **In defense** Colloids are used in warfare for smoke screens. Smoke screens are colloidal dispersion of substances like $SiCl_4$ or titanium oxide in the air.
- **In rocket technology** Colloid thruster is used in rocket engines. A thruster is a propulsive device used by spacecraft for low thrust acceleration.

Q.6 How do colloids acquire a charge? Why is ferric hydroxide/aluminium hydroxide sol prepared in the experiment, positively charged while arsenious sulphide sol is negatively charged?

Ans. The sol particles adsorb preferentially positive or negative ions present in the dispersion medium. When two or more ions are present in the dispersion medium, preferential adsorption of the ion common to the colloidal particle usually takes place resulting in the formation of positively or negatively charged particles in a colloidal solution.

If $FeCl_3$ is added to the excess of hot water, a positively charged sol of hydrated ferric oxide is formed due to the adsorption of Fe^{3+} ions ($Fe_2O_3 \cdot xH_2O/Fe^{3+}$) from the solution.

In the colloidal solution of arsenious sulphide, each particle is surrounded by HS^- ions produced by the dissociation of H_2S and hence, arsenious sulphide sol is negatively charged.

Q.7 Identify some sols (colloids) that you use in your daily life and mention their importance.

Ans. Most of the substances, we come across in our daily life, are colloids. Some are following

(i) Pigmented ink: used to colour a surface to produce an image.
(ii) Paints: used to protect, colour or provide texture to objects.
(iii) Starch colloid or sol: used in paper industries.

Experiment 1.2

AIM

To purify prepared sol by dialysis.

Theory/Principle

The purification of sols by dialysis is based upon the fact that the colloidal particles being larger in size are unable to pass through a cellophane or parchment paper (i.e., semi-permeable membrane) whereas, NaCl can do so. Thus, NaCl can be completely removed from egg-albumin sol without affecting its stability.

Materials Required

• Parchment/cellophane paper (30 cm × 30 cm)	:	One sheet
• Trough	:	1
• Thread	:	As per need
• Test tubes	:	2
• Colloidal dispersion of egg albumin	:	Prepared in experiment 1.1
• Distilled water	:	As per need
• Uranyl zinc acetate	:	As per need
• Silver nitrate	:	As per need

Procedure

1. Take a square sheet of parchment/cellophane paper and soak the sheet in water. Fold the soaked sheet in a conical shape.
2. Pour all the colloidal dispersion of egg albumin in the cone of parchment/cellophane paper.
3. Tie the cone with a thread and suspend it in a trough containing distilled water as shown in the [Fig. 1.7].

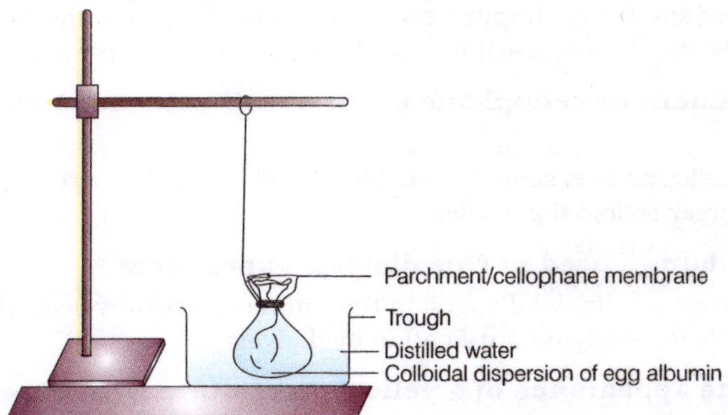

Fig. 1.7 *Purification of a colloid*

4. After about half an hour, test for the presence of ions in the trough water.
5. To check the presence of Na^+ and Cl^- ions, take water from the trough in two test tubes. To one test tube, add uranyl zinc acetate and to the other, add silver nitrate solution. A yellow precipitate with uranyl zinc acetate indicates the presence of Na^+ ions while a white precipitate with silver nitrate indicates the presence of chloride ions.

6. Change the water present in the trough after every half an hour and check for the ions again. The process is repeated till it is free of the impurities of Na^+ and Cl^- ions.
7. Note the time required for the purification of colloidal dispersion.

Note 1. *In some process, dialysis may be a very slow process. Therefore, in such cases, it is advisable to change the water of the trough twice or thrice till the colloidal dispersion is free of ions.*

2. *Hot water may be used in the dialysis of starch to speed up the process of dialysis. But hot water cannot be used for the purification of egg albumin by dialysis as egg albumin undergoes coagulation on heating.*

Result

Total time required for the purification of colloidal dispersion = ...

PRECAUTIONS

- *Fill upto two-third level of the cellophane/parchment bag with sol.*
- *In this process, make the parchment bag air tight to prevent the entry of water into the bag. Keep the neck of the parchment bag above the surface of water.*
- *Use distilled water for dialysis.*
- *Change the water in trough from time to time during dialysis.*
- *Avoid disturbing the setup while the process is ongoing to ensure efficient removal of ions.*

Viva-Voce

Q.1 What is the purpose of dialysis in the purification of colloids?

Ans. Dialysis removes small ionic impurities (like Na^+ and Cl^-.) from the colloidal solution through a semi-permeable membrane, leaving behind only the colloidal particles.

Q.2 Why is parchment or cellophane paper specifically used for making the dialysis bag?

Ans. Parchment or cellophane is semi-permeable that allows only small ions to diffuse out, while retaining the larger colloidal particles.

Q.3 Why is egg albumin used in this dialysis experiment?

Ans. Egg albumin forms a colloidal dispersion that mimics naturally occurring colloids and thus makes it suitable for studying purification by dialysis.

Q.4 What does the appearance of a yellow precipitate with uranyl zinc acetate indicate?

Ans. It indicates the presence of sodium ions (Na^+) in the water surrounding the dialysis bag.

Q.5 What confirms the presence of chloride ions in the surrounding water during dialysis?

Ans. A white precipitate with silver nitrate confirms the presence of chloride ions (Cl^-).

Q.6 How does the size of colloidal particles affect their retention in dialysis?

Ans. Colloidal particles are too large to pass through the semi-permeable membrane, so they remain inside the bag while smaller ions will escape

Q.7 What safety precautions are necessary while handling silver nitrate in this experiment?

Ans. Silver nitrate can cause skin staining and is light-sensitive, so it should be handled with gloves and stored in a dark bottle.

Q.8 Why is dialysis considered a physical method of purification rather than a chemical one?

Ans. It involves physical separation by selective diffusion based on particle size without any chemical reaction.

Questions From NCERT Lab Manual

Q.1 How can we make dialysis process quick?

Ans. The ordinary process of dialysis is slow. To make the process of dialysis quick, an electric field can be applied around the cellophane bag containing impure colloidal solution.

Experiment 1.3

AIM

To study the role of emulsifying agents in stabilising the emulsions of different oils.

Theory/Principle

Emulsions of oil in water are unstable and sometimes they are separated into two layers on standing. The stability of oil in water emulsion is increased by an addition of certain **emulsifying agents** such as, soap solution.

For complete emulsification, an optimum concentration of soap is required. If the amount is less or more than the optimum concentration, then effective stabilisation does not occur.

In presence of optimum amount of soap solution, oil in water emulsion is more stable and thus, takes more time for separation of oil and water layers.

Materials Required

- Test tubes : 6
- Droppers : 5
- Glass rod : 1
- Soap/detergent : 5 g
- Test tube stand : 1
- Stopwatch : 1
- Linseed oil, mustard oil, castor oil and machine oil : 10 mL each oil brand

Procedure

1. Dissolve 1g of soap/detergent in 10 mL of distilled water in a test tube with vigorous shaking and heat the content of the test tube if needed. Label it as *A*.
2. Take four test tubes. Mark these as *B*, *C*, *D* and *E* and to each of these test tubes, add 5 mL of distilled water followed by 10 drops of mustard oil in test tube *B*, linseed oil in test tube *C*, castor oil in test tube *D* and machine oil in test tube *E*, respectively.
3. Shake test tube *B* vigorously for five minutes, keep it in a test tube stand and simultaneously start the stopwatch. Record the time taken for the separation of the two layers.
4. Repeat the step 3 with test tubes *C*, *D* and *E* and record the time for the separation of the layers in each case.
5. Now, add two drops of soap/detergent solution from test tube *A* into each test tube (*B*, *C*, *D* and *E*). Shake each test tube for five minutes and record the time of separation of the layers in each case again.
6. Record your observations in a tabular form.

ALERT

All oils are flammable and should be kept away from Bunsen flame.

Observations

Emulsification of different oils by soap/detergent

Test tube	Name of oil used for emulsification	Time taken for the separation of layers	
		Without soap/detergent	With soap/detergent
B	Mustard oil		
C	Linseed oil		
D	Castor oil		
E	Machine oil		

Result

The longer the time taken for separation of two liquids, the more stable is the emulsion. Therefore, it is clear from the above observations that .... oil will take long time to get separated from its emulsion and is rated as (1) and .... oil will take minimum time and is rated as (5). Hence, the decreasing order of stability of above formed emulsions is ....

PRECAUTIONS

- *Add equal number of drops of soap/detergent solution to all the test tubes.*
- *Each test tube should be shaken vigorously for identical time span, so as to minimise the errors while recording the time required for the separation of layers in different systems.*
- *Volume of the liquids should be accurately measured.*
- *The time should be recorded carefully. Start the stopwatch immediately after shaking is stopped and stop it immediately when two layers separate.*
- *Avoid using excessive soap/detergent as excess may lead to incorrect results due to overstabilisation or breaking of the emulsion.*

Viva-Voce

Q.1 What type of colloidal system is an emulsion?

Ans. An emulsion is a colloidal system in which both the dispersed phase and the dispersion medium are liquids.

Q.2 Why is soap used as an emulsifying agent in this experiment?

Ans. Soap is a salt of long-chain carboxylic acid with a polar carboxyl group that interacts with water and oil and helps form a stable emulsion.

Q.3 How is the optimum concentration of soap related to emulsion stability?

Ans. Optimum concentration gives maximum emulsification and either less or more than the required amount results in decreased stability.

Q.4 Why is the time of layer separation recorded before and after adding soap solution?

Ans. To compare the stability of emulsions without and with the emulsifying agent and to assess the effect of soap on emulsion stability.

Q.5 What indicates the formation of a stable emulsion during the experiment?

Ans. A milky, homogeneous mixture that does not separate into layers quickly indicates a stable emulsion.

Q.6 Which factor other than the nature of oil influences emulsion stability in this experiment?

Ans. The method of shaking i.e., vigorous or mild also affects the degree of emulsification and hence the stability of the emulsion.

Q.7 What is observed when soap solution is added to the oil-water mixture?

Ans. The emulsion becomes more stable and the time taken for separation of layers increases.

Q.8 What would happen if more than the optimum amount of soap is added?

Ans. The emulsion may become unstable again due to excess emulsifier disrupting the balance at the oil-water interface.

Questions From NCERT Lab Manual

Q.1 Can two miscible liquids form an emulsion?

Ans. No, two miscible liquids cannot form an emulsion rather they form a solution.

Q.2 Give some examples of emulsions that you come across in daily life.

Ans. Milk, butter, vanishing cream, cold cream, etc.

Q.3 What are the points of similarity and dissimilarity among sol, gel and emulsion?

Ans. Depending upon the nature of interaction between dispersed phase and dispersion medium, sol, gel and emulsion are similar. But depending upon the physical state of dispersed phase and dispersion medium, sol, gel and emulsion are dissimilar. Sol is a colloidal system of solid (dispersed phase) and liquid (dispersion medium), gel is a colloidal system of liquid and solid and emulsion is a colloidal system of two liquids.

Q.4 **Name the reagents other than soap which can be used as an emulsifying agent in the oil in water type emulsion.**

Ans. Gelatin, protein, agar-agar and egg albumin.

Q.5 **How will you identify the type of an emulsion?**

or

Suggest a test to distinguish between oil in water and water in oil type of emulsions?

Ans. There are three methods to identify the type of emulsion:

(i) **Dye test** To the emulsion, add oil soluble dye and shake. If the droplets become coloured, then the emulsion is oil in water and if the medium or background becomes coloured, then the emulsion is water in oil.

(ii) **Spreading test** Place a drop of emulsion on an oily surface. If it spreads easily, then the emulsion is water in oil type otherwise, it is oil in water.

(iii) **Dilution test** To the emulsion, add few drops of oil. If the oil forms a separate layer, then the emulsion is oil in water, otherwise it is water in oil type.

Q.6 **Milk is said to be a stable emulsion. What provides stability to milk?**

Ans. Milk is an emulsion of soluble fats in water and stabilised by a protein casein which itself is a lyophilic colloid. Milk is naturally occurring emulsion.

Q.7 **Dettol forms an emulsion in water. How does this emulsion get stabilised?**

Ans. Dettol is light yellow in colour in the concentrated form but as several of the ingredients are insoluble in water, it produces a milky emulsion of oil droplets when diluted with water, exhibiting ouzo effect. Ouzo effect is the appearance of cloudiness in the solution due to the formation of oil in water micro-emulsions. The presence of pine oil in dettol stabilises the emulsion formed in water

Q.8 **Why do separation of layers of different oils forming an emulsion with water take different time?**

Ans. The mixing capacity of different oils with water is different and hence, their emulsions have different stability. The different stabilities is due to different physical properties and chemical composition of the oils. Thus, some oils form emulsions readily with water and many others form emulsions with great difficulty. Hence, their separation takes different time.

Unit 2

Chemical Kinetics

The branch of chemistry which deals with the study of the speed or the rate of chemical reactions and the mechanism by which the reactions proceed is known as **chemical kinetics**.

Rate of a reaction

"The rate of reaction is the change in concentration of any one of the reactants or products with time".

In general, for any hypothetical reaction of the type

$$P + Q \longrightarrow R + S$$

$$\text{Rate of reaction} = \frac{-\Delta[P]}{\Delta t} = \frac{-\Delta[Q]}{\Delta t} = +\frac{\Delta[R]}{\Delta t} = +\frac{\Delta[S]}{\Delta t}$$

(Here, (–ve) sign represents decrease in concentration of reactant and (+ve) sign represents increase in concentration of product).

The above equation represents the **average rate of a reaction** (r_{av}).

To know the rate of a reaction at a particular moment of time, term **instantaneous rate of a reaction** is used. It is expressed as $(r_{inst}) = \frac{-d[P]}{dt} = -\frac{d[Q]}{dt} = +\frac{d[R]}{dt} = +\frac{d[S]}{dt}$

The unit of rate of reaction is mol $L^{-1}s^{-1}$.

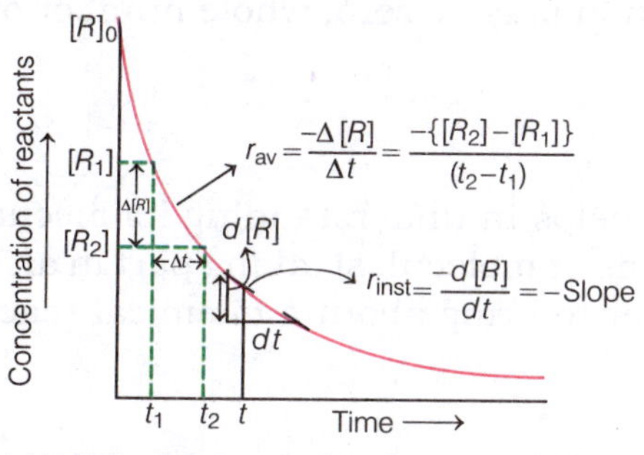

(a) Variation in concentration of reactant with time

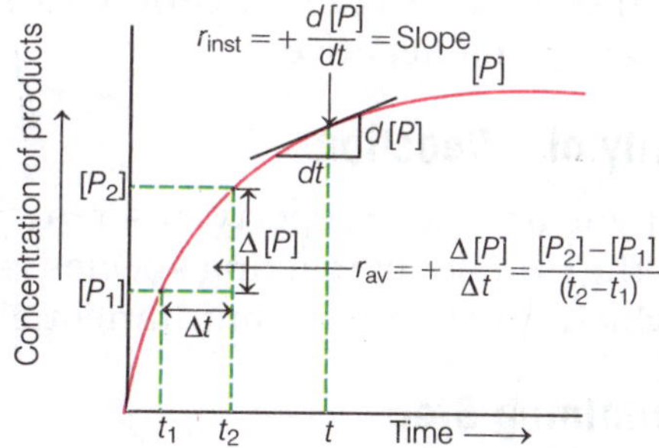

(b) Variation in concentration of product with time

Fig. *Determination of average and instantaneous rate of a reaction*

Factors Affecting Rate of Reaction

The rate of reaction is affected by the number of factors. Some of them are

1. **Concentration of the reactants** Greater are the concentrations of the reactants, faster is the reaction. Conversely, as the concentration of the reactants decrease, the rate of reaction also decreases.
2. **Temperature** The rate of reaction increases with increase of temperature. In most of the cases, this happens due to an increase in the number of collisions. The rate of reaction becomes nearly double for 10° rise of temperature.

   In some cases, reactions do not take place at room temperature but take place at higher temperature.
3. **Presence of catalyst** A catalyst generally increases the rate of reaction without itself being consumed in the reaction.
4. **Surface area of the reactants** Smaller the surface area of the reactants, faster is the reaction.
5. **Nature of the reactants** The rate varies with different types of reactants.
6. **Presence of radiation** The rate of some reactions can be increased when radiation of suitable frequency is available otherwise they are very slow or do not occur.

In this unit, we will study only the effect of concentration and temperature on the rate of the reaction.

Rate Law

The rate law is the expression in which the reaction rate is given in terms of molar concentration of reactants with each term raised to some power, which may or may not be same as the stoichiometric coefficient of the reacting species in a balanced chemical equation.

e.g. $$2NO(g) + O_2(g) \longrightarrow 2NO_2(g)$$

Rate $= k\,[NO]^2\,[O_2]$

where, k is the proportionality constant called **rate constant**.

Order of a Reaction

The sum of the powers of the concentration of the reactants in the rate law expression is called the **order of the chemical reaction**. Order of reaction may be zero, whole number or fractional values. It cannot be negative.

Molecularity of a Reaction

Molecularity is another property of a reaction that helps in understanding its mechanism. It is defined as the number of reacting species (atoms, ions or molecules) taking part in an elementary reaction which must collide simultaneously in order to bring about a chemical reaction.

Rate Determining Step

A balanced chemical equation never gives us a true picture of how reaction takes place since rarely a reaction gets completed in one step. The reaction taking place in one step is called **elementary reaction.** When a sequence of elementary reactions (called mechanism) gives us the products, the reactions are called **complex reactions.** Out of these steps, the slowest step of the reaction is considered as the **rate determining step** of the chemical reaction and decides the overall rate of the reaction.

Experiment 2.1

AIM

To study the effect of concentration and temperature on the rate of reaction between sodium thiosulphate and hydrochloric acid.

Theory/Principle

The reaction between sodium thiosulphate and hydrochloric acid yield the colloidal solution of sulphur with the evolution of sulphur dioxide gas. The reaction can be represented in molecular form as follows

$$\underset{\text{Sodium thiosulphate}}{Na_2S_2O_3(aq)} + 2HCl\,(aq) \longrightarrow 2NaCl\,(aq) + S(s) + SO_2(g) + H_2O(l)$$

In ionic form, the above equation can be represented as follows

$$S_2O_3^{2-}(aq) + 2H^+(aq) \longrightarrow S(s) + SO_2(g) + H_2O(l)$$

The formation of colloidal solution of sulphur makes the solution **translucent**. This property is used to study the rate of precipitation of sulphur. The rate of precipitation of sulphur increases with an increase in the concentration of the reacting species or with an increase in the temperature of the system.

The effect of change in concentration is determined by turnwise changing the concentration of $Na_2S_2O_3$ and HCl. However, the rate of reaction can be studied by measuring the time taken to produce enough sulphur to make some mark invisible on a paper kept below the reaction vessel. With an increase in the concentration, the number of molecular collisions per unit time between the reacting species increase and consequently chances of product formation increase. This results in an increase in the rate of precipitation of sulphur.

The effect of temperature on the rate of reaction can be studied by taking the same quantity of the reactants at different temperatures and noting the time taken for the cross to become invisible as shown in the Fig 2.1. On increasing the temperature, the kinetic energy of the reacting species increases, so the number of collisions that result in the formation of products increases, leading to a faster rate of reaction.

Materials Required

- Conical flask (100 mL) : 5
- Burette (50 mL) : 1
- Pipette (25 mL) : 1
- Pipette (5 mL) : 1
- Burette stand : 1
- Stopwatch : 1
- Thermometer (110°C) : 1
- Tripod stand : 1
- Wire gauze : 1
- Trough : 1
- 0.1 M sodium thiosulphate : As per need
- 1.0 M hydrochloric acid : As per need

Procedure

A. The effect of concentration on the rate of reaction

1. Take a trough and fill half of it with water. This will provide a constant temperature bath to all the reaction samples, maintained at room temperature.
2. Rinse and fill the burette with 1.0 M HCl solution, after rinsing it with little amount of 1.0 M HCl solution.
3. Take a 100 mL conical flask and mark a point 'x' in the centre of the outer surface of the bottom of conical flask with the help of a glass marker. Fill the flask with 50 mL of 0.1 M sodium thiosulphate solution using a 25 mL graduated pipette.
4. Place the conical flask in the trough for few minutes to attain the temperature of the bath. The mark 'x' is visible to the naked eye from the top of the conical flask [Fig. 2.1] on account of the transparent nature of the system.

⚠ ALERT

- *Hydrochloric acid is corrosive and irritant.*
- *Sodium thiosulphate solution is pungent smelling and irritant.*

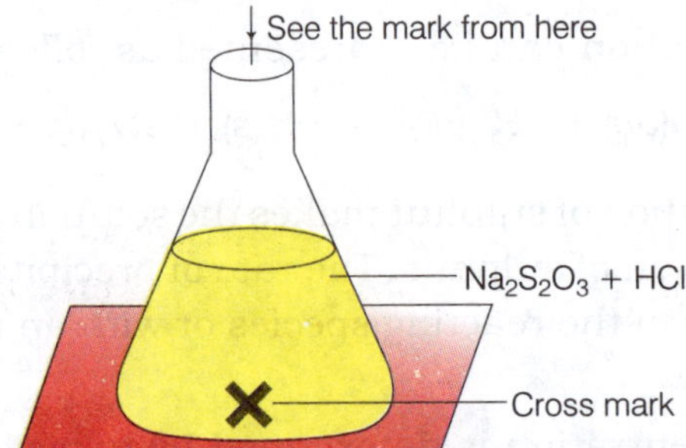

Fig. 2.1 *Reaction mixture with a cross mark 'x'*

5. Add 1.0 mL of 1.0 M HCl solution to the conical flask from the burette with swirling the conical flask. Start the stopwatch when half of HCl solution (i.e. 0.5 mL) has been transferred to the conical flask.
6. Stop the stopwatch immediately when the mark 'x' become invisible and record the reading shown by the stopwatch. This is considered as a stage of the completion of the reaction.
7. Repeat the procedure (i.e. steps 3-6) by adding 2 mL, 4 mL, 8 mL and 16 mL of 1.0 M HCl solution to the fresh 50.0 mL of 0.1 M sodium thiosulphate solution every time and record the time required for the disappearance of the mark 'x' in each case separately.
8. Record your observations in a tabular form and plot a graph between volume of HCl added on *Y*-axis and the time taken for the completion of reaction, i.e. time required for the disappearance of the mark 'x' on *X*-axis.

B. The effect of temperature on the rate of reaction

1. Take a thermostat and maintain it at 30°C.
2. Take a 100 mL conical flask and fill it with 50 mL of 0.1 M sodium thiosulphate solution. Put a mark 'x' on the outer surface of the bottom of the conical flask. Then, keep the flask in a thermostat maintained at 30°C.
3. Add 5.0 mL of 1.0 M HCl solution to the conical flask from the burette with swirling the contents in the flask and start the stopwatch immediately when the half of HCl (i.e. 2.5 mL) has been transferred to the conical flask.
4. Stop the stopwatch immediately when the mark 'x' become invisible and note down the total time elapsed in the reaction.

5. Repeat the above procedure (i.e. steps 1-4) by maintaining the temperature of thermostat at 40°C, 50°C, 60°C and 70°C using fresh sodium thiosulphate solution each time and record the time required for the disappearance of the mark 'X'.
6. Record your observations in a tabular form and plot a graph between the temperature of reaction on *Y*-axis and the time taken for the mark to become invisible, i.e. the time elapsed in the completion of reaction on *X*-axis.

Note *If thermostat (constant temperature bath) is not available in the laboratory then while studying the effect of temperature on the rate of reaction, ordinary water bath can be used. Heat the water in a water bath by placing it on the flame of the burner to raise the temperature and a thermometer should be inserted in the water bath to notice its temperature. When the temperature of the water bath increases from the desired temperature then removed the burner and when the temperature comes down then again keep it on the burner. The water in water bath should be stirred from time to time to maintain the constant temperature across water bath.*

Observations

A. **Effect of concentration of HCl on the rate of reaction**

Volume of 0.1M $Na_2S_2O_3$ solution taken each time = 50 mL

Concentration of HCl solution used in the reaction mixture = 1.0 M

Room temperature = ... °C

S. No.	**Volume of HCl added** (in mL)	**Time taken for the mark 'X' to become invisible** (in s)
1.	1.0	
2.	2.0	
3.	4.0	
4.	8.0	
5.	16.0	

B. **Effect of temperature on the rate of reaction**

Volume of 0.1 $Na_2S_2O_3$ solution used each time= 50 mL

Volume of 1.0 M HCl used each time = 5 mL

S. No.	**Temperature of the reaction mixture** (°C)	**Time taken for the mark 'X' to become invisible** (in s)
1.	30	
2.	40	
3.	50	
4.	60	
5.	70	

1. Plot a graph between the volume of hydrochloric acid added and time taken for the disappearance of the mark 'x' in each case.
2. Plot a graph between temperature of reaction mixture and time taken for the disappearance of the mark 'x' in each case.

Result

1. On increasing concentration of HCl, the rate of reaction .... (increases/decreases/remains constant).
2. On increasing temperature of reaction mixture, the rate of reaction .... (increases/decreases/remains constant).

PRECAUTIONS

- *Start the stopwatch immediately when half of HCl solution has been transferred to the conical flask and again immediately stop it when the mark 'X' becomes invisible.*
- *Keep the conical flask containing sodium thiosulphate solution in a thermostat/trough water bath for enough time to maintain its temperature constant.*
- *During the study of effect of temperature, the temperature should be constant throughout, i.e. from beginning to the completion of a reaction.*
- *Select a suitable scale for plotting the graph.*

Viva-Voce

Q.1 Why is it important to start the stopwatch when only half of the HCl has been added?

Ans. Starting the stopwatch at the halfway mark ensures that the timing reflects the active mixing phase when the reaction begins and not the delay during complete addition.

Q.2 How does increasing the concentration of HCl affect the rate of reaction?

Ans. Increasing HCl concentration increases the number of H^+ ions thus resulting in more frequent effective collisions and hence a faster rate of reaction.

Q.3 Why is the volume of sodium thiosulphate kept constant in the concentration variation part?

Ans. To isolate and observe the effect of changing only one variable i.e., HCl concentration while keeping the other constant for accurate comparison.

Q.4 What happens to the rate of reaction when the temperature is increased?

Ans. As temperature increases, the kinetic energy of particles increases, leading to more frequent and energetic collisions, which increases the reaction rate.

Q.5 What is the role of the water bath or thermostat in this experiment?

Ans. The thermostat maintains a constant temperature environment, allowing accurate measurement of how temperature affects reaction rate.

Q.6 Why is it important to use fresh sodium thiosulphate solution each time?

Ans. Reusing the solution may result in decreased reactivity due to dilution, contamination, or prior decomposition, affecting the reliability of results.

Q.7 What is the observable sign of sulphur formation in the reaction mixture?

Ans. The solution becomes cloudy and the 'X' mark beneath the beaker becomes invisible due to the colloidal suspension of sulphur.

Q.8 What type of reaction is studied in this experiment?

Ans. It is a precipitation reaction involving the formation of an insoluble product (sulphur) from soluble reactants.

Q.9 Why do we plot reaction time instead of rate directly?

Ans. The rate is inversely proportional to the time taken for the reaction to complete; hence time gives a practical indication of rate changes.

Q.10 Which gas evolves during the reaction and what is its property?

Ans. Sulphur dioxide (SO_2) evolved, which is a pungent-smelling and acidic gas.

Questions From NCERT Lab Manual

Q.1 How does the rate constant of a reaction vary with temperature?

Ans. The rate constant of a reaction increases with temperature because on increasing the temperature, the number of collisions per unit time increases that increases the chances of product formation.

Q.2 Can the order of a reaction be a fractional quantity?

Ans. Yes, the order of a reaction can be a fractional quantity.

e.g. $CH_3CHO \longrightarrow CH_4 + CO$, order $= \frac{3}{2}$

Q.3 What is the difference between the order and the molecularity of a reaction?

Ans. Order of a reaction is the sum of powers raised to the concentration terms in the rate law expression. While molecularity of a reaction is the number of molecules which collide simultaneously in an elementary reaction to form products.

Q.4 The molecularity of the reaction cannot be zero but the order can be zero. Explain.

Ans. The molecularity of the reaction cannot be zero because molecularity is the atoms, species or molecules present in the reaction. If it is zero, there is no meaning of molecularity. But order is the sum of power of concentration terms, hence it may be zero/fractional.

Q.5 Why is the stopwatch/stopclock started when half of the reactant is delivered into the beaker?

Ans. To measure the time taken to produce enough sulphur to make the solution translucent.

Q.6 Comment on the statement that for a given reaction, rate of the reaction varies but the rate constant remains constant at a particular temperature.

Ans. The rate of reaction depends on the concentration of reactants, temperature and catalyst. When reaction starts, the concentration of reactants is high and as the reaction proceeds, concentration of reactants decreases, thus rate of reaction decreases even at a fixed temperature. However, rate constant is fixed until the temperature conditions are not changed.

Q.7 The reaction under examination is as follows:

$$S_2O_3^{2-}(aq) + 2H^+(aq) \longrightarrow H_2O(l) + SO_2(g) + S(s)$$

Write the conditions under which the rate law expression for this reaction can be written in the following manner

Rate of precipitation of sulphur = $k[S_2O_3^{2-}][H^+]^2$

Ans. The conditions are as follows

(i) The reaction should be an elementary reaction.

(ii) None of the reactant should be used in very high quantity with respect to other. If the concentration is very high, then its concentration remains constant practically. If this happens then the factor of its concentration should be omitted from the rate law expression.

Q.8 Suppose the rate law expression for the precipitation of sulphur is $k[S_2O_3^{2-}][H^+]^2$, then on doubling the concentration of $S_2O_3^{2-}$ ion and H^+ ion, by how many times will the rate of the reaction increase?

Ans. Rate law expression, $r = k[S_2O_3^{2-}][H^+]^2$

On doubling the concentration of both $S_2O_3^{2-}$ and H^+ ions, the rate law expression becomes

$$r' = k(2[S_2O_3^{2-}])(2[H^+])^2$$
$$= 2 \times 4 \cdot k[S_2O_3^{2-}][H^+]^2$$
$$= 8k[S_2O_3^{2-}][H^+]^2 = 8r$$

Thus, the rate of the reaction becomes 8 times.

Q.9 Suppose the reaction given below follows third order kinetics, then in what units, will the rate of the reaction and the rate constant be expressed?

$$S_2O_3^{2-} + 2H^+ \longrightarrow H_2O + SO_2 + S$$

Ans. The unit of the rate of reaction is mol $L^{-1}s^{-1}$. While rate constant is a measure of rate of reaction. The unit of the rate constant depends upon the order of reaction. The unit of rate constant for third order kinetics is $mol^{-2}L^2s^{-1}$.

Q.10 The structure of $S_2O_3^{2-}$ ion is described as follows

S(2)
‖
$^-$O—S(1)—O$^-$
‖
O

The two sulphur atoms are marked here as (1) and (2).

Which of the sulphur atoms, according to you, is precipitated as colloidal sulphur? How can you verify your answer experimentally?

Ans. Here, sulphur atom marked as (2) precipitated as colloidal sulphur when reacts with dilute acid.

$$S_2O_3^{2-}(aq) + 2H^+(aq) \longrightarrow S(s) + SO_2(g) + H_2O(l)$$

$^-$O—S(=S)(=O)—O$^-$ ⟶ O$^-$—S(—S$^-$)(=O)=O ⟶ O=S(—S$^-$)(—O$^-$)=O ⟶ S(s) + SO_3

$$SO_3 + 2H^+ \longrightarrow SO_2(g) + H_2O(l)$$

Experiment 2.2

AIM

To study the rate of reaction of iodide ions with hydrogen peroxide at room temperature using different concentrations of iodide ions.

Theory/Principle

In the reaction between hydrogen peroxide and iodide ions, hydrogen peroxide oxidises iodide ions (I^-) to molecular iodine (I_2) in acidic medium. The reaction can be represented as follows :

$$2I^-(aq) + H_2O_2(l) + 2H^+(aq) \longrightarrow I_2(g) + 2H_2O(l)$$

If a definite amount of thiosulphate ions (i.e. sodium thiosulphate solution) is added in the presence of starch solution (as an indicator) to the reaction mixture, then the iodine which is produced in the reaction will react with thiosulphate ions instantaneously to give iodide ions till all the thiosulphate ions are oxidised to tetrathionate ions. Due to the formation of iodide ions, iodine cannot give blue colouration with starch.

$$I_2 + 2S_2O_3^{2-} \xrightarrow{\text{Fast}} S_4O_6^{2-} + 2I^-$$

After the complete consumption of thiosulphate ions, the concentration of iodine liberated in the reaction of hydrogen peroxide with iodide ions increases rapidly to a point where iodine reacts with starch to give an intense blue complex.

$$I_2 + \text{Starch} \longrightarrow \underset{\text{Blue}}{\text{Starch - } I_2 \text{ complex}}$$

This reaction is called **indicator reaction**.

Time of appearance of blue colour depends upon

(i) Initial rate of formation of iodine which depends on the concentration of hydrogen peroxide and iodide ions.

(ii) Amount of thiosulphate added.

If the amount and the concentration of thiosulphate is kept constant, then the time difference in the appearance of blue colour would depend on the concentrations of I^- and H_2O_2. Further, if the concentration of H_2O_2 is also kept constant, the rate of reaction with variable concentration of iodide ions can be studied. Since, time for the appearance of colour is noted, the reaction is usually called a **clock reaction**.

Materials Required

- Conical flasks (250 mL) : 5
- Conical flask (500 mL) : 1
- Stopwatch : 1
- Measuring cylinder (100 mL) : 1
- Trough : 1
- Starch solution : As per need
- 2.5 M sulphuric acid (H_2SO_4) solution : As per need
- 0.1 M potassium iodide (KI) solution : As per need
- 0.04 M sodium thiosulphate ($Na_2S_2O_3$) solution : As per need
- 3% hydrogen peroxide solution : As per need

Procedure

1. Take a 500 mL conical flask and mark it as *A*. Pour 25 mL of 3% H_2O_2, 25 mL of 2.5 M H_2SO_4 solution, 5 mL of freshly prepared starch solution and 195 mL distilled water into it. Stir this solution and place it in a water bath maintained at room temperature.
2. Take four 250 mL conical flasks and label them as *B*, *C*, *D* and *E*. Taking help of a measuring cylinder, put the solutions in these flasks in accordance with the following measurements given in the table:

⚠ ALERT

- *Hydrogen peroxide being flammable may cause fire when comes in contact with combustible material.*
- *Sulphuric acid is irritant.*
- *Sodium thiosulphate solution is irritant but it is of low hazard.*
- *Starch solution is of low hazard.*

Conical flask	Volume of the solution (in mL)			Total volume (in mL)
	0.04 M $Na_2S_2O_3$	0.1 M KI	Distilled water	
B	10.0	10.0	80.0	100.0
C	10.0	20.0	70.0	100.0
D	10.0	30.0	60.0	100.0

3. Shake all the conical flasks, i.e. *B*, *C* and *D* well and put them into water bath maintained at room temperature.
4. In flask *E*, pour 25 mL of solution from flask *A* and 25 mL of solution from flask *B* with the help of measuring cylinder. Keep stirring the solution. Start the stopwatch when half of the solution from flask *B* has been transferred. Keep the flask *E* in a water bath to maintain the constant temperature and record the time required for the appearance of blue colour.
5. Repeat the experiment with the solutions of flasks *C* and *D* separately by using once again 25 mL of the solution of these flasks and 25 mL of solution from flask *A*. Note the time required for the appearance of blue colour in each case.
6. Repeat the experiment with solutions of flasks *B*, *C* and *D* twice and calculate the average time for the appearance of blue colour.
7. Record your observations in a tabular form.
8. Compare the time required for the appearance of blue colour for all the three systems and make a generalisation about the variation in the rate of the reaction with concentration of iodide ions.

Observations

Temperature of water in the trough =...... °C

Volume of solution *A* taken for each study = 25 mL

Volume of either of the solution *B*, *C* and *D* taken =25 mL

Total volume of reaction mixture = 50 mL

S. No.	Total volume of reaction mixture	Time taken for the appearance of blue colour		Mean time $\left(\frac{t_1 + t_2}{2}\right)$ s
		t_1 (s)	t_2 (s)	
1.	25 mL solution from flask *A* + 25 mL solution from flask *B*			
2.	25 mL solution from flask *A* + 25 mL solution from flask *C*			
3.	25 mL solution from flask *A* + 25 mL solution from flask *D*			

Alternatively, if we plot a graph between relative rate of reaction $(1/t)$ and volume of solution of KI, we get a straight line as shown in the figure 2.2.

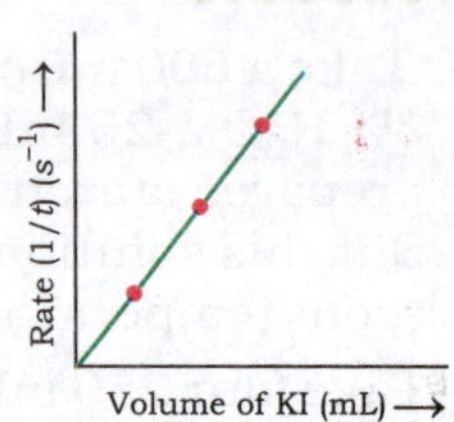

Fig 2.2

Result

It is observed that the time taken for the blue colour to appear goes on decreasing with increase in concentration of iodide ions. Thus, the rate of reaction between hydrogen peroxide and iodide ions increases with the increase in concentration of iodide ions.

PRECAUTIONS

- *Always keep the concentration of sodium thiosulphate solution less than that of potassium iodide solution.*
- *Use only freshly prepared starch solution.*
- *Sodium thiosulphate solution should be kept separate from acidic medium before the reaction proceeds.*
- *All the solutions should be maintained at same temperature.*
- *Stopwatch should be started immediately when half of the solution from flasks B, C and D are delivered into the solution A.*
- *Time of the appearance of the blue colour should be noted immediately and accurately.*
- *Always use the same measuring cylinders for measuring solutions in two different sets of observations. If after measuring one solution, the cylinder is used for measuring another solution, clean it before using.*

Viva-Voce

Q.1 What is the purpose of using starch in this experiment?

Ans. Starch acts as an indicator, it forms a blue complex with iodine which signals the end-point of the reaction.

Q.2 Why does the blue colour not appear immediately when the reaction begins?

Ans. Because iodine is formed and it is immediately reduced back to iodide by sodium thiosulphate until all the thiosulphate is consumed. The blue colour appears only when free iodine accumulates.

Q.3 Why is this experiment called a clock reaction?

Ans. Because the blue colour appears after a fixed and reproducible time interval which acts like a "clock" for measuring reaction rate.

Q.4 What does a shorter time for the appearance of blue colour indicate?

Ans. A shorter time means the reaction occurred faster thus indicating a higher rate of reaction.

Q.5 Why is a freshly prepared starch solution used each time?

Ans. Starch solution degrades over time and may not give a clear or accurate indication of iodine presence if it is old.

Q.6 Which ions are directly responsible for reducing iodine to iodide during the reaction?

Ans. Thiosulphate ions ($S_2O_3^{2-}$) reduce iodine (I_2) back to iodide (I^-) during the early stage of the reaction.

Q.7 Why is it important to maintain the temperature constant throughout the experiment?

Ans. Because temperature affects the rate of reaction and a constant temperature ensures that only the iodide concentration is being tested.

Q.8 What would be the effect on reaction time if less H_2O_2 is used?

Ans. The reaction would proceed slower and delay the appearance of blue colour.

Q.9 What would be the effect on reaction time if less H_2O_2 is used?

Ans. The reaction would proceed slower, delaying the appearance of blue colour.

Questions From NCERT Lab Manual

Q.1 Why does iodine impart blue colour to starch?

Ans. When starch is mixed with iodine in water, a blue-black coloured complex is formed. This complex is formed when iodine (in the form of I_3^- ions) gets into the coils of amylose molecules of starch and on the absorption of visible light, the complex appears as blue-black in colour.

Q.2 Why is the reaction given the name clock reaction?

Ans. Iodine clock refers to a group of reactions which involves the mixing of two colourless solutions to produce a solution which remains colourless for a precise amount of time and then suddenly changes to a deep blue colour. These are given name 'clock reactions' as they can be easily timed and progressed with clock work precision.

Q.3 Calculate the oxidation number of sulphur in tetrathionate ion ($S_4O_6^{2-}$). Can the oxidation number be a fractional number?

Ans. The oxidation number of sulphur in $S_4O_6^{2-}$ ion can be determined by considering its structure as

$$^{-}O-\overset{O}{\underset{O}{\overset{\|}{\underset{\|}{S}}}}{}^{+5}-\overset{0}{S}-\overset{0}{S}-\overset{O}{\underset{O}{\overset{\|}{\underset{\|}{S}}}}{}^{+5}-O^{-}$$

Since, each of the two terminal sulphur atoms has (+5) oxidation state and each of the two central sulphur atoms has zero oxidation state, the average oxidation state of the four sulphur atoms is

$$\frac{(2 \times 5) + (2 \times 0)}{4} = 2.5$$

Thus, we can conclude that the idea of fractional oxidation state is unconvincing, since electrons are never transferred or shared in fractions. Infact, fractional oxidation state is only the average oxidation state of an element when two or more of its atoms are present in different oxidation states in a given compound.

Q.4 Distinguish between the role of iodine and iodide ions in this experiment.

Ans. In this experiment, iodide ions act as a reducing agent and reduces H_2O_2 solution to produce water and iodine in an acidic medium.

$$H_2O_2 + 2I^- + 2H^+ \longrightarrow 2H_2O + I_2$$

Iodine imparts blue colour in the presence of starch solution but before that can actually happen, it reacts with thiosulphate ions present in the solution and reduces itself into iodide ions again.

$$I_2 + 2S_2O_3^{2-} \longrightarrow S_4O_6^{2-} + 2I^-$$

Once the thiosulphate ions are used up by iodine, the iodine liberated due to the reaction of H_2O_2 with I^- ions increases rapidly, the solution turns blue as now the iodine and starch are present in the solution.

Q.5 Why should the concentration of sodium thiosulphate solution taken be always less than that of potassium iodide solution?

Ans. As sodium thiosulphate solution acts as a delaying agent in the reaction between H_2O_2 and I^- ions and it prevents the instant completion of reaction by reducing I_2 produced in this reaction to I^- ions. So, as long as thiosulphate ions are present in solution, it reacts with iodine and I_2 is not able to form starch-I_2 blue complex but the moment at which all the thiosulphate ions get consumed with I_2, the I_2 produced gives blue colour with starch solution.

That's why, the concentration of sodium thiosulphate solution should always be taken less than that of potassium iodide solution.

Q.6 Explore the possibility of using an oxidant other than H_2O_2 in this experiment.

Ans. We can replace H_2O_2 by other oxidising agents such as $KMnO_4$, $K_2Cr_2O_7$ and NaOCl for iodine clock reaction.

$$2\,MnO_4^- + 16H^+ + 10I^- \longrightarrow 2Mn^{2+} + 5I_2 + 8H_2O$$
$$Cr_2O_7^{2-} + 14H^+ + 6I^- \longrightarrow 2Cr^{3+} + 3I_2 + 7H_2O$$
$$OCl^- + 2I^- + 2H^+ \longrightarrow I_2 + Cl^- + H_2O$$

Experiment 2.3

AIM

To study the rate of reaction between potassium iodate (KIO_3) and sodium sulphite (Na_2SO_3) using starch solution as an indicator.

Theory/Principle

Potassium iodate acts as a powerful oxidising agent in acidic medium and oxidises sulphite ions to sulphate ions. The reaction proceeds in the following steps

$$\underset{\text{Iodate ion}}{IO_3^-} + \underset{\text{Sulphite ion}}{3SO_3^{2-}} \xrightarrow{\text{Slow}} \underset{\text{Iodide ion}}{I^-} + \underset{\text{Sulphate ion}}{3SO_4^{2-}}$$

$$\underset{\text{Iodide ion}}{5I^-} + 6H^+ + \underset{\text{Iodate ion}}{IO_3^-} \xrightarrow{\text{Fast}} 3H_2O + \underset{\text{Iodine}}{3I_2}$$

$$I_2 + \underset{\text{Sulphite ion}}{SO_3^{2-}} + H_2O \xrightarrow{\text{Very fast}} \underset{\text{Sulphate ion}}{SO_4^{2-}} + \underset{\text{Iodide ion}}{2I^-} + 2H^+$$

It is a slow reaction and the rate of reaction may be observed by noting the appearance of blue colour due to the formation of starch-iodine complex. The above reaction takes place in three steps

I. Sulphite ions first reacts with iodate ions to produce iodide ions.

II. The iodide ions so formed gets oxidised by more of iodate ions in acidic medium generating iodine.

III. Iodine so produced immediately reacts with sulphite ions to form sulphate and iodide ions.

This is a **clock reaction**, as the rate of reaction is determined by the sudden appearance of the blue colour.

Materials Required

- Conical flasks (250 mL) : 6
- Measuring cylinder (100 mL) : 1
- Stopwatch : 1
- Trough : 1
- 2.0 M sulphuric acid : As per need
- 5% starch solution : As per need
- 6% potassium iodate solution : As per need
- 6% sodium sulphite solution : As per need
- Distilled water : As per need

Procedure

1. Take 25 mL of 6% KIO_3 solution, 25 mL of 2.0 M H_2SO_4 and 50 mL of distilled water into a 250 mL conical flask and mark it as 'A'. Shake the content of the flask *A* well and keep it in a trough half-filled with water (which serves as constant temperature bath) so as to keep its temperature constant.
2. Take five 250 mL conical flasks and mark these as *B*, *C*, *D*, *E* and *F* respectively. Take 6% sodium sulphite solution, 5% starch solution and distilled water in flasks *B*, *C*, *D* and *E* in the proportion given in the following table and keep flask *F* for carrying out the reaction.

> **⚠ ALERT**
> - *Potassium iodate solution is harmful and irritant.*
> - *Sodium sulphite solution is irritant.*
> - *Sulphuric acid is harmful, irritant and corrosive.*

Conical flask	Volume of the solution (in mL)			Total volume (in mL)
	6% Na_2SO_3 solution (mL)	5% starch solution (mL)	Distilled water (mL)	
B	20.0	5.0	75.0	100.0
C	15.0	5.0	80.0	100.0
D	10.0	5.0	85.0	100.0
E	5.0	5.0	90.0	100.0

3. Shake the solutions of all the conical flasks, i.e. *B*, *C*, *D* and *E* and keep them in a trough of water so that these acquire room temperature.
4. Now, take conical flask *F*. In this flask, add 25 mL of the solution from conical flask *A* and 25 mL of the solution from conical flask *B*. Start the stopwatch when half of the solution from flask *B* has been added. Mix these two solutions thoroughly by constant stirring and keep it in the water bath. Record the time required for the appearance of blue colour.
5. Repeat the experiment in a similar manner with the solutions in flasks C, *D* and *E* respectively by using 25 mL of the solution as in the experiment with solution from flask *B* and record the time required for the appearance of blue colour in each case.
6. Repeat the whole experiment for each case twice and calculate the average time for the appearance of blue colour in each set.
7. Record your observations in a tabular form.
8. From the tabulated results, find out the relationship between the time of appearance of blue colour and the variation in concentration of sodium sulphite.

Observations

Room temperature =...... °C

Volume of solution 'A' taken in each study = 25 mL

Volume of either of the solution *B*, *C*, *D* and *E* taken = 25 mL

Total volume of reaction mixture = 50 mL

S. No.	Composition of the solution taken in flask F	Time taken for the appearance of blue colour		Mean time, $\frac{t_1 + t_2}{2}$ (s)
		t_1 (s)	t_2 (s)	
1.	25 mL solution from flask A+ 25 mL solution from flask B			
2.	25 mL solution from flask A+ 25 mL solution from flask C			
3.	25 mL solution from flask A+ 25 mL solution from flask D			
4.	25 mL solution from flask A+ 25 mL solution from flask E			

Comparison of the time of appearance of blue colour points out that the rate of reaction of iodate and sulphite ions decreases with decrease in sulphite ion concentration.

Result

The rate of reaction is directly proportional to the concentration of reactants as it increases with the increase in concentration of sodium sulphite solution.

PRECAUTIONS

- *Always use a freshly prepared solution of sodium sulphite because it is easily oxidised by air.*
- *Concentration of KIO_3 solution should be higher than the concentration of sodium sulphite (Na_2SO_3) solution.*
- *Use a freshly prepared starch solution.*
- *Start the stopwatch when half of the solution from conical flasks B, C, D or E is added to the conical flask F containing 25 mL solution from flask A.*
- *Use the same measuring cylinder for accurate measurement.*
- *Record your observations carefully.*

Viva-Voce

Q.1 What would happen if starch is added too early before any iodine is formed?

Ans. No colour will appear initially, but the starch will still be present to form a blue complex as soon as free iodine accumulates.

Q.2 Why is flask A prepared with excess potassium iodate and sulphuric acid?

Ans. To ensure a constant oxidising environment so that the rate of reaction is influenced only by the concentration of sodium sulphite.

Q.3 Why is it important to start the stopwatch when only half of the solution from flask B, C, D or E is added?

Ans. To synchronise timing with the start of the mixing and reaction process and to ensure consistency across trials.

Q.4 What happens if the potassium iodate concentration is not kept higher than sodium sulphite?

Ans. The rate of reaction may become inconsistent and less iodine may be produced, affecting the visibility and timing of the blue colour.

Q.5 What is the importance of using the same volume (100 mL) in all conical flasks?

Ans. To ensure that the only variable affecting the rate is the concentration of sodium sulphite and not the volume of the reaction mixture.

Q.6 The blue colour observed at the end of the reaction due to ....

Ans. It is due to the formation of a starch-iodine complex when free iodine accumulates in the reaction mixture.

Q.7 What would happen if potassium iodate and sodium sulphite were mixed without an acidic medium?

Ans. The oxidation-reduction reactions would not proceed efficiently and iodine may not be liberated or detected properly.

Q.8 Why is this experiment suitable for studying reaction kinetics?

Ans. Because the appearance of colour occurs at a reproducible, measurable time interval, allowing direct observation of how changes in reactant concentration affect reaction rate.

Questions From NCERT Lab Manual

Q.1 Mention the factors that affect the rate of reaction in the present study.

Ans. Concentration of reactants (potassium iodate and sodium sulphite), pH of reaction mixture and room temperature are the factors which affect the rate of reaction.

Q.2 How would the time for the appearance of blue colour vary if the temperature of the experiment in the above case is enhanced by 10°C?

Ans. The rate of reaction increases with increase in temperature because with the increase in temperature, the kinetic energy of the molecules increases, thereby the number of effective collisions increases which leads to the formation of more products. Thus, it will take comparatively less time for the appearance of blue colour if the temperature of the experiment is enhanced by 10°C.

Q.3 Which of the acids, hydrochloric or nitric, would be suitable to make the medium acidic in this experiment? Explain your answer with reasons.

Ans. Hydrochloric acid is suitable to make medium acidic in this experiment because nitric acid is a powerful oxidising agent and oxidises iodide ions into iodine. Hence, it affects the rate of reaction and can change the results. So, it should not be used in this reaction.

Q.4 Out of the reactions (i) and (ii) given below

$IO_3^- + 3SO_3^{2-} \longrightarrow I^- + 3SO_4^{2-}$ ...(i) $5I^- + IO_3^- + 6H^+ \longrightarrow 3H_2O + 3I_2$ ...(ii)

Which could be the rate determining reaction? What is the molecularity of the rate determining reaction?

Ans. As reaction (i) is slow step, hence it is a rate determining step. As 4 molecules are participating in the rate determining step thus, the molecularity of the reaction is 4.

Q.5 Can AsO_3^{3-} be used in place of SO_3^{2-} in the above reaction? Support your answer with proper reasoning.

Ans. In the reaction between potassium iodate and sodium sulphite, potassium iodate gives iodine, which acts as an oxidising agent and sulphite ions act as a reducing agent. As arsenite ion also acts as a reducing agent when reacts with potassium iodate, it can replace the former one.

$$I_2 + \underset{\text{Arsenite ion}}{AsO_3^{3-}} + H_2O \longrightarrow 2I^- + \underset{\text{Arsenate ion}}{AsO_4^{3-}} + 2H^+$$

Unit 3

Thermochemistry

Most of the reactions carried out at atmospheric pressure are accompanied by the heat or enthalpy changes. The reactions may involve either absorption or evolution of heat. The branch of chemistry which involves the study of heat changes taking place in reactions is called **thermochemistry.**

Enthalpy (*H*) and Enthalpy Change (ΔH)

Total heat content at constant pressure is called **enthalpy** and is represented by *H*.

The enthalpy changes (or heat changes) are directly related to the temperature changes by the relation:

$$\begin{aligned}\Delta H &= q_p \\ &= mC_p\Delta T \\ &= Vd\ C_p\Delta T \quad [\because d = m/V \Rightarrow m = V\times d]\end{aligned} \quad \text{...(i)}$$

Where, V= Volume of the solution

d = Density of the solution

C_p = Heat capacity

ΔT = Change in temperature

Enthalpy Change of a Reaction or Reaction Enthalpy (ΔH_r)

It is the enthalpy change accompanying a chemical reaction or it can also be defined as the enthalpy change when the moles of reactants have reacted completely.

e.g. $$2H_2(g) + O_2(g) \longrightarrow 2H_2O(l),\ \Delta H = -572\ \text{kJ}$$

Enthalpies for Different Types of Reactions

(i) **Enthalpy of solution** ($\Delta_{sol} H$)

Enthalpy of solution (or dissolution) is the amount of heat liberated or absorbed when one mole of a solute (liquid/solid) is dissolved in such a large quantity of solvent (usually water) that further dilution does not make any heat changes. It is positive when heat is absorbed and negative when heat is given out during dissolution.

e.g. $$KCl(s) + aq \longrightarrow KCl(aq),\ \Delta_{sol} H = +28.6\ \text{kJ/mol}$$

(ii) **Enthalpy of neutralisation** ($\Delta_{neut} H$)

In general, **enthalpy of neutralisation** is defined as the amount of heat liberated when 1 mole of H^+ ions furnished by acid combine with 1 mole of OH^- ions furnished by base to form water. Thus,

$$\underset{\text{Acid}}{H^+(aq)} + \underset{\text{Base}}{OH^-(aq)} \longrightarrow H_2O(l),\ \Delta_{neut} H = -57.1\ \text{kJ}$$

Enthalpy of neutralisation is also defined as the amount of heat liberated, when 1g equivalent of an acid is completely neutralised by 1 g equivalent of a base in dilute solution.

When both acid and base are strong, the heat released for the formation of 1 mol $H_2O(l)$ is maximum which is equal to 13.7 kcal or 57.3 kJ mol^{-1}. This value is always a fixed amount of heat liberated in the reaction of strong acid and strong base. It is evident from the following data

S.No.	Acid	Base	Heat of neutralisation (in kJ)
1.	HCl	KOH	– 57.45 ≈ 57.3
2.	HNO_3	NaOH	– 57.28 ≈ 57.3
3.	HNO_3	KOH	– 57.3

Calorimeter and Calorimeter Constant

The vessels in which measurement of heat changes are carried out are called **calorimeters.** Reactions may also be carried out in beakers placed in thermos flask or in thermally insulated box or in styrofoam cup. Metallic calorimeters are not used for measuring thermochemical changes because metals may react with substances. Stainless steel or gold plated copper calorimeters may be used.

During measurement of heat changes, calorimeter, thermometer and stirrer also absorb some heat. This amount of heat should also be known and it is called **calorimeter constant**. There is minimum loss of heat to the surroundings in calorimeter.

In the case of a glass vessel, (e.g., beaker) calorimeter constant for that part is found, which is actually in contact with the reaction mixture. This is so because when thermal conductivity of the material of calorimeter is low, only the area of the calorimeter in contact with the liquid absorbs maximum heat. Method of mixtures is used to determine the calorimeter constant.

To determine calorimeter constant, known volume of hot water at a specified temperature is added to known volume of water contained in the calorimeter at room temperature.

Experiment 3.1

AIM

To determine the enthalpy of dissolution of copper sulphate or potassium nitrate.

Theory/Principle

Dissolution of one mole of hydrated copper sulphate ($CuSO_4 \cdot 5H_2O$) can be represented as:

$$CuSO_4 \cdot 5H_2O(s) + H_2O(l) \longrightarrow CuSO_4 \cdot 5H_2O\,(aq)\ ;\ \Delta H = +\ 11.7\ kJ/mol$$

Also, dissolution of KNO_3 is represented as

$$KNO_3(s) + H_2O(l) \longrightarrow KNO_3(aq);\ \Delta H = 35.4\ kJ/mol$$

It can be determined by putting a known volume of water in a vessel called **calorimeter** and then finding out its change in temperature on adding a known weight of the substance into it. From the change in temperature, heat absorbed or evolved can be calculated. The amount of heat changes, absorb by calorimeter, thermometer and stirrer which is called **calorimeter constant** should also be known.

Generally, aqueous solutions are mixed in thermochemical measurements. Thus, water in the reaction medium and the temperature changes result due to the chemical reactions taking place in solution.

Note *According to the law of conservation of energy, the sum of enthalpy changes occurs in the calorimeter (loss and gain of energy) is equal to zero. Therefore, equation for enthalpy change is,*

$$(\Delta H_1) + (\Delta H_2) + (\Delta H_3) + (\Delta H_4) = 0$$

(ΔH_1)	(ΔH_2)	(ΔH_3)	(ΔH_4)
Heat gained by calorimeter, thermometer and stirrer	Enthalpy change of solution (water) in calorimeter	Enthalpy change of added solution (water) in calorimeter	Enthalpy change of reaction

Materials Required

- Beakers (250 mL) : 3
- Beaker (500 mL) : 1
- Thermometer (110°C) : 1
- Glass rod : 1
- Cotton wool : As per need
- Small wooden block : 1
- Small piece of cardboard : 1
- Stirrer : 1
- Hydrated copper sulphate/ potassium nitrate : 2 g

Procedure

A. Determination of Calorimeter Constant or Water Equivalent of Calorimeter (Beaker)

1. Take 100 mL of water in the inner beaker of calorimeter (250 mL) which is placed on a wooden block kept in a large beaker (500 mL).
2. Pack the empty space between the larger beaker and the smaller beaker with some insulating material such as cotton wool to prevent the heat loss by conduction.

ALERT

- *Hydrated copper sulphate is harmful, poisonous and dangerous for the environment.*
- *Potassium nitrate is harmful.*

Cover the larger beaker with a cardboard which has two holes, one for thermometer and another for stirrer as shown in the figure 3.1.

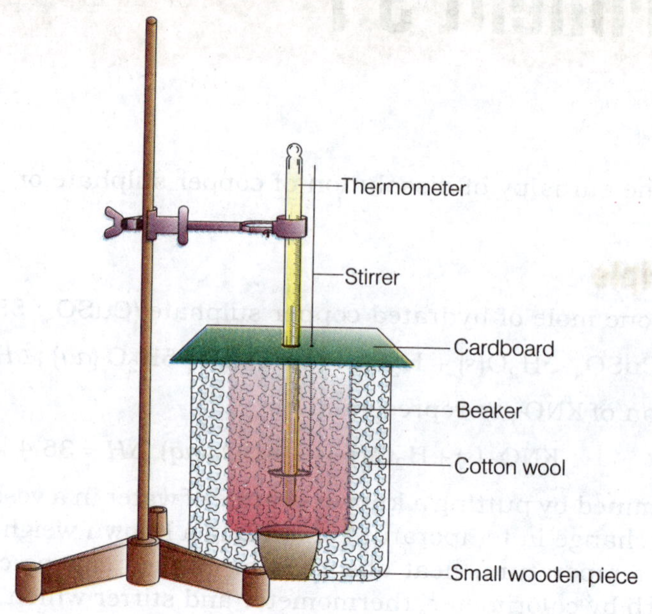

Fig. 3.1 *Sectional view of calorimeter for the determination of water equivalent (W) or calorimeter constant*

3. Allow it to attain a steady temperature and note it accurately. Let this temperature be t_1°C.
4. Take 100 mL of water in a separate 250 mL beaker and heat it upto about 60°C and note the temperature of hot water accurately. Let this temperature be t_2°C.
5. Lift the cardboard and transfer the entire hot water to the inner beaker of calorimeter and stir it slowly.
6. Note down the highest temperature attained by the mixed water. Let this temperature be t_3°C.
7. Note that the three temperatures follow the order : t_2 °C > t_3 °C > t_1 °C

Observations

1. Volume of the cold water = 100 mL
2. Assuming specific density of water = 1g/mL
3. Mass of the cold water = 100 g
4. Mass of the hot water = 100 g
5. Temperature of cold water = t_1°C
6. Temperature of hot water = t_2°C
7. Temperature attained after mixing = t_3° C

Calculation

Increase in temperature of cold water = $(t_3 - t_1)$°C

[As the three temperatures are in the order $t_2 > t_3 > t_1$]

Decrease in temperature of hot water = $(t_2 - t_3)$°C

By applying the principle of calorimetry,

Heat given out by hot water = Heat taken by calorimeter + Heat taken by cold water

$$100 \times (t_2 - t_3) \text{ cal} = W \times (t_3 - t_1) \text{ cal} + 100 \times (t_3 - t_1) \text{ cal}$$

or

$$W = \frac{100\,(t_2 - t_3) - 100\,(t_3 - t_1)}{(t_3 - t_1)} \text{ g}$$

Now, as we know, heat gained or lost by a substance (heat capacity)

= Mass × Specific heat × Rise or fall in temperature

and specific heat capacity of water = 1 cal/g°C or 4.18 J/g°C

Therefore, $$W = \frac{100 \times 4.18\,(t_2 - t_3) - 100 \times 4.18\,(t_3 - t_1)}{(t_3 - t_1)}\,\text{g}$$

Thus, water equivalent (W) = Heat capacity of calorimeter (beaker)

= Mass of beaker × Specific heat of beaker

B. Determination of Enthalpy of Dissolution

1. Now, remove water from calorimeter and dry it.
2. Take 200 mL of distilled water measured by means of graduated cylinder in the inner beaker and fix the cover with two holes in it.
3. Insert thermometer in one hole and stirrer in the other. Note down the temperature of water. Let it be t_1'°C.
4. Weigh accurately about 7g of the powdered salt of $CuSO_4 \cdot 5H_2O$ or 5.5 g powdered KNO_3 and add it to the water in a calorimeter. Put the cover back quickly.
5. Stir the solution with a stirrer till the entire amount of $CuSO_4$ or KNO_3 dissolves but the speed of stirring should not be high and vigorous. As stirring may introduce error in temperature reading by increasing the temperature.
6. Note down the temperature (t_2'°C) attained by the $CuSO_4$ or KNO_3 solution till the mercury in the thermometer stem is steady atleast for 5 min.

Observations

1. Weight of the hydrated copper sulphate added = w g (7 g in this case) or weight of potassium nitrate added = w g (5.5 g in this case).
2. Volume of the distilled water taken (or solvent) = 200 mL = 200 g (assuming specific density = 1g/mL)
3. Temperature of water = t_1'°C
4. Final temperature of solution = t_2'°C
5. Water equivalent of calorimeter (calorimeter constant) = W g (given)

Calculation

The enthalpy of dissolution of copper sulphate is calculated as:

Total mass of the solution = Mass of solvent + mass of solute = $(200 + w)$g

Change in temperature = $(t_1' - t_2')$°C [$\because t_1 > t_2$ as when $CuSO_4 \cdot 5H_2O$ dissolves in water, heat is absorbed by it from water]

Enthalpy change of the calorimeter (beaker) = $W(t_1' - t_2')$

where, W = calorimeter constant

Enthalpy change of solution = $[(200 + w)(t_1' - t_2')] \times 4.184$ J for $(t_1' - t_2')$°C fall in temperature

Total enthalpy change of the calorimeter (beaker) and solution

$$= [W(t_1' - t_2') + (200 + w)(t_1' - t_2')] \times 4.184\text{ J}$$

Heat change on dissolution of 1g hydrated copper sulphate

$$= \frac{[W(t_1' - t_2') + (200 + w)(t_1' - t_2')] \times 4.184\text{ J}}{w}$$

As 1 mole of $CuSO_4 \cdot 5H_2O$ weighs 249.5 g. Thus, heat change on dissolution of 1 mole of

$$CuSO_4 \cdot 5H_2O = \frac{249.5 \times [W(t_1' - t_2') + (200 + w)\ (t_1' - t_2')] \times 4.184}{w} \text{ J mol}^{-1}$$

Note *To find out the enthalpy change for the dissolution of potassium nitrate in place of $CuSO_4 \cdot 5H_2O$ in the above calculations and molar mass is taken as 101 g.*

Result

The enthalpy of dissolution of $CuSO_4 \cdot 5H_2O$ in water is .... J mol^{-1} at t_1'°C.

Or, the enthalpy of dissolution of KNO_3 in water is .... J mol^{-1} at t_1'°C.

Note *The students are not required to find the value of water equivalent or calorimeter constant (W). This value will be given to the students in the practical examination but students are required to know what is water equivalent, how is it different from calorimeter constant and how to determine its value in laboratory?*
In all simple calorimeters used in laboratories, some of the heat released by reaction is absorbed by the components of calorimeter itself. Thus, the calorimeter constant is regarded as heat capacity of calorimeter and expressed in J/°C or J/K

PRECAUTIONS

- To record the temperature of water, use a thermometer with 0.10°C graduation.
- Be sure that thermometer dips in water for each case.
- In the determination of water equivalent or calorimeter constant record the temperature of hot water just before mixing.
- Weigh copper sulphate carefully as it is hygroscopic in nature.
- Addition of salt should be quick without splashing or spilling water and put the lid of calorimeter back quickly.
- Avoid excessive and unnecessary stirring to prevent heating due to friction.
- Insulate the calorimeter thermally as perfectly as possible. Use cotton wool to create insulation between the two beakers.

Viva-Voce

Q.1 Which principle is used in thermochemical measurement for this experiment?

Ans. The principle used is the law of conservation of energy which states that the total enthalpy change in the system must be zero.

Q.2 Why is cotton wool placed between the two beakers?

Ans. Cotton wool is placed to provide insulation and reduce heat loss during the experiment.

Q.3 How is the calorimeter constant calculated in this experiment?

Ans. It is calculated by mixing known volumes of hot and cold water and observing the temperature change using the heat balance equation.

Q.4 Why do we use a thermometer with 0.1 C graduation?

Ans. Because small temperature changes need to be measured accurately during the experiment.

Q.5 **What does the term 'enthalpy of solution' refer to?**

Ans. It refers to the heat absorbed or released when one mole of solute dissolves in a large amount of solvent such that further dilution causes no heat change.

Q.6 **Why is copper sulphate weighed carefully before adding to water?**

Ans. Because copper sulphate is hygroscopic and can absorb moisture from air, affecting the accuracy.

Q.7 **Why is it advised to avoid using a very large amount of solute?**

Ans. Using a large amount may cause excessive temperature change or incomplete dissolution.

Q.8 **State why is it advised to avoid using a very large amount of solute?**

Ans. Using a large amount may cause excessive temperature change or incomplete dissolution.

Q.9 **What are the units of the enthalpy of dissolution obtained in this experiment?**

Ans. Joules per mole ($J\ mol^{-1}$).

Q.10 **Which two components contribute to the total enthalpy change in the experiment?**

Ans. The calorimeter (beaker) and the solution.

Q.11 **Is the method of determining ΔH different for potassium nitrate than for copper sulphate?**

Ans. No, the same procedure is used with potassium nitrate instead of copper sulphate.

Q.12 **Why is the thermometer inserted through a cardboard cover?**

Ans. To reduce heat loss and maintain a closed insulated environment.

Questions From NCERT Lab Manual

Q.1 **What is meant by the term calorimeter constant?**

Ans. In all simple calorimeters used in laboratory, some of the heat released by the reaction is absorbed by the components of calorimeter such as beaker, thermometer and stirrer. Thus, the calorimeter constant is regarded as the amount of heat absorbed by the calorimeter for one degree celsius rise of temperature. It is expressed in J/°C or J/K.

Q.2 **How does $\Delta_{sol} H$ vary with temperature?**

Ans. For the substances having $\Delta_{sol}H$ positive, the dissolution of substance and $\Delta_{sol}H$ increases with increase in temperature while for the substances having $\Delta_{sol}H$ negative, the dissolution of substance and $\Delta_{sol}H$ decreases with increase in temperature.

Q.3 **Why is $\Delta_{sol} H$ for some substances negative while for others, it is positive?**

Ans. The enthalpy of solution of a substance depends upon the lattice enthalpy and hydration enthalpy of the substance according to the formula,

$$\Delta_{sol}H = \Delta_{lattice}H + (-\Delta_{hyd}H)$$

If the lattice enthalpy of the salt is higher than hydration enthalpy, the salt has a positive $\Delta_{sol}H$ and it produces cooling on dissolving in water, whereas if the hydration enthalpy of salt is higher than lattice enthalpy, it has a negative $\Delta_{sol}H$ and it produces heating on dissolving in water.

Q.4 How will the solubility of copper sulphate and potassium nitrate be affected by increasing the temperature? Explain.

Ans. The thermochemical equations for the dissolution of anhydrous $CuSO_4$, hydrated $CuSO_4$ and KNO_3 may be represented as

$$KNO_3(s) + aq \longrightarrow KNO_3(aq), \Delta_{sol}H = +\ 35.4\ kJ\ mol^{-1}$$

$$CuSO_4(s) + aq \longrightarrow CuSO_4(aq), \Delta_{sol}H = -\ 66.5\ kJ\ mol^{-1}$$

$$CuSO_4 \cdot 5H_2O(s) + aq \longrightarrow CuSO_4 \cdot 5H_2O\ (aq), \Delta_{sol}H = +\ 11.5\ kJ mol^{-1}$$

As the dissolution of KNO_3 and hydrated $CuSO_4$ is an endothermic reaction, thus its solubility in water increases on increasing the temperature while the dissolution of anhydrous $CuSO_4$ is an exothermic reaction, thus, its solubility in water decreases on increasing the temperature.

Note *Since, $CuSO_4$ may be anhydrous or hydrated, so in this question, we mentioned the effect of temperature on solubility for both the salts.*

Q.5 Will the enthalpy change for dissolution of same amount of anhydrous copper sulphate and hydrated copper sulphate in the same amount of water be the same or different? Explain.

Ans. The dissolution of anhydrous copper sulphate in water is an exothermic process.

$$CuSO_4(s) + aq \longrightarrow CuSO_4\ (aq), \Delta_{sol}H = -\ 66.5\ kJ\ mol^{-1}$$

But when $CuSO_4$ is present in the hydrated state (i.e. $CuSO_4 \cdot 5H_2O$), it dissolves with the absorption of heat.

$$CuSO_4 \cdot 5H_2O + aq \longrightarrow CuSO_4(aq), \Delta_{sol}H = +11.7\ kJ\ mol^{-1}$$

Hence, the enthalpies of dissolution of both forms are different. It can be explained as when the hydrated salt is dissolved in water, only degradation of crystal lattice occurs which is an endothermic reaction whereas in case of anhydrous salt, the enthalpy of dissolution corresponds to the difference between lattice enthalpy and hydration enthalpy. So, the resulting enthalpy of dissolution may be endothermic or exothermic, depending upon the above two processes, i.e. degradation of lattice and hydration of ions.

Experiment 3.2

AIM

To determine the enthalpy of neutralisation of a strong acid (HCl) with a strong base (NaOH).

Theory/Principle

A neutralisation reaction involves the combination of $H^+(aq)$ ions furnished by an acid and $OH^-(aq)$ ions furnished by a base, evidently leading to the formation of $H_2O(l)$. Since, the reaction involves bond formation, therefore, this reaction is always **exothermic**.

In case of HCl and NaOH, it can be shown by an equation:

$$HCl + NaOH \longrightarrow NaCl + H_2O + 13.7 \text{ kcal (or 57.3 kJ)}$$

As both of these are strong, they dissociate 100% and the reaction is precisely.

$$\underset{\text{Acid}}{H^+} + \underset{\text{Base}}{OH^-} \longrightarrow H_2O + 13.7 \text{ kcal (or 57.3 kJ)}$$

From the above expression, we can evaluate another definition of heat of neutralisation, i.e. the amount of heat released when one mole of water is produced from complete reaction of an acid and base. It may be noted that if any of the species, acid or base is a weak electrolyte, heat evolved or heat of neutralisation will be less than 57 kJ mol^{-1}. Because some heat liberated is used for the ionisation of acid or base or both of them. It will be the least when both are weak.

ALERT

Hydrochloric acid and sodium hydroxide are irritants.

In this experiment, known volumes of the standard solutions of an acid and alkali are mixed and the change in temperature is observed and from this, enthalpy of neutralisation is calculated.

Materials Required

- Beakers (250 mL) : 3
- Beaker (500 mL) : 1
- Thermometer (110°C) : 1
- Glass rod : 1
- Cotton wool : As per need
- Small wooden block : 1
- Piece of cardboard : 1
- Stirrer : 1
- Calorimeter : 1
- 1 M HCl : 100 mL
- 1 M NaOH : 100 mL
- Dropper : 1

Procedure

A. Determination of Water Equivalent (or Calorimeter Constant)

Water equivalent of calorimeter or calorimeter constant may be determined by following the procedure as detailed in experiment 3.1.

B. Determination of Enthalpy of Neutralisation

1. Clean and dry the calorimeter completely and take 100 mL of 1.0 M HCl solution in it.
2. Cover it with cardboard and wait for some time and note its steady temperature.
3. Take 100 mL of 1.0 M NaOH solution in another 250 mL beaker and note down its steady temperature (t_1°C).
4. Both the solutions should have the same temperature, otherwise wait for sometime so that they attain the same temperature.

5. Transfer 100 mL of 1 M NaOH solution into the calorimeter containing 100 mL of 1M HCl solution quickly, put the lid of calorimeter back and stir the solutions well.
6. Note the final temperature (t_2°C) of the mixture after small intervals till it becomes constant. Record the highest temperature reached.

Observations

1. Initial temperature of acid and base = t_1°C (it should be room temperature here)
2. Temperature attained after mixing the two solutions (HCl and NaOH) = t_2°C
3. Change in temperature, $\Delta t = (t_2 - t_1)$°C
4. Mass of mixture solution after neutralisation = 200 g (as the solution has same density as water)
5. Water equivalent of calorimeter = W g (given)

Calculation

1. The rise in temperature = $(t_2 - t_1)$ °C.
2. Heat liberated during the neutralisation of 100 mL of 1M HCl with 100 mL of 1 M NaOH = $-(200 + W)(t_2 - t_1)$ cal [Here, negative sign represents the evolution of heat]
$$= -(200 + W)(t_2 - t_1) \times 4.18 \text{ J}$$
where, W is water equivalent of calorimeter or calorimeter constant.
3. The enthalpy of neutralisation ($\Delta_{neut} H$), i.e. heat evolved when 1000 mL of 1 M of HCl neutralised with 1000 mL of 1 M base, NaOH
$$= \frac{-(200 + W)(t_2 - t_1) \times 4.184 \times 1000}{1.0 \times 1000} \text{ J} = \frac{-(200 + W)(t_2 - t_1) \times 4.184}{1000} \text{ kJ}$$
$$\therefore \text{Enthalpy of neutralisation, } \Delta_{neut} H = \frac{(200 + W)(t_2 - t_1) \times 4.184}{1000} \text{ kJ}$$
[for calculations, you can neglect the (–ve) sign]
4. Percentage error = $\frac{[-57.3 - (\text{observed enthalpy of neutralisation})]}{-57.3} \times 100$

Result

The enthalpy change in neutralisation of HCl solution with NaOH solution is .... kJ mol^{-1}.

PRECAUTIONS

- *Record the temperature carefully with the help of a thermometer graduated upto 0.1°C.*
- *Measure the volume of HCl and NaOH solution to be taken for the experiment carefully.*
- *Both HCl and NaOH should be at the same temperature and should have an equal molarity or normality.*
- *Heat loss due to conduction, convection and radiation should be negligible.*
- *The liquids should not spurt while mixing or stirring.*
- *Avoid unnecessary and excessive stirring to prevent heating due to friction.*
- *Proper insulation should be made between the two beakers.*
- *If dilution is needed, always add acid to water slowly to avoid splashing or exothermic reactions.*

Viva-Voce

Q.1 How do you define the enthalpy of neutralisation?

Ans. Enthalpy of neutralisation is the amount of heat liberated when one mole of H^+ ions furnished by an acid combines with one mole of OH^- ions furnished by a base to form one mole of water.

Q.2 Which type of chemical reaction is neutralisation — exothermic or endothermic?

Ans. Neutralisation is an exothermic reaction as it results in the release of heat.

Q.3 What is the value of enthalpy of neutralisation for strong acid–strong base reactions?

Ans. The enthalpy of neutralisation of a strong acid with a strong base is always 57 kJ mol^{-1}

Q.4 What kind of bond formation causes the release of energy in neutralisation?

Ans. The release of energy is due to the formation of a bond between H^+ and OH^- ions, resulting in the formation of H_2O.

Q.5 Why is the value of ΔH negative in this experiment?

Ans. ΔH is negative because the reaction is exothermic and releases heat.

Q.6 When does the heat released in the reaction reach its maximum?

Ans. The heat released reaches maximum at complete neutralisation, when equal moles of HCl and NaOH have reacted.

Q.7 How is the calorimeter constant (W) determined in this experiment?

Ans. It is determined by mixing hot and cold water in the calorimeter and applying the heat balance equation.

Q.8 What is the significance of the calorimeter constant?

Ans. It accounts for the heat absorbed by the calorimeter and is essential for accurate enthalpy calculation.

Q.9 What is the purpose of using equal volumes of acid and base in this experiment?

Ans. Equal volumes of 1 M HCl and 1 M NaOH ensure that the number of moles is equal for complete neutralisation.

Q.10 Why is it important to insulate the beaker setup using cotton wool?

Ans. Insulation minimizes heat loss to the surroundings, ensuring accurate temperature measurement.

Q.11 Why is temperature measured before and after mixing the solutions?

Ans. It is because the temperature difference gives the rise in temperature needed to calculate heat evolved.

Questions From NCERT Lab Manual

Q.1 Why does the reaction $H_2O(l) \rightleftharpoons H^+(aq) + OH^-(aq)$ proceed in the forward direction with rise in temperature of the system?

Ans. This is obviously because of the fact that with increase in temperature, the degree of ionisation of water increases. In other words, more of H_2O molecules dissociate into H^+ and OH^- ions with the increase in temperature.

Q.2 Why do we calculate the heat evolved for the neutralisation of 1000 mL of an (1 M) acid by 1000 mL of a (1 M) monoacidic base?

Ans. As per definition of neutralisation, 1M of acid reacts with 1M of base. When we multiply 1000 mL with 1M acid or base, we get 1 mole of acid or base. In other words, 1000 mL of 1M acid or base is equivalent to 1 mole of acid or base.

Q.3 In comparison to heat evolved in neutralisation reaction between a strong acid and a strong base, why is lesser quantity of heat evolved when any one of the acid or the base is weak and still less when both are weak?

Ans. Heat of neutralisation of a weak acid or weak base is less than 57.3 kJ .The lower value is because of consumption of some of the heat liberated during the neutralisation for ionisation of weak acid or weak base. Thus, if any of the species, acid or base is a weak electrolyte, then heat evolved will be less and will be the least when both are weak.

Experiment 3.3

AIM

To determine the enthalpy change during the interaction (hydrogen bond formation) between acetone and chloroform.

Theory/Principle

In the pure state, only weak van der Waals' forces hold molecules of chloroform as well as acetone. The hydrogen bonding between the molecules of acetone and chloroform is depicted as follows:

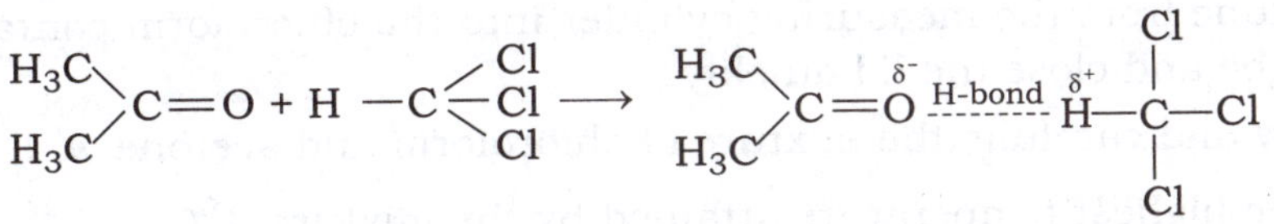

$$(H_3C)_2C{=}O + H{-}CCl_3 \longrightarrow (H_3C)_2C{=}\overset{\delta^-}{O} \cdots\text{H-bond}\cdots \overset{\delta^+}{H}{-}CCl_3$$

Hydrogen bonding between chloroform and acetone

Acetone and chloroform forms non-ideal liquid pair system which shows negative deviation from Raoult's law. Enthalpy change will be negative on interaction of acetone with chloroform, i.e. heat will be given out on this interaction as the two associate and get stabilised due to hydrogen bond formation.

The heat evolved from the system depends upon the amount of the liquid components mixed. Therefore, enthalpy change during mixing of 1 mole chloroform with 1 mole acetone is given by,

$$(\Delta H_1) + (\Delta H_2) + (\Delta H_3) + (\Delta H_4) = 0$$

where (ΔH_1) = Heat gained by calorimeter, thermometer and stirrer; (ΔH_2) = Enthalpy change of chloroform; (ΔH_3) = Enthalpy change for acetone; (ΔH_4) = Enthalpy change of reaction

$$\Delta H_4 = -(\Delta H_1 + \Delta H_2 + \Delta H_3)$$

Materials Required

- Beaker (250 mL) : 1
- Boiling tube : 1
- Thermometer (110°C) : 1
- Glass rod : 1
- Cotton wool : As per need
- Measuring cylinder (250 mL) : 1
- Piece of cardboard : As per need
- Stirrer : 1
- Chloroform : 20 mL
- Acetone : 10 mL

Procedure

A. Determination of Calorimeter Constant (or Water Equivalent)

Water equivalent of calorimeter or calorimeter constant is determined in the same manner as detailed in previous experiment 3.1 but the difference is, here 8 mL of cold water and 7.5 mL of hot water is used instead of 100 mL. Also, instead of inner beaker, boiling tube is used here.

⚠ ALERT

- *Acetone is volatile, flammable and irritant.*
- *Chloroform causes drowsiness and is a harmful irritant.*

B. Determination of Enthalpy Change on Mixing Chloroform and Acetone

1. For the determination of enthalpy change on mixing chloroform and acetone, take a clean and dry calorimeter.
2. Transfer the volume of chloroform equivalent to 0.1 mole (≈ 8.14 mL) after measuring with the help of a measuring cylinder into the insulated boiling tube of the calorimeter as shown in the [Fig. 3.2]. Let the mass of the chloroform taken be m_1 g.
3. Record the temperature of the chloroform. Let it be t_1°C.
4. Now, transfer the volume of acetone equivalent to 0.1 mole of acetone (≈ 7.34 mL) in a clean measuring cylinder. Let its mass be m_2 g.
5. Record the temperature of acetone. Both the solutions should have the same temperature i.e. t_2°C.
6. Pour acetone from the measuring cylinder into the chloroform contained in an insulated boiling tube and close the lid quickly.
7. Stir gently and carefully the mixture of chloroform and acetone with the help of stirrer.
8. Record the highest temperature attained by the mixture, t_3°C.

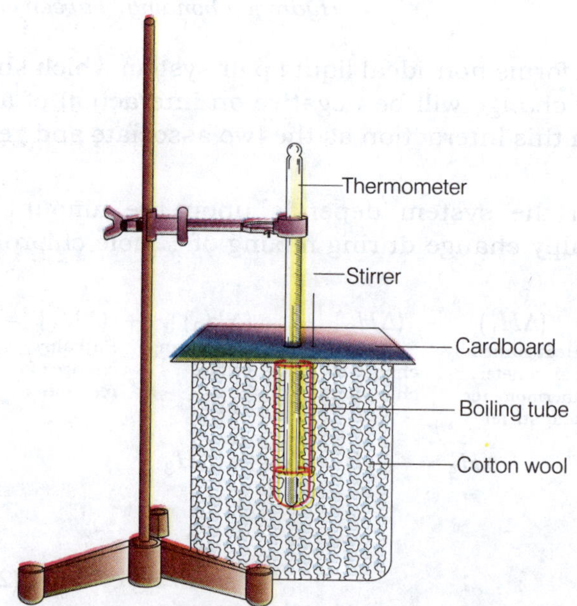

Fig. 3.2 *Determination of enthalpy of interaction of chloroform and acetone.*

Observations

1. Initial temperature of acetone = t_1°C
2. Initial temperature of chloroform = t_2°C
3. Final temperature after mixing the two liquids = t_3°C
4. Water equivalent of calorimeter = W g (given)
5. Molar mass of chloroform = 119.5 g
6. Density of chloroform = 1.47 g/mL

7. Specific heat of chloroform, $S_1 = 0.96$ J/gK
8. Molar mass of acetone = 58.0 g
9. Density of acetone = 0.79 g/mL
10. Specific heat of acetone, $S_2 = 2.18$ J/gK

Calculation

Volume of 1 mole of chloroform $= \dfrac{\text{Molar mass of chloroform}}{\text{Density of chloroform}} = \dfrac{119.5}{1.47} = 81.4$ mL

$\therefore$ Volume of 0.1 mole of chloroform = 8.14 mL

Similarly, volume of 1 mole of acetone $= \dfrac{58}{0.79} = 73.4$ mL

$\therefore$ Volume of 0.1 mole of acetone = 7.34 mL

Total volume of acetone and chloroform = 8.14 + 7.34 = 15.48 mL

Let the room temperature be t°C, heat gained by calorimeter (boiling tube) is

$$W \times (t_3 - t) \times 4.184 \text{ J}$$

Heat gained by chloroform $= m_1 S_1 (t_3 - t_1) = 8.14 \times 1.47 \times 0.96 (t_3 - t_1) \text{ J} = 11.49 (t_3 - t_1)$

Heat gained by acetone $= m_2 S_2 (t_3 - t_2) = 7.34 \times 0.79 \times 2.18 (t_3 - t_2) \text{ J} = 12.64 (t_3 - t_2)$

Therefore, heat evolved on mixing 0.1 mole of each acetone and chloroform

$$= -[4.184\, W (t_3 - t) + 11.49 (t_3 - t_1) + 12.64 (t_3 - t_2)] \text{ J}$$

Or, heat evolved on mixing 1 mole of acetone and 1 mole of chloroform

$$= -\frac{[4.184\, W(t_3 - t) + 11.49 (t_3 - t_1) + 12.64 (t_3 - t_2)]}{0.1} \text{ J}$$

$$\therefore \quad \Delta_{\text{mixing}} H = -[4.184\, W(t_3 - t) + 11.49 (t_3 - t_1) + 12.64 (t_3 - t_2)] \times 10 \text{ J mol}^{-1}$$

Here, negative sign implies that the mixing of chloroform and acetone is an exothermic process.

Note *Here, care should be taken that the total volume of acetone and chloroform is equal to the volume of water for which water equivalent of the calorimeter has been calculated.*

Result

Enthalpy change during the interaction between 1 mole of acetone and 1 mole of chloroform is .... J.

PRECAUTIONS

- Measure chloroform and acetone carefully.
- Acetone is a flammable liquid and eye and skin irritant, so, handle it carefully.
- Chloroform has high vapour pressure and evaporates readily. Inhalation of it irritates respiratory tract and affects the central nervous system including headache, drowsiness, dizziness. So, handle it carefully.
- The liquids should not spurt while mixing or stirring.
- Avoid unnecessary and excessive stirring to prevent heating due to friction.
- Record the temperature very carefully with a thermometer graduated upto 0.1° C.

Viva-Voce

Q.1 Why do acetone and chloroform form a non-ideal liquid pair?

Ans. Acetone and chloroform exhibit strong intermolecular hydrogen bonding upon mixing, which causes deviation from Raoult's law and making them a non-ideal liquid pair.

Q.2 What kind of deviation from Raoult's law is shown by acetone and chloroform?

Ans. They show a negative deviation from Raoult's law due to strong intermolecular attraction via hydrogen bonding, leading to lower vapour pressure than expected.

Q.3 What is the thermodynamic significance of the enthalpy change in this experiment?

Ans. The enthalpy change represents the amount of heat evolved or absorbed when 0.1 mol of acetone is mixed with 0.1 mol of chloroform, indicating the extent of interaction between their molecules.

Q.4 What is the significance of the negative sign in the enthalpy of interaction?

Ans. A negative sign indicates that the process is exothermic, i.e., energy is released when acetone and chloroform interact.

Q.5 How is the calorimeter constant determined in this setup?

Ans. It is calculated using the temperature change caused by mixing known volumes of hot and cold water in the same boiling tube used for the actual experiment.

Q.6 Why are 0.1 mol quantities of acetone and chloroform used?

Ans. These quantities are used to standardise the calculation and to ensure that the enthalpy change corresponds to interaction of 1 mol total (0.1 mol each).

Q.7 State the importance of using equal total volume as water equivalent during calorimeter calibration?

Ans. This ensures consistent heat capacity of the system so that the heat change measured during mixing accurately reflects the interaction enthalpy.

Q.8 What are the specific heat values used for in the calculation?

Ans. They are used to calculate the heat absorbed by each liquid component individually based on their temperature rise during mixing.

Q.9 Why is a boiling tube used instead of a beaker for this experiment?

Ans. A boiling tube is preferred due to the smaller volume of liquids used, which helps minimise heat loss and ensures a better-insulated system.

Q.10 What is the impact of molecular interactions on vapour pressure in this case?

Ans. Strong intermolecular hydrogen bonding reduces vapour pressure, causing negative deviation from Raoult's law.

Q.11 Can the same procedure be used for other liquid pairs? Why or why not?

Ans. No, because not all liquid pairs show significant interactions like hydrogen bonding. The enthalpy change would be negligible or absent in ideal systems.

Q.12 Why must temperature readings be taken carefully and quickly?

Ans. To prevent heat exchange with surroundings which can introduce errors in calculating enthalpy change due to inaccurate temperature difference.

Questions From NCERT Lab Manual

Q.1 Give two examples of each of the liquid pairs for which $\Delta_{mixing} H$ is negative and positive, respectively.

Ans. Ethanol-water and ethanol-acetone liquid pair shows positive deviation from Raoult's law and its $\Delta_{mixing} H$ is positive. On the other hand, chloroform-acetone and phenol-aniline liquid pair shows negative deviation from Raoult's law and its $\Delta_{mixing} H$ is negative.

Q.2 Chloroform and acetone do not form an ideal liquid pair, whereas acetone and benzene do form. Why?

Ans. Acetone and benzene form ideal solution because the interactions (repulsion or attraction) between the molecules of both the components are of the same magnitude as the intermolecular interactions found in the pure acetone and pure benzene. On the other hand, when chloroform and acetone are mixed, the hydrogen bonding takes place between these two molecular species due to which the mixture deviates from ideal behaviour.

Q.3 Why does liquid pair of ethanol and water show positive deviation from Raoult's law?

Ans. In pure ethanol, a very high fraction of the molecules are hydrogen bonded. On adding water, its molecules get in between the molecules of ethanol, thus, breaking of hydrogen bonds and reducing ethanol-ethanol attractions takes place considerably.

Thus, more molecules change into vapour state and total vapour pressure is greater than that corresponding to an ideal solution of the same composition. Hence, ethanol-water mixture shows positive deviation from Raoult's law.

Q.4 How is the vapour pressure of the liquids related to interaction pattern between the molecules of the components of a liquid mixture?

Ans. There may be three cases:

(i) For a liquid mixture of two pure components, if the intermolecular interactions between the components are of the same magnitude as the intermolecular interactions found in pure components, the total vapour pressure of the mixture is equal to the sum of the vapour pressures of pure components.

(ii) If the intermolecular interactions between the components of liquid mixture are lower than that between the molecules of pure components, the total vapour pressure is greater than that corresponding to an ideal solution of same composition.

(iii) In case, the forces of attraction between the molecules of components of mixture are more than that between pure components, the total vapour pressure of the solution will be less than that expected from Raoult's law.

Unit 4

Electrochemistry

The branch of chemistry which deals with the study of relationship between electrical energy and chemical energy and interconversion of one form of energy into another is called **electrochemistry**. The device in which chemical energy is converted into electrical energy is called an **electrochemical** cell or **galvanic cell**. Basically, in galvanic cells, the chemical energy of a spontaneous redox reaction is converted into electrical energy.

Cell Potential

The electrode potential may be defined as the tendency of an electrode to lose or gain electron when it is in contact with a solution of its own ions.

The difference between the electrode potential of two electrodes forming an electrochemical cell is called **cell potential** of the cell. Thus, the potential difference between two electrodes of a galvanic cell is called cell potential. It is measured in **volts**. Hence, we can say that cell potential is the difference between the reduction potentials (or oxidation potentials) of the cathode and anode. When no current is drawn from the cell, it is called **electromotive force** (emf) of the cell.

$$E_{cell} = E_{cathode} - E_{anode}$$

Measurement of Electrode Potential

The standard potential of individual half-cells cannot be measured. We can measure only the difference between the two half-cell potentials that gives emf of the cell. According to convention, standard hydrogen electrode (SHE) represented by Pt, H_2 (g, 1 bar)/ H^+ (aq, 1 M) is assigned zero potential at all temperatures corresponding to the reaction.

$$H^+(aq) + e^- \longrightarrow \frac{1}{2}H_2(g)$$

Half-cell potentials are measured with respect to **standard hydrogen electrode.**

A cell is constructed by taking standard hydrogen electrode as anode (reference half-cell) and under standard conditions of which cell potential is to be measured, is made cathode as the other half-cell. Then, the cell potential is equal to the standard electrode potential of the other half cell.

$$E^\circ_{cell} = E^\circ_{cathode} \text{ because, } E^\circ_{anode} = 0 \qquad [\because E^\circ_{cell} = E^\circ_{cathode} - E^\circ_{anode}]$$

Nernst Equation

Nernst showed that electrode potential of cell with respect to standard hydrogen electrode can be measured at any concentration.

For the electrode reaction of the type, $M^{n+}(aq) + ne^- \longrightarrow M(s)$

The electrode potential at any concentration measured with respect to standard hydrogen electrode can be represented by

$$E_{M^{n+}/M} = E^{\circ}_{M^{n+}/M} - \frac{RT}{nF}\text{In}\frac{[M]}{[M^{n+}]}$$

The concentration of solid M is taken as unity and we have,

$$E_{M^{n+}/M} = E^{\circ}_{M^{n+}/M} - \frac{RT}{nF}\text{In}\frac{1}{[M^{n+}]}$$

Here, R is gas constant (8.314 $JK^{-1}mol^{-1}$), F is Faraday constant (96487 C mol^{-1}), T is temperature in Kelvin and $[M^{n+}]$ is the concentration of species, M^{n+}.

Putting $R = 8.314\ JK^{-1}\ mol^{-1}$, $F = 96487\ C\ mol^{-1}$ and $T = 298K$, we get,

$$E = E^{\circ} - \frac{0.059}{n}\log\frac{1}{[M^{n+}]}$$

This equation is called **Nernst equation.**

While applying Nernst equation, standard electrode potential is always taken as standard reduction potential.

Experiment 4

AIM

To study the variation in cell potential of the cell $Zn|Zn^{2+}||Cu^{2+}|Cu$ with the change in concentration of electrolytes ($CuSO_4/ZnSO_4$) at room temperature.

Theory/Principle

The electrochemical cell of zinc and copper is represented as follows:

$$Zn(s)|Zn^{2+}(aq,\ 1.0\ M)\ ||\ Cu^{2+}(aq,\ x\,M)|Cu(s)$$

Here, xM represents varying concentrations of Cu^{2+} (*aq*) ions.

Hence, to study the variation in cell potential with concentration, the concentration of Cu^{2+} (*aq*) ions is varied, while that of Zn^{2+} (*aq*) is kept constant. The measured cell potential enables us to calculate the electrode potential of Cu^{2+}/Cu electrode for each concentration of Cu(II) ions.

For Cu^{2+}/Cu electrode, the electrode potential for each concentration of Cu^{2+} ions theoretically can be calculated by

$$E_{Cu^{2+}/Cu} = E^{\circ}_{Cu^{2+}/Cu} + \frac{0.059}{2}\log[Cu^{2+}] \quad ...(i)$$

The variation in the electrode potential of Cu^{2+}/Cu electrode ($E_{Cu^{2+}/Cu}$) consequently brings variation in the cell potential according to the relation:

$$E_{cell} = E_{cathode} - E_{anode}$$

or

$$E_{cell} = E_{Cu^{2+}/Cu} - E_{Zn^{2+}/Zn} \quad ...(ii)$$

Eq. (ii) suggests that while keeping $E_{Zn^{2+}/Zn}$ constant, the variation in $E_{Cu^{2+}/Cu}$ brings corresponding variation in E_{cell} (cell potential).

Similarly, keeping the concentration of Cu^{2+} ions constant, one can study the variations in the cell potential with the variation in the concentration of Zn^{2+} ions.

Materials Required

▪ Beakers (50 mL)	:	6	▪ 1.0 M zinc sulphate solution	:	40 mL
▪ Voltmeter (Potentiometer)	:	1	▪ 0.25 M, 0.1 M, 0.05 M, 0.025 M and 0.0125 M copper sulphate solutions	:	40 mL each
▪ Zinc plate	:	1			
▪ Copper plate	:	1			
▪ Salt bridge	:	1			

Procedure

1. Take two beakers and add 1.0 M $ZnSO_4$ and 0.25 M $CuSO_4$ solutions separately (40 mL volume of each).
2. Immerse the cleaned zinc and copper rods in the solution of that metal.
3. Connect the copper rod with the positive terminal and zinc rod with negative terminal of a voltmeter through the key with the help of connecting wires.
4. Place the salt bridge in the beakers such that it connects both the solutions as shown in the [Fig. 4.1].
5. Note down the voltmeter readings that gives the EMF or cell potential of the cell and also keep record of polarity of the electrodes (this will enable us to give a sign to the cell potential, E_{cell}).
6. Remove the salt bridge as soon as the cell potential measurement is over.
7. Replace the beaker of 0.25 M $CuSO_4$ with 0.10 M $CuSO_4$ solution in the beaker. Place the salt bridge in position and note the voltmeter reading.
8. Repeat the procedure with different decreasing order of concentrations of $CuSO_4$ but keep the same 1.0 M concentration of $ZnSO_4$.
9. Calculate log[Cu^{2+} *(aq)*] and then $E_{Cu^{2+}/Cu}$ for each variation in the concentration of copper (II) in the solution.
10. Record electrode potential values of Cu^{2+} *(aq)* /Cu(s) electrode for different concentrations of Cu^{2+} ions in tabular form.

ALERT

- *Copper sulphate solution is irritant, harmful and poisonous.*
- *Zinc sulphate is of low hazard.*

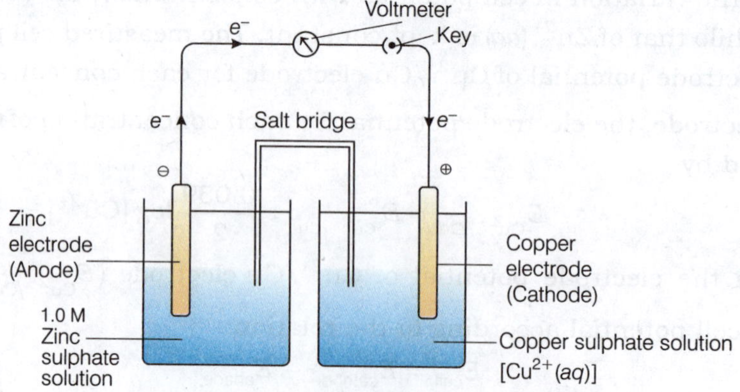

Fig. 4.1 *Zn-$CuSO_4$ reaction in a Daniell cell*

Note *To prepare salt-bridge, take a U-shaped glass tube. Heat 3.0 g of agar-agar and 30 g of pure potassium chloride in a 100 mL water taken in a beaker. Suck to fill the U-shaped tube with this solution and plug both ends of U-tube with cotton plugs.*

Observations

S.No.	$[Zn^{2+}(aq)]$ (in mol L^{-1})	$[Cu^{2+}(aq)]$ (in mol L^{-1})	log $[Cu^{2+}(aq)]$ (in mol L^{-1})	Cell potential (in volt)	
				Experimental value ($E_{Cu^{2+}/Cu}$)	Calculated from Nernst equation (E_{cell})
1.	1.0	0.25			
2.	1.0	0.10			
3.	1.0	0.05			
4.	1.0	0.025			
5.	1.0	0.0125			

Plot a graph for the variation of cell potential (or emf) with concentration by taking ($E_{Cu^{2+}/Cu}$) on *Y*-axis and log $[Cu^{2+}(aq)]$ on *X*-axis.

Calculation

1. When $[Cu^{2+}(aq)] = 0.25M$,

$$E_{Cu^{2+}/Cu} = E^{\circ}_{Cu^{2+}/Cu} - \frac{0.059}{2}\log\ [Cu^{2+}] = 0.34 + \frac{0.059}{2}\log 0.25 = 0.32\ V$$

When $[Zn^{2+}(aq)] = 1M$,

$$E_{Zn^{2+}/Zn} = E^{\circ}_{Zn^{2+}/Zn} + \frac{0.059}{2}\log\ [Zn^{2+}]$$

$$E_{Zn^{2+}/Zn} = -0.76 - 0$$

$$E_{Zn^{2+}/Zn} = -0.76\ V$$

Theoretical value of E_{cell},

$$E_{cell} = E_{cathode} - E_{anode} = [0.32 - (-0.76)]\ V = 1.08\ V$$

2. When $[Cu^{2+}(aq)] = 0.1\ M$

$$E_{Cu^{2+}/Cu} = E^{\circ}_{Cu^{2+}/Cu} + \frac{0.059}{2}\log[Cu^{2+}] = 0.34 + \frac{0.059}{2}\log 0.10 = 0.31\ V$$

As $E_{Zn^{2+}/Zn} = E^{\circ}_{Zn^{2+}/Zn} = -0.76V$ $\quad [\because [Zn^{2+}] = 1M]$

$$\therefore \quad E_{cell} = E_{Cu^{2+}/Cu} - E_{Zn^{2+}/Zn} = 0.31 - (-0.76) = 1.07\ V$$

Result

The $E_{Cu^{2+}/Cu}$ electrode potential decreases with decrease in the concentration of electrolyte around cathode, i.e. copper sulphate [or $Cu^{2+}(aq)$]. Hence, the graph between $E_{Cu^{2+}/Cu}$ and log $[Cu^{2+}(aq)]$ is a straight line.

PRECAUTIONS

- *Clean copper, zinc strips and connecting wires with sand paper before use.*
- *Place the salt bridge immediately in distilled water after its use.*
- *Carry out dilution of the solution to another concentration very carefully.*
- *Use a new salt bridge for every cell.*
- *The concentrations of copper sulphate and zinc sulphate should neither be too low nor too high.*
- *Connect copper rod with positive terminal of voltmeter and zinc rod with the negative terminal.*
- *No connection in the circuit should be loose.*
- *Note down the voltmeter reading only when the pointer becomes stable.*
- *Choose appropriate scales for plotting the graph.*

Viva-Voce

Q.1 Which instrument is used to measure the potential difference of the cell?

Ans. A voltmeter or potentiometer is used to measure the cell potential.

Q.2 What will happen to E_{cell} if the Zn^{2+} concentration is also increased?

Ans. Increasing Zn^{2+} will increase the electrode potential of the $\frac{Zn}{Zn^{2+}}$ electrode, thus decreasing the overall E_{cell}.

Q.3 What type of chemical cell is studied in this experiment-galvanic or electrolytic?

Ans. A galvanic (voltaic) cell is studied, which produces electricity from spontaneous redox reactions.

Q.4 What is the direction of electron flow in this cell?

Ans. Electrons flow from zinc (anode) to copper (cathode) through the external circuit.

Q.5 Why is sandpaper used before immersing the metal strips?

Ans. Sandpaper removes surface oxide layers from the metal strips, ensuring better conductivity and reaction efficiency.

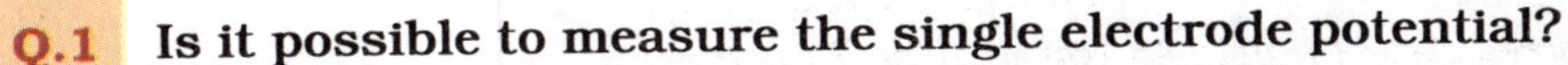

Questions From NCERT Lab Manual

Q.1 Is it possible to measure the single electrode potential?

Ans. The absolute value of the electrode potential of a single electrode cannot be determined because oxidation or reduction half-cell reaction cannot take place alone.

Q.2 What factor is kept in mind while selecting an electrolytic solution for the construction of a salt bridge?

Ans. Factors for selecting an electrolytic solution are as follows:

(i) Inert electrolyte

(ii) Concentration of electrolytes

The ions of the electrolyte in the salt bridge should not react with ions of the electrolytes around the electrodes.

Q.4 For the reaction given below, apply Le-Chatelier's principle to justify the results obtained by you and also bring about mathematical rationalisation of your results.

$$Zn(s) + Cu^{2+}(aq) \rightleftharpoons Zn^{2+}(aq) + Cu(s)$$

Ans. According to Le-Chatelier's principle, if a system in equilibrium is subjected to a change of concentration, the equilibrium shifts in a direction that tends to undo the effect of the change imposed. Hence, for the following reaction,

$$Zn(s) + Cu^{2+}(aq) \rightleftharpoons Zn^{2+}(aq) + Cu(s)$$

If the concentration of Cu^{2+} ions is increased, the equilibrium will be shifted towards forward reaction. Hence, the electron flow from zinc electrode to copper electrode increases and so as EMF of the cell also increased.

Apply Nernst equation, we have

$$E_{cell} = E^{\circ}_{cell} - \frac{0.0591}{2}\log\frac{[Zn^{2+}(aq)]\,[Cu\,(s)]}{[Cu^{2+}(aq)]\,[Zn\,(s)]}$$

For pure solids, i.e. [Zn(s)] and [Cu (s)] = 1

$$\therefore \quad E_{cell} = E^{\circ}_{cell} - \frac{0.0591}{2}\log\frac{[Zn^{2+}(aq)]}{[Cu^{2+}(aq)]}$$

Q.5 Devise another experiment to study the variation in cell potential with concentration of one of the ions involved in a cell reaction.

Ans. In the above given experiment, if we keep the conc. of $CuSO_4$ constant and different concentration of $ZnSO_4$ is used, then the variation in E_{cell} can be studied. It will be noted that the E°_{cell} will decrease with increase in molar concentration of $[Zn^{2+}]$, i.e., $ZnSO_4$ solution.

Unit 05

Chromatography

The word chromatography is derived from latin word chroma meaning colour and graphy for writing. This method was first discovered by a Russian botanist, Tswett. Now, **chromatography** is a widely used technique employed for the separation, purification and identification of compounds.

In accordance to IUPAC, chromatography is a physical method of separation in which the components to be separated are distributed between two phases, one of which is stationary while the other moves in a definite direction.

Thus, chromatography is based on the **principle** of differential migration of the individual components of a mixture through the stationary phase under the influence of a moving phase. The **stationary phase** may be a porous solid (such as alumina or silica) usually in the form of a packed column (column chromatography) but may take other forms also such as flat sheet or a thin layer adhering to a suitable form of backing material such as glass (thin layer chromatography). The **moving** or **mobile phase** may be some solvent or a gas which is commonly known as **eluent.** Hence, in chromatography, a substance equilibrates between a mobile and a stationary phase. The more the interaction of substance with the stationary phase, slower is its movement.

Types of Chromatography

Different possible combinations of these phases give rise to techniques of chromatography. All chromatographic techniques work on the principle of adsorption or partition.

1. Adsorption Chromatography

In adsorption chromatography, the stationary phase is a finely divided solid adsorbent and the mobile phase is a liquid. The process of separation depends upon the selective adsorption of the components of a mixture on the surface of a solid. Thus, in this technique, the components of a mixture are separated by their different adsorption abilities on the solid adsorbent. This type of chromatography is commonly called **liquid-solid chromatography**. Column chromatography and thin layer chromatography comes under adsorption chromatography.

Column Chromatography

In column chromatography, the stationary phase, i.e. the adsorbent (alumunium or silica gel) is packed in a long glass column held in a vertical position. The mixture of components dissolved in a suitable solvent like hexane, alcohol, ether act as **mobile phase.** The mixture is poured from the top of the column which is filled with adsorbing material like alumina, chalk, charcoal, silica gel. The process of addition of the mixture to the column is called **loading**.

As the mobile phase flows, several bands are developed. The most highly adsorbed component forms the topmost band while the least adsorbed component forms the lowermost band (Fig. 5.1). Different components are washed down by passing another liquid through the column. This process is known as **elution.** Evaporation or distillation of solvent from different fractions gives the pure form of the various components of the mixture.

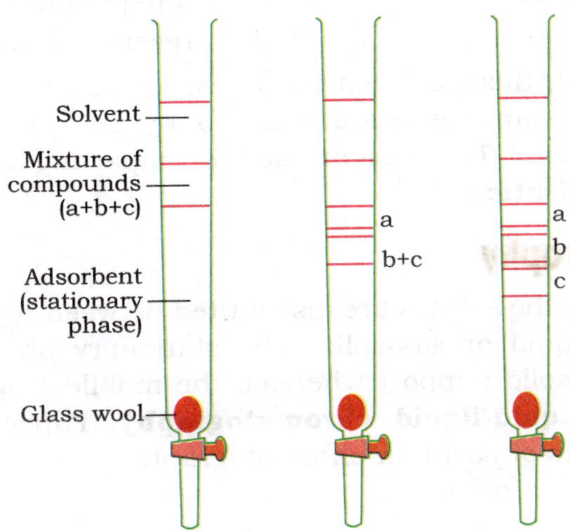

Fig. 5.1 *Column chromatography*

Thin Layer Chromatography (TLC)

In thin layer chromatography, a thin layer of adsorbent like alumina or silica gel (stationary phase) is spread on a glass plate or plastic sheet. In TLC, the mobile phase is a liquid which moves by capillary action.

A mixture of components is dissolved in a suitable solvent. A drop of this solution is placed at one end of the glass plate. It is then placed vertically in a vessel containing the solvent. The solvent rises up by capillary action and carries the components of the mixture which get adsorbed at different distances on thin layer of the adsorbent depending upon the extent of adsorption.

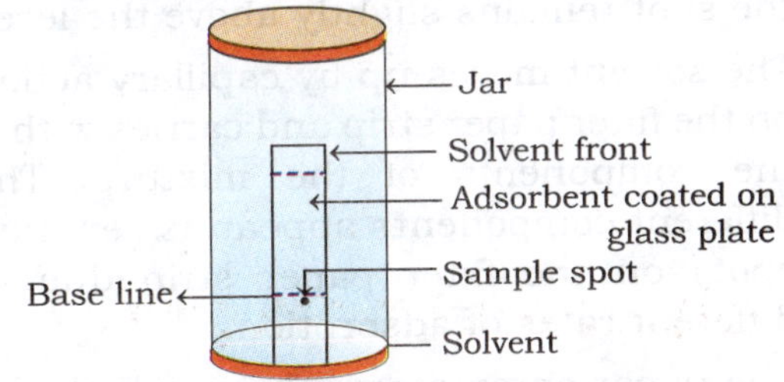

Fig. 5.2 *Thin layer chromatography*

The strongly adsorbed components remain at the lower level while the weakly adsorbed components rise to greater heights [Fig. 5.2].

The various components on the developed TLC plate are identified by their R_f values.

R_f value

At a constant temperature (generally room temperature), it is possible to determine the characteristic rate of movement of each component of mixture on the chromatographic paper for a given solvent or eluent. This is represented by **relative front** or **retention factor** or **retardation factor (R_f value)**. Thus, R_f value is the ratio of the distance travelled by the solute from the origin to the distance travelled by the solvent from the same point.

It can be calculated as

$$R_f = \frac{\text{Distance travelled by the solute from the original or reference line (cm)}}{\text{Distance travelled by the solvent from the original or reference line (cm)}}$$

Since, solvent front moves faster than the compounds, the R_f value of a substance will always be less than one. Also, R_f value has no unit.

R_f values of different compounds are different even if the mobile phase (solvent) is same. Furthermore, R_f value of a compound may be different in different solvents.

R_f value of a substance depends upon :

1. Nature of the mobile phase (solvent)
2. Quality of the filter paper used (in paper chromatography)
3. Nature of the substance
4. Temperature
5. Presence of impurities

If the compound is coloured, then its position on the chromatographic paper may be easily located. However, if the substance is colourless, it may be treated with the reagent, which imparts its characteristic colour. The reagent used for imparting a colour is called **developer.** This process is called **visualisation.**

2. Partition Chromatography

In partition chromatography, the solutes are distributed between two immiscible phases, which may be liquid-liquid, gas-liquid or gas-solid. The stationary phase is a thin film of liquid adsorbed on the surface of solid support whereas, the mobile phase is a liquid. This type of chromatography is called **liquid-liquid chromatography**. Paper chromatography and gas chromatography are the types of partition chromatography.

Paper Chromatography

Paper chromatography technique was devised by Martin and Synge in 1941. It is an example of liquid-liquid partition chromatography in which a special adsorbent paper is used.

It is a chromatography in which liquid present in the pores of paper is **stationary phase** and solvent serves as **mobile phase.** The mixture to be analysed is placed in the form of a spot at one end of the filter paper. The filter paper is suspended in a cylinder containing a solvent such that the spot remains slightly above the level of the solvent. [Fig. 5.3]

The solvent moves up by capillary action on the filter paper strip and carries with it the components of the mixture. The different components appear as separate spots on the filter paper strip due to different rates of adsorption.

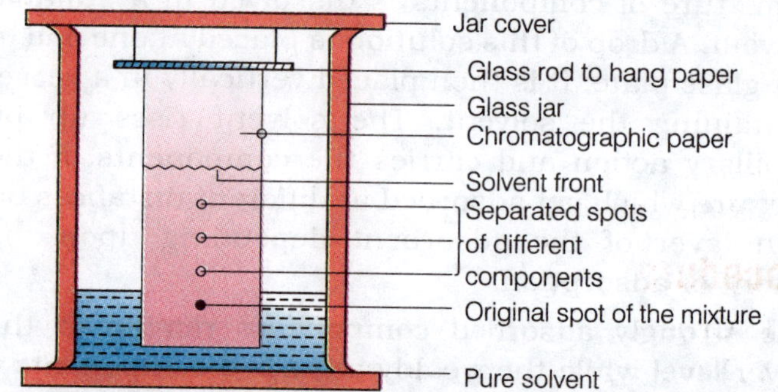

Fig. 5.3 *Paper chromatography*

The paper chromatography in which the solvent rises up is known as **ascending paper chromatography.** On the other hand, if the solvent is taken on the top in a container and allowed to come down on the paper, is known as **descending paper chromatography.**

The chromatographic paper can also be folded in the form of a cylinder and is dipped in a solvent. This is called radial chromatography. The different spots formed after the separation of the mixture are made visible by placing the paper on the plate in an iodine chamber. This process is called **visualisation** as discussed earlier. Spots of separated coloured components are identified by their R_f values.

Gas Chromatography

It is a type of partition chromatography used to separate mixture of gases, liquids and volatile liquids. A small amount of mixture is introduced into a stream of gas which acts as mobile phase. The stream of gas along with the various components to be separated passes through a column. Various components get separated and collected one by one at different intervals and are recorded automatically on a chromatogram.

Experiment 5.1

AIM

Separation of pigments from extracts of leaves and flowers by paper chromatography and determination of R_f value of components.

Theory/Principle

Flower juice contains organic compounds which are covalent in nature and thus, soluble in organic solvents. In this experiment, moving or mobile phase (eluent) can be a solvent like hexane, toluene, acetone or a mixture of solvents such as methanol-water mixture, etc. and water molecules present in the pores of the filter paper act as the stationary phase. The mixture (here, mixture refers to the mixture of pigments present in the extract of leaves and flowers) to be separated is placed at one end of the small filter paper strip as a small spot.

As the moving phase passes through the spot on which sample has been absorbed, it dissolves the components more or less readily, depending upon the solubility and carries them along with it while moving on the support. The filter paper showing the separation of the components is called **chromatogram**.

Materials Required

- Whatman's filter paper no.1 of size 4 cm × 17 cm : 1
- Glass jar of size 5 cm × 20 cm : 1
- Rubber cork fixed with hook in the centre : 1
- Test tubes : As per need
- Capillary tube with fine tip : As per need
- Pestle and mortar : 1
- Scale and pencil : 1 each
- Extract of flowers and leaves : As per need
- Distilled water : As per need
- Methanol or acetone : As per need
- Petroleum ether boiling range (60-80°C) : As per need
- Chloroform/acetone : As per need

Procedure

1. Crush few petals of coloured flowers with about 1 mL of acetone or methanol in a mortar with the help of pestle.
2. Transfer the semiliquid paste into a test tube and then close it with an appropriate cork and shake it well. Filter it and collect the filtrate in a test tube and cork the test tube.
3. Grind some leaves in the same manner and make their solution.
4. Take the strip of Whatman's filter paper no. 1 of size 4 cm × 17 cm and draw a line at about 3 cm from the bottom end of the paper strip with a soft pencil. [Fig. 5.4]
5. Using a finely drawn capillary, put one spot '*a*' for the extract of leaves and one spot '*b*' for the extract of flowers. [Fig. 5.4]
6. Let the spots dry in air, put another drops on the same spots and dry again. Repeat this step 2-3 times so that the spot is rich in mixture. [Fig. 5.4]

⚠ ALERT

- *Petroleum/ether is flammable.*
- *Acetone is flammable and irritant.*
- *Chloroform is harmful as it is a potent anaesthetic and depresses central nervous system when inhaled.*

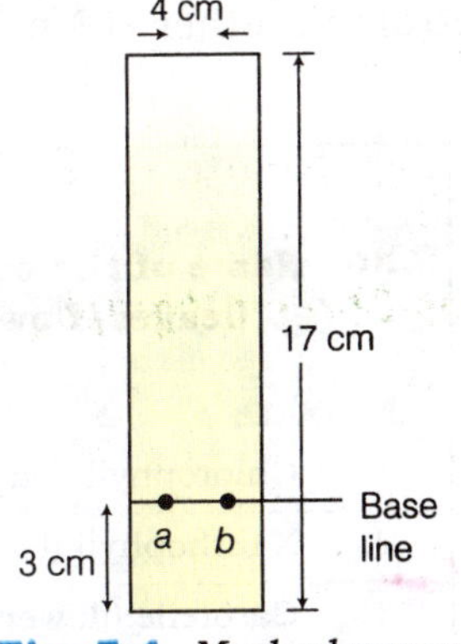

Fig. 5.4 *Marked paper*

7. Pour the mobile phase or solvent (eluent) into the jar to a depth of about 2 cm. The solvent is 20 mL mixture of petroleum ether and chloroform (19 mL petroleum ether + 1 mL chloroform) or mixture of petroleum ether and acetone in the ratio 9 : 1 (18 mL petroleum ether + 2 mL acetone).
8. Suspend the filter paper vertically in the jar with the help of a hook in such a way that solvent does not touch the reference line or base line as well as spots. Filter paper should stand straight and should not touch the sides of the jar as shown in [Fig. 5.5].
9. Cover the jar and leave it undisturbed till the mobile phase (solvent) rises upto two-third of the length of the paper [Fig. 5.6].

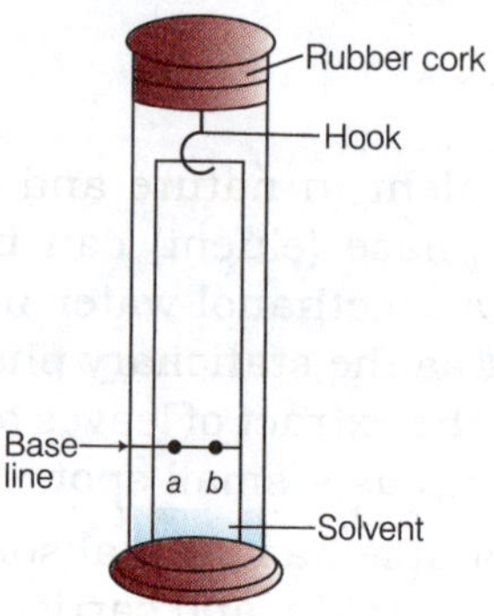

Fig. 5.5 *Dipping the filter paper in the solvent*

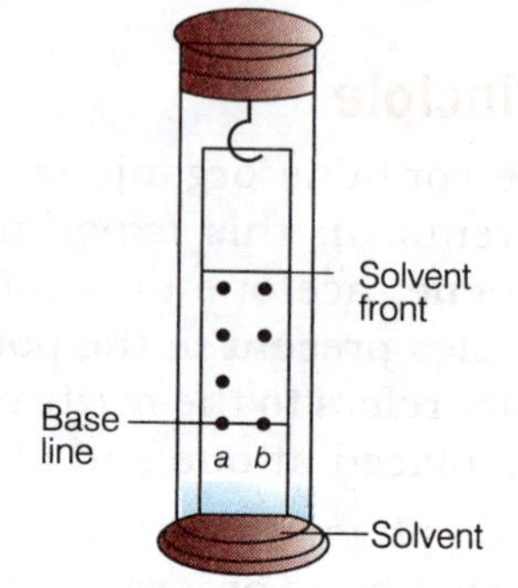

Fig. 5.6 *Developing chromatogram*

10. Remove the filter paper from the jar, mark the solvent front (i.e. the distance that the solvent has travelled on the paper), outline the spots with the help of pencil and allow the filter paper to get dry.
11. Measure the distance travelled by the solvent front and the centre of different spots with respect to the reference line as marked with the pencil. [Fig. 5.7]
12. Identify the number of pigments which are present in the extract of leaves and flowers.
13. Calculate the R_f values of different spots with the help of the expression mention earlier.
14. Compare the calculated and theoretical R_f values of various pigments and ascertain their presence.
15. Record your observations in the table.

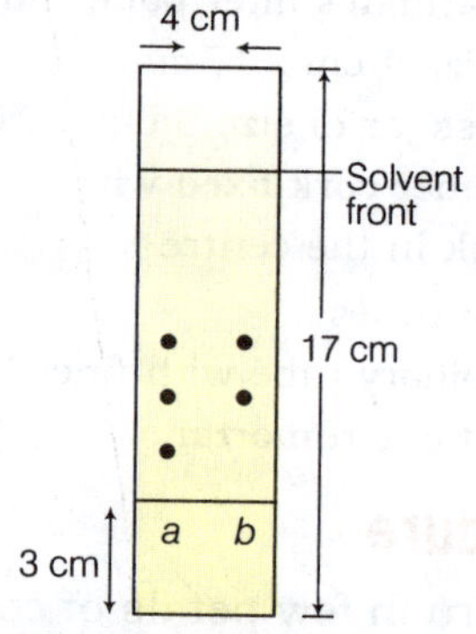

Fig. 5.7 *Developed chromatogram*

Note *Attach chromatogram in your practical file.*

Observations

Name of the flower .... Name of the plant from which leaves are obtained ....

Mobile phase (in mL) =mixture of 19 mL petroleum ether + 1 mL chloroform / mixture of petroleum ether (18 mL) + acetone (2 mL) in the ratio 9 : 1. Running time is 4 hours.

Separation of pigments of leaves and flowers

S.No.	Name of the extract (leaves/flower)	Colour of the spot	Distance travelled by the components of the spots *a* or *b* from the reference line (in cm)	Distance travelled by the solvent from reference line (in cm)	R_f values
1.	Chlorophyll (leaves)	Green	*A* cm	*X* cm	*A*/*X*
2.	Xanthophyll (leaves)	Yellow	*B* cm	*X* cm	*B*/*X*
3.	Carotene (flower)	Red	*C* cm	*X* cm	*C*/*X*

Calculation

$$R_f \text{ value of pigments} = \frac{\text{Distance moved by the pigment}}{\text{Distance moved by the solvent}}$$

$$\text{e.g. } R_f \text{ value of chlorophyll} = \frac{A}{X} = \frac{\text{Distance moved by the chlorophyll}}{\text{Distance moved by the solvent}}$$

Result

1. Number of coloured constituents present in the extract of flowers are ....
2. Number of coloured constituents present in the extract of leaves are ....
3. R_f values of components of flowers are ....
4. R_f values of components of leaves are ....

PRECAUTIONS

- *Use good quality pencil for drawing the reference line so that the mark does not dissolve in the solvent in which the chromatography is carried out.*
- *Always make use of a very fine capillary for applying the spot on the paper. Diameter of the spot should not exceed 2 to 4 mm.*
- *While spotting the test solution on the paper, do not allow the spots to spread.*
- *Dip the paper strip in the solvent in such a way that the spot of the mixture is above the solvent level and the movement of the solvent front is not zig-zag.*
- *The distance of the spot from the end should not be more than 3 cm and should be small and rich in mixture.*
- *Ensure that the filter paper hangs freely in the jar.*
- *Do not put the strip over flame for drying. Keep the strip erect and do not let it to be curled.*
- *The spot should not dip in the mobile phase.*
- *Once the experiment is started, do not disturb the jar as long as the chromatogram is being developed. Keep the jar covered with the lid when the chromatogram is being developed.*
- *Make the paper strip perfectly dry before developing the spots.*
- *Handle the organic solvents with care.*

Viva-Voce

Q.1 Define chromatography.

Ans. Chromatography is a technique used to separate, obtain and purify different components of a mixture.

Q.2 What is the basis of classification of different chromatographic techniques?

Ans. The chromatographic techniques are classified on the basis of difference in the nature of mobile and stationary phase.

Q.3 Name different chromatographic techniques.

Ans. Column chromatography, partition chromatography, thin layer chromatography, paper chromatography and gas chromatography.

Q.4 What type of solvents are used to separate the organic and inorganic compounds?

Ans. Organic solvents like acetone are used to separate organic compounds whereas polar solvents like water, HCl are used to separate inorganic compounds.

Q.5 What is the basic principle involved in paper chromatography?

Ans. Partition between two miscible liquids.

Q.6 What are moving and stationary phases in paper chromatography?

Ans. Both phases are liquids, water adsorbed on cellulose constituting the paper serves as stationary phase and organic solvent acts as mobile phase.

Q.7 What is the difference between ascending, descending and radial paper chromatography?

Ans. When the movement of mobile phase is in upward direction, it is ascending chromatography, when it is downward, it is descending chromatography, and when it is horizontal and outward from a central spot, it is radial chromatography.

Q.8 Can we use the ordinary filter paper for paper chromatography?

Ans. Though we can use the ordinary filter paper for paper chromatography but it does not yield effective separation of components because the pores of ordinary filter paper are not regular and it may also contain impurities which may hinder in the separation of components.

Q.9 Why did you allow the sample spot to dry?

Ans. If sample spot is not dried and dipped in the solvent, then the spot widely spreads and making the separation of components impossible.

Q.10 What is the significance of R_f values?

Ans. R_f values help in the identification of the components of a sample mixture.

Q.11 Can R_f value be greater than one?

Ans. R_f value cannot be greater than one because

$$R_f = \frac{\text{Distance travelled by the component}}{\text{Distance travelled by the solvent}}$$

Thus, the distance travelled by the solvent is always greater than the distance travelled by each component.

Q.12 Why is the R_f value of pigments in flower petal juice different?

Ans. Because the different pigments have different rates of movement.

Experiment 5.2

AIM

To study the separation of constituents present in an inorganic mixture containing two cations, Pb^{2+} and Cd^{2+}(constituents having large difference in R_f values to be provided).

Theory/Principle

The separation of cations and anions present in an inorganic mixture is based on the fact that the cations or anions move with different speeds on stationary phase (i.e. silica gel or alumina) on developing with a particular solvent.

If the compound is coloured, then its position on the chromatographic paper may be easily located. However, if the substance is colourless, the spot is then made visible by using a suitable visualising reagent, called **developer**. In the separation of Pb^{2+} and Cd^{2+} ions, the paper strip can be sprayed by ammonium sulphide $[(NH_4)_2S]$ or sodium sulphide $[Na_2S]$ solution so that Pb^{2+} forms black spot and Cd^{2+} forms yellow spot.

$$Pb^{2+} + S^{2-} \longrightarrow \underset{\text{Black spot}}{PbS}$$

$$Cd^{2+} + S^{2-} \longrightarrow \underset{\text{Yellow spot}}{CdS}$$

Note *Ammonium sulphide is prepared by passing H_2S gas through the mixture containing 100 mL water and 10 mL liuquor ammonia for about 45 minutes.*

Materials Required

- Whatman's filter paper no.1 of size 4 cm × 17 cm : 1
- Glass jar of size 5 cm × 20 cm : 1
- Rubber cork fixed with hook in the centre : 1
- 1-2% solution of $Pb(NO_3)_2$ and $Cd(NO_3)_2$: As per need
- Ethanol : As per need
- Test tubes : As per need
- 6.0 M HNO_3 : As per need

Procedure

1. Take a strip of Whatman's filter paper no.1 of size 4 cm × 17 cm and draw a line at about 3 cm from one end of the paper strip with a soft pencil.
2. Apply a spot '*a*' of a mixture containing Pb^{2+} and Cd^{2+} ions at the centre of the initial line with the help of a fine capillary tube. Allow the spot to dry.
3. Hang the filter paper strip vertically in the jar containing a mixture of ethanol, 6.0 M HNO_3 and distilled water in the ratio of 8:1:1.
4. Keep the jar as such till the mobile phase (solvent) rises upto two-third of the length of the paper.
5. Remove the filter paper from the jar and mark the solvent front.
6. Allow the paper to dry and then spray 1% aqueous solution of ammonium sulphide (or sodium sulphide) solution on the chromatography paper to obtain spots of yellow and black colour.

⚠ ALERT

- *Lead nitrate, $Pb(NO_3)_2$ and cadmium nitrate, $Cd(NO_3)_2$ are harmful irritant, toxic and carcinogenic, prevent inhalation, ingestion and skin contact.*
- *Ethanol is highly flammable so keep it away from flames or fire in the laboratory.*

7. Dry the paper and after that mark the positions of the spots with a pencil and measure the distance moved by the solvent front and the different spots of the cations with respect to the reference base line. This distance is the shortest distance between the reference line and the centre of different spots.
8. Record the observations in tabular form to calculate the R_f value for each cation.

Observations

Mobile phase = Ethanol + 6.0 M HNO_3 + water = 8 : 1 : 1

Developing agent = 1% aqueous solution of ammonium sulphide or sodium sulphide

Running time = ...

Separation of Pb^{2+} and Cd^{2+} ions by paper chromatography

S. No.	Colour of the spot	Distance of spot from the origin line (in cm)	Distance of solvent front from the origin line (in cm)	R_f value
1.	Black (PbS)	n cm	X cm	$\frac{n}{X}$
2.	Yellow (CdS)	m cm	X cm	$\frac{m}{X}$

Note Actual standard R_f value for Pb^{2+} is 0.27 and Cd^{2+} is 0.77.

Calculation

$$R_f \text{ value of } Pb^{2+} \text{ ion} = \frac{n}{X} = \frac{\text{Distance moved by } Pb^{2+} \text{ ion}}{\text{Distance moved by solvent}}$$

$$R_f \text{ value of } Cd^{2+} \text{ ion} = \frac{m}{X} = \frac{\text{Distance moved by } Cd^{2+} \text{ ion}}{\text{Distance moved by solvent}}$$

Result

R_f value of Pb^{2+} ion is .... R_f value of Cd^{2+} ion is ....

Precautions

Same as described in experiment 5.1.

Viva-Voce

Q.1 Who invented chromatography? Also name the scientist who introduced paper chromatography?

Ans. Russian botanist M. Tswett discovered chromatography in 1906. Paper chromatography was invented by Martin and Synge in 1941.

Q.2 Can we separate colourless substances by chromatography?

Ans. Yes, in case of colourless substances, the components will not be visible on the chromatogram. Their presence can be detected by spraying a suitable reagent on the chromatogram called developer which makes the constituents visible.

Q.3 What is meant by the term developing in chromatography?

Ans. During chromatography, if the components to be separated are colourless, then these are not visible on chromatogram. Their presence is detected by developer which involves spraying a suitable reagent (called developing reagent) on the chromatogram, so that the various components become visible. This process is called developing of chromatogram.

Q.4 What is a visualising agent?

Ans. The colourless components of a mixture are not visible on the paper or the column, thus the reagents are used to develop the chromatogram so that the spots become visible. These reagents are called visualising agents. e.g. Ninhydrin spray is used for amino acids and ammonium sulphide is used to detect Cu^{2+}, Pb^{2+} and Cd^{2+} ions.

Q.5 What is resolution?

Ans. The degree of separation of the components after developing of the chromatogram is called resolution.

Q.6 What is loading or spotting?

Ans. The application of mixture as a spot on the reference line on chromatographic paper by using fine capillary tube is called loading or spotting.

Q.7 What is reference line or origin line or base line?

Ans. It is a line drawn near one end of the strip with a pencil for spotting. The sample spot is applied at the centre of this line.

Q.8 How does the liquid rise through the filter paper in paper chromatography?

Ans. By means of capillary action.

Q.9 Which will travel more distance, one which has more adsorbing power or one, which has less adsorbing power?

Ans. The one which has less adsorbing power will travel more distance.

Q.10 Is distance moved by spots measured from top or bottom or centre of spot?

Ans. It is measured from the centre of spot.

Q.11 Which colour of ink has more adsorbing power–red or blue?

Ans. Red.

Q.12 Is it possible to separate a mixture of amino acids? What is the commonly used solvent?

Ans. Yes, it is possible to separate the mixture of amino acids. The solvent used is a mixture of n-butanol (25 mL), glacial acetic acid (5 mL) and water (20 mL). The visualising agent used for amino acids is ninhydrin solution.

Q.13 Is it possible to separate isotopes of elements by chromatography? Give reason.

Ans. No, since isotopes have same chemical properties, they cannot be separated by using this technique.

Q.14 Mention some important biochemical applications of chromatography.

Ans. Separation of amino acids, peptides, proteins, nucleic acids, etc.

Questions From NCERT Lab Manual

Q.1 How is the phenomenon of adsorption applied in the separation of compounds by chromatography?

Ans. Chromatography is based on the principle of different rates of adsorption of components from a moving phase (solvent) into stationary phase (silica gel or alumina) under the influence of solvent.

Q.2 What are the essential characteristics of the substance used as developer?

Ans. The essential characteristics of the substance used as developer are:

(i) It should be volatile.

(ii) It should impart colour to the different spots.

(iii) It should not react with various compounds which are being separated.

Unit 6

Preparation of Inorganic Compounds

Generally, the inorganic compounds prepared in laboratory at this level are double salts. These are made up of two single salts which are crystallised together with a definite number of water of crystallisation. Thus, **double salt** is a substance obtained by the combination of two different salts which crystallise together as a single substance but ionise as two distinct salts when dissolved in water.

The constituent salts are always taken in some definite molecular proportions. The most common examples of double salts are alums and Mohr's salt.

Crystallisation is a process of cooling slowly the hot saturated solution of a substance to form crystals of well defined geometrical forms. Crystals are solid particles having well defined geometrical shapes which separate when a hot saturated solution of the solid is cooled slowly. Crystallisation is carried out for the purification of solids and preparation of double salts.

Alums

Alums are double sulphates possessing a general formula $X_2SO_4 \cdot M_2(SO_4)_3 \cdot 24H_2O$

where, X = monovalent cation like Na^+, K^+ and NH_4^+

M = trivalent cation like Al^{3+}, Cr^{3+} and Fe^{3+}

Some common alums are listed below

Ferric alum : $(NH_4)_2SO_4 \cdot Fe_2(SO_4)_3 \cdot 24H_2O$

Potash alum : $K_2SO_4 \cdot Al_2(SO_4)_3 \cdot 24H_2O$

Chrome alum : $K_2SO_4 \cdot Cr_2(SO_4)_3 \cdot 24H_2O$

Soda alum : $Na_2SO_4 \cdot Al_2(SO_4)_3 \cdot 24H_2O$

Alums are isomorphous crystalline solids which are soluble in water. Due to hydrolysis, their aqueous solutions have acidic character.

Mohr's Salt

Mohr's salt is a doube salt of formula $FeSO_4 \cdot (NH_4)_2SO_4 \cdot 6H_2O$. It is used as primary standard in volumetric analysis. Its crystals neither lose water of crystallisation by efflorescence nor it is oxidised by air. It is a stable salt unlike green vitriol ($FeSO_4 \cdot 7H_2O$) which gets oxidised by air.

Experiment 6.1

AIM

To prepare double salts : ferrous ammonium sulphate (Mohr's salt) and potash alum.

Theory/Principle

Ferrous Ammonium Sulphate (Mohr's Salt)

Mohr's salt having the formula $FeSO_4 \cdot (NH_4)_2SO_4 \cdot 6H_2O$, furnishes Fe^{2+}, NH_4^+, SO_4^{2-} ions on dissolving in water. It is prepared by dissolving equimolar quantities of ferrous sulphate and ammonium sulphate in water containing a little amount of dilute sulphuric acid, and then subjecting the resulting solution to crystallisation when light green crystals of ferrous ammonium sulphate [$FeSO_4 \cdot (NH_4)_2SO_4 \cdot 6H_2O$] separate out. Dilute sulphuric acid is added to prevent the hydrolysis of ferrous sulphate.

$$\underset{\substack{1\ \text{mol} \\ = 152\ \text{g mol}^{-1}}}{FeSO_4} + \underset{\substack{1\ \text{mol} \\ = 132\ \text{g mol}^{-1}}}{(NH_4)_2SO_4} + \underset{\substack{6\ \text{mol} \\ = 108\ \text{g mol}^{-1}}}{6H_2O} \longrightarrow \underset{\substack{1\ \text{mol} = 392\ \text{g mol}^{-1} \\ \text{(Mohr's salt)}}}{FeSO_4 \cdot (NH_4)_2SO_4 \cdot 6H_2O}$$

The light green crystals of Mohr's salt are **monoclinic** in shape.

Potash Alum

Potash alum furnishes K^+, Al^{3+} and SO_4^{2-} ions in aqueous solution. It can be prepared by concentrating equimolar quantities of potassium sulphate (K_2SO_4) and aluminium sulphate [$Al_2(SO_4)_3$] dissolved in minimum amount of water containing a little amount of sulphuric acid and subjecting the resulting solution to crystallisation point. The solution is allowed to cool and the colourless **octahedral crystals** of potash alum are obtained.

$$\underset{\substack{1\ \text{mol} \\ = 174\ \text{g mol}^{-1}}}{K_2SO_4} + \underset{\substack{1\ \text{mol} \\ = 342\ \text{g mol}^{-1}}}{Al_2(SO_4)_3} + \underset{\substack{24\ \text{mol} \\ = 432\ \text{g mol}^{-1}}}{24H_2O} \longrightarrow \underset{\substack{1\ \text{mol} = 948\ \text{g mol}^{-1} \\ \text{(Potash alum)}}}{K_2SO_4 \cdot Al_2(SO_4)_3 \cdot 24H_2O} \text{ or } 2KAl(SO_4)_2 \cdot 12H_2O$$

Materials Required

- Beaker (100 mL) : 1
- Beakers (50 mL) : 3
- Conical flasks (50 mL) : 2
- Trough : 2
- Glass rod : 1
- Tripod stand : 1
- Funnel : 1
- Wire gauze : 1
- Potassium sulphate : As per need
- Aluminium sulphate : As per need
- Ferrous sulphate : As per need
- Ammonium sulphate : As per need
- Dilute sulphuric acid : As per need
- Ethanol : As per need

Procedure

A. Preparation of Double Salt : Ferrous Ammonium Sulphate (Mohr's Salt)

For the preparation of ferrous ammonium sulphate, proceed in the following steps:

ALERT

- *Ethanol is flammable liquid.*
- *Sulphuric acid is corrosive.*

Preparation of Solution

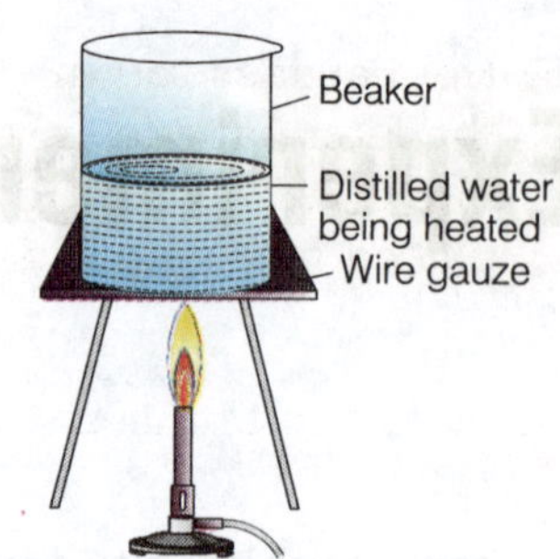

Fig. 6.1 *Boiling of distilled water*

1. Dissolve 3.5 g of ferrous sulphate and 1.7 g of ammonium sulphate (weighed separately) in 5 mL of distilled water contained in 100 mL beaker by heating. Add about 0.5-1 mL of dilute sulphuric acid to the beaker to mix the contents (H_2SO_4 prevents the hydrolysis of ferrous sulphate).
2. In another 50 mL beaker, boil about 10 mL of water for about 5 min to expel dissolved air [Fig. 6.1].
3. Add the boiling water to the contents in the first beaker in small instalments at a time. Stir with a glass rod giving circular motion (as shown in the Fig. 6.2) until the salts are completely dissolved.

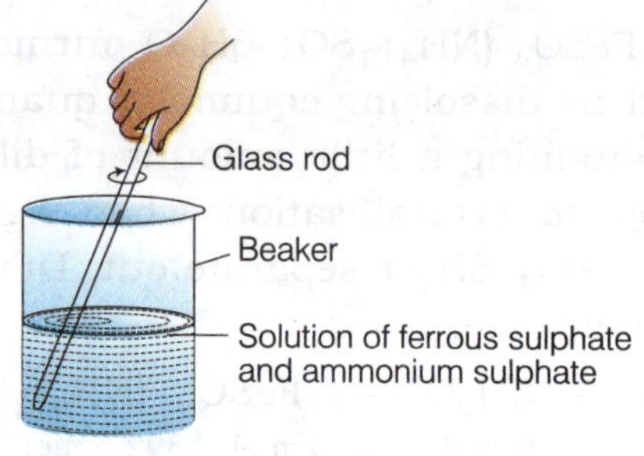

Fig. 6.2 *Stirring of solution with glass rod*

Filtration of Hot Solution

4. Take a circular filter paper. First fold it one-half, then fold it one-fourth. Open the filter paper folds, holding three on one side and one fold on the other side to get a cone.
5. Take a funnel and fit the filter paper cone in such a way that the upper half of the cone fits well into the funnel and the lower part is slightly away from the bottom of the funnel.
6. Wet the filter paper cone with a spray of water from a wash bottle. Gently press the upper part of the filter paper cone against the wall of the funnel with the thumb. So that no air gap is left between the paper cone and the funnel.
7. Keep the funnel on a funnel stand. Place a clean China dish below the funnel for collecting the filtrate. For smooth flow of the filtrate, place the funnel in such a way so that its stem touches the wall of the dish. [Fig. 6.3]

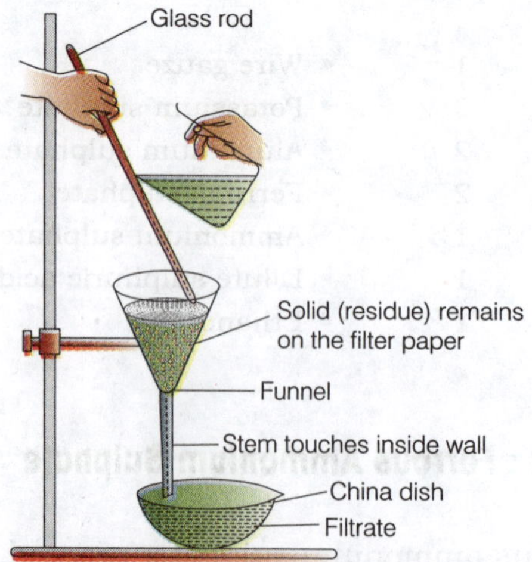

Fig. 6.3 *Filtration process for removing insoluble impurities*

8. Hold a glass rod in slanting position taking care that the lower end of the rod reaches into the filter paper cone but does not touch it. Pour the solution along the glass rod as shown in Fig. 6.3. The filtrate passes through the filter paper and is collected into the China dish placed below and insoluble impurities are left on the filter paper.

Concentration of Filtrate

9. Place the China dish containing the filtrate over a wire gauze on a tripod stand and heat it gently. Do not boil the solution. Keep stirring the solution with a glass rod. [Fig. 6.4]

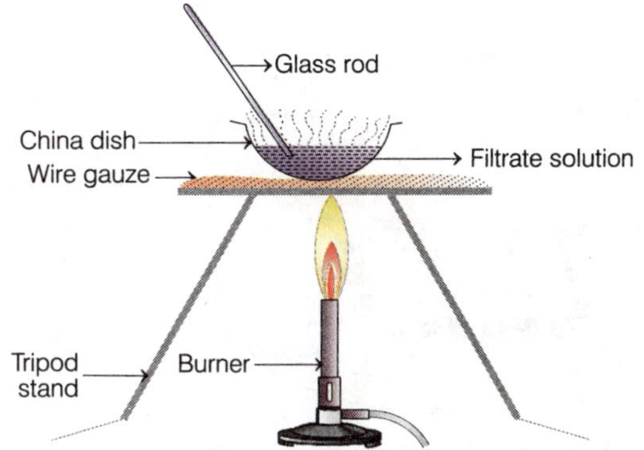

Fig. 6.4 *Concentration (Evaporation) of the solution*

Checking the Crystallisation Point

10. When the volume of the solution reduces to one-half, dip one end of the glass rod into the concentrated solution and cool it by blowing air. Formation of thin crust on the glass rod indicates that crystallisation point has attained. [Fig. 6.5]

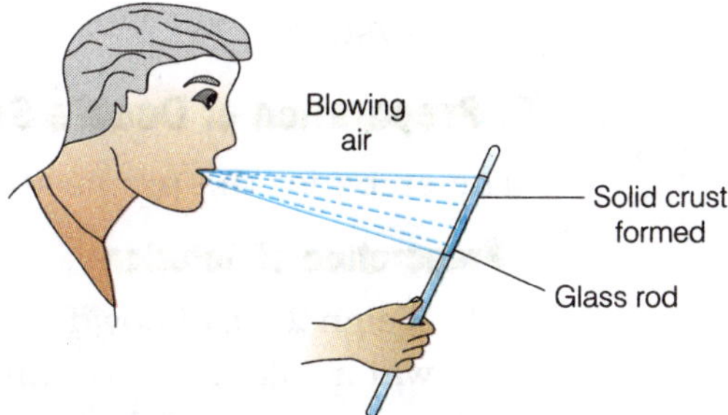

Fig. 6.5 *Checking the crystallisation point*

Cooling the Hot Concentrated Solution followed by Separation

11. Remove the China dish from the flame and cover it with a watch glass and keep the contents of dish undisturbed for cooling. As the solution cools, the crystals separate out. Slow cooling of concentrated solution is preferred for better yield of crystals.

12. If crystals are not separated, then the China dish containing the concentrated solution is cooled by placing it on a beaker filled with cold water [Fig. 6.6]. Seeding may be done if needed.

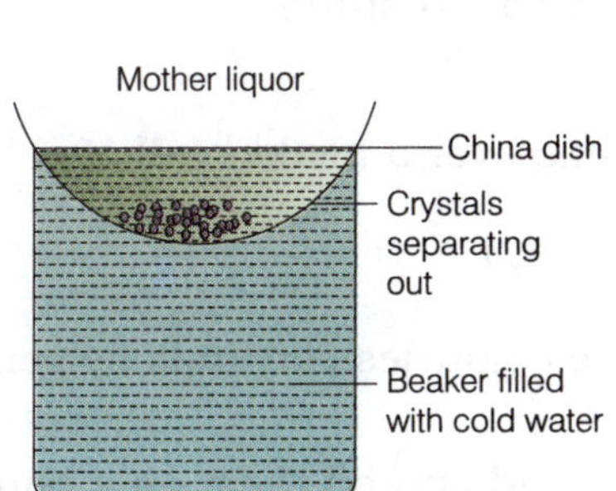

Fig. 6.6 *Cooling by keeping the china dish on a cold water beaker*

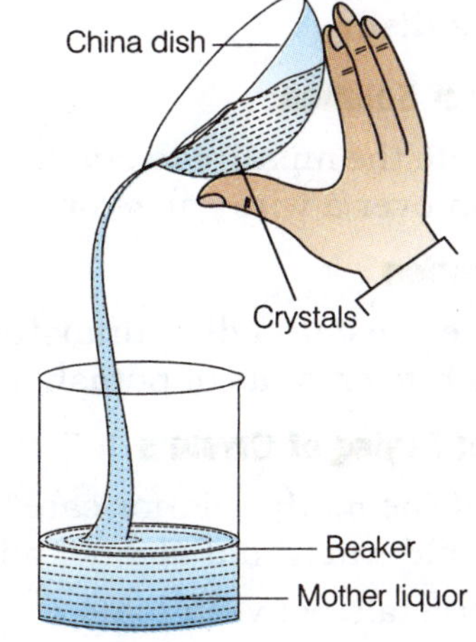

Fig. 6.7 *Decanting the mother liquor*

13. When enough crystals grow, decant off the mother liquor carefully without disturbing the crystals [Fig. 6.7]. Light green crystals of ferrous ammonium sulphate separate out.
14. Wash the crystals by shaking with very small amounts of 1 : 1 cold water and alcohol mixture to remove sticking mother liquor.

Drying of Crystals

15. Dry the crystals by pressing them gently between the folds of filter paper [Fig. 6.8] and by spreading them on a porous plate.

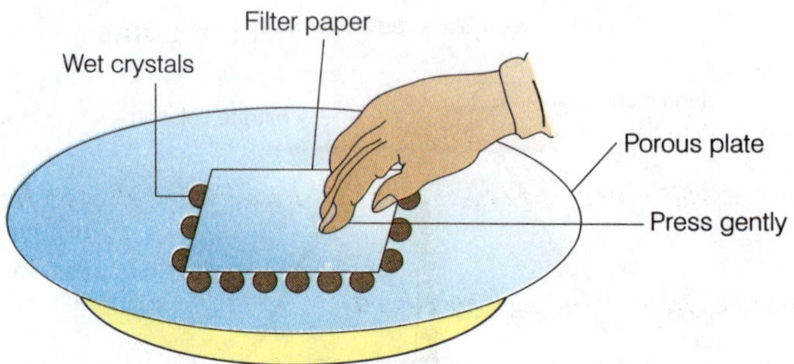

Fig. 6.8 *Crystals pressed gently between the pads of filter paper*

16. Observe the colour and shape of crystals and weigh them. Note the yield of the prepared crystals.

B. Preparation of Double Salt: Potassium Aluminium Sulphate (Potash Alum)

The steps for the preparation of potash alum are as follows

Preparation of Solution

1. Weigh 2.4 g of powdered potassium sulphate and dissolve it in minimum volume of distilled water taken in a 50 mL beaker. Heat the solution with constant stirring with glass rod till potassium sulphate dissolves completely.
2. Take 10 mL of distilled water in an another 50 mL beaker and heat it to about 40°C. Dissolve 6.6 g of aluminium sulphate in it and add about 0.4 mL of dilute sulphuric acid.
3. Heat the beaker on wire gauze with occasional stirring. If the solution is still turbid, then filter it. Mix the filtered solution of aluminium sulphate and solution of potassium sulphate in a China dish.

Concentration of Solution

4. Concentrate the mixture to crystallisation point by gently heating the solution contained in china dish over a wire gauze or sand bath kept on a tripod stand.

Cooling of Solution

5. Now, place the china dish undisturbed for some time over a beaker full of cold water. On cooling, white crystals of potash alum separate out.

Separation and Drying of Crystals

6. Decant off the mother liquor carefully and wash the colourless crystals by gently shaking with 1 : 1 cold water and alcohol mixture.
7. Dry the crystals between folds of rough filter paper and spread them on a porous plate.
8. Observe the colour and shape of crystals and weigh them. Also note the yield of the prepared crystals.

Observations

1. **For Mohr's salt**
   (i) Colour of the crystals = Light green
   (ii) Shape of the crystals = Monoclinic
   (iii) Theoretical yield = 4.94 g

2. **For potash alum**
   (i) Colour of the crystals = Colourless
   (ii) Shape of the crystals = Octahedral
   (iii) Theoretical yield = 13.10 g

Result

1. Yield of Mohr's salt is .... g.
2. Yield of potash alum is .... g.

PRECAUTIONS

- *Cooling should be done slowly, otherwise crystals of good quality would not form. Avoid rapid cooling.*
- *Do not disturb the solution while it is getting cooled.*
- *While doing filtration of hot solution, to avoid splashing of the filtrate, adjust the funnel so that its stem touches the wall of the dish.*
- *Dilute H_2SO_4 must be added in both preparations to prevent hydrolysis of ferrous sulphate and aluminium sulphate.*
- *Potassium sulphate and aluminium sulphate should be dissolved in separate beakers and in minimum volume of distilled water.*
- *Avoid prolonged heating while preparing crystals of ferrous ammonium sulphate, as it may oxidise ferrous ions to ferric ions and change the stoichiometry of the crystals.*
- *Handle the chemicals carefully in laboratory as ethanol is a flammable liquid and concentrated sulphuric acid is a highly corrosive liquid and it can cause burns upon skin contact.*
- *Weigh the desired quantities of different substances accurately.*

Viva-Voce

Q.1 What do you mean by equimolecular proportion?

Ans. Proportion of the substances in the ratio of their molecular masses, i.e., 1 : 1 mole ratio.

Q.2 What are alums?

Ans. Alums are hydrated double sulphates having general formula $X_2SO_4 \cdot M_2(SO_4)_3 \cdot 24H_2O$.
where, X = monovalent cation such as Na^+, K^+ etc.
M = trivalent cation such as Al^{3+}, Cr^{3+} etc.

Q.3 Which ions are furnished by Mohr's salt in an aqueous solution?

Ans. Aqueous solution of Mohr's salt contains Fe^{2+}, NH_4^+ and SO_4^{2-} ions.

Q.4 Why we add dilute sulphuric acid to the solution during the preparation of Mohr's salt crystals?

Ans. Dilute sulphuric acid is added to prevent hydrolysis of ferrous sulphate.

Q.5 Does lithium sulphate combine with aluminium sulphate to form alum?

Ans. No, lithium ion being very small in size does not form alums.

Q.6 Why is water used for the preparation of Mohr's salt solution boiled for 5 mins?

Ans. To expel dissolved oxygen from the water which otherwise, it will oxidise ferrous salt to ferric salt.

Q.7 Mohr's salt crystals are washed with alcohol, not water. Why?

Ans. Mohr's salt crystals are readily soluble in water but insoluble in alcohol.

Q.8 What is the colour and shape of potash alum crystals?

Ans. Potash alum crystals are colourless and have octahedral shape.

Q.9 What are crystals?

Ans. These are solid particles having well-defined geometrical shapes.

Q.10 What is seeding?

Ans. Seeding is a technique to start crystallisation by suspending few crystals of the substance in its concentrated solution.

Q.11 What is mother liquor?

Ans. The liquor left behind after the separation of crystals from a saturated solution is known as mother liquor. It contains soluble impurities.

Questions From NCERT Lab Manual

Q.1 Why do we take equimolar quantities of reacting compounds in the preparation of double salts?

Ans. Because double salts are formed only when two salts crystallise together in simple molecular proportions.

Q.2 What is the difference between a complex compound and a double salt?

Ans. In complex compound, the properties of all individual ions of the constituent salts may not be exhibited whereas in double salts, properties of the ions of the constituent salts are exhibited in solution. Examples of complex compound and double salt are

Complex compound : $K_4[Fe(CN)_6]$ Double salt : $FeSO_4 \cdot (NH_4)_2SO_4 \cdot 6H_2O$

Q 3 Give the name of some of the alums where cations are other than Al^{3+}.

Ans. Chrome alum : $K_2SO_4 \cdot Cr_2(SO_4)_3 \cdot 24H_2O$ Ferric alum : $(NH_4)_2SO_4 \cdot Fe_2(SO_4)_3 \cdot 24H_2O$

Q.4 In the preparation of ferrous ammonium sulphate, can concentrated acid be used in place of dilute sulphuric acid? Explain.

Ans. No, because concentrated sulphuric acid is a powerful oxidising agent. It will oxidise ferrous ions to ferric ions.

Q.5 Why does an aqueous solution of potash alum turn blue litmus red?

Ans. Because the aqueous solution of potash alum is acidic due to hydrolysis of salt, as it is a double salt of strong acid (H_2SO_4) and weak base [$Al(OH)_3$].

Q.6 What are the isomorphous substances?

Ans. The substances having similar crystal structure are known as isomorphous substances.

Q.7 What is the difference between iron compounds: $K_4[Fe(CN)_6]$ and $FeSO_4 \cdot (NH_4)_2SO_4 \cdot 6H_2O$?

Ans. $K_4[Fe(CN)_6]$ is a coordination complex. In aqueous solution, it furnishes K^+ and $[Fe(CN)_6]^{4-}$ ions, whereas $FeSO_4 \cdot (NH_4)_2SO_4 \cdot 6H_2O$ is a double salt and it furnishes Fe^{2+}, NH_4^+ and SO_4^{2-} ions in aqueous solution.

Q.8 What is the action of heat on potash alum?

Ans. Potash alum on heating to 365 K, loses all the 24 molecules of water of crystallisation to yield a porous mass, which swells and known as 'burnt alum'. It is light and fluffy. Its formula is $K_2SO_4 \cdot Al_2(SO_4)_3$

Experiment 6.2

AIM

To prepare potassium ferric oxalate [potassium trioxalatoferrate(III)].

Theory/Principle

When freshly prepared reddish brown coloured **ferric hydroxide** (obtained by the reaction of ferric chloride and potassium hydroxide) is treated with an aqueous solution of oxalic acid, ferric oxalate is formed. This soluble ferric oxalate in the presence of excess of oxalate ion (which is obtained by the reaction of ferric oxalate with potassium oxalate) gives rise to green coloured crystals of **potassium ferric oxalate** or **potassium trioxalatoferrate(III)**. The reactions involved in the formation of these green crystals are as follows:

$$\underset{162.5\text{ g mol}^{-1}}{FeCl_3} + 3KOH \longrightarrow \underset{\substack{107\text{ g mol}^{-1}\\ \text{Ferric hydroxide}}}{Fe(OH)_3} + 3KCl$$

$$\underset{2\times107\text{ g mol}^{-1}}{2Fe(OH)_3} + \underset{3\times126\text{ g mol}^{-1}}{3\begin{array}{c}COOH\\ |\\ COOH\end{array}\cdot 2H_2O} \longrightarrow \underset{\substack{376\text{ g mol}^{-1}\\ \text{Ferric oxalate}}}{Fe_2(C_2O_4)_3} + 12H_2O$$

$$\underset{376\text{ g mol}^{-1}}{Fe_2(C_2O_4)_3} + \underset{3\times184\text{ g mol}^{-1}}{3\begin{array}{c}COOK\\ |\\ COOK\end{array}\cdot H_2O} \longrightarrow \underset{\substack{\text{Potassium trioxalatoferrate (III)}\\ 2\times437\text{ g mol}^{-1}}}{2K_3[Fe(C_2O_4)_3]} + 3H_2O$$

Materials Required

Beakers (250 mL)	:	3	Tripod stand	:	1
Porcelain or China dish	:	1	Ferric chloride	:	3.5 g
Water bath	:	1	Potassium hydroxide	:	8.0 g
Glass rod	:	1	Oxalic acid	:	4.0 g
Funnel	:	1	Ethanol	:	As per need
Funnel stand	:	1			

Procedure

Preparation of Ferric Hydroxide

1. Dissolve 3.5 g of anhydrous ferric chloride in 50 mL of distilled water in a 250 mL beaker.
2. In another beaker, dissolve 4 g of potassium hydroxide in 50 mL of distilled water.
3. Add potassium hydroxide solution to ferric chloride solution in small installments with constant stirring. Wait for sometime and then filter the reddish-brown precipitate of ferric hydroxide so formed through a funnel. Wash the precipitate with distilled water.

⚠ ALERT

- *Potassium hydroxide is corrosive.*
- *Ethanol is flammable and oxidising.*
- *Oxalic acid is irritant.*

Preparation of Potassium Trioxalatoferrate (III)

4. In another 250 mL beaker, take 4 g of oxalic acid in 14 mL of water. In this solution, add 4g pellets of potassium hydroxide and stir thoroughly to get the clear solution of potassium oxalate.

5. Add the freshly prepared ferric hydroxide precipitate in small amounts to the above solution with constant stirring. The precipitate get dissolved and a green coloured solution is obtained. If precipitate does not dissolve, then warm it and leave the contents for sometime.

Concentration of Filtrate and Cooling of Concentrated Solution

6. Filter and transfer the green filtrate to the China dish and concentrate the green filtrate by heating on a water bath (or sand bath) to obtain crystallisation point.
7. Now, place the China dish on a beaker full of cold water and keep it aside for crystallisation.
8. Cover the China dish with a black paper or place the China dish in dark room as the complex formed is photosensitive.
9. Filter the crystals so formed.
10. Wash the crystals with 1: 1 mixture of cold water and ethanol.
11. Dry the crystals by pressing them gently between the folds of filter paper.
12. Observe the colour and shape of the crystals and find out their weight on a physical balance. Also, note the yield of the crystals so obtained.

Observations

1. Colour of the crystals = Emerald green
2. Shape of the crystals = Octahedral
3. Theoretical yield = 5.28 g

Result

1. Yield of potassium trioxalatoferrate(III) = ...g
2. Percentage yield of potassium trioxalatoferrate(III) = ...%

PRECAUTIONS

- *Add potassium hydroxide to the oxalic acid solution in small lots.*
- *Do not evaporate the entire solvent when the solution is being concentrated.*
- *Maintain the temperature of hot water around 40°C.*
- *Let the concentrated solution cool slowly and left undisturbed to get large crystals.*
- *Crystals of potassium trioxalatoferrate(III) trihydrate must be protected from light as they are photosensitive.*
- *Weigh the desired quantities of different substances accurately.*

Viva-Voce

Q.1 Mention one merit of double salts over single salts.

Ans. Double salts are more stable as compared to single salts and can be obtained in state of high purity.

Q.2 Why the complex $K_3[Fe(C_2O_4)_3] \cdot 3H_2O$ is paramagnetic?

Ans. In this complex, iron is present in (+3) oxidation state, i.e., Fe^{3+}, it has five unpaired electrons in its 3*d* orbitals that's why this complex is paramagnetic in nature.

Q.3 What is the geometry of the complex $K_3[Fe(C_2O_4)_3] \cdot 3H_2O$? What type of isomerism does it exhibit?

Ans. Octahedral and it can exhibit optical isomerism.

Q.9 Why did you add potassium hydroxide to the reaction mixture with constant stirring?

Ans. To dissolve the potassium hydroxide completely so that it reacts easily and speedly with ferric chloride to give ferric hydroxide.

Q.4 State the principle of crystallisation.

Ans. It is based on the difference in the solubility of the compounds and the impurities present in a suitable solvent.

Q.5 Mention the purpose of crystallisation.

Ans. (i) Crystallisation is done to obtain pure alum crystals from an impure alum.

(ii) It is done for purification of salts.

Q.6 What is crystallisation point?

Ans. The stage at which the solution becomes saturated with respect to its solute is called crystallisation point.

Q.7 Why must the flask and funnel be heated before the hot solution is filtered?

Ans. To prevent premature precipitation of the solid on the funnel.

Q.8 Why does the filtrate is not heated strongly?

Ans. Because on strong heating, the crystals are not obtained in proper shape.

Q.9 At what temperature, the best crystals obtained? What is the disadvantage of using ice temperature for crystallisation?

Ans. At room temperature, the best crystals are obtained. If the flask is cooled in an ice bath, crystallisation time is shortened but crystal size may become smaller.

Q.10 What are some another methods to initiate crystal growth?

Ans. Scratching the walls of beaker, seeding and reducing the volume of the solvent through evaporation.

Questions From NCERT Lab Manual

Q.1 Give the IUPAC name of the compound called potassium ferrioxalate, $K_3[Fe(C_2O_4)_3] \cdot 3H_2O$.

Ans. Potassium trioxalatoferrate(III) trihydrate.

Q.2 What is the coordination number of iron in potassium trioxalatoferrate(III)?

Ans. Six.

Q.3 Give two examples of bidentate ligands other than oxalate ion.

Ans. (i) Ethylene diamine (en), $H_2\ddot{N} — CH_2—CH_2—\ddot{N}H_2$

(ii) Glycinate, $H_2\ddot{N} — CH_2— COO^-$

Q.4 What are chelates?

Ans. Multidentate ligands are known as chelates.

Q.5 Why does the compound, potassium trioxalatoferrate (III), not give the test for ferric ions?

Ans. Because it contains Fe (III) as complex ion, $[Fe(C_2O_4)_3]^{3-}$ and not as Fe^{3+} ions.

Unit 7

Preparation of Organic Compounds

Organic compounds are widely used in our daily life. Many of the medicines which we take, are composed of mainly organic compounds. Many flavouring agents and sweeteners are also organic in nature. Therefore, in experimental organic chemistry, the preparations are very important. The preparation should give a good yield, the product must be pure and crystalline.

Experiment 7.1

AIM

To prepare acetanilide ($C_6H_5NHCOCH_3$)

Theory/Principle

The replacement of one hydrogen atom of the $—NH_2$ group of aniline by an acetyl, $CH_3CO—$ group in the presence of glacial acetic acid gives acetanilide. This reaction is called **acetylation**.

$$C_6H_5-NH_2 + CH_3-\overset{O}{\overset{\|}{C}}-O-\overset{O}{\overset{\|}{C}}-CH_3 \xrightarrow{\text{Glacial acetic acid}} C_6H_5-NH-\overset{O}{\overset{\|}{C}}-CH_3 + CH_3COOH$$

Aniline; Acetic anhydride; Acetanilide; Acetic acid

Note If acetic anhydride is not available, then acetylation may also be carried out with acetyl chloride in the presence of pyridine.

$$C_6H_5-NH_2 + CH_3COCl \xrightarrow{\text{Pyridine}} C_6H_5-NHCOCH_3 + HCl$$

Aniline; Acetyl chloride; Acetaniline

Materials Required

- Round bottomed flask (100 mL) : 1
- Beakers (250 mL) : 2
- Air condenser : 1
- Sand bath : 1
- Clamps : 2
- Funnel : 1
- Tripod stand : 1
- Wire gauze : 1
- Burner : 1
- Iron stand : 1

Procedure

1. Take 10 mL of acetic anhydride in a clean dry 100 mL round bottom flask and add 10 mL of glacial acetic acid and shake the contents thoroughly. This mixture is called acetylating mixture. Alternatively, take 10 mL of acetyl chloride and 5 mL of dry pyridine as the acetylating mixture.

2. Add 10 mL of aniline to the above acetylating mixture taken in a flask and fit an air condenser on the mouth of the round bottom flask after adding a few pumice stones.
3. Place the flask on a sand bath placed on a tripod stand as shown in the [Fig. 7.1].
4. Reflux the mixture for 10-15 mins.
5. Cool the reaction mixture. Detach the condenser and pour the reaction mixture slowly into about 200 mL of ice-cold water contained in a beaker. During addition, stir vigorously the contents of the beaker with the help of glass rod.
6. Filter the white precipitate or powder which separates out and wash it with cold water.
7. Take the white powder of crude acetanilide into a beaker. Dissolve this in minimum amount of 2% hot rectified spirit. Now, add about 1 g of activated charcoal into the solution. Heat to dissolve acetanilide in it and filter.

   Collect the filtrate into another clean beaker and cool it in ice. Filter off the crystals and dry them by pressing them between the folds of filter paper.
8. Weigh the crystals, determine its melting point and record its yield.

⚠ ALERT

- *Acetic anhydride is highly toxic, corrosive and harmful eye irritant. Do not inhale their vapours while using.*
- *Pyridine is highly toxic, flammable and eye irritant, harmful to the environment, wear gloves while using pyridine.*
- *Aniline is toxic and eye irritant.*
- *Glacial acetic acid is corrosive, irritant and pungent smelling so, handle with care. It can cause serious burns.*

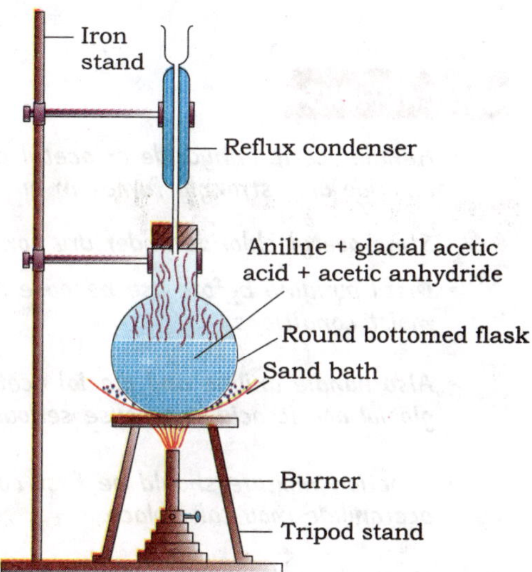

Fig. 7.1 *Preparation of acetanilide*

Alternative Method for the Preparation of Acetanilide

If acetic anhydride or pyridine is not available then the following method can be used.

Materials Required

▪ Boiling tube	:	1	▪ Water bath	:	1
▪ Funnel	:	1	▪ Melting point assembly	:	1
▪ Aniline	:	1 mL	▪ Glacial acetic acid	:	1 mL
▪ Acetyl chloride	:	1 mL			

Procedure

1. Take 1mL of aniline in a dry boiling tube, add 1mL of glacial acetic acid and mix the solution thoroughly.
2. Add 1mL of acetyl chloride in lots (0.3 mL at a time) to the above mixture.
3. The mixture becomes warm, cool it under tap water.
4. Heat the mixture for 5 minutes in a boiling water bath.
5. Cool the boiling tube and add ice cold water (10 mL) into the tube with constant stirring.
6. Filter the acetaniline separated as white powder and wash with water till filtrate is neutral to litmus.

7. Crystallise the crude acetanilide with hot water.
8. Report the yield and melting point of compound.

Observations

1. Colour of crystals = colourless to white 2. Expected yield = 14.5 g
3. Appearance of crystals = shiny flakes like or plate shaped

Result

1. Yield of acetanilide is ...... g.
2. Percentage yield of acetanilide is ......%.
3. Melting point of acetanilide is ......°C.

Note *The melting point of pure acetanilide is* 113°C.

PRECAUTIONS

- *Handle acetic anhydride or acetyl chloride carefully as they cause irritation to the eyes and acetyl chloride also strongly fumes in air.*
- *Store acetyl chloride under dry conditions.*
- *Distil pyridine before use because it absorbs moisture and the reaction does not take place under moist conditions.*
- *Also handle aniline and glacial acetic acid carefully as aniline is a toxic organic compound and glacial acetic acid can cause serious burns.*
- *Reaction mixture should be first cooled and then poured in ice-cold water otherwise hydrolysis of acetanilide may take place.*
- *Wash the solid 2-3 times with cold water till the filtrate is neutral to litmus.*
- *Determine the melting point of perfectly dried and recrystallised sample.*

Viva-Voce

Q.1 Which type of reaction is involved in the preparation of acetanilide?

Ans. It is an acetylation reaction, in which the ($—NH_2$) group of aniline is acetylated by ($CH_3CO—$) group forming acetanilide.

Q.2 What is the role of glacial acetic acid in this reaction?

Ans. Glacial acetic acid acts both as a solvent and a mild acid to catalyse the acetylation reaction.

Q.3 What precaution should be taken while handling acetyl chloride?

Ans. Acetyl chloride is highly corrosive, causes irritation to the eyes, and fumes in moist air hence, it should be handled in a fume hood and stored in dry conditions.

Q.4 Why is pyridine used in acetylation reactions involving acetyl chloride?

Ans. Pyridine is used to absorb the HCl evolved during the reaction and also acts as a base catalyst.

Q.5 What is the appearance of the product obtained?

Ans. Acetanilide forms as white, needle-shaped, shining crystals after recrystallisation.

Q.6 **Why is recrystallisation done in this preparation?**

Ans. Recrystallisation is done to purify the crude product and remove impurities for accurate yield and melting point determination.

Q.7 **What is the significance of washing the product with cold water?**

Ans. Cold water is used to remove unreacted reagents and acidic impurities, ensuring the filtrate is neutral to litmus.

Q.8 **What is the expected melting point of pure acetanilide?**

Ans. The melting point of pure acetanilide is around 114°C to 116°C.

Q.9 **What type of apparatus is used for heating in this experiment?**

Ans. A sand bath is used to provide uniform heating during the reflux process.

Q.10 **Why are pumice stones added before refluxing?**

Ans. Pumice stones prevent bumping and ensure smooth boiling during the heating process.

Q.11 **Why must apparatus be dry when acetyl chloride is used?**

Ans. Acetyl chloride reacts vigorously with water, forming acetic acid and releasing HCl gas which can affect the yield and safety.

Q.12 **Can coloured aniline be directly used in the experiment?**

Ans. No, coloured aniline should be distilled first, as impurities reduce the yield of acetanilide.

Q.13 **Why is the product dried before determining melting point?**

Ans. Moisture affects the accuracy of melting point, so the product must be perfectly dry and recrystallised.

Questions From NCERT Lab Manual

Q.1 **How phenol and aniline can be distinguished chemically?**

Ans. Phenol is soluble in aqueous NaOH solution, whereas aniline is not. Aniline is soluble in dilute HCl, whereas phenol is not.

Q.2 **Why is aniline soluble in hydrochloric acid while it is insoluble in water?**

Ans. Aniline is an organic compound, hence it is insoluble in water. However, if HCl is added to the mixture of aniline and water, then it forms acid-base pair or salt of aniline hydrochloride, because aniline is a base. Hence, aniline is soluble in hydrochloric acid.

Q.3 **Why is aniline a weaker base than ammonia?**

Ans. Because lone pair of nitrogen in aniline is delocalised over benzene ring and it is not fully available for sharing with acids.

Q.4 **Why is acetic anhydride preferred over acetyl chloride for acetylation reaction?**

Ans. Because it is cheaper than acetyl chloride, less easily hydrolysed, gives less violent reaction and good yield. Moreover, acetyl chloride releases corrosive fumes of HCl when reacts but acetic anhydride releases a carboxylic acid which is less hazardous.

Experiment 7.2

AIM

To prepare Di-benzalacetone or Dibenzylideneacetone (C_6H_5—CH=CH—CO—CH=CHC_6H_5)

Theory/Principle

Dibenzalacetone is prepared by Claisen-Schmidt reaction.

$$C_6H_5\text{—CHO} + H_2C(H)\text{—}\overset{O}{\overset{\|}{C}}\text{—}C(H)H_2 + \text{OHC—}C_6H_5 \xrightarrow[-2H_2O]{NaOH} C_6H_5\text{—CH=CH—}\overset{O}{\overset{\|}{C}}\text{—CH=CH—}C_6H_5$$

Benzaldehyde + Acetone + Benzaldehyde → Dibenzalacetone

This is a base catalysed cross aldol condensation between an aromatic aldehyde and an aliphatic aldehyde or an aliphatic ketone.

Materials Required

▪ Conical flask (250 mL)	: 1		▪ Ethanol	: 25 mL
▪ Beaker (250 mL)	: 1		▪ Sodium hydroxide	: 3.15 g
▪ Funnel	: 1		▪ Benzaldehyde	: 3.2 mL
▪ Melting point assembly	: 1		▪ Acetone	: 2.3 mL
▪ Ethyl acetate	: As per need		▪ Ice	: As per need

Procedure

1. Prepare a solution of 3.15g sodium hydroxide in a mixture of 25 mL ethanol and 30 mL distilled water taken in a 250 mL beaker.

   Cool the beaker in an ice bath maintained at a temperature of about 20-25°C along with shaking of the solution.

2. Prepare a mixture of 3.2 mL of benzaldehyde and 2.3 mL of acetone in 250 mL conical flask and add half of this mixture slowly in ice cooled NaOH solution prepared in step 1 with vigorous stirring. A fluffy precipitate is formed within 1-2 mins. Stir the mixture gently for about 15 mins.
3. After 15 mins, add remaining mixture of benzaldehyde and acetone and stir for 30 mins more.
4. Filter the pale yellow solid so obtained and wash with cold water to remove the traces of sodium hydroxide.
5. Dissolve the yellow crude solid in minimum amount of ethyl acetate or 2% hot rectified spirit (or ethanol) and then allow it to cool slowly. Pale yellow crystals separate out.
6. Filter the crystals and dry.
7. Weigh and calculate the product yield and also determine the melting point of the compound.

⚠ ALERT

- *Ethanol is flammable and oxidising.*
- *NaOH is corrosive and irritant. [NaOH in aqueous ethanol is corrosive and particularly dangerous to the eyes. If contacted, remove with plenty of water]*
- *Benzaldehyde is harmful and toxic.*
- *Acetone is flammable and irritant.*
- *Ethyl acetate is flammable.*

Observations

1. Colour of crystals = yellow
2. Theoretical yield = 3.69 g

Result

1. Yield of dibenzalacetone is .... g.
2. Percentage yield is ....%.
3. Melting point of dibenzalacetone is ....°C.

Note *Melting point of pure dibenzalacetone* is 111°C.

PRECAUTIONS

- *NaOH solution should be added dropwise to the reaction mixture with constant shaking.*
- *Maintain the temperature around 20°C while shaking the reaction mixture.*
- *Always use freshly distilled benzaldehyde or the sample from a freshly opened bottle.*
- *Wash the precipitate with water to remove NaOH.*
- *Use minimum amount of ethanol or ethyl acetate or rectified spirit to dissolve crude product for crystallisation.*
- *Determine the melting point of perfectly dried and recrystallised sample.*

Viva-Voce

Q.1 What is the IUPAC name of dibenzalacetone?

Ans. (1*E*, 4*E*) 1, 5-diphenylpenta-1,4-dien-3-one.

Q.2 What is the essential condition for aldol condensation to occur?

Ans. The presence of α-hydrogen atom within the aldehyde or ketone is the essential condition for molecules to undergo aldol condensation.

Q.3 What is Claisen-Schmidt reaction?

Ans. It is the cross-aldol condensation reaction of aromatic aldehyde with an aliphatic aldehyde or a ketone (or aryl-alkyl ketones) in the presence of dil. NaOH solution (that acts as a base).

Q.4 Why does the acetone carbanion react with benzaldehyde rather than another molecule of acetone?

Ans. Benzaldehyde is more reactive than acetone.

Q.5 Why is ethyl acetate used in the preparation of dibenzalacetone?

Ans. Ethyl acetate helps in the recrystallisation of pale yellow solid dibenzalacetone.

Q.6 Name the organic compound which has almonds like odour.

Ans. Benzaldehyde has a characteristic pleasant almond like odour.

Q.7 What happens if the reaction flask is not stoppered and some of the acetone evaporates during the synthesis of dibenzalacetone?

Ans. If acetone evaporates, there will not be enough acetone to contribute enough α-hydrogens, preventing the reaction from occurring.

Experiment 7.3

AIM

To prepare *p*-nitroacetanilide ($NO_2—C_6H_4—NHCOCH_3$)

Theory/Principle

Acetanilide undergoes nitration giving mainly the colourless *p*-nitroacetanilide and yellow *o*-nitroacetanilide. Among these two, *p*-nitroacetanilide is the major product. The reaction yields 80% *p*-nitroacetanilide and 20% *o*-nitroacetanilide.

$$\text{Acetanilide } (C_6H_5NHCOCH_3) \xrightarrow[\text{Below } 20°C,\ -H_2O]{\text{Conc. } HNO_3/\text{Conc. } H_2SO_4} p\text{-nitroacetanilide (80\%)} + o\text{-nitroacetanilide (20\%)}$$

Acetanilide

p-nitroacetanilide (80%)

o-nitroacetanilide (20%)

Recrystallisation from ethanol readily removes the soluble *ortho* compound and the *para* compound separates as fine crystals.

Materials Required

▪ Conical flask (100 mL)	: 1	▪ Acetanilide	:	5 g
▪ Beaker (100 mL)	: 1	▪ Glacial acetic acid	:	5 mL
▪ Funnel	: 1	▪ Conc. H_2SO_4	:	7 mL
▪ Glass rod	: 1	▪ Conc. HNO_3	:	2 mL
▪ Ice bath	: 1	▪ Ethanol or methanol or 2% rectified spirit	:	As per need
▪ Ice	: As per need			

Procedure

1. Take 5 g of powdered acetanilide in a 100 mL conical flask. Add 5 mL of glacial acetic acid to it and dissolve acetanilide by stirring the mixture using a glass rod.
2. Add 5 mL of concentrated sulphuric acid dropwise to the conical flask containing acetanilide and glacial acetic acid. Stir the contents with the glass rod. The temperature of the mixture will rise to about 40°C. Cool the reaction mixture in an ice bath maintained at 0-5°C. The solution will become very viscous.

⚠ ALERT

- *Concentrated sulphuric acid (H_2SO_4) is corrosive.*
- *Fuming nitric acid (HNO_3) is corrosive and irritant.*
- *Glacial acetic acid (CH_3COOH) is corrosive and can cause severe burns. It is a skin irritant and pungent smelling liquid so, handle with care.*
- *Acetanilide ($C_6H_5NHCOCH_3$) is highly toxic and may cause cyanosis.*

3. Mix 2 mL of conc. or fuming nitric acid and 2 mL of conc. sulphuric acid in a boiling tube and cool it also in an ice bath.

4. When both the solutions are cold then, add nitrating mixture prepared in step 3 drop by drop to the cold contents of flask with constant stirring.
5. During the addition, keep the reaction flask in an ice bath so that the temperature of the reaction mixture is maintained at 10°C.
6. Stir the reaction mixture carefully after the addition of each drop. The entire addition requires about 15 mins.
7. After the addition is completed, remove the flask from the ice bath and allow the reaction mixture to attain room temperature and stand it for 30 mins. Meanwhile, monitor the temperature, if it rises above 25°C, cool the flask in an ice bath.
8. Pour the contents of the flask on 100 g crushed ice taken in a beaker. Stir it and filter the crude product.
9. Wash the compound thoroughly with cold water to remove acid.
10. Dissolve the pale yellow crude product obtained above in about 20-30 mL of methylated spirit or ethyl alcohol. Warm it to get a clear solution. Filter while hot and cool the filtrate in ice, yellow *o*-nitroacetanilide formed in small amounts goes in the filtrate (mother liquor) as it is soluble in alcohol while *p*-nitroacetanilide is obtained as colourless crystals on the filter paper.
11. Wash the solid on the filter paper with cold water. Dry it in hot air oven at 100°C.
12. Weigh it and record its yield. Also determine its melting point.

Note
- *Here, glacial acetic acid is used because it is a polar solvent and thus, capable of dissolving acetanilide and the acetate ion is a poor nucleophile, so no substitution is possible.*
- *To prevent dinitration of the acetanilide, the nitrating mixture is added in small portions to the acetanilide solution so that the concentration of* HNO_3 *is kept at minimum.*
- *Traces of acid should be removed because hydrogen ion catalyse the hydrolysis of amide group to p-nitroaniline. The last traces of acid can be removed by using a neutralising agent, i.e.* Na_2HPO_4.

Observations

1. Appearance of *p*-nitroacetanilide = crystalline solid
2. Colour of *p*-nitroacetanilide = white
3. Theoretical yield = 5 g (80%)

Result

1. Yield of *p*-nitroacetanilide is .... g. 2. Percentage yield of *p*-nitroacetanilide is ....%.
3. Melting point of *p*-nitroacetanilide is .... °C.

Note *The melting point of pure p-nitroacetanilide is 214°C.*

PRECAUTIONS

- *Do not allow the temperature of the reaction mixture to exceed 10°C during the addition of nitrating mixture.*
- *Add mixture of concentrated nitric acid and sulphuric acid into the solution of acetanilide slowly and carefully.*
- *Use perfectly dry apparatus.*
- *Wash the solid for many times till the filtrate is neutral to litmus.*
- *Determine the melting point of perfectly dried and recrystallised sample.*

Viva-Voce

Q.1 The nitronium ion is the electrophile in the nitration of acetanilide. Write an equation to show how is it formed?

Ans. The nitrating mixture (conc. H_2SO_4 and conc. HNO_3) releases nitronium ion (NO_2^+) which acts as an electrophile in the nitration of acetanilide.

$$HNO_3 + 2H_2SO_4 \longrightarrow NO_2^+ + H_3O^+ + 2HSO_4^-$$

Q.2 In the presence of H_2SO_4, whether HNO_3 acts as a base or acid?

Ans. HNO_3 acts as a base by accepting H^+ from an acid H_2SO_4

Q.3 Name the reactive species that bring about nitration when nitrating mixture is used.

Ans. NO_2^+ (nitronium ion).

Q.4 What is the function of conc. H_2SO_4, in nitration?

Ans. It reacts with HNO_3 to generate nitronium ion (NO_2^+).

Q.5 In the preparation of *p*-nitroacetanilide from acetanilide, what will happen if the amount of glacial acetic acid is increased from 5 mL to 10 mL?

Ans. If the volume of the solvent is increased, then the concentration of the compound is halved. As the rate of reaction depends upon the concentration of reactants, hence it will also be reduced to halved.

Q.6 Why glacial acetic acid is used as a solvent for the nitration of acetanilide?

Ans. (i) Glacial acetic acid is a poor nucleophile (CH_3COO^- ion) which indicates a relatively low possibility of causing unwanted substitution reactions.

(ii) Glacial acetic acid is a polar solvent which can dissolve polar acetanilide.

(iii) Glacial acetic acid provides acidic environment which would not neutralise nitric acid.

Q.7 Why is sometimes *p*-nitroacetanilide yellow in colour?

Ans. Because of the presence of *o*-nitroacetanilide.

Experiment 7.4

AIM

To prepare 2-naphthol aniline or phenyl-azo-β-naphthol dye.

Theory/Principle

Phenyl azo-β-naphthol or 2-naphthol aniline is an orange-red dye. It belongs to a class of azo compounds, all of which contain the characteristic grouping, —N=N—.

All azo compounds are coloured compounds. This dye is prepared from aniline through diazotisation.

Aniline is an aromatic primary amine. It forms diazonium salt when treated with nitrous acid at 0-5°C. Nitrous acid is generated *in situ* by the reaction of sodium nitrite with hydrochloric acid. This process is called **diazotisation**. The diazonium salt is coupled with an alkaline solution (pH = 9 to 10) of β-naphthol to form an orange-red azo dye.

$$C_6H_5NH_2 + NaNO_2 + 2HCl \xrightarrow{0\text{-}5°C} C_6H_5\overset{+}{N}\equiv NCl^- + NaCl + H_2O$$

Aniline → Benzene diazonium chloride

$$C_6H_5\overset{+}{N}\equiv NCl^- + \beta\text{-naphthol} \xrightarrow[0\text{-}5°C]{NaOH} C_6H_5\text{—N=N—}C_{10}H_6OH$$

β-naphthol → 1-phenyl-azo-β-naphthol (Orange-red dye)

Materials Required

Item		Quantity	Item		Quantity
Conical flask (100 mL)	:	1	Conc. HCl	:	6.5 mL
Beakers (100 mL)	:	2	Sodium hydroxide	:	2.0 g
Glass rod	:	1	Glacial acetic acid	:	25 mL
Thermometer (210°C)	:	1	Ice	:	As per need
Filter paper	:	As per need	Aniline	:	2 mL
Distilled water	:	As per need	Sodium nitrite	:	1.6 g
Funnel	:	1	β-naphthol	:	3.2 g
Melting point assembly	:	1	Ethanol	:	As per need

Procedure

1. In 100 mL conical flask, add 6.5 mL conc. HCl and dilute it with 6.5 mL of water. Dissolve 2 mL of aniline to this diluted acid.
2. Cool the above mixture by placing the flask in an ice bath maintaining the temperature at 0-5°C.
3. In another 100 mL beaker, dissolve 1.6 g of sodium nitrite in 8 mL of water and cool this solution also to 5°C.

⚠ **ALERT**

- *Glacial acetic acid is corrosive and irritant.*
- *Aniline is carcinogenic (wear gloves to handle the aniline).*
- *Sodium nitrite and β-naphthol are toxic and flammable.*
- *HCl and NaOH are corrosive.*

4. Now, diazotise the mixture of aniline by adding the above mixture (prepared in step 3) slowly with continuous stirring.
5. Dissolve 3.2 g of β-naphthol in 18 mL of 10% sodium hydroxide solution taken in another 100 mL beaker. Cool this solution to 5°C by placing in an ice bath. Some crushed ice (about 25 g) may be added directly to facilitate cooling of the reaction mixture.
6. Now, add the prepared diazonium chloride solution very slowly to the β-naphthol solution with constant stirring. The mixed solutions immediately develop a deep red colour.
7. When the addition of diazo solution is complete, allow the mixture to stand in ice bath for 30 mins with occasional stirring.
8. 1-phenyl-azo-β-naphthol rapidly separates as orange-red crystals then filter the crystals obtained.
9. Wash the crystals of 1-phenyl-azo-β-naphthol with cold water and dry the crystals obtained by pressing them between the folds of filter paper.
10. Dissolve the crude product, i.e. orange-red crystals obtained above in 20-25 mL of glacial acetic acid. Warm it to get a clear solution. Filter the solution while hot and cool the filtrate to get the orange-red crystals of dye.
11. Wash this recrystallise sample with few mL of ethanol to remove acetic acid. Dry it between the folds of filter paper.
12. Weigh to calculate the yield of the reaction and determine the melting point of the compound.

Note *Nitrous acid* (HONO) *is a weak, unstable acid that's why, it is always prepared 'in situ'. So, the role of* $NaNO_2$ *and* HCl *is to produce the nitrous acid and nitrosonium cation* (NO^+).

$$NO_2^- \xrightarrow{H_3O^+} HNO_2 \xrightarrow{H_3O^+} H_2\overset{+}{N}O_2 \xrightarrow{-H_2O} \underset{\text{Nitrosonium ion}}{NO^+}$$

After the formation of nitrosonium ion, the diazotisation reaction starts and after diazotisation, coupling takes place.

Observations

1. Appearance of 1-phenyl-azo-β-naphthol = crystalline solid
2. Colour of crystals = orange-red
3. Theoretical yield = 5.4 g (approximately)

Result

1. Yield of phenyl-azo-β-naphthol is ...... g.
2. Percentage yield of phenyl-azo-β-naphthol is ......%.
3. Melting point of phenyl-azo-β-naphthol is ...... °C.

Note *The melting point of pure phenyl-azo-β-naphthol is 131°C.*

PRECAUTIONS

- *1-phenyl-azo-β-naphthol is carcinogenic and might enter your system. So, wear gloves and mask throughout the experiment.*
- *The solution of aniline hydrochloride should be cooled in the range of 0-5°C and this temperature is maintained throughout the addition of the sodium nitrite solution.*
- *Addition of sodium nitrite should be very slow because the reaction is exothermic and may cause rise in temperature of reaction mixture.*
- *Always add diazonium chloride solution to β-naphthol solution for the dye formation and not vice-versa.*
- *Determine the melting point of perfectly dried and recrystallised sample.*

Viva-Voce

Q.1 What is the process of diazotisation?

Ans. Diazotisation is the process of converting an aromatic primary amine into a diazonium salt by treating it with nitrous acid at 0–5°C.

Q.2 How is nitrous acid prepared in situ in this experiment?

Ans. Nitrous acid is prepared in situ by reacting sodium nitrite with hydrochloric acid.

Q.3 Why should the temperature be maintained between 0-5 C during diazotisation?

Ans. This temperature range prevents decomposition of the diazonium salt as it is unstable at higher temperatures.

Q.4 What is the role of β-naphthol in this experiment?

Ans. β-naphthol acts as the coupling component that reacts with the diazonium salt to form the azo dye.

Q.5 What is the characteristic colour of phenyl-azo-β-naphthol?

Ans. It is orange-red in colour.

Q.6 What type of chemical reaction is used to form phenyl-azo-β-naphthol?

Ans. A coupling reaction between diazonium salt and β-naphthol under alkaline conditions.

Q.7 Give a reason why ice is used while preparing the β-naphthol solution?

Ans. Ice helps maintain low temperature and prevents premature decomposition of the diazonium salt.

Q.8 Why is the diazonium chloride solution added slowly to β-naphthol and not vice versa?

Ans. Slow addition prevents sudden reaction and ensures controlled dye formation.

Q.9 Why is glacial acetic acid used for recrystallisation?

Ans. Glacial acetic acid dissolves impurities and helps obtain pure crystals of the dye.

Q.10 What is the molecular interaction responsible for the colour of the azo dye?

Ans. The extended conjugation in the azo linkage (—N = N—) causes absorption in the visible region, giving colour.

Q.11 What is the role of sodium hydroxide in this experiment?

Ans. It creates an alkaline medium required for coupling the diazonium salt with β-naphthol.

Q.12 What will happen if the temperature rises above 5 C during diazotisation?

Ans. The diazonium salt may decompose, reducing yield and affecting dye formation.

Q.13 How do you ensure the removal of excess acid after recrystallisation?

Ans. The recrystallised sample is washed with a small amount of alcohol to remove glacial acetic acid.

Questions From NCERT Lab Manual

Q.1 In contrast to aromatic primary amines, aliphatic primary amines do not form stable diazonium salts. Why?

Ans. Because alkyl carbocation formed on the decomposition of diazonium salt is more stable than phenyl carbocation.

Q.2 Why are diazonium chlorides usually soluble in water?

Ans. Because diazonium chlorides are polar in nature having formula, $Ar-\overset{+}{N}\equiv NX^-$, where Ar is an aryl group and X^- is the anion of a strong acid such as HSO_4^-, Cl^-, BF_4^-, Br^- or NO_3^-.

Q.3 Which of the following compounds on diazotisation followed by coupling with β-naphthol will form an azo dye?

(i) *p*-toluidine **(ii) Benzylamine** **(iii) N-methylaniline**

Ans. *p*-toluidine because it is a primary aromatic amine.

Q.4 How is methyl orange prepared in the laboratory?

Ans. The chemical name of methyl orange is sodium *p*-dimethylaminophenyl azobenzene-*p*′-sulphonate. It is an acidic azo dye and obtained by coupling between diazotised sulphanilic acid with dimethyl aniline.

$$Na^+O_3^-S-C_6H_4-NH_2 \xrightarrow[0-5^\circ C]{NaNO_2/HCl} Na^+O_3^-S-C_6H_4-N^+\equiv NCl^- \xrightarrow{C_6H_5N(CH_3)_2} Na^+O_3^-S-C_6H_4-N=N-C_6H_4-N(CH_3)_2$$

Sodium salt of sulphanilic acid

N, N-Dimethyl aniline

(Methyl orange)

Experiment 7.5

AIM

To prepare aniline yellow (*p*-aminoazobenzene)

Theory/Principle

Aniline yellow can also be prepared by direct diazotisation and coupling of aniline as followed for the preparation of phenyl-azo-β-naphthol dye. However, the diazotisation is carried out in a weakly acidic medium.

$$C_6H_5{-}NH_2 + NaNO_2 + 2HCl \xrightarrow{0\text{-}5^\circ C} C_6H_5{-}\overset{+}{N}{\equiv}NCl^- + NaCl + H_2O$$

Aniline → Benzene diazonium chloride

$$C_6H_5{-}\overset{+}{N}{\equiv}NCl^- + H_2N{-}C_6H_5 \xrightarrow[273\text{-}278\ K\ (-HCl)]{H^+(pH=4\text{-}5)} C_6H_5{-}N{=}N{-}NH{-}C_6H_5 \xrightarrow[H^+,\ \Delta]{(Rearrange)} C_6H_5{-}N{=}N{-}C_6H_4{-}NH_2$$

Benzene diazonium chloride + Aniline → Diazoaminobenzene → *p*-aminoazobenzene (Aniline yellow)

Materials Required

- Conical flask (100 mL) : 1
- Funnel : 1
- Thermometer : 1
- Melting point assembly : 1
- Aniline : 6 mL
- 1.0 M HCl : 4 mL
- Glacial acetic acid : 9 mL
- Carbon tetrachloride : As per need

Procedure

1. Prepare a solution of benzene diazonium chloride using 2 mL of aniline in accordance to the method as described in experiment 7.4, i.e. preparation of phenyl-azo-β-naphthol dye.
2. Prepare a solution of 4 mL aniline in 4 mL of 1.0 M HCl.
3. Add the cold solution of aniline hydrochloride slowly into the cold solution of benzene diazonium chloride.
4. Add 9 mL of glacial acetic acid diluted with an equal volume of water and shake the reaction mixture thoroughly to convert excess aniline to its acetate which is water soluble.
5. Allow the mixture to stand for 15 minutes with occasional stirring.
6. Filter the yellow compound *p*-aminobenzene, wash with a little cold water and dry it between the folds of filter paper.
7. Recrystallise the small amounts of crude sample, (*p*-aminobenzene) from carbon tetrachloride and report the yield and melting point.

⚠ ALERT

- *Aniline is highly toxic and harmful to skin.*
- *Carbon tetrachloride is harmful and carcinogenic.*
- *HCl is corrosive.*

Observations

1. Appearance of aniline yellow = crystalline solid
2. Colour of crystals = yellow colour
3. Theoretical yield = 8.6 g (approximately)

Result

1. Yield of aniline yellow is .... g.
2. Percentage yield of aniline yellow is .... %.
3. Melting point of aniline yellow is .... °C.

Note *Melting point of pure aniline yellow is* 123-126°C.

PRECAUTIONS

- *During diazotisation, temperature should be maintained in the range of 0-5°C.*
- *The crude product should be washed with a small volume of water repeatedly.*
- *Determine the melting point of perfectly dried and recrystallised sample.*
- *During this coupling reaction, the pH should be 4-5.*

Viva-Voce

Q.1 Which type of reaction is involved in this preparation?

Ans. It involves a rearrangement reaction of diazoaminobenzene under weakly acidic conditions.

Q.2 Why is aniline used as a solvent in the rearrangement reaction?

Ans. Aniline is used as a solvent because it stabilises the intermediate and enhances the yield of the desired product.

Q.3 At what temperature is the rearrangement reaction carried out?

Ans. The rearrangement is carried out at about 40-45°C in a water bath.

Q.4 Why is the reaction mixture allowed to stand after heating?

Ans. Standing allows the rearranged product to crystallise and stabilise before separation.

Q.5 How is excess aniline removed from the reaction mixture?

Ans. Excess aniline is converted to aniline acetate by shaking with glacial acetic acid diluted with water, which is water-soluble and gets washed away.

Q.6 Why is recrystallisation carried out from carbon tetrachloride?

Ans. Carbon tetrachloride is used as it dissolves impurities but allows pure aniline yellow to crystallise out.

Q.7 What colour is the product obtained in this reaction?

Ans. The product obtained is yellow in colour, hence called aniline yellow.

Q.8 What precautions are necessary while handling glacial acetic acid?

Ans. Glacial acetic acid causes severe burns, so it must be handled with gloves and in a fume cupboard.

Q.9 Why is diazoaminobenzene finely powdered before use?

Ans. Finely powdered diazoaminobenzene ensures better dissolution and improves reaction efficiency.

Q.10 Is aniline yellow water-soluble?

Ans. No, aniline yellow is not water-soluble and must be filtered and washed thoroughly.

Q.11 Give a reason as to why melting point determination is important?

Ans. The melting point helps to check the purity of the compound prepared.

Q.12 **How is carbon tetrachloride handled safely in the lab?**

Ans. Carbon tetrachloride should be used in a well-ventilated area as it is toxic and harmful on inhalation.

Q.13 **How can azo dyes be classified based on solubility?**

Ans. Azo dyes may be water-soluble or water-insoluble depending on their substituents and structural groups.

Q.14 **What is the importance of maintaining accurate proportions of reactants in azo dye synthesis?**

Ans. Excess reactants may lead to decomposition, low yield, or formation of tar-like impurities.

Questions From NCERT Lab Manual

Q.1 **How is crude solid compound purified?**

Ans. Crude solid compound is purified by recrystallisation. This process is based on the difference in solubilities of desired product and impurities of solids in a given solvent system.

Q.2 **How is an organic compound recrystallised?**

Ans. In this technique, an impure solid compound is dissolved in minimum amount of a solvent by heating and then allowed to slowly crystallise out as the solution cools. As the compound crystallises from the solution, the molecules of the other compounds (impurities) dissolved in solution are excluded from the growing crystal lattice, giving a pure solid

Q.3 **Is it necessary to recrystallise the compound obtained from the reaction? Explain why?**

Ans. Yes, because this is a primary method of purifying crude solid compounds.

Unit 8

Tests for Functional Groups Present in Organic Compounds

All the organic compounds comprises of two parts. **Functional group** and skeleton of carbon atoms commonly called as **alkyl group**. Functional group is the most reactive part of the organic compound which determines the properties of a compound. Different compounds with same functional group have similar properties and belongs to a family of compounds. In contrast, compounds having different functional groups have different properties and belong to different families of compounds. There exist a homologous series of compounds containing each type of functional group, e.g. homologous series of aldehydes like CH_3CH_2CHO, $CH_3CH_2CH_2CHO$, etc. Some of the important functional groups are listed below.

Class of compounds	Functional group	Examples
Alkenes	$>C=C<$ (Carbon - carbon double bond)	$CH_2=CH_2$ (Ethene)
Alkynes	$-C\equiv C-$ (Carbon-carbon triple bond)	$CH\equiv CH$ (Ethyne)
Alcohols	— OH (Hydroxyl)	C_2H_5OH (Ethanol)
Aldehydes	$-\overset{H}{\overset{\mid}{C}}=O$ (Aldehydic)	CH_3CHO (Ethanal)
Ketones	$>C=O$ (Keto)	$(H_3C)_2C=O$ (Propanone)
Carboxylic acids	$-\overset{O}{\overset{\parallel}{C}}-OH$ (Carboxylic)	CH_3COOH (Ethanoic acid)
Amines Primary amines (1°)	$-NH_2$ (Amino)	CH_3NH_2 Methanamine(1° amine)
Secondary amines (2°)	$R-\underset{R}{\underset{\mid}{N}}H$ or R_2NH	$(H_3C)_2NH$ N-methyl methanamine (2°amine)
Tertiary amines (3°)	$R-\underset{R}{\underset{\mid}{N}}-R$ or R_3N	$CH_3-\underset{CH_3}{\underset{\mid}{N}}-CH_3$ N, N - dimethyl methanamine (3° amine)

Significance of Functional Groups

(a) Identification of organic compounds based on functional group becomes easy.

(b) The study of huge number of known organic compounds become systematic.

(c) The properties and nature of a newly synthesised compound can be established if the presence of functional group is established.

Experiment 8.1

AIM

Test for unsaturation.

Theory/Principle

Organic compounds having double bond ($>C=C<$) or triple bond ($-C \equiv C-$) (or both) between the two adjacent carbon atoms are called **unsaturated compounds**.

Materials Required

- Test tubes : 2
- Test tube holder : 1
- Potassium hydroxide solution : 1-2 mL
- Carbon tetrachloride (CCl_4)/ chloroform ($CHCl_3$) : 2 mL
- Bromine water/solution of bromine in CCl_4 or $CHCl_3$: 2 mL
- Potassium permanganate solution : As per need
- Compound to be tested : As per need

Procedure and Observations

Experiment	Observation	Inference	Chemistry involved
1 Br_2 WATER TEST			
Add aqueous solution of compound (2 mL CCl_4 + 0.1 g or 5-6 drops of given compound) + Br_2 water or solution of Br_2 in CCl_4 or $CHCl_3$ (2%) + shake.	Orange-red colour (of Br_2 water) turns colourless.	Disappearance of orange-red colour or decolourisation of bromine solution, indicates the presence of unsaturated compound.	• $R(H)C=CH_2$ (Alkene) + Br_2 (Reddish orange) → $R(H)C(Br)-C(Br)H_2$ *Vicinal* dibromide (Colourless) • $H-C\equiv C-H$ (Alkyne) + $2Br_2$ (Reddish orange) $\xrightarrow{CCl_4}$ $H-CBr_2-CBr_2-H$ Tetrabromide (Colourless)

2 BAEYER'S TEST			
Add aqueous solution of compound (2 mL H_2O + 25-30 mg organic compound) + 1% alk. $KMnO_4$ solution+1% KOH solution or 1% Na_2CO_3 solution.	Purple or pink colour (due to $KMnO_4$) turns colourless.	Disappearance of purple colour confirms the presence of unsaturated bond(s) in the given compound.	• $3\ R(H)C{=}C(H)H + 4H_2O + 2MnO_4^-$ (Alkene; MnO_4^- Purple) $\rightarrow 3R{-}CH(OH){-}CH(OH){-}H + 2OH^- + 2MnO_2$ Vicinal glycols (Colourless) • $3H{-}C{\equiv}C{-}H + 4H_2O + 2MnO_4^-$ (Alkyne; MnO_4^- Purple) $\rightarrow 3H{-}C(=O){-}C(=O){-}H + 2O\bar{H} + 2MnO_2$ Diketone (Colourless)

Note (i) *Unsaturation in an organic compound is confirmed only when both of the above tests are positive.*
(ii) *In place of CCl_4 any other solvent such as $CHCl_3$/dioxan and even water can be used to dissolve the organic compound for carrying out the reaction.*

Result

The given compound gives the tests .... (positive/negative) for having unsaturated bond(s).

PRECAUTIONS

- *Be careful while handling any chemical mentioned in this experiment. Avoid inhalation of vapours of bromine and direct contact with skin.*
- *Perform all the reactions at room temperature.*

Viva-Voce

Q.1 Which reagents are commonly used to test unsaturation in organic compounds?

Ans. Bromine water and alkaline potassium permanganate solution (Baeyer's reagent) are commonly used to detect unsaturation.

Q.2 What observation confirms the presence of a double bond when using bromine water?

Ans. Disappearance of the reddish-orange colour of bromine solution indicates the presence of unsaturation.

Q.3 Why is bromine used in carbon tetrachloride or chloroform during unsaturation tests?

Ans. These solvents are non-polar and help dissolve organic compounds and bromine without reacting, allowing addition reactions to be observed clearly.

Q.4 What is the chemical name of Baeyer's reagent?

Ans. Baeyer's reagent is an alkaline solution of potassium permanganate ($KMnO_4$) in sodium carbonate.

Q.5 What is the expected result of the Baeyer's test in the presence of an alkene?

Ans. The purple colour of $KMnO_4$ decolourises, indicating the presence of a double bond due to the formation of vicinal diols.

Q.6 Why must Baeyer's test be conducted under alkaline conditions?

Ans. Alkaline conditions prevent oxidation of aromatic compounds and make the test specific for alkenes.

Q.7 What is the role of carbon tetrachloride in bromine water test?

Ans. Carbon tetrachloride acts as a non-reactive solvent that helps in dissolving the organic compound and bromine for reaction observation.

Q.8 What does the disappearance of pink or purple colour in Baeyer's test signify?

Ans. It indicates that the permanganate ions have been reduced, usually due to reaction with a double or triple bond in the compound.

Q.9 What functional groups interfere with Baeyer's test?

Ans. Some aldehydes and phenols can also decolourise $KMnO_4$, so cross-verification with bromine test is important.

Q.10 How is the test for unsaturation different from tests for aromatic substitution?

Ans. Unsaturation tests involve addition reactions, while aromatic compounds undergo substitution and usually do not react with $KMnO_4$ under alkaline conditions.

Q.11 What indicates a negative test for unsaturation in both bromine and $KMnO_4$ tests?

Ans. Persistence of bromine's orange colour and the purple colour of $KMnO_4$ indicates the compound is saturated.

Questions From NCERT Lab Manual

Q.1 What is Baeyer's reagent?

Ans. Baeyer's reagent is 1% alkaline potassium permanganate solution.

Q.2 Why do alkenes and alkynes decolourise bromine water and alkaline $KMnO_4$?

Ans. Unsaturated hydrocarbons form bromoalkanes when treated with orange-red bromine water. These bromoalkanes are colourless compounds hence, bromine water appears decolourised. Also, unsaturated hydrocarbons decolourised purple or pink colour of alkaline $KMnO_4$ and form glycol and diketone, respectively with alkene and alkyne which are colourless.

Q.3 Explain why for the confirmation of unsaturation in a compound both the tests namely test with bromine water and test with Baeyer's reagent should be performed.

Ans. Because only unsaturated organic compounds can give both the tests positive. Other unknown compounds may give either of these tests positive hence, leave a possibility of doubt.

Q.4 Why does benzene not decolourise bromine water although it is highly unsaturated?

Ans. Due to the delocalisation of π-electrons in benzene, it does not undergo addition reactions of typical unsaturated hydrocarbons like alkenes and alkynes. Hence, it does not decolourise bromine water and undergoes substitution reactions with bromine water.

Experiment 8.2

AIM

Test for alcoholic (*R*—OH) group.

Theory/Principle

Organic compounds having **hydroxyl**, i.e. —OH group attached to the chain of C-atoms are called **alcoholic compounds** or alcohols and the hydroxyl (—OH) functional group is called **alcoholic group**. It is denoted by *R*—OH, where, *R* represents a carbon chain.

Materials Required

- Test tubes : As per need
- Test tube holder : 1
- Ceric ammonium nitrate solution : As per need
- Piece of sodium metal : As per need
- Glacial acetic acid : As per need
- Anhydrous calcium sulphate, $CaSO_4$: As per need
- Conc. sulphuric acid : As per need
- Iodine solution : As per need
- Sodium hydroxide : As per need
- Lucas reagent : As per need

Procedure and Observations

Experiment	Observation	Inference	Reactions involved
1 CERIC AMMONIUM NITRATE TEST			
Add Organic compound (2 mL) + ceric ammonium nitrate. (3-4 drops)	The solution changes to the red or pink colour.	Appearance of pink or red colour confirms the presence of —OH group in the given compound. **Note** *The red colour disappears after keeping the reaction mixture for sometime. The colour also disappears if excess of ceric ammonium nitrate solution is added. Therefore, use of excess ceric ammonium nitrate solution should be avoided.*	$(NH_4)_2[Ce(NO_3)_6]$ + 3 ROH (Alcohol) ⟶ Ceric ammonium nitrate (Yellow) $[Ce(NO_3)_4(ROH)_3]$ Red complex + $2NH_4NO_3$ Ammonium nitrate

Experiment	Observation	Inference	Reactions involved
2 SODIUM METAL TEST			
Add organic compound (2 mL) + anhyd. $CaSO_4$ (2 g) +Filter + Na metal. **Note** *Anhydrous $CaSO_4$ is added to absorb the moisture if present.*	Effervescence noticed due to the liberation of H_2 gas. This gas can be detected by bringing the burning matchstick near the mouth of the test tube. If pop sound comes, it shows that H_2 gas is released.	Brisk effervescence confirms the presence of — OH group.	$\underset{\text{Alcohol}}{R\text{—}OH} + \underset{\text{Sodium}}{Na} \longrightarrow \underset{\text{Sodium alkoxide}}{R\text{—}O^-Na^+} + \frac{1}{2}H_2\uparrow$
3 ESTER TEST			
Add organic compound (2 mL or 0.1 g) + glacial acetic acid (2 mL) + conc. sulphuric acid (4-5 drops) + heat.	Fruity smell of ester is noticed.	A fruity smell confirms the presence of — OH group.	$\underset{\text{Alcohol}}{R\text{—}OH} + \underset{\text{Carboxylic acid}}{R'\text{—}\overset{O}{\overset{\|\|}{C}}\text{—}OH} \overset{H^+}{\rightleftharpoons} \underset{\text{Ester (Fruity smell)}}{R'\text{—}\overset{O}{\overset{\|\|}{C}}\text{—}O\text{—}R} + H_2O$
4 IODOFORM TEST			
First method Warm organic compound (0.2 mL or 0.1 g) + 10% aqueous KI solution (10 mL) + Freshly prepared NaOCl solution (10 mL)	Yellow crystals of iodoform separate out	Yellow ppt. confirms the presence of alcoholic, —OH group.	$CH_3CH_2OH \xrightarrow{KOI} CH_3CHO \xrightarrow{KOI} CI_3CHO \xrightarrow{NaOH} \underset{\text{Iodoform}}{CHI_3} + HCOONa$

Experiment	Observation	Inference	Reactions involved
Second method ▪ Add organic compound (0.1 g or 4-5 drops of compound + 2 mL water) + I_2 solution (1%) + *aq.* NaOH (2 mL of 5%) + heat.	Yellow precipitate of iodoform is obtained.	The formation of yellow precipitate confirms the presence of —OH group.	$H_3C—CH(OH)—CH_3$ (Propan-2-ol) + I_2 (Iodine) + 2NaOH (Sodium hydroxide) → CHI_3 (Iodoform) + CH_3COONa (Sodium acetate) + NaI + H_2O (water)
Note ▪ *If organic compound does not dissolve in water add dioxane drop by drop to get a homogeneous solution.* ▪ *I_2 solution is also known as potassium iodide-iodine reagent and is prepared by dissolving 20 g of potassium iodide and 10 g of iodine in 100 mL of water.*			
5 LUCAS TEST			
Compound (1 mL) + Lucas reagent (anhyd. $ZnCl_2$ + HCl) (10 mL) + shake. **Note** *Lucas test is applicable to only those alcohols which are soluble in the reagent because the test is based on separation of alkyl halides as separate layer.*	Separate cloudy layers of insoluble alkyl halides are obtained. (i) Cloudy layers separate immediately.	Separate cloudy layer of alkyl halide confirms the presence of —OH group. (i) Immediate separation of cloudy layer confirms the presence of tertiary alcohol.	$CH_3—C(CH_3)_2—OH$ (*tert*-butyl alcohol) $\xrightarrow{\text{anhydrous } ZnCl_2 + HCl}$ $CH_3—C(CH_3)_2—Cl$ (*tert*-butyl chloride)
	(ii) Cloudy layers separate in 1-5 mins.	(ii) Delayed cloudy separation of layer confirms the presence of secondary alcohol.	$CH_3—CH(OH)—CH_2—CH_3$ (*sec*-butyl alcohol) $\xrightarrow{\text{anhydrous } ZnCl_2 + HCl}$ $CH_3—CH(Cl)—CH_2—CH_3$ (*sec*-butyl chloride)
	(iii) No layer is formed.	(iii) No formation of layer means either there is a primary alcohol or no alcoholic group.	CH_3CH_2OH Ethyl alcohol (Primary) $\xrightarrow{\text{anhydrous } ZnCl_2 + HCl}$ No reaction in cold

Result

The given organic compound gives the above test .... (positive/negative) for having —OH group.

PRECAUTIONS

- *Avoid the contact of NaOH and H_2SO_4 with any body part.*
- *Do not throw unreacted sodium metal into the sink or waste bin.*
- *Test tubes should be dry and clean otherwise result might be altered.*

Viva-Voce

Q.1 What kind of colour change is observed during a positive ceric ammonium nitrate test?

Ans. A red colouration is observed due to the formation of a red complex between the alcohol and ceric ammonium nitrate.

Q.2 Give a reason as to why excess ceric ammonium nitrate is not recommended in the test?

Ans. Excess ceric ammonium nitrate may cause the red colour to disappear, leading to false negative results.

Q.3 What is the role of iodine in the iodoform test?

Ans. Iodine iodinates the methyl ketone formed during oxidation and helps in the formation of yellow iodoform precipitate.

Q.4 Which type of alcohols give a positive iodoform test?

Ans. Ethanol and secondary alcohols having the $CH_3—CH(OH)—R$ structure give a positive iodoform test.

Q.5 What is the appearance of the iodoform formed during the test?

Ans. Iodoform appears as a yellow crystalline precipitate with a characteristic medicinal odour.

Q.6 What is the function of sodium hypochlorite in the iodoform test?

Ans. Sodium hypochlorite oxidises potassium iodide to potassium hypoiodite, which facilitates the reaction.

Q.7 What is Lucas reagent composed of?

Ans. Lucas reagent is a mixture of concentrated hydrochloric acid and anhydrous zinc chloride.

Q.8 What observation confirms a tertiary alcohol using Lucas test?

Ans. Immediate formation of a second layer or cloudiness indicates the presence of a tertiary alcohol.

Q.9 What is the underlying principle of the Lucas test?

Ans. It is based on the difference in reactivity of primary, secondary, and tertiary alcohols with HCl in the presence of $ZnCl_2$, leading to alkyl halide formation.

Q.10 What solvent is used if the compound is not soluble in water for the iodoform test?

Ans. Dioxane is used dropwise to obtain a homogeneous solution of the compound.

Q.11 What is the role of $ZnCl_2$ in Lucas reagent?

Ans. Zinc chloride acts as a Lewis acid and helps in protonating the —OH group, making it a better leaving group.

Q.12 What precaution must be taken while handling iodine solution in an iodoform test?

Ans. Iodine solution should be handled carefully to avoid skin contact and inhalation of vapours.

Q.13 Why is a red complex formed in ceric ammonium nitrate test?

Ans. The red complex forms due to coordination between cerium ions and the lone pair of electrons on the oxygen of the alcohol group.

Questions From NCERT Lab Manual

Q.1 What is haloform reaction? What type of compounds generally give this reaction.

Ans. In haloform reaction (iodoform test), when organic compounds are warmed with NaOH and iodine solution, a yellow precipitate is formed. This test is given by acetaldehyde, methyl ketones and alcohols containing $CH_3—\underset{\underset{OH}{|}}{CH}—$ group.

Q.2 How can CH_3OH and C_2H_5OH be distinguished chemically?

Ans. Methyl alcohol (CH_3OH) does not give iodoform test while ethyl alcohol (C_2H_5OH) gives the iodoform test.

Q.3 Why is solution of iodine prepared in potassium iodide but not in water?

Ans. Potassium iodide (KI) dissociates into K^+ and I^- ions and I^- ion forms I_3^- with iodine (I_2) which reacts with different functional groups to form iodoform (CHI_3).

Experiment 8.3

AIM

Test for phenolic (Ar—OH) group.

Theory/Principle

The —OH **group** attached directly to the carbon atom of a benzene ring (or aromatic ring) is called **phenolic** (Ar—OH) group and the compounds possess phenolic group are collectively called **phenols**. Phenols are weakly acidic. Phenols give coloured complex with neutral ferric chloride solution.

Materials Required

- Test tubes : As per need
- Test tube holder : 1
- Beakers (250 mL) : As per need
- Blue litmus paper : As per need
- Ferric chloride solution: As per need
- Conc. sulphuric acid : As per need
- Sodium hydroxide : As per need
- Phthalic anhydride : As per need
- Organic compound containing phenolic (Ar—OH) group : As per need

Procedure and Observations

Experiment	Observation	Inference	Reactions involved
1 LITMUS TEST			
Add 2-3 drops of aqueous solution of organic compound on blue litmus paper.	Colour of blue litmus paper changes to red.	Phenolic group may be present.	
2 FERRIC CHLORIDE TEST			
Add aqueous solution of compound (2 mL) + 4-5 drops of neutral $FeCl_3$ solution. ***Note*** *Neutral ferric chloride is prepared by adding dil. NaOH solution to ferric chloride solution drop by drop till a small but permanent brown ppt. appears. Solution is filter and clear filtrate is used for the test.*	Appearance of blue, green, violet, red etc., colour is observed.	Presence of phenolic group is confirmed.	$\underset{\text{Phenol}}{6C_6H_5OH} + FeCl_3 \longrightarrow$ $[Fe(C_6H_5O)_6]^{3-} + 3HCl + 3H^+$ Ferric phenoxide (Violet complex)

Experiment	Observation	Inference	Reactions involved
3 PHTHALEIN DYE TEST			
▪ Add 0.2 g of organic compound +0.2 g of phthalic anhydride + 2-3 drops of conc. H_2SO_4 + heat about 1 min in an oil bath. ▪ Cool the reaction mixture and pour carefully into a beaker containing 15 mL of dil. NaOH solution. ***Note*** *Different colours by the given organic compounds in this test is as follows :* • ***o-cresol****-red;* *m-cresol-bluish-purple;* • ***p-cresol****-colourless,* • *Catechol-blue* • ***Resorcinol****-green fluorescent colour of fluorescein*	Appearance of pink, red, blue, green etc., colour is observed. ***Note*** *The colour disappears on adding excess amount of NaOH solution.*	Presence of phenolic group is confirmed.	2 Phenol + Phthalic anhydride → (Conc. H_2SO_4) Phenolphthalein → (NaOH) (Pink) → (Excess NaOH) (Colourless)
4 BROMINE WATER TEST			
Add organic compound (1 g) + water (2 mL) + bromine solution (1-2 mL).	A white precipitate is formed.	Formation of white precipitate confirms the presence of phenolic group.	Phenol + $3Br_2(aq)$ → 2, 4, 6-tribromophenol (white ppt.) + 3HBr

Result

The given compound shows all mentioned tests .... (positive/negative) for having phenolic (Ar—OH) group.

PRECAUTIONS

- *Always use freshly prepared, neutral and dilute solution of ferric chloride.*
- *Use dry and clean test tubes.*
- *Phenol is toxic and corrosive in nature and should be handled with care.*

Viva-Voce

Q.1 Why are phenols soluble in NaOH but not in $NaCHO_3$?

Ans. Phenols are weak acids and can react with strong bases like NaOH to form phenoxide ions (soluble), but they are not acidic enough to react with weaker bases like sodium hydrogen carbonate.

Q.2 What is the colour change observed with neutral ferric chloride in the presence of phenol?

Ans. Phenol forms a violet-coloured complex with neutral ferric chloride solution due to the formation of ferric phenoxide complex.

Q.3 What is the principle behind the phthalein dye test?

Ans. Phenols react with phthalic anhydride in presence of concentrated H_2SO_4 to form a dye-like compound such as phenolphthalein, which gives a pink colour in alkaline solution.

Q.4 Why is it necessary to use neutral ferric chloride solution in the test?

Ans. Neutral ferric chloride prevents false results, as acidic or basic conditions can interfere with complex formation or cause hydrolysis.

Q.5 What is the significance of the colour in the phthalein dye test?

Ans. The appearance of pink, red, or green colour upon addition of dilute NaOH confirms the presence of phenolic (—OH) group due to dye formation.

Q.6 Why do some phenols like 2,4-dinitrophenol dissolve in sodium bicarbonate solution?

Ans. Due to the presence of strong electron-withdrawing groups, these phenols become stronger acids and can release H^+ even in the presence of weaker bases like $NaHCO_3$.

Q.7 What is the role of conc. H_2SO_4 in the phthalein dye test?

Ans. Conc. H_2SO_4 acts as a dehydrating and condensing agent, facilitating the condensation between phenol and phthalic anhydride to form the dye.

Q.8 Can the colour produced in ferric chloride test be used to identify specific phenols?

Ans. Yes, different phenols produce different characteristic colours with ferric chloride, which helps in their identification.

Q.9 Why is use of excess NaOH avoided in the phthalein dye test?

Ans. Excess NaOH can destroy the coloured dye formed, leading to disappearance of colour and giving a false negative result.

Q.10 Why must phenol be handled with care in the lab?

Ans. Phenol is toxic and corrosive; it can cause severe burns and systemic poisoning on skin contact or inhalation.

Q.11 What is the nature of the ferric-phenol complex?

Ans. It is a coordination complex where ferric ion coordinates with phenoxide ions, producing coloured compounds.

Q.12 **Name a phenol which gives green colour with ferric chloride?**

Ans. Catechol gives a green colour with neutral ferric chloride solution, which rapidly darkens upon standing.

Q.13 **Name one phenol that does not give characteristic colour with ferric chloride.**

Ans. 1-Naphthol does not give a characteristic colour in the ferric chloride test.

Q.14 **How does electron-withdrawing substitution affect phenol acidity?**

Ans. Electron-withdrawing groups stabilise the phenoxide and thus increasing the acidity of phenol and enhancing solubility in weaker bases like $NaHCO_3$.

Q.15 **What safety precautions should be taken while performing the dye test?**

Ans. One must handle conc. H_2SO_4 with extreme care as it is highly corrosive and can cause severe burns.

Q.16 **How does the phthalein dye test confirm phenolic —OH?**

Ans. The formation of a coloured dye product in basic medium confirms that the compound is phenolic in nature.

Questions From NCERT Lab Manual

Q.1 **Why does phenol decolourise bromine water?**

Ans. Because phenol is ortho and para-directing. After bromination, it forms white precipitate of 2, 4, 6-tribromophenol so, brown colour of bromine is decolourised.

$$\text{Phenol} + 3Br_2 \longrightarrow \text{2, 4, 6-tribromophenol (White ppt.)} + 3HBr$$

Experiment 8.4

AIM

Test for aldehydic (—CHO) and ketonic ($-\overset{O}{\overset{\|}{C}}-$) groups

Theory/Principle

Aldehydes and ketones both have **carbonyl group** ($>C{=}O$) and commonly known as carbonyl compounds.

Identification of aldehydes and ketones is done by two important reactions of carbonyl group, i.e.

(i) addition reaction on double bond of ($>C{=}O$) group.

(ii) oxidation of carbonyl group.

Addition reactions of derivatives of ammonia are important for the identification of carbonyl compounds. Addition is followed by elimination resulting, in the formation of unsaturated compound.

$$>C{=}O + RNH_2 \longrightarrow >C\begin{matrix} OH \\ NHR \end{matrix} \xrightarrow{-H_2O} >C{=}NR$$

(R = alkyl, aryl or C_6H_5 NH, etc.)

These reactions are catalysed by an acid or a base and do not occur under strongly acidic or basic conditions. Maintenance of pH is very important because each reaction requires an optimum pH for its occurrence.

As far as oxidation is concerned, aldehydes are easily oxidised to carboxylic acids while ketones require relatively stronger oxidising agents. These two types of carbonyl compounds can be distinguished on the basis of difference in their reactivity.

Materials Required

- Beaker (250 mL) : As per need
- Test tube holder : 1
- Test tubes : As per need
- Schiff's reagent : As per need
- Fehling's solutions *A* and *B* : As per need
- Silver nitrate : As per need
- Dilute ammonium hydroxide solution : As per need
- 2,4-dinitrophenyl hydrazine reagent : As per need
- *m*-dinitrobenzene : As per need
- Sodium nitroprusside : As per need
- NaOH : As per need
- Sodium bisulphite : As per need

Procedure and Observations

Experiment	Observation	Inference	Reactions involved
1 TESTS FOR CARBONYL GROUP			
2, 4-DNP test Add organic compound (3-4 drops) + alcoholic solution of 2, 4-dinitrophenyl hydrazine (4-5 drops).	Yellow, orange or orange-red ppt. is formed. ***Note*** *If precipitate does not appear at room temperature, then warm the reaction mixture in a water bath for few minutes and cool it*	Confirms the presence of >C=O group.	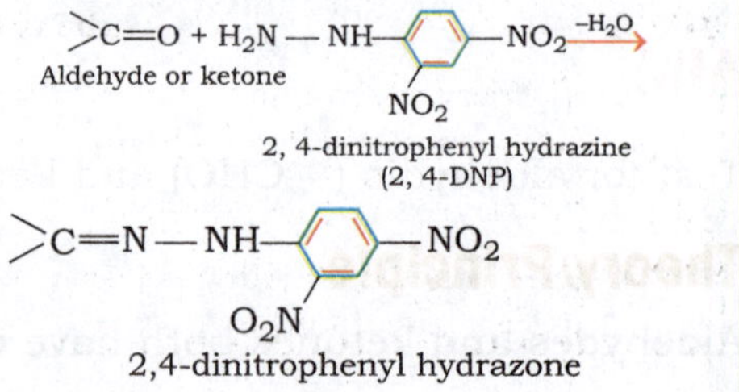 >C=O + H_2N—NH—$C_6H_3(NO_2)$—NO_2 $\xrightarrow{-H_2O}$ (Aldehyde or ketone; 2, 4-dinitrophenyl hydrazine (2, 4-DNP)) >C=N—NH—$C_6H_3(O_2N)$—NO_2 2,4-dinitrophenyl hydrazone
Sodium bisulphite test Add given organic compound (2 mL or 2 g) + sodium bisulphite (2 mL).	Crystalline white ppt. is formed.	Confirms the presence of >C=O group.	>C=O + $Na\overset{+}{H}SO_3^-$ ⟶ (Aldehyde or ketone; Sodium bisulphite) >C(OH)(SO_3Na^+) Bisulphite addition product
2 TESTS FOR ALDEHYDIC GROUP			
Schiff's test Add given organic compound (4-5 drops or 0.5 g) + Schiff's reagent (3-4 drops). [Schiff's reagent-prepared by decolourising *aq.* solution of *p*-rosaniline hydrochloride dye by adding sodium sulphite or by passing SO_2 gas]	Solution turns to pink colour.	Confirms the presence of —CHO group.	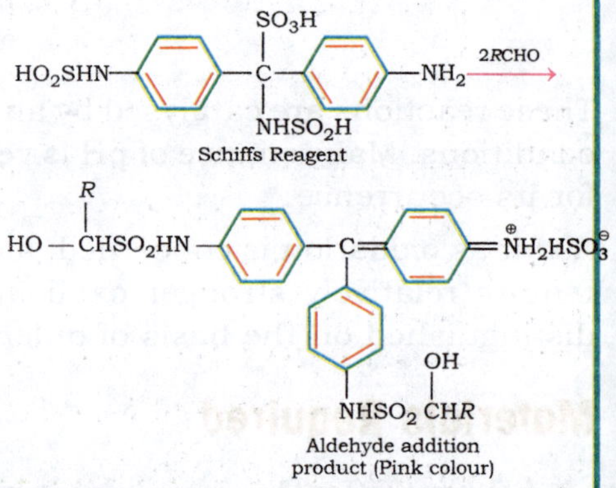 HO_2SHN—C_6H_4—C(SO_3H)($C_6H_4NHSO_2H$)—C_6H_4—NH_2 $\xrightarrow{2RCHO}$ (Schiffs Reagent) HO—CH(*R*)SO_2HN—C_6H_4—C(=C_6H_4=$\overset{\oplus}{N}H_2HSO_3^{\ominus}$)—$C_6H_4$—$NHSO_2CH(OH)R$ Aldehyde addition product (Pink colour)
Fehling's test Add fehling's solution *A*, *aq.* $CuSO_4$ solution(1 mL) + Fehling's solution *B*, Rochelle salt (sodium potassium tartarate) in NaOH (1 mL) + Given organic compound (3-4 drops) + Heat [Fehling reagent-alkaline solution of cupric ions complexed with tartarate]	Brick red ppt. of Cu(I) oxide is formed.	Confirms the presence of —CHO group. ***Note*** *This test is not given by aromatic aldehydes.*	$RCHO + 2Cu^{2+} + 5OH^- \longrightarrow$ (Aldehyde; Fehling's solution (complexed)) $Cu_2O(s)\downarrow + RCOO^- + 3H_2O$ (Red ppt.)

Experiment	Observation	Inference	Reactions involved
Tollen's test Add $AgNO_3$ (2 mL of 2%) + NaOH (3-4 drops) + NH_4OH solution (dropwise) + given organic compound (aqueous or alcoholic solution) + Heat [Tollen's reagent-alkaline solution of silver cation complexed with ammonia]	A mirror like layer of silver metal at the bottom of the test tube is observed.	Confirms the presence of —CHO group.	$\underset{\text{Tollen's reagent}}{2[Ag(NH_3)_2]^+} + 2OH^- + \underset{\text{Aldehyde}}{RCHO} \downarrow$ $RCOONH_4 + \underset{\text{Silver mirror}}{2Ag\downarrow} + 3NH_3 + H_2O$
Benedict's test Add organic compound(1 pinch) + alcohol (1 mL) + Benedict's solution (2 mL) + Heat [Benedict's reagent-alkaline solution containing a mixture of $CuSO_4$ and $2Na_3C_6H_5O_7 \cdot 11H_2O$ (sodium citrate)	Appearance of orange-red ppt. of Cu (I) oxide.	Confirms the presence of —CHO group.	$\underset{\text{Aldehyde}}{RCHO} + \underset{\text{Copper (II) citrate complex (Benedict's reagent)}}{2Cu^{2+}} \longrightarrow$ $\underset{\text{Carboxylate ion}}{RCOO^-} + \underset{\text{(Orange-red ppt.)}}{Cu_2O\downarrow}$
3 TESTS FOR KETONIC GROUP			
Sodium nitroprusside test Sodium nitroprusside (0.1 g) + distilled water (1mL) + organic compound (0.5 mL or 0.5 g) + shake + NaOH solution (dropwise). ***Note*** *If we perform Schiff's reagent test, Tollen's test and fehling's test for organic compounds containing ketones; then no pink colour, silver mirror and brick red ppt. of Cu(I) oxide is observed respectively. This confirms the presence of ketonic group.*	Red colouration is produced.	Confirms the presence of $R_2C{=}O$ group.	$\underset{\text{Ketone}}{CH_3COCH_3} + OH^- \longrightarrow CH_3COCH_2^- + H_2O$ $\underset{\text{Nitroprusside ion}}{[Fe(CN)_5NO]^{2-}} + CH_3COCH_2^- \downarrow$ $[Fe(CN)_5NO \cdot (CH_3COCH_2)]^{3-}$ Red colouration

Result

1. The given compound tested .... (positive/negative) for the presence of carbonyl ($>C{=}O$) group.
2. Presence of ...... (aldehydic/ketonic group) is confirmed for the given sample.

PRECAUTIONS

- *Always use freshly prepared reagents (like $AgNO_3$ solution, Fehling's solution, etc) to perform the test.*
- *Heat the reaction mixture on water bath and not directly on the flame.*
- *After performing the experiment, add dil. HNO_3 to silver mirror layer in order to destroy the silver mirror and flush off the solution with excess of water.*

Viva-Voce

Q.1 What is the basic difference between aldehydes and ketones in terms of oxidation?

Ans. Aldehydes are easily oxidised to carboxylic acids with mild oxidising agents, while ketones are resistant to oxidation and require stronger agents for oxidation.

Q.2 Which test is common to both aldehydes and ketones and what does it indicate?

Ans. The 2,4-DNP (2,4-dinitrophenylhydrazine) test is common to both and confirms the presence of a carbonyl group through the formation of a yellow to orange-red precipitate.

Q.3 Why do aldehydes give a positive Tollen's test but ketones do not?

Ans. Tollen's reagent is a mild oxidising agent that oxidises aldehydes to acids and itself gets reduced to metallic silver, but ketones do not undergo this oxidation and hence do not give the test.

Q.4 What is observed in a positive Fehling's test and what does it signify?

Ans. A brick-red precipitate of Cu_2O forms in a positive Fehling's test which indicates the presence of an aldehyde group (though aromatic aldehydes may not respond).

Q.5 Which reagent is more stable between Fehling's and Benedict's and why is it preferred?

Ans. Benedict's reagent is more stable as it is a single solution, unlike Fehling's which needs mixing two parts. Benedict's reagent is preferred for its convenience and shelf-life.

Q.6 What is the purpose of the Schiff's test in identifying carbonyl compounds?

Ans. Schiff's test helps detect aldehydes specifically; they give a pink colour with Schiff's reagent, while ketones do not react.

Q.7 Why must Tollen's reagent be freshly prepared before use?

Ans. Tollen's reagent decomposes on standing and may form explosive silver fulminate, hence it should be prepared fresh for safety and accuracy.

Q.8 Why do aromatic aldehydes often fail to give Fehling's test?

Ans. Aromatic aldehydes are less reactive due to resonance stabilisation and hence do not reduce Fehling's reagent easily.

Q.9 Which compound is formed when aldehydes react with Tollen's reagent?

Ans. Carboxylate salts are formed, and silver ions are reduced to metallic silver, which appears as a mirror on the test tube's inner surface.

Q.10 How can we distinguish between acetone and acetaldehyde using chemical tests?

Ans. Acetaldehyde, being an aldehyde, gives positive Schiff's, Fehling's, and Tollen's tests, while acetone (a ketone) does not.

Questions From NCERT Lab Manual

Q.1 How would you distinguish an aldehyde from a ketone by chemical tests?

Ans. We shall first perform the 2,4-DNP test to confirm the presence of carbonyl ($>C=O$) group. Then we will perform Tollen's test to confirm the aldehyde (if it gives the test positive) or ketone (if it gives the test negative). However, sodium nitroprusside can be used to confirm the presence of ketonic group.

Q.2 How can you distinguish the compounds $CH_3-\overset{O}{\overset{\|}{C}}-C_2H_5$ and $C_2H_5-\overset{O}{\overset{\|}{C}}-C_2H_5$ by simple chemical test?

Ans. Such compounds are distinguished by iodoform test which is a reaction of compound containing $CH_3-\underset{O}{\underset{\|}{C}}-$ group with I_2 and NaOH. The reaction produces a yellow ppt. of CHI_3 (iodoform).

Thus, only methyl ketones like $CH_3-\overset{O}{\overset{\|}{C}}-C_2H_5$ gives iodoform test while compounds like $C_2H_5-\overset{O}{\overset{\|}{C}}-C_2H_5$ do not respond to this test.

Q.3 Why does formic acid give a positive test with Tollen's reagent?

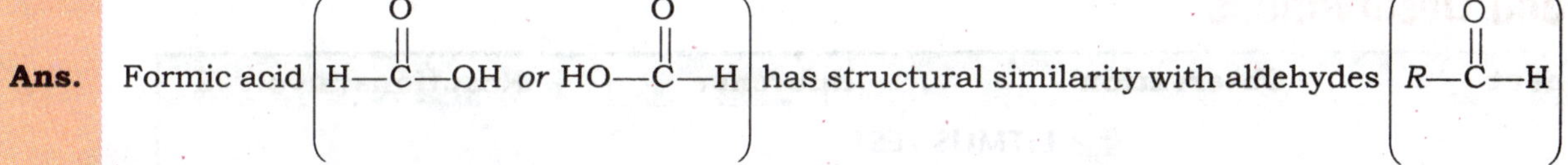

Ans. Formic acid $\left(H-\overset{O}{\overset{\|}{C}}-OH \text{ or } HO-\overset{O}{\overset{\|}{C}}-H\right)$ has structural similarity with aldehydes $\left(R-\overset{O}{\overset{\|}{C}}-H\right)$ hence, it also gives the Tollen's test positive.

Q.4 Outline the principle of testing glucose in a sample of urine in a pathological laboratory.

Ans. Pathologists use Fehling's reagent or Benedict's solution to detect the presence of glucose in a urine sample. When a sample of urine is boiled with these reagents, then — CHO group in glucose gets oxidised to — COOH and Cu^{2+} gets reduced to red colour Cu_2O. This confirms the presence of glucose in urine.

Q.5 Why is Benedict's reagent more stable than Fehling's reagent?

Ans. In Benedict's reagent, cupric ions are complexed with citrate ions whereas in Fehling's reagent, cupric ions (Cu^{2+}) are complexed with tartarate ions. Since, citrate complex in Benedict's reagent is much more stable than Cu^{2+}-tartarate complex.

Thus, Benedict's reagent does not precipitate on standing for long and hence more stable than Fehling's reagent.

AIM

Test for carboxylic (—COOH) group.

Experiment 8.5

Theory/Principle

Organic compounds possessing carboxyl $\left(-\overset{\overset{\displaystyle O}{\|}}{C}-OH\right)$ functional groups are called **carboxylic acids**. The term carboxyl, derives its name from the combination of words carbonyl and hydroxyl because carboxylic functional group contains both of these groups $\left(-\overset{\overset{\displaystyle O}{\|}}{C}-OH\right)$.

Materials Required

- Test tube holder : 1
- Glass rod : 1
- Test tubes : As per need
- Blue litmus paper/solution : As per need
- Ethyl alcohol : As per need
- Sodium hydrogen carbonate solution : As per need

Procedure and Observations

Experiment	Observation	Inference	Reactions involved
1 LITMUS TEST			
Put a drop of given organic compound on blue litmus paper	Colour of blue litmus paper changes to red.	Indicates the presence of carboxylic acid or phenolic group.	
2 SODIUM HYDROGEN CARBONATE TEST			
Add *aq.* $NaHCO_3$ (2 mL solution) + given organic compound (4-5 drops or 0.5 g)	Brisk effervescence of CO_2 is observed.	Confirms the presence of carboxylic group.	$\underset{\text{Carboxylic acid}}{RCOOH} + \underset{\text{Sodium bicarboante}}{NaHCO_3} \longrightarrow \underset{\text{Sodium salt of carboxylic acid}}{RCOONa} + \underset{\text{(Brisk effervescence)}}{CO_2 \uparrow} + H_2O$
3 ESTER TEST			
Add given organic compound (0.5 g) + ethanol (5 mL) + conc. H_2SO_4 (4-5 drops) + heat. Pour the reaction mixture to a beaker containing aqueous Na_2CO_3 solution in order to neutralise excess of —COOH and H_2SO_4.	Sweet smell of ester is observed.	Confirms the presence of carboxylic group.	$\underset{\text{Carboxylic acid}}{R\text{–}\overset{\overset{\displaystyle O}{\|}}{C}\text{–}OH} + \underset{\text{Alcohol}}{R'OH} \xrightleftharpoons{H^+} \underset{\text{Ester}}{R\text{–}\overset{\overset{\displaystyle O}{\|}}{C}\text{–}OR'} + H_2O$

Result

The given organic compound gives the tests .... (positive/negative) for the presence of carboxylic group.

PRECAUTIONS

- *Add given compound to $NaHCO_3$ solution slowly so that the effervescence is easily noticeable.*
- *Use properly washed, clean and dry equipments.*

Viva-Voce

Q.1 Which reaction confirms the evolution of carbon dioxide in this experiment?

Ans. The reaction between carboxylic acid and sodium hydrogencarbonate releases carbon dioxide:

$$RCOO + HNaHCO_3 \longrightarrow RCOONa + H_2O + CO_2 \uparrow$$

Q.2 What does the evolution of brisk effervescence indicate?

Ans. It indicates the release of carbon dioxide gas, confirming the presence of a carboxyl group.

Q.3 Why does phenol not give effervescence with $NaHCO_3$?

Ans. Phenols are weakly acidic and do not react with sodium hydrogencarbonate to produce carbon dioxide gas.

Q.4 How can you distinguish between phenol and a carboxylic acid?

Ans. A carboxylic acid gives brisk effervescence with sodium hydrogencarbonate whereas phenol does not.

Q.5 What is the esterification test for carboxylic acids?

Ans. A carboxylic acid is heated with ethanol and concentrated H_2SO_4 to form an ester with a fruity odour, indicating the presence of —COOH group.

Q.6 What is the role of sulphuric acid in the esterification test?

Ans. Sulphuric acid acts as a dehydrating agent and catalyst in the esterification reaction.

Q.7 What observation confirms a positive ester test?

Ans. A sweet or fruity smell indicates a positive esterification test.

Q.8 What is the precaution while adding the compound to $NaHCO_3$ solution?

Ans. The compound should be added slowly to clearly observe the effervescence.

Q.9 Is the litmus test conclusive for identifying carboxylic acids?

Ans. No, as phenols also turn blue litmus red; further tests like $NaCHO_3$ and esterification are needed for confirmation.

Q.10 Why do we neutralise the esterification reaction mixture after heating?

Ans. To remove excess acid and carboxylic acid, and to isolate the ester product.

Q.11 Can acetic acid be identified using this experiment?

Ans. Yes, acetic acid gives all the positive tests for carboxylic group - effervescence, red litmus, and fruity ester smell.

Q.12 Which solvents are used in the ester test for dissolving the compound?

Ans. Ethanol or methanol are used in combination with concentrated sulphuric acid.

Q.13 What does a negative sodium bicarbonate test indicate?

Ans. It may suggest that the compound is not a carboxylic acid or the acid is too weak to liberate CO_2.

Q.14 Can the ester test be used to confirm alcohols too?

Ans. No, ester test primarily confirms the presence of carboxylic acids when reacted with alcohol; separate tests confirm alcohols.

Questions From NCERT Lab Manual

Q.1 How will you distinguish between phenol and benzoic acid?

Ans. Phenol gives ferric chloride test positive while benzoic acid does not. Again, benzoic acid gives ester test positive while phenol does not. Hence, by performing these tests, we can distinguish between phenol and benzoic acid.

Q.2 How would you separate a mixture of phenol and benzoic acid in the laboratory by using chemical method of separation?

Ans. Dissolve the mixture of phenol and benzoic acid in distilled water. Then, add little amount of dil. HCl into it. The benzoic acid precipitates out while phenol remains dissolved in aqueous medium.

Experiment 8.6

AIM

Test for amino (primary), [R—NH_2] group.

Theory/Principle

Organic compounds containing an **amino** (—NH_2) group are basic in nature due to the presence of a lone pair of electrons on nitrogen atom of amino group. This lone pair attacks on Lewis acids and hence, amines itself act as a Lewis base. This is the reason that it readily reacts with an acid to form a salt which is soluble in water. On the basis of this solubility, its presence can be tested by the solubility test in an acid.

Materials Required

- Test tubes : As per need
- Test tube holder : 1
- Bunsen burner : 1
- Chloroform : As per need
- Potassium hydroxide : As per need
- Sodium nitrite solution : As per need
- Aniline : As per need
- β-naphthol : As per need
- Dilute HCl : As per need
- NaOH solution : As per need
- Ice : As per need

Procedure and Observations

Experiment	Observation	Inference	Reactions involved
1 TESTS FOR AMINO GROUP			
Solubility test Organic compound (1mL) + dil. HCl (2-3 drops) in a test tube and shake well the contents.	Organic compound dissolves in dil. HCl.	Amino group may be present.	C_6H_5—NH_2 + HCl ⟶ C_6H_5—$\overset{+}{N}H_3Cl^-$ Anilinium chloride soluble in water.
Carbylamine test Add given compound (2-3 drops) + chloroform (2-3 drops) + alcoholic KOH (2-3 drops of 0.5 M) + heat.	Offensive or obnoxious smell is observed.	Offensive smell confirms the presence of primary amino group.	R—NH_2 + $CHCl_3$ + 3KOH ⟶ (Δ) RNC + 3KCl + $3H_2O$ (1°amine; Chloroform; Potassium hydroxide; Isocyanide/Carbylamine)
Azo dye test Add Organic compound (0.2 g) + dil. HCl (2 mL) + cool + cold *aq.* $NaNO_2$ (2 mL of 2.5%) + β-naphthol (0.2 g) + dil. NaOH + shake.	Scarlet red dye is obtained.	Formation of red dye confirms the presence of aromatic primary amine.	C_6H_5—NH_2 + $NaNO_2$+HCl (1°aromatic amine) ⟶ ($-2H_2O$) C_6H_5—$\overset{+}{N}\equiv NCl^-$ (Benzene diazonium chloride) + β-naphthol (OH) ⟶ C_6H_5—N=N—(OH)naphthyl β-naphthol azo-dye (Scarlet red dye)

Result

The given compound is tested .... (positive/negative) for having —NH_2 group.

PRECAUTIONS

- *Do not inhale or expose yourself to the vapours of carbylamine during carbylamine test as isocyanide/carbylamine is toxic in nature and it should be destroyed immediately by adding conc. HCl and flush it into the sink.*
- *For diazotisation, temperature should be maintained in the range of 0-5°C, otherwise diazonium chloride salt formed decomposes at higher temperature.*
- *Do not add β-naphthol solution to diazonium chloride solution. Always add diazonium chloride solution into alkaline β-naphthol solution slowly with shaking.*

Viva-Voce

Q.1 How can the solubility test help in detecting an amino group in an organic compound?

Ans. The solubility of the compound in dilute hydrochloric acid confirms the presence of a basic functional group such as —NH_2, which forms a soluble salt.

Q.2 What is the principle behind the carbylamine test?

Ans. In the carbylamine test, primary amines react with chloroform and alcoholic potassium hydroxide on heating to form foul-smelling isocyanides thus confirming the presence of a primary amino group.

Q.3 Why is the carbylamine reaction considered specific for primary amines only?

Ans. Because only primary amines have two hydrogen atoms on nitrogen, which are necessary for forming the isocyanide during the carbylamine reaction.

Q.4 What is the chemical identity of the unpleasant-smelling compound formed in the carbylamine test?

Ans. The compound is isocyanide (or carbylamine), which is highly toxic and has a pungent odour.

Q.5 How is the toxicity of the carbylamine handled after the test is completed?

Ans. The test tube is cooled and an excess of concentrated hydrochloric acid is added to neutralise the isocyanide and render it harmless.

Q.6 What is the azo dye test used for?

Ans. The azo dye test is used to confirm the presence of an aromatic primary amine through the formation of a brightly coloured azo dye via diazotisation and coupling with β-naphthol.

Q.7 Why is the temperature maintained between 0–5 C during diazotisation in the azo dye test?

Ans. Because diazonium salts are unstable above 5°C and may decompose therefore the temperature is kept low to ensure the stability of the intermediate.

Q.8 What is the observed indication of a positive azo dye test?

Ans. Formation of a scarlet red or brightly coloured azo dye confirms the presence of an aromatic primary amine.

Q.9 How does the structure of secondary and tertiary amines affect the carbylamine test?

Ans. Secondary and tertiary amines lack the required hydrogen atoms on nitrogen, so they do not undergo the carbylamine reaction.

Q.10 What safety precautions must be observed during the carbylamine test?

Ans. One must avoid inhaling the vapours and immediately neutralise the isocyanide formed using concentrated HCl.

Q.11 What reagent is used to generate nitrous acid in situ for the azo dye test?

Ans. Sodium nitrite and dilute hydrochloric acid are used together to generate nitrous acid in *situ*.

Q.12 What is the role of β-naphthol in the azo dye test?

Ans. β-naphthol acts as a coupling component, reacting with the diazonium salt to form the coloured azo dye.

Q.13 Can aliphatic amines give a positive azo dye test?

Ans. No, only aromatic primary amines give a positive azo dye test due to the requirement of an aromatic ring for stable diazonium salt formation.

Q.14 How can the presence of a primary amine be confirmed using more than one test?

Ans. By performing both the solubility test and the carbylamine test; solubility in acid confirms basic nature, and carbylamine confirms the presence of a primary $—NH_2$ group.

Q.15 How is diazonium salt prepared in the azo dye test?

Ans. By treating the aromatic primary amine with cold nitrous acid (generated from $NaNO_2$ and HCl) at 0–5°C.

Q.16 What happens if the diazonium salt is warmed beyond 5° C during the azo dye test?

Ans. The diazonium salt decomposes, which prevents the formation of the azo dye and may release nitrogen gas.

Questions From NCERT Lab Manual

Q.1 How can you distinguish between ethylamine and diethylamine?

Ans. Ethylamine (CH_3CH_2— NH_2) is a primary alkyl amine and diethylamine (C_2H_5—NH — C_2H_5) is a secondary alkyl amine. Thus, ethylamine gives positive carbylamine test but diethylamine does not give positive carbylamine test.

Q.2 Write the chemistry of diazotisation and coupling reactions.

Ans. A primary aromatic amine such as aniline undergoes diazotisation with nitrous acid at 0-5°C. Here, a lone pair of electrons on nitrogen in aromatic amine attacks on positively charged nitrogen of nitrosonium ion to undergo diazotisation.

$$O{=}N{-}\ddot{O}H + H^+ \rightleftharpoons O{=}N{-}\overset{+}{\ddot{O}}H_2 \longrightarrow \overset{+}{N}{=}O + H_2\ddot{O}$$

Nitrous acid   Nitrosonium ion

$$C_6H_5{-}\ddot{N}H_2 + \overset{+}{N}{=}O \longrightarrow C_6H_5{-}\overset{+}{N}H_2{-}N{=}O \xrightarrow{-H^+} C_6H_5{-}NH{-}N{=}\ddot{O}: \overset{+H^+}{\rightleftharpoons}$$

$$C_6H_5{-}NH{-}N{=}\overset{+}{O}H \xrightarrow{-H^+} Ar{-}N{=}N{-}\ddot{O}H \xrightarrow{+H^+} Ar{-}\ddot{N}{=}N{-}\overset{+}{O}H_2 \longrightarrow Ar{-}\overset{+}{N}{\equiv}N + H_2O$$

Diazonium cation

During coupling reaction, diazonium salt reacts with another organic compound having labile hydrogen that means the hydrogen which can be easily removed and form a coupled product.

$$C_6H_5{-}\overset{+}{N}{\equiv}N + H{-}C_{10}H_6{-}OH \xrightarrow{-H^+} C_6H_5{-}N{=}N{-}C_{10}H_6{-}OH$$

Diazonium cation   Azo dye

Unit 9

Tests for Carbohydrates, Fats and Proteins

Food is an important substance which must be supplied to the body for its normal functioning and proper development. Within the body, food undergoes complex biological reactions and produces energy to promote growth; replace worn out tissues; regulate metabolic processes like assimilation and digestion and to sustain life.

Food contains the following essential components:

(i) Carbohydrates
(ii) Proteins
(iii) Oils and fats
(iv) Vitamins and minerals

I. Carbohydrates

Carbohydrates are the hydrates of carbon having a general formula $C_x(H_2O)_y$. e.g. Glucose ($C_6H_{12}O_6$), sucrose ($C_{12}H_{22}O_{11}$), etc. It is defined as, 'The carbohydrates are optically active polyhydroxy aldehydes or polyhydroxy ketones, or the compounds which produce these units on hydrolysis'.

Classification of Carbohydrates

Carbohydrates can be classified on the basis of number of polyhydroxy aldehyde or ketone units that it gives after hydrolysis. Thus, the three broad classes of carbohydrates are :

(i) **Monosaccharides** These carbohydrates cannot be hydrolysed to simpler carbohydrates hence, these are the simplest carbohydrates. e.g. Glucose, fructose, galactose, etc.

(ii) **Oligosaccharides** These carbohydrates can be hydrolysed to give 2-10 monosaccharide units. e.g. Sucrose is a disaccharide as it gives 2 monosaccharide units, i.e. glucose and fructose.

(iii) **Polysaccharides** These carbohydrates give a large number of monosaccharides on hydrolysis. e.g. Starch $(C_6H_{10}O_5)_n$ produces '*n*' number of glucose units where, *n* has very high value.

Monosaccharides are further classified on the basis of number of carbon atoms and functional group present in the carbohydrate. If aldehyde group is present, then it is called **aldose** and if ketone group is present, then it is called **ketose**. The general term for all monosaccharides is glycose.

Sugars and Non-sugars Carbohydrates are sweet in taste, infact the table sugar which we use is sucrose, the sugar in fruits is fructose. On the basis of sweetness, carbohydrates are also classified as sugars and non-sugars. Carbohydrates like glucose, fructose, sucrose that are crystalline, water soluble and sweet in taste are called **sugars**. Whereas carbohydrates like starch, cellulose that are amorphous, insoluble in water and not sweet in taste are called **non-sugars**.

Further, sugars can also be further classified according to their reducing and non-reducing nature. The carbohydrates which can reduce Tollen's reagent or Fehling's solution are called **reducing sugars.** All monosaccharides are reducing sugars. Disaccharides which contain a free hemi-acetal group $\left(\begin{array}{c} H \diagup C - OR \\ | \\ OH \end{array} \right)$ are also mild reducing sugars.

Mostly naturally occurring disaccharides are reducing sugars except sucrose. Thus, reducing sugars can be tested with the help of Fehling's test, Benedict's test and Tollen's test.

II. Oils and Fats

Oils and fats are the esters of long chain fatty acids and glycerol (propan-1,2,3-triol) and are also called as **triglycerides**. These are the glycerides of unsaturated fatty acids, i.e. contain double or triple bonds. Triglycerides which are liquids at room temperature are oils while triglycerides which are solids at room temperature are called **fats**.

$$\begin{array}{l} CH_2{-}O{-}\overset{O}{\overset{\|}{C}}{-}R_1 \\ | \\ CH{-}O{-}\overset{O}{\overset{\|}{C}}{-}R_2 \\ | \\ CH_2{-}O{-}\overset{O}{\overset{\|}{C}}{-}R_3 \end{array}$$

Here, R_1, R_2 and R_3 are long chain saturated or unsaturated groups that may be same or different.

Most of the naturally occurring fats or oils are polyunsaturated as their fatty acids have two or three double bonds in their alkyl chain. As compared to fats, oils contain a large proportion of unsaturated acid radicals. We use *trans*-form of oil. At the high temperature, *trans* oil converts into *cis*- form of oil which is not good for our body.

III. Proteins

Proteins are high molecular mass complex organic compounds containing nitrogen. These are the long chain polymers of **α-amino acids** which contains both **amine** ($-NH_2$) and **carboxylic acid** ($-COOH$) group.

The **amino acids** in proteins are called **α-amino acids** because the amino group is attached to the α-carbon atom.

$$\begin{array}{c} R \\ | \\ H_2N - C - COOH \\ | \\ H \end{array}$$

α - amino acid

The product formed by the combination of the number of amino acid molecules is called **polypeptide**. A polypeptide having molecular mass greater than 10,000 is called a **protein**.

Thus, the $-\overset{O}{\overset{\|}{C}}-NH$ linkage that joins the two amino acids is called **peptide linkage**.

Note *Proteins* $\xrightarrow{\text{Hydrolysis}}$ *Peptides* $\xrightarrow{\text{Hydrolysis}}$ *α-amino acids*

Chemistry of Some Tests of Carbohydrates, Proteins and Fats

A. TESTS FOR CARBOHYDRATES

1. Molisch's Test

Carbohydrates of all classes gives Molisch's test. When concentrated sulphuric acid is added to the aqueous solution of carbohydrate, it hydrolyses glycosidic bonds of carbohydrate to give monosaccharides which are dehydrated to form an aldehyde which is called **furfural**, which reacts with 1-naphthol to give a deep violet coloured unstable condensation product. This violet colour is visible at the junction of two liquids, aqueous solution and organic solution of 1-naphthol.

Molisch's reagent 10% alcoholic solution of α-naphthol.

The reactions taking place during Molisch's test are:

For Aldohexose

CHO–CHOH–CHOH–CHOH–CHOH–CH_2OH $\underset{\beta\text{-elimination}}{\xrightleftharpoons{-H_2O}}$ CHO–C(OH)=C(H)–CHOH–CHOH–CH_2OH ⇌ CHO–C=O–CH_2–CHOH–CHOH–CH_2OH ⇌ HOH_2C, H, O, CHO, OH, OH (cyclic) $\xrightarrow{-2H_2O}$ 5-hydroxymethyl furfural (HOH_2C, O, CHO; ring positions 1–5) $\xrightarrow{\text{1-naphthol}}$ Violet coloured product

For Ketohexose

CH_2OH–C=O–CHOH–CHOH–CHOH–CH_2OH ⇌ HOH_2C, H, O, CH_2OH, OH, OH OH (cyclic) $\xrightarrow[-H_2O]{H^+}$ HOH_2C, H, O, CHO, OH OH (cyclic) $\xrightarrow{-2H_2O}$ 5-hydroxymethyl furfural (HOH_2C, O, CHO) $\xrightarrow{\text{1-naphthol}}$ Violet coloured product

2. Fehling's Test and Benedict's Test

Black copper (II) oxide is formed on heating a suspension of copper hydroxide in alkaline solution.

$$Cu(OH)_2 \longrightarrow \underset{\text{Copper (II) oxide (Black)}}{CuO} + H_2O$$

If some reducing agent is present in the reaction medium then orange-red copper (I) oxide is precipitated.

$$2Cu(OH)_2 \longrightarrow \underset{\substack{\text{Copper (I) oxide} \\ \text{(Orange - red)}}}{Cu_2O\downarrow} + 2H_2O + [O]$$

Reducing sugars, because of aldehydic group or α-hydroxy ketonic group are reducing in nature. Thus, in alkaline medium, these sugars reduce Cu^{2+} ions to Cu^{+} ions which is orange-red in colour. But Cu^{2+} ions in the presence of an alkali form $Cu(OH)_2$ (copper hydroxide) which get precipitated in the solution.

Thus, to prevent this precipitation, copper (II) ions are complexed with tartarate ions (in Fehling's test) or citrate ions (in Benedict's test). These complexes being soluble in alkaline medium gives very low concentration of Cu^{2+} so that solubility product of copper (II) hydroxide is not reached and it cannot be precipitated.

The reaction between reducing sugars and Fehling's reagent or Benedict's reagent is as follows

$$RCHO + 2Cu^{2+} + 5OH^- \xrightarrow[\text{or citrate ions}]{\text{Tartarate ions}} RCOO^- + \underset{\substack{\text{Orange - red} \\ \text{ppt.}}}{Cu_2O} + 3H_2O$$

The discharge of **blue colour** due to Cu^{2+}ions and **appearance of orange-red precipitate** of Cu_2O, indicates the reducing property of sugars. It is to be noted that in Benedict's test, colour of the precipitate of Cu_2O may vary from **orange** to **brick-red**.

$$\text{D-glucose} + Cu^{2+}\text{ (citrate)} \xrightarrow{Na_2CO_3\,(aq)} \text{D-gluconic acid} + \underset{\text{Orange-red ppt.}}{Cu_2O}$$

$$\text{D-maltose} + Cu^{2+}\text{(tartarate)} \xrightarrow{NaOH\,(aq)} \text{D-maltobionic acid} + \underset{\text{Orange-red ppt.}}{Cu_2O}$$

$$\text{Sucrose (disaccharide)} \xrightarrow[\text{solution}]{\text{Fehlings}} \text{No reaction}$$

Sometimes, the cuprous precipitate comes down as yellow cuprous hydroxide but on warming, this is converted to orange-red copper (I) oxide.

In some cases, this reaction may be used as quantitative analytical process for the determination of reducing sugars in blood and urine.

3. Tollen's Test

Tollen's reagent is the ammoniacal solution of silver nitrate. It is prepared by adding NaOH solution to $AgNO_3$ solution. Then ammonium hydroxide (NH_4OH) is added to this solution dropwise till all the precipitate formed become dissolved and a clear solution is formed.

When a reducing sugar solution is added to Tollen's reagent then silver ion of Tollen's reagent gets reduced to metallic silver. This metallic silver gets deposited on the inner walls of the test tube to form a **silver mirror**.

The reactions involved in the formation of silver mirror are as follows

$$AgNO_3 + NH_4OH \longrightarrow NH_4NO_3 + AgOH$$

$$2AgOH \longrightarrow Ag_2O + H_2O$$

$$Ag_2O + 2NH_4OH \longrightarrow 2[Ag(NH_3)_2]OH$$

$$\underset{\text{Reducing sugar}}{RCHO} + 2[Ag(NH_3)_2]^+ \longrightarrow \underset{\text{Silver mirror}}{2Ag\downarrow} + RCOONH_4 + H_2O + 3NH_3$$

4. Barfoed's test

Cupric acetate in acetic acid solution is weakly acidic and is reduced by only monosaccharides. Monosachharides react with this reagent within 5 minutes and forms brick red precipitate of Cu_2O whereas dissacharides take a longer time to react because aldehyde function is masked in the acetal linkage.

$$\underset{\text{Monosaccharide}}{RCHO} + 2Cu^{2+} \longrightarrow RCOOH + \underset{\text{Brick-red}}{Cu_2O}$$

5. Seliwanoff's test

Keto sugars dehydrate very rapidly in the presence of concentrated acids to yield furfurals which react with resorcinol (1,3-dihydroxy benzene) to given a coloured product.

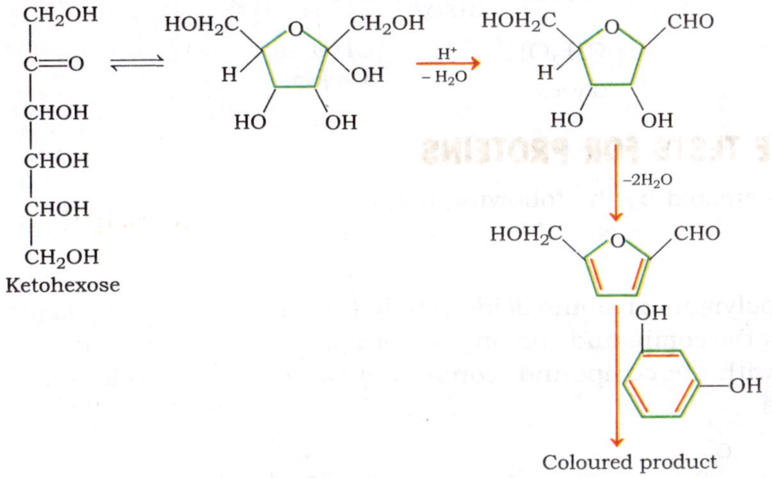

Ketohexose

Coloured product

Aldoses takes longer time to produce colour as aldoses form furfural slowly under same conditions. This is because β-elimination is required before dehydration to furfural. Hence, prolonged heating should be avoided.

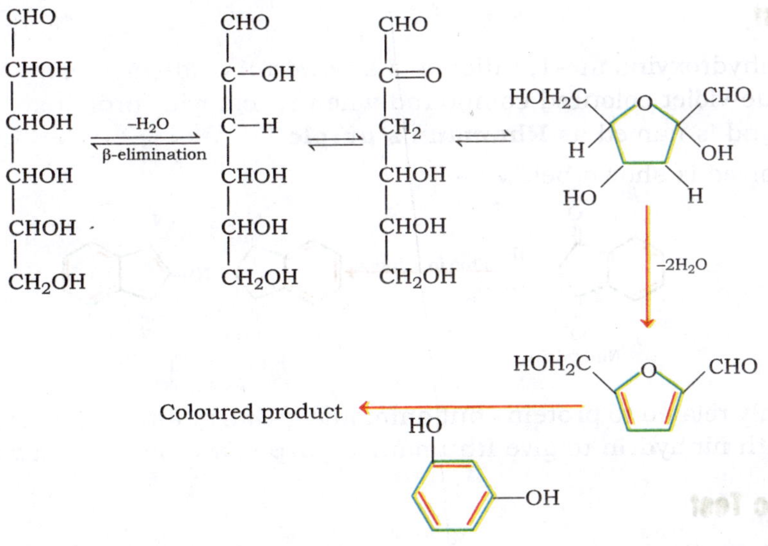

Coloured product

6. Iodine Solution Test

Starch when reacts with iodine solution gives a blue coloured complex known as starch-iodine complex.

$$Starch + I_2 \longrightarrow \underset{\text{Blue colour}}{Starch\text{-}I_2 \text{ complex}}$$

B. QUALITATIVE TESTS FOR FATS AND OILS

1. **Solubility Test** Fats and oils are soluble in organic solvents like chloroform, alcohol but are insoluble in water. We can check the solubility of fats and oils by dissolving them in water and organic solvents.

2. **Acrolein Test** Oils or fats are hydrolysed to form glycerol and fatty acids, then glycerol reacts with $KHSO_4$ and dehydrates to give a pungent smelling scompound, acrolein.

e.g.

$$\text{Oils or fats} \xrightarrow{\Delta} \text{Glycerol + Fatty acids}$$

$$\underset{\text{Glycerol}}{CH_2OH-CHOH-CH_2OH} \xrightarrow[KHSO_4]{\text{Heat}} \underset{\text{Acrolein}}{CH_2=CH-CHO} + 2H_2O$$

C. QUALITATIVE TESTS FOR PROTEINS

Proteins can be detected by the following tests.

1. Biuret Test

Proteins are the polymers of amino acids which are joined together by peptide bonds. Biuret test is used to identify the compounds having two or more peptide bonds. In this test, alkaline copper sulphate reacts with the compound, containing two or more peptide bonds and forms a violet colour complexes.

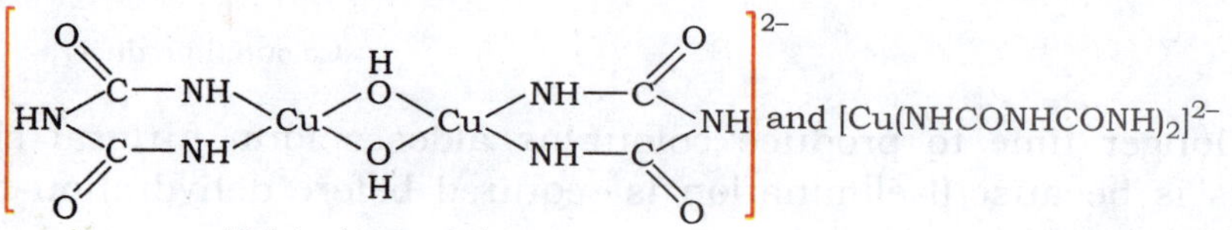

$[HN(C(=O)NH)_2Cu(OH)_2Cu(NHC(=O))_2NH]^{2-}$ and $[Cu(NHCONHCONH)_2]^{2-}$

Violet colour complexes

2. Ninhydrin Test

Ninhydrin (2,2-dihydroxyindane-1,3-dione) is a powerful oxidising agent. It gives a characteristic blue-violet coloured compound when reacts with proteins. This characteristic coloured compound is named as **Rhumann's purple**.

The reaction involved is shown below :

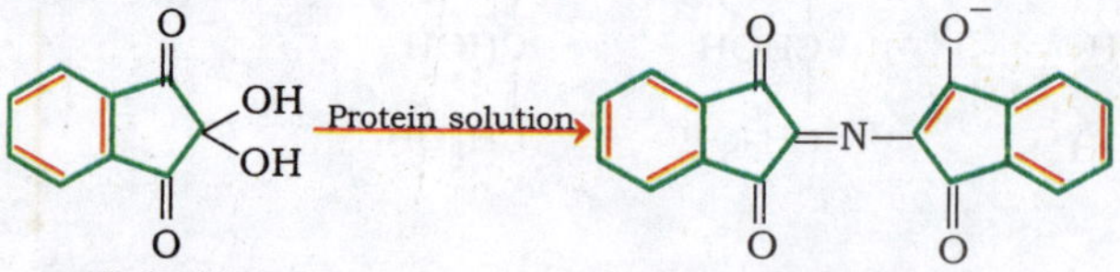

Ninhydrin $\xrightarrow{\text{Protein solution}}$ Rhumann's purple (Blue-violet)

This test is not only related to proteins but ammonia, primary amines, amino acids and peptides can also react with ninhydrin to give Rhumann's purple, a violet coloured compound.

3. Xanthoproteic Test

This test is used for the proteins or amino acids carrying aromatic groups. Aromatic group undergoes nitration with concentrated nitric acid. The product or salt formed after the nitration of aromatic group is either yellow or orange in colour.

While performing xanthoproteic test, initially on heating, a yellow colour is observed. This yellow coloured compound is xanthoproteic acid, which is formed by the nitration of amino acids.

Experiment 9.1

AIM

To study the characteristics of carbohydrates in pure sample and their detection in the given foodstuffs.

Theory/Principle

In general, carbohydrates are detected by Molisch's test. Reducing sugar reduces Tollen's and Fehling's reagent. Further, Barfoed's test and Seliwanoff's test is used to distinguish monosaccharides from disaccharides and ketoses from aldoses respectively. Starch is a polysaccharide which can be easily tested by iodine test. The presence of carbohydrates in any given food stuff can be easily detected by the particular chemical test prescribed for them.

I. MOLISCH'S TEST

Materials Required

- Test tubes : As per need
- Test tube stand : 1
- Test tube holder : 1
- Beaker (100 mL) : 1
- Glucose, fructose, sugar (sucrose) : As per need
- Alcoholic solution of 1-naphthol : As per need
- Concentrated H_2SO_4 : As per need

Procedure

1. Prepare 1% stock solution (or aqueous solution) of glucose/fructose/sugar (any of these) by shaking 0.5 g of sugar with 1-2 mL of water.
2. Then, add 2-3 drops of Molisch's reagent (1% alcoholic solution of 1-naphthol) to it.
3. Add 2 mL of concentrated H_2SO_4 along the sides of the test tube in such a manner that it forms a separate layer at the bottom of the test tube.

⚠ ALERT

- *1-naphthol in high concentration is hazardous to body tissues. So, handle it with care.*
- *Alcohol is flammable.*
- *Conc. H_2SO_4 is corrosive.*

Observation

Violet coloured ring forms at the junction (or interface) of two liquids.

Result

The formation of violet ring at the interface of the two layers (or liquids) confirms the presence of carbohydrates.

II. TESTS FOR REDUCING SUGARS

Materials Required

- Test tubes : As per need
- Test tube stand : 1
- Test tube holder : 1
- Beaker (100 mL) : 1
- Water bath : 1
- Bunsen burner : 1
- Fehling's solution A and B : As per need
- Benedict's reagent : As per need
- Tollen's reagent : As per need

Procedure and Observations

S.No.	Experiment	Observation	Inference
1.	**Fehling's test** (i) Prepare 1% stock solution (or aqueous) solution of carbohydrate (sugar) by shaking 0.5 g of carbohydrate with 1-2 mL of water. (ii) Then add 1 mL each of Fehling's solution *A* and *B* to the carbohydrate solution. (iii) After that, heat the content of the test tube on a water bath and observe the colour of the precipitate if formed. ***Note* : Preparation of Fehling's solution** *Fehling's solution A is prepared by dissolving 3.5 g of* $CuSO_4$ *in 50 mL of distilled water containing few drops of* H_2SO_4. *Fehling's solution B is prepared by dissolving 1.7 g of sodium potassium tartarate and 35 g of NaOH in 150 mL of distilled water.*	Orange-red colour precipitate is formed.	Presence of reducing sugar.
2.	**Benedict's Test** (i) Prepare 1% stock solution (or aqueous solution) of carbohydrate (sugar) in a test tube by shaking 0.5 g of carbohydrate with 1-2 mL of distilled water. (ii) Add 1 mL of Benedict's reagent to the test tube having carbohydrate solution. (iii) Then allow the contents of test tube to heat till boiling on a water bath for 2 mins and observe the colour of the precipitate. ***Note* : Preparation of Benedict's Reagent** *Dissolve 17.3 g of sodium citrate and 9 g of anhydrous* Na_2CO_3 *in about 80 mL of distilled water. Heat, if necessary. Dissolve 1.73 g of* $CuSO_4$ *in 100 mL of water. Mix the two solutions and add water to make 250 mL of volume.*	A brick red colour precipitate is formed.	Presence of reducing sugar.
3.	**Tollen's Test** (i) Prepare Tollen's reagent by taking 1 mL of aqueous silver nitrate in a test tube. (ii) Add sodium hydroxide to it dropwise such that the precipitate of silver oxide forms. (iii) Then add ammonium hydroxide solution dropwise with shaking such that the precipitate of silver oxide dissolves completely to form a clear solution which is the Tollen's reagent. (iv) Now, add 1-2 mL of this Tollen's reagent to 1 mL of aqueous sample (or 1% stock solution) of carbohydrate (sugar) in a test tube. (v) Warm the contents of the test tube on a water bath and observe for the precipitate formation.	A silver mirror on the wall of the test-tube is formed.	Presence of reducing sugar.

III. TEST TO DISTINGUISH MONOSACCHARIDES FROM DISACCHARIDES (BARFOED'S TEST)

Materials Required

- Test tubes : As per need
- Test tube holder : 1
- Water bath : 1
- Glucose, fructose, sugar (sucrose) : As per need
- Barfoed's reagent : As per need
- Test tube stand : 1
- Beaker (100 mL) : 1
- Bunsen burner : 1

Procedure

1. Take 10 drops of 1% sugar solution in a test tube and then add 1 mL of Barfoed's reagent into it.
2. After that, heat the content of the test tube on a water bath for 5 mins and observe the colour of the precipitate formed.

Observations

An orange-red precipitate is formed.

Result

It indicates the presence of monosaccharides.

Note *Disaccharides do not give this test.*

IV. TEST TO DISTINGUISH BETWEEN KETOSE FROM ALDOSE

Materials Required

- Test tubes : As per need
- Test tube holder : 1
- Water bath : 1
- Glucose, fructose, sugar (sucrose) : As per need
- Seliwanoff's reagent : As per need
- Test tube stand : 1
- Beaker (100 mL) : 1
- Bunsen burner : 1

Procedure

1. Take 10 drops of 1% sugar solution in a test tube and then add 2 mL of Seliwanoff's reagent it.
2. After that, heat the test tube on a water bath for 2 mins and observe the colour of the solution.

Observations

Ketohexoses gives red colour and ketopentoses gives blue-green colour.

Result

It indicates the presence of ketohexoses and ketopentoses.

Note *Aldoses do not give colour within 2 mins.*

V. TEST FOR POLYSACCHARIDES (STARCH)

Materials Required

▪ Test tubes	: As per need	▪ Water bath	: 1
▪ Test tube stand	: 1	▪ Bunsen burner	: 1
▪ Test tube holder	: 1	▪ Starch solution	: As per need
▪ Beaker (100 mL)	: 1	▪ Iodine solution	: As per need

Procedure

1. Make a suspension of starch (0.5 g) in 5 mL water.
2. Pour it in 50 mL boiling water to get an aqueous colloidal solution.
3. Add few drops of aqueous iodine solution and shake the mixture to observe for the colour of the solution.

⚠ ALERT

Iodine is pungent smelling, eye and skin irritant and harmful to the environment.

Observation

Blue colour of the solution is obtained.

Result

The appearance of blue colour indicates the presence of starch.

VI. TEST FOR CARBOHYDRATES IN FOODSTUFFS

Materials Required

▪ Test tubes	: As per need	▪ Foodstuffs like milk, wheat flour, rice flour, powdered legumes and gram flour	: As per need
▪ Test tube stand	: 1	▪ Molisch's reagent	: As per need
▪ Test tube holder	: 1	▪ Conc. H_2SO_4	: As per need
▪ Beaker (100 mL)	: 1	▪ Fehling's solution A and B	: As per need
▪ Water bath	: 1	▪ Benedict's reagent	: As per need
▪ Bunsen burner	: 1	▪ Barfoed's reagent	: As per need
▪ Tollen's reagent	: As per need		

Procedure

1. Take the food samples like milk, wheat flour, rice flour, gram flour and powdered legumes of which test for the presence of carbohydrates has to be done in a test tube.
2. Take 0.5 mL of milk in a test tube for test of the carbohydrates.
3. For powdered food samples, make a colloidal solution of it. Colloidal solution can be prepared by adding 100 mg of the sample in 10 mL of distilled water and boil the suspension to get the desired solution. This solution is used to perform the carbohydrates test mentioned as in section I, II, III, IV and V.

Observations

Sample	Carbohydrate present/absent
Milk	
Wheat flour	
Rice flour	
Powdered legumes	
Gram flour	

Result

Foodstuffs which shows the presence of carbohydrates are ....

PRECAUTIONS

- *While performing the Tollen's test, do not heat the test tube directly otherwise it may cause explosion.*
- *While preparing the extract of flours and powdered legumes, shake the mixture thoroughly.*
- *The reagents used to carry out the tests must be freshly prepared.*
- *While performing Barfoed's and Seliwanoff's test, do not heat the contents prolonged as it may give wrong interpretation.*

Viva-Voce

Q.1 Mention the structural difference between glucose and fructose.

Ans. Fructose is a polyhydroxy ketone whereas glucose is a polyhydroxy aldehyde.

Q.2 What is the composition of Molisch' reagent?

Ans. Molisch' reagent is 10% alcoholic solution of α-naphthol.

Q.3 How violet colour ring is formed in Molisch's test?

Ans. Conc. H_2SO_4 produces furfural or its derivative on reacting with aqueous solution of carbohydrate. This furfural reacts with α-naphthol to give a deep violet colour unstable condensation product which is visible at the junction of the two liquids.

Q.4 How silver mirror is formed in Tollen's test?

Ans. A reducing sugar reduces silver (I) ions from ammoniacal solution of silver nitrate into silver metal. This silver metal is deposited on the walls of the test tube forming a silver mirror.

Q.5 Why Cu_2O precipitate appears orange-red in Fehling's and Benedict's test but brick-red colour in Barfoed's test?

Ans. In Barfoed's test, the precipitate of Cu_2O formed is less dense and hence, it appears brick-red instead of orange-red as in Fehling's and Benedict's test.

Q.6 Why on prolonged heating disaccharides may also give positive Barfoed's test?

Ans. On prolonged heating, disaccharides may hydrolyse and reduce Cu^{2+} ion to Cu^{+} to give false positive Barfoed's test.

Q.7 Name the test by which a ketose and an aldose can be distinguished. What is the role of resorcinol in the test?

Ans. Seliwanoff's test is useful in distinguishing between a ketose and an aldose. Furfural formed upon dehydration of the carbohydrates reacts with resorcinol to form a coloured complex that distinguish between a ketose and an aldose.

Q.8 Why on prolonged heating aldoses may also give positive Seliwanoff's test?

Ans. On prolonged heating, aldoses undergo β-elimination before dehydration to furfural which later reacts with resorcinol to give positive Seliwanoff's test.

Questions From NCERT Lab Manual

Q.1 How will you distinguish between glucose and sucrose?

Ans. Glucose is a monosaccharide and sucrose is a disaccharide. Hence, these two sugars can be distinguished by Barfoed's test. Glucose gives brick-red coloured precipitate of Cu_2O in the test while sucrose cannot.

Q.2 Explain, why does fructose reduce Fehling's solution and Tollen's reagent inspite of the presence of ketonic group?

Ans. In the presence of alkaline medium by NaOH , the fructose undergoes rearrangement to form glucose and an equilibrium is set between the two. Then, glucose being a reducing sugar gives Fehling's test.

Q.3 What is the role of tartarate and citrate ions in Fehling's reagent and Benedict's reagent respectively?

Ans. Rochelle salt is sodium potassium tartarate salt. The principle behind Fehling's and Benedict's test is the reduction of Cu^{2+} ions to Cu^{+} ions of Cu_2O (orange-red) but in the presence of NaOH, the Cu^{2+} precipitate as $Cu(OH)_2$.

Thus, to prevent precipitation of Cu^{2+} ions, tartarate ions (from Rochelle salt) form a soluble complex with Cu^{2+}ions. Hence, Fehling's test is helpful in identifying reducing sugar.

Similarly, in Benedict's test, citrate ions form a soluble complex with Cu^{2+} ions and decrease the solubility product of $Cu(OH)_2$, so that Cu^{2+} ions cannot precipitate.

Experiment 9.2

AIM

To study the characteristics of oils and fats in pure samples and their detection in the given foodstuffs.

Theory/Principle

Oils and fats can be tested by solubility test and acrolein test. The presence of oils and fats in any food stuff can be easily detected by the specified chemical tests for them.

I. TEST FOR FATS IN PURE FORM

Materials Required

- Test tubes : As per need
- Test tube holder : 1
- Test tube stand : 1
- Beaker (100 mL) : 1
- Water bath : 1
- Chloroform : As per need
- Bunsen burner : 1
- Mustard oil or ghee : As per need
- Potassium hydrogen sulphate : As per need

Procedure and Observations

S. No.	Experiment	Observation	Inference
1.	**Solubility Test** (i) Water (5 mL) +oil sample (ii) Chloroform (5 mL) + oil sample	Sample is immiscible. Sample is miscible.	Oil or fat is present. Oil or fat is present in a given sample.
2.	**Acrolein Test** Mustard oil or ghee sample (3 mL) + $KHSO_4$ (0.5 g) + heat	Pungent irritating smell of acrolein is observed.	Pungent irritating odour of acrolein confirms the presence of oil or fat.

PRECAUTIONS

- *Do not inhale the vapours of acrolein.*
- *Oils and fats are highly flammable, so heating should be done on water bath and do not heat on direct flame.*

II. TEST FOR FATS IN FOODSTUFFS

Materials Required

- Test tubes : As per need
- Test tube holder : 1
- Test tube stand : 1
- Beaker (100 mL) : 1
- Water bath : 1
- Bunsen burner : 1
- Potassium hydrogen sulphate : As per need
- Foodstuffs like milk, wheat flour, rice flour, gram flour and powdered legumes : As per need

Procedure

1. Take 1-2 mL of milk in a test tube and carry out the acrolein test.
2. For powdered foodstuffs, 100 mg of the sample is added to 10 mL of distilled water. Then, boil the suspension to get a colloidal solution.
3. Then, perform the acrolein test by taking 1-2 mL of each colloidal solution in a test tube.

Observations

Sample	Fats present/absent
Milk	
Wheat flour	
Rice flour	
Gram flour	
Powdered Legumes	

Result

Foodstuffs in which fats or oils present are ....

Note *While preparing the extracts of solid foodstuffs, shake the mixture thoroughly.*

Viva-Voce

Q.1 Explain the difference between the terms oils and fats.

Ans. Oils are the triglycerides that have higher proportion of unsaturated fatty acids and exist as liquid at room temperature. While fats are the triglycerides that have higher proportion of saturated fatty acids and exist as solid at room temperature.

Q.2 Why fats and oils are called triglycerides?

Ans. Fats and oils are called triglycerides as they are esters composed of three fatty acid units joined to glycerol, a trihydroxy alcohol.

Q.3 Give the molecular structure of acrolein.

Ans. $CH_2{=}CH{-}CHO$ (Acrolein)

Q.4 If instead of fats or oils, glycerol is tested for acrolein test, then what will be the result of the test?

Ans. The test shows positive result because acrolein test is done for glycerol either in free form or substituted (as in case of fats or oils).

Q.5 What is the role of $KHSO_4$ in acrolein test?

Ans. $KHSO_4$ dehydrates glycerol to form acrolein having pungent smell.

Q.6 Is there any other test that indicates the presence of fats or oils?

Ans. Yes, solubility test is the another test that indicates the presence of oils or fats. Fats or oils are soluble in organic solvents and insoluble in water.

Experiment 9.3

AIM

To study the characteristics of tests of proteins in the pure samples and their detection in the given foodstuffs.

Theory/Principle

Proteins can be tested by Biuret tests, ninhydrin test and xanthoproteic test. Its presence in the food stuff can also be detected by these tests.

A. TEST FOR PROTEINS IN PURE FORM

Materials Required

- Test tube : As per need
- Test tube stand : 1
- Test tube holder : 1
- Beaker (100 mL) : 1
- Water bath : 1
- Bunsen burner : 1
- Egg albumin/casein : As per need
- NaOH solution : As per need
- Ninhydrin : As per need
- Conc. HNO_3 : As per need
- Copper reagent ($CuSO_4$ solution) : As per need
- Alcohol : As per need

Procedure and Observations

S.No.	Experiment	Observation	Inference
1.	**Biuret Test** Take egg albumin (0.5% *w/v*) in 0.1 M NaOH solution (2mL) + 10% NaOH (2 mL) + $CuSO_4$ (dropwise) + heat (5 mins)	Violet coloured complex appears.	Appearance of violet colour due to the formation of a complex species of Cu^{2+} ions with —CONH— group confirms the presence of proteins in the sample.
2.	**Ninhydrin Test** Aqueous solution of egg albumin (2-3 mL) + 3 - 4 drops of ninhydrin + heat	Blue colouration appears in the solution.	This blue colouration confirms the presence of protein.
3.	**Xanthoproteic Test** Egg albumin (*aq*) (1 mL) + conc. HNO_3 (few drops)+ heat	A yellow colour appears first. On addition of NaOH sol, an orange coloured solution is obtained.	Appearance of yellow colour indicates protein may be present. Formation of orange coloured solution confirms the presence of protein.

PRECAUTIONS

- *Freshly prepared reagents should be used while performing the tests.*
- *The reagents should be taken in required amount.*

B. TEST FOR PROTEINS IN FOODSTUFFS

Materials Required

- Test tubes : As per need
- Test tube stand : 1
- Test tube holder : 1
- Beaker (100 mL) : 1
- Water bath : 1
- Bunsen burner : 1
- Ninhydrin : As per need
- Foodstuffs like milk, wheat flour, rice flour, gram flour and powdered legumes : As per need
- $CuSO_4$ solution : As per need
- Conc. HNO_3 : As per need
- Alcohol : As per need
- NaOH solution : As per need

Procedure

1. Take the foodstuffs like milk, wheat flour, rice flour, gram flour and powdered legumes to detect the presence of proteins.
2. 0.5 mL of milk is taken in a test tube and carry out the tests (Biuret test, Ninhydrin test, Xanthoproteic test) for proteins.
3. For powdered samples like wheat, rice and gram flour, powdered legumes, prepare the aqueous solution for each sample by taking 100 mg of each sample in separate test tubes and add 10 mL of distilled water to them and boil them to get a colloidal solution. Then take 1-2 mL of each sample solution and perform tests for protein.

Observations

Sample	Protein present or absent
Milk	
Wheat flour	
Rice flour	
Gram flour	
Powdered legumes	

Result

Foodstuffs which show the presence of proteins are ....

PRECAUTIONS

- *While preparing the extracts of solid foodstuffs, shake the mixture thoroughly.*
- *Same as mentioned for part I.*

Viva-Voce

Q.1 Name the basic unit of proteins.

Ans. Amino acids

Q.2 How amino acids are linked to form a protein?

Ans. α-amino acids are linked to each other through peptide bonds $\left(-\underset{\underset{O}{\|}}{C}-NH-\right)$ to form a complex molecule of high molecular weight greater than 10000. This complex molecule is protein.

Q.3 What is meant by the term peptide linkage?

Ans. Peptide linkage $\left(-\underset{\underset{O}{\|}}{C}-NH\right)$ is a chemical bond formed between two molecules when the carboxyl group of one amino acid reacts with the amino group of the another amino acid.

Q.4 How are proteins affected by conc. HNO_3?

Ans. Proteins give yellow colour with conc. HNO_3 (i:e. nitration of amino acids occur).

Q.5 What type of other compounds give positive Biuret test except the compounds containing peptide bonds (proteins)?

Ans. Compounds having two carbonyl groups attached through a carbon or nitrogen atom also give positive Biuret test.

Q.6 Which compound is responsible for blue-violet colour in Ninhydrin test? Give its structure.

Ans. Rhumann's purple is the blue-violet coloured compound formed in ninhydrin test.

Rhumann's purple
(Blue-violet)

Q.7 In Xanthoproteic test, a yellow colour is observed on heating initially. Which compound is responsible for this colour?

Ans. Xanthoproteic acid is formed upon the nitration of aromatic amino acids which gives yellow colour on heating.

Q.8 What is Millon's test?

Ans. Proteins containing phenolic amino acids can be detected by the test called Millon's test. In this test, reagent used is the solution of mercuric nitrate in dilute nitric acid. This reagent is called Millon's reagent. When few drops of Millon's reagent is added to the protein sample, a white precipitate is formed which turns red on heating (after boiling the solution on water bath).

Q.9 Name the food stuff which contains carbohydrates, fats as well as proteins.

Ans. Milk.

Unit 10

Titrimetric Analysis I

(Apparatus used in Titrimetric Analysis)

Titrimetric analysis involves determination of the volume of a solution of accurately known concentration which is required to react quantitatively with the measured volume of the solution of a substance, concentration of which is to be determined.

The mass of the substance dissolved in the solution of unknown concentration is calculated from the volume of the standard solution used, the chemical equation and the relative molecular masses of the reacting compounds.

- To carry out titrimetric analysis, the solution of unknown concentration is usually added from the long graduated tube called **burette**.
- The solution taken in burette is called **titrant**.
- The process of adding the solution of unknown concentration to the solution of known concentration until the reaction is just complete is called **titration**.
- The point at which reaction is completed is called **equivalence point** or the **theoretical** or **stoichiometric end point**.

Volumetric Apparatus used for Measuring Volume of Liquids

In titrimetric analysis, the volume of the various solutions should be measured accurately. The apparatus used for measuring the volume of liquids are graduated and calibrated apparatus.

Graduated Cylinder

Before using a graduated cylinder [Fig. 10.1], it should be cleaned because dirt may chemically contaminate the substance being measured and it may alter the volume of the liquid. Hence, it may affect the accurate determination of volume. Further, dirty glassware does not drain properly and the volume delivered may not be equal to that indicated by calibration mark.

These are available in various capacity of 5 mL, 10 mL, 25 mL, 100 mL, 250 mL, 500 mL, 1000 mL and 2000 mL. Measuring cylinders used for delivering the volume actually contain slightly more than the volume read. This compensates for the film of liquid left on the walls when liquid is poured out.

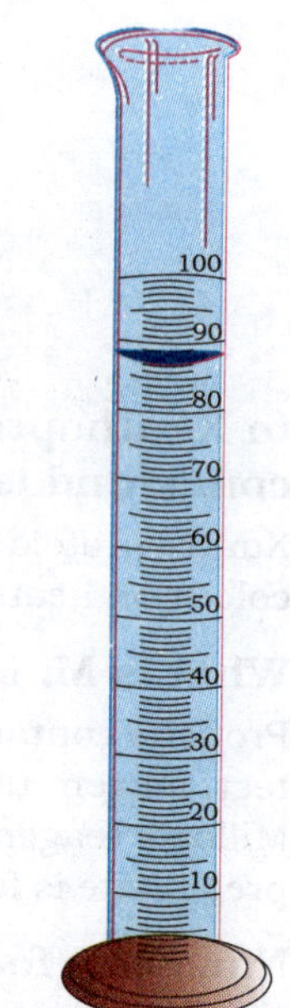

Fig. 10.1 *Measuring cylinder*

Burette

A burette is a long, graduated and cylindrical tube of uniform bore. It is fused at the lower end with a stopcock or pinch-cock and a fine nozzle. [Fig. 10.2] It is used for measuring volume in a quantitative (titrimetric) estimation. It is graduated in millilitres from 0 to 50. Each division is subdivided into ten equal parts. Therefore, each subdivision reads 0.1 mL.

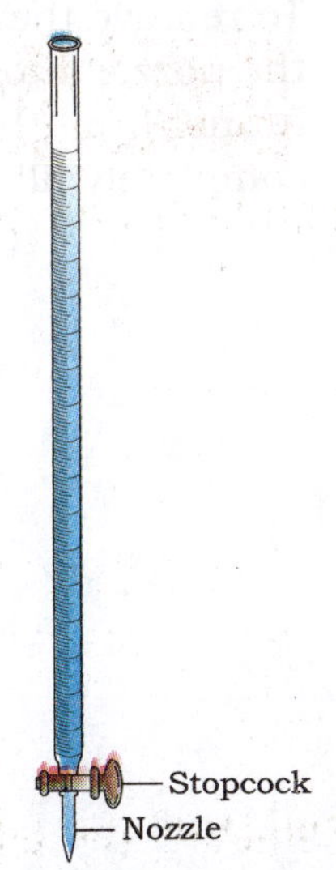

Fig. 10.2 *Burette*

Rinsing and Filling of Burette

Before filling a burette with the solution, it is thoroughly washed with chromic acid ($K_2Cr_2O_7$ + Conc. H_2SO_4) then with distilled water so that no greasy matter remains sticked inside or outside the burette.

After cleaning the burette, it should be rinsed with the solution to be filled. For rinsing the burette, few millilitres of solution is taken into it [Fig. 10.3(i)].

Close the upper mouth of the burette with the thumb and hold in horizontal position [Fig. 10.3(ii)]. The burette is rotated so as to wet the inner walls of the burette with the solution [Fig. 10.3(iii)]. After rinsing, the solution is drained out from the nozzle of the burette [Fig. 10.3 (iv)].

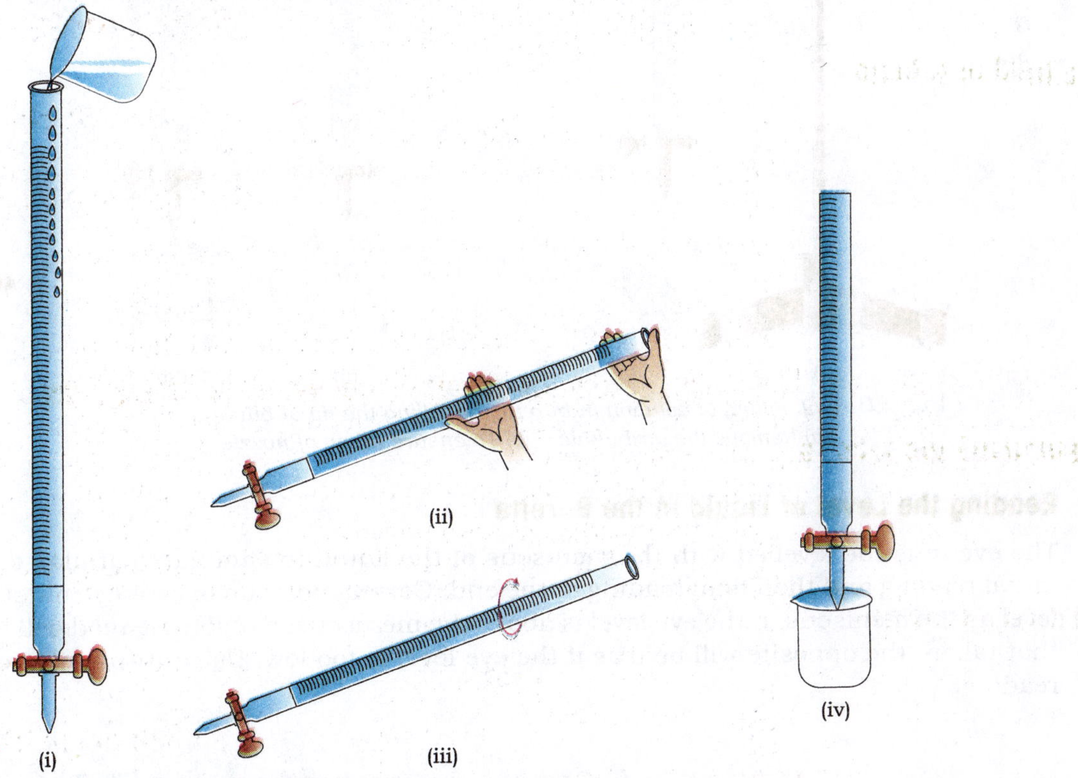

Fig. 10.3 *(i) Filling a small volume of burette with the help of beaker*
(ii) Holding of burette
(iii) Rotating the burette
(iv) Draining of the solution used for rinsing

After rinsing, fit the burette carefully and properly on the clamp stand at a convenient height, which makes you convenient in taking the reading. Then, fill the solution in the burette with the help of funnel which is inserted at the top of the burette above zero mark [Fig. 10.4(i)]. The stopcock is opened so that the solution can also be filled in the tip [Fig. 10.4(ii)].

Make sure no air bubbles remain in narrow bottom tip of the burette because they may cause an error at the time of reading.

To remove the air bubbles, stopcock is opened wide and the solution is allowed to run through the nozzle into the beaker or flask until there are no air bubbles in it. [Fig. 10.4 (iii)] Remove the funnel from the burette before noting the reading of the burette and ensure that the nozzle is completely filled [Fig. 10.4 (iv)].

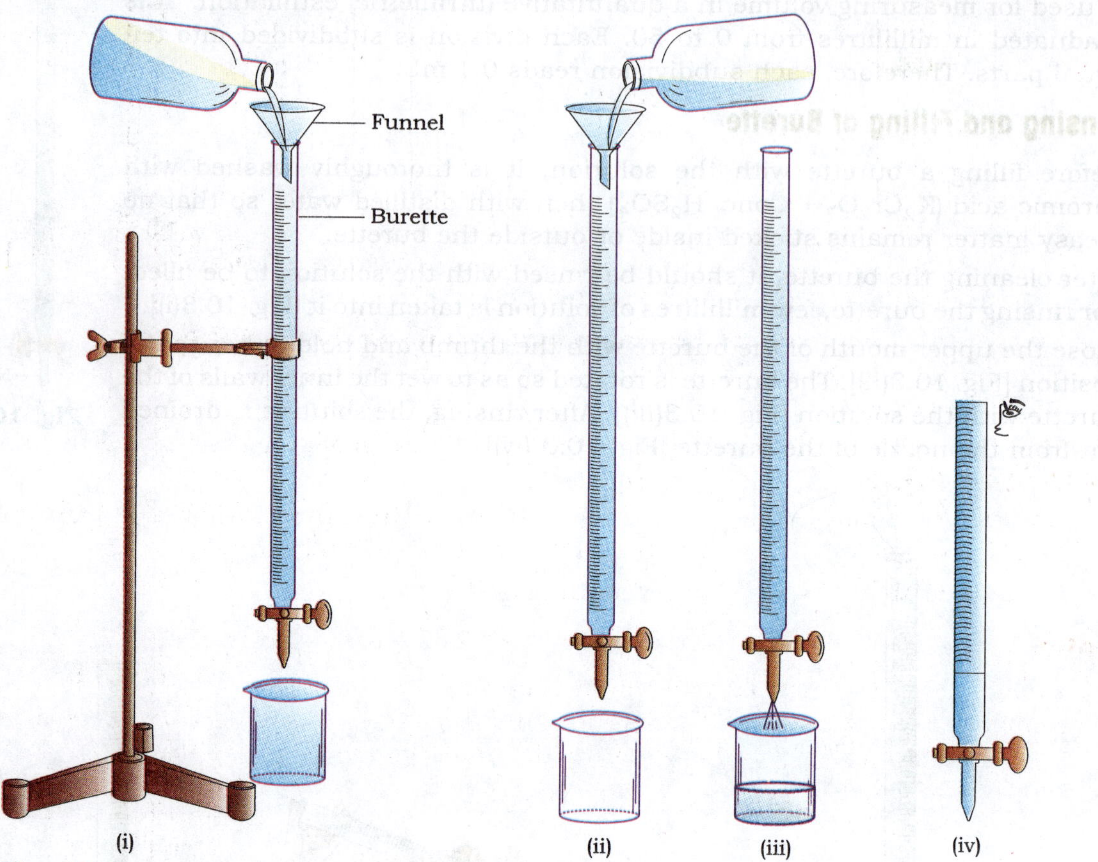

Fig. 10.4 *(i) Filling of solution in burette, (ii) Filling the tip of burette (iii) Remove the air bubble , (iv) To ensure filling of nozzle.*

Reading the Level of Liquid in the Burette

The eye must be levelled with the meniscus of the liquid to eliminate parallax errors for taking initial reading and then final reading at the end. Correct position is your eye must be at the same level as the meniscus. If the eye level is above the meniscus, the volume read will be smaller than that taken, the opposite will be true if the eye level is too low. Use anti-parallax card for correct reading.

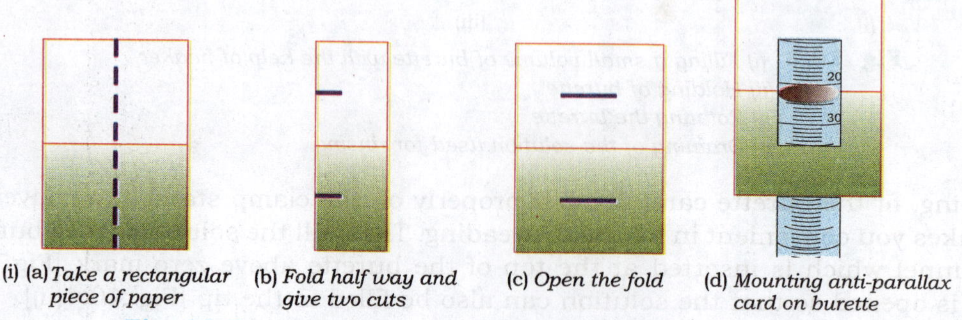

(i) (a) *Take a rectangular piece of paper* (b) *Fold half way and give two cuts* (c) *Open the fold* (d) *Mounting anti-parallax card on burette*

Fig. 10.5 *(i) Making and mounting anti-parallax card on burette*

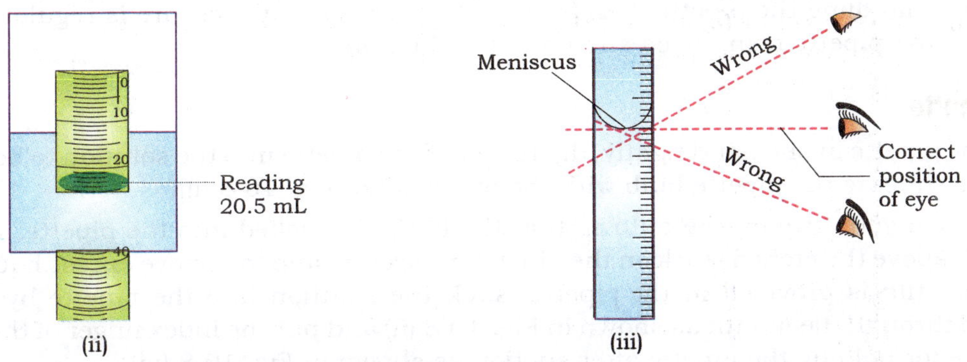

Fig. 10.5 (ii) *Using antiparallax card for noting correct reading*
(iii) *Correct way of reading burette*

Some important points should be remembered while working with burette

1. Fix burette exactly vertical.
2. Make sure stopcock does not leak.
3. While noting the reading, take care that no drop is hanging from the nozzle of the burette.
4. The liquid should be delivered dropwise.
5. If the liquid is allowed to run too fast, the walls of the burette will not drain properly and some liquid may remain stick to the surface of the walls which may lead to faulty reading.
6. Hot liquids should not be poured in the burette.

Pipette

It is a small and handy apparatus used for accurate measurements of definite volume of solution. It consists of a long narrow tube with cylindrical bulb in the middle and a jet (or nozzle) at its lower end.

On the upper part of the stem, there is an etched circular mark which represents the definite volume upto which the pipette can deliver when filled upto the circular mark. [Fig. 10.6]

Pipettes are used for measuring the volumes when these are to be transferred to a flask or some other apparatus.

Various capacity of pipettes 1 mL, 2 mL, 5 mL, 10 mL, 20 mL, 25 mL etc., are available in laboratory.

> **ALERT**
>
> *Liquids are sucked into the pipette by applying suction through mouth or by using a pipette filler bulb or a pipette filler pump [Fig. 10.7 (i)]. It is always safe to use pipette filler bulb or pipette filler pump to fill the pipette. When poisonous and corrosive solutions are to be drawn into the pipette, never suck by mouth rather use a pipette filler bulb to draw the liquid up into the pipette.*

Cleaning and Rinsing of Pipette

If the pipette is greasy, wash it with chromic acid and then thoroughly with water. After this, the pipette should always be rinsed with the solution which is to be measured by it.

For this, fill the pipette with few millilitres of solution and wet the inner surface of the pipette with the solution by rotating it [Fig. 10.7 (ii) and (iii)]. After rinsing, drain out the whole amount of solution taken in it through the nozzle [Fig. 10.7(iv)]. Now, it is ready for measuring the solution.

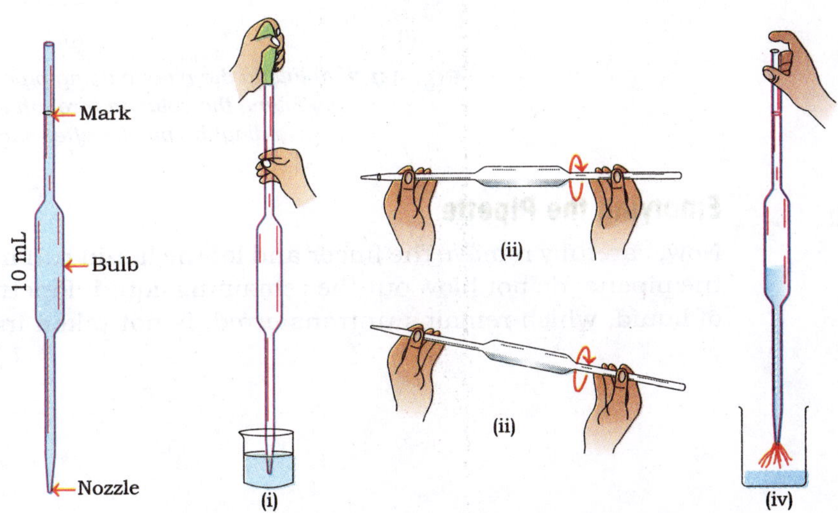

Fig. 10.6 *Pipette* **Fig. 10.7** *(i) Filling of pipette through pipette filler pump (ii), (iii) Wetting the inner walls by rotating it (iv) Draining out solution through nozzle*

Note that while handling the pipette, hands should be dry so that pressure is regulated easily. Also, nozzle of the pipette being used should not be broken.

Filling of Pipette

(i) Hold the pipette in one hand tightly, dip the jet of the pipette into the solution to be pipetted out and squeeze the pipette bulb with the other hand [Fig. 10.8 (i)].

(ii) Now loosen your grip on the bulb so that the liquid is sucked into the pipette. When the liquid is above the etched mark on the pipette, press the bulb to remove excess liquid. But if no filler bulb is provided in the pipette, suck the solution into the pipette by applying suction through the mouth as shown in Fig. 10.8 (ii) and put the index finger of the hand at its place for holding the pipette after suction as shown in Fig. 10.8 (iii).

(iii) Loosen the finger carefully to allow the excess liquid to flow out so that the curvature of the meniscus reaches the mark.

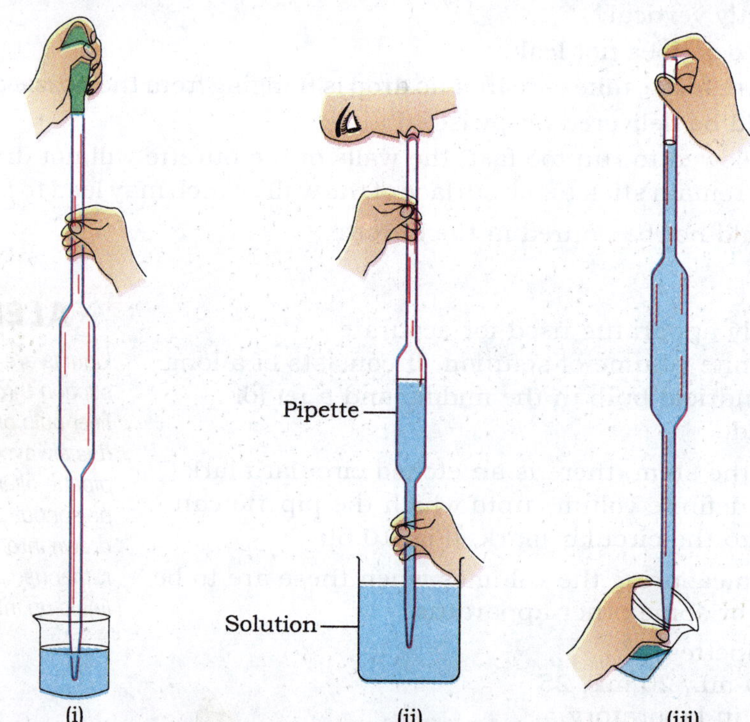

Fig. 10.8 *(i) Filling the pipette using pipette bulb*
(ii) Filling the solution through suction
(iii) Holding the pipette after suction

Emptying the Pipette

Now, carefully remove the finger and let the liquid run into the flask [Fig. 10.9 (i)]. After emptying the pipette, do not blow out the remaining liquid. Pipettes are so designed that the little amount of liquid, which remains untransferred, is not taken into calibration [Fig. 10.9 (ii)].

To take out the maximum volume after complete transfer, simply touch the pipette to the side or base of the container into which the liquid is being transferred.

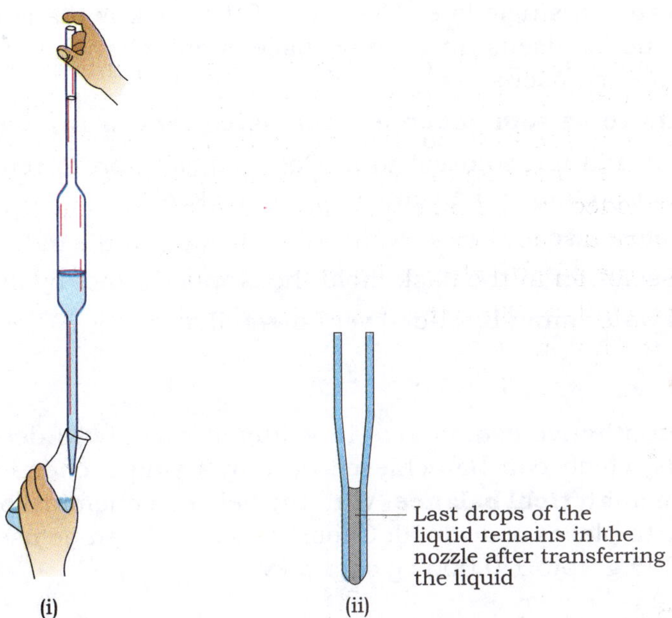

Fig. 10.9 *(i) Transferring the liquid to the flask*
(ii) Nozzle of the pipette after measuring solution

Some important points to be remembered while using a pipette

1. The pipette should be washed well before use.
2. The pipette should be rinsed before filling it up with the solution to be measured.
3. Always use the fore-finger and not the thumb to close the upper end of the pipette.
4. The solution should not be sucked too fast as it may go into the mouth.
5. Do not blow off the last drop remaining in the pipette. Pipettes are so designed that the little amount of liquid, which remains untransferred, is not taken into calibration.
6. While handling the pipette, hands should be dry so that the pressure is regulated easily. Also, nozzle of the pipette being used should not be broken.

Measuring Flasks

These are employed for making specific volumes of solutions (mainly standard solutions). This is also called **graduated flask** or **volumetric flask**. It is a pear shaped vessel with a long narrow neck and flat bottom.

A thin circle etched around the neck indicates the volume of the liquid that it holds at a definite temperature.

Measuring flasks of various capacity are available. Usually, at this level of experimentation, flasks of capacity 50 mL, 100 mL and 250 mL are employed in the work [Fig. 10.10].

The temperature and the capacity of the flask at that temperature are marked on the flask. The mark around the neck helps in avoiding errors due to parallax when making the final adjustment of meniscus.

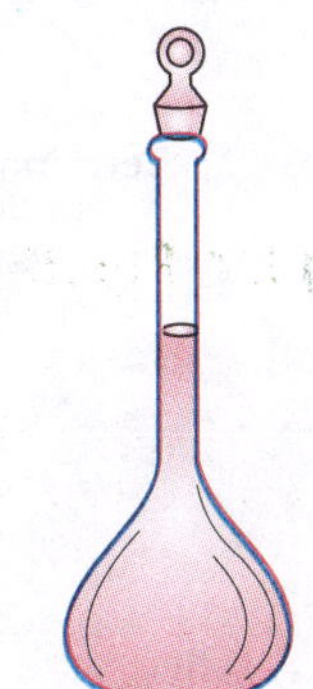

Fig. 10.10 *Measuring flask*

The lower edge of the meniscus of the liquid should be tangential to the graduated mark. While making final adjustment of the meniscus, the front and the back portion of the circular mark should be observable in single line. The neck of the flask is made narrow to reduce error in adjustment of the meniscus. In narrow space, small change in volume makes large effect on the height of the meniscus.

Some important points to be remembered while using measuring flask:

1. Neither heat it nor add hot solution to it. Cool the solution to room temperature before pouring. Heating may change the volume of the flask.
2. Clean the flask before use.
3. While mixing the solution in the flask, hold the stopper intact by pressing it down.
4. Last few drops of water must be added very carefully.

Chemical Balance

The accuracy of the quantitative estimations in volumetric analysis depend upon the correct weighing of compounds which can be achieved only by using a chemical balance. Chemical balance is also called an **analytical balance**. With the help of a chemical balance, one can weigh accurately upto the fourth places of decimal. Chemical balance can be used to weigh the objects not heavier than 100-200 g upto ± 0.0002 g accuracy.

A. Description of the Apparatus

It is a delicate and sensitive instrument. The analytical balance used in quantitative microanalysis can be used for weighing objects not heavier than 100-200 g to a precision of 0.0002 g, i.e. 0.2 mg.

The main parts of the chemical balance are:

Beam is the most important part of the balance. The beam is mounted on a centre knife edge which appears like a prism and rest upon a plate made up of very hard material such as agate or corundum. At equal distances from the centre edge of the beam, two terminal agate knife edges are present. From the centre of the beam, a long and sharp pointer is attached which swings over a scale below [Fig. 10.11].

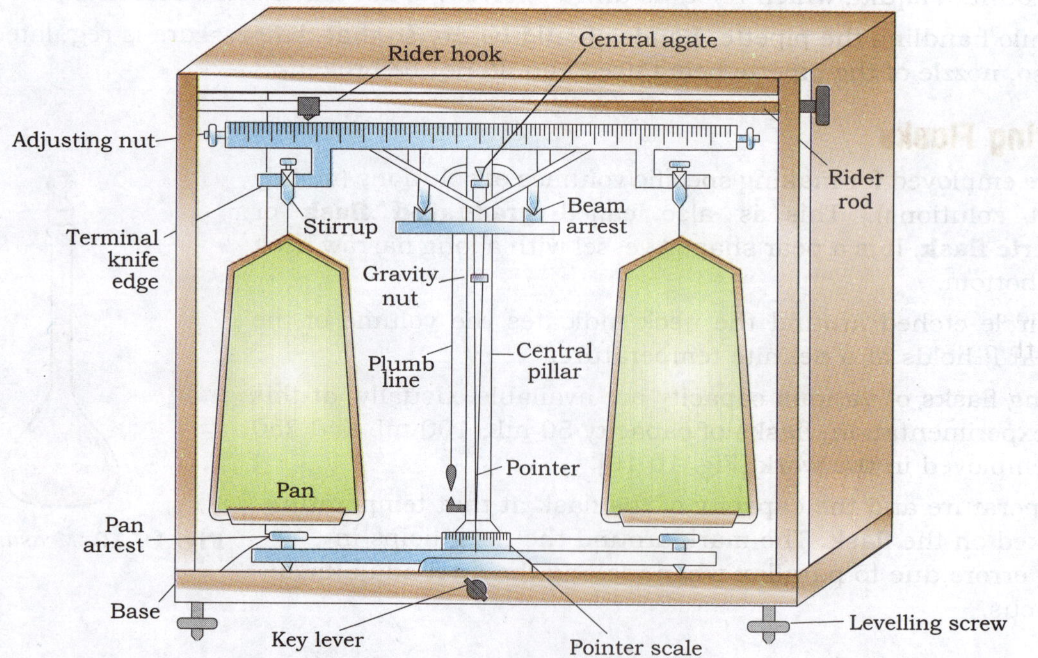

Fig. 10.11 *Chemical or analytical balance*

The pointer serves to point out the deflection of the beam from central position when the balance is in operation. The pointer moves equally on both the sides, when the weight on both the pans weighs same.

Central pillar The central edge plate is attached to the central beam support called central pillar.

Stirrups The terminal knife edges support a suspension called stirrups, which are used to suspend or hang the pans.

Balance pans are made up of a light metal. Two pans on each side are hung by hooks or stirrups. Right pan is generally used for placing the weights and left pan is used for placing the things (or chemicals) to be weighed. The chemicals should never be placed directly on the pan. It must be weighed in pre-weighed watch glass or weighing bottle.

Rider rod is a rod provided at the top of the balance. It carries a rider hook for carrying a rider.

All the three knife edges must be kept parallel and in the same plane for correct weighing. Further, the precision of weighing depends to a large extent on the sharpness of the three knife edges and the smoothness of the plates on which they rest.

With use, the knife edges and plates slowly wear out and the balance becomes less precise. To reduce wear and tear of the knife edges, the balance is provided with beam arrest which raises the balance beam and the balance is in arrested position. When the balance is 'arrested', the knife edges do not touch their plates and thereby reducing the wear and tear of the knife edges.

Rider

Chemical samples less than 10 mg are weighed by rider. Rider is a U-shaped thin wire (usually made up of aluminium). Its weight itself is 10 mg (0.01 g). The rider is placed easily in the grooves (or hooks) of the balance beam with the help of forceps. The hook is fixed to a horizontal rider rod. This rod is rotated or moved to place the rider at any desired point on the beam. The balance beam is divided into 10 equal parts each of which is further sub-divided into 5 parts. One bigger division corresponds to 1 mg (1/10) and one small division reads 0.2 mg (1/5).

B. Weight Box Including Fractional Weights and Riders

Weight box is a special box which contains all the types of weights that are required for measuring the compounds on analytical balance [Fig. 10.12 (i)]. It is a wooden box having grooves of various sizes containing different types of weights.

The weight box of a chemical (or analytical) balance generally contains:

1. **Weights for weighing in grams** These are cylindrical in shape and provided with knobs to pick them up with a force. These are arranged in the following order:

   100 g 50 g 20 g 20 g 10 g
   1 g 2 g 2 g 5 g

   The value of each weight is stamped on its surface. These are made up of copper and nickel with or without coating of chromium.

2. **Weights for weighing in milligrams** These are made up of different shapes so that small weights can be easily distinguished [Fig. 10.12 (ii)]. These are arranged in three rows:

   500 mg 200 mg 200 mg 100 mg
   50 mg 20 mg 20 mg 10 mg
   5 mg 2 mg 2 mg 1 mg

   These are made up of aluminium or stainless steel or German silver.

3. **Rider** A loop made up of aluminium or platinum wire to weigh 0.2 mg to 10 mg.

4. **Forceps** It is used to transfer the weights.

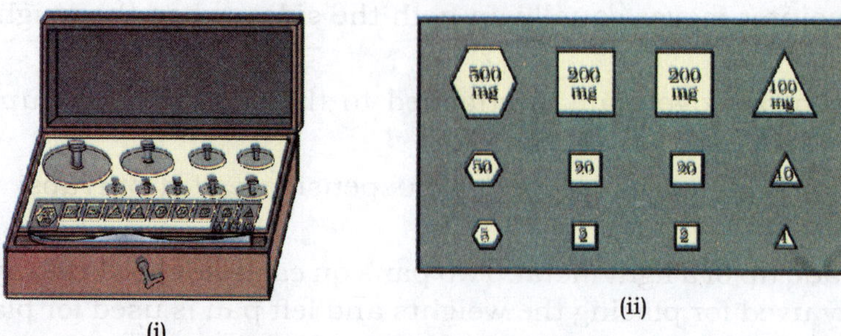

(i) (ii)

Fig. 10.12 (i) *Weight box* (ii) *Fractional weights*

C. Setting of a Chemical Balance and Weighing

1. Setting the Balance

Before weighing the substance, the balance should be cleaned and set in a proper position. It can be done as:

(i) With the help of levelling screws and plumb line, level the balance.

(ii) Ensure that the beam is horizontal. If it is not then, balance it using levelling screw.

(iii) Check (by raising the beam gently) that pointer of the beam oscillate equal divisions on both sides. If it is not so then arrest the beam and move the adjusting screws till the pointer oscillates equally on both sides of zero mark.

2. Weighing of the Substance

Remember the following points, when weighing a substance:

(i) Place a clean and dry watch glass or weighing bottle on the left pan in which weighing material is kept. With the help of forceps, put approximate weights from the weight box on the right pan.

(ii) Note the movement of the pointer on the scale by raising the beam slowly. If its weight is not appropriate, the pointer will move towards the lighter side.

(iii) According to the requirement, add or remove weights after bringing the pans to rest by arresting the beam with the help of knob located near the base. When weight on both the pans becomes equal, the pointer moves equal divisions on both sides of the zero of the base scale.

(iv) For adjustment of weight below 10 mg, use the rider.

(v) Arrest the beam and record the correct weight of substance (or compound).

3. Using Rider

For weighing chemicals by using the rider, principle of moment is applied. Weight is equal to the arm length from the centre of the beam multiplied by the weight of the rider. Length of the beam from the centre to one side of the beam is taken as unit length.

On both sides from the centre, the balance beam is divided into ten equal parts through equidistant marks, each of which corresponds to $\frac{1}{10}$th of the length of the beam. Hence, each big division corresponds to $\frac{1}{10} \times 0.01\,g = 0.001$ g or 1 mg weight. Each big division is further divided into five parts.

Thus, each small division corresponds to only 1/5 milligram, i.e. 0.2 mg or 0.0002 g. Thus, the rider placed at 4.2 mark [Fig. 10.13] will weigh 0.0044 g [i.e. $4 \times 0.001 + 2 \times 0.0002 = 0.0044$ g].

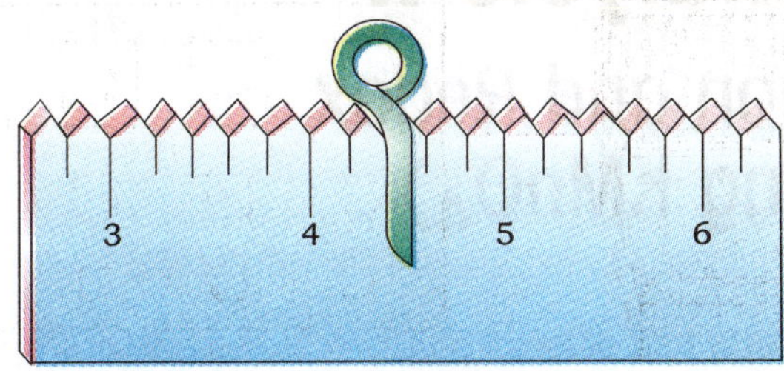

Fig. 10.13 *Rider resting on groove of balance beam*

Precautions while Handling the Balance

While weighing, it must be kept in mind that the analytical balance is a precise and sensitive instrument. It must be handled with care, as the results can be easily spoiled by improper handling. Thus, to obtain precise weighing, following precautions should be taken while handling the balance:

1. Before and after weighing, pans must be properly cleaned.
2. Place the gram weights and fractional weights back into the weight box after weighing the substance.
3. Chemicals should never be placed directly on the pans for weighing.
4. Do not overload the balance as overloading may damage the instrument.
5. Always keep weights on the right pan and object on the left pan of the balance.
6. Never weigh a hot or cold object on the balance.
7. Always transfer the weights by forceps.
8. Always release the beam gently.
9. Do not allow the weights to get spoiled by corrosion.
10. Hygroscopic substances must be weighed in closed weighing bottles.
11. Always make necessary adjustments in the balance before weighing.
12. To insert or remove weights and to keep the object on the pans always use the side doors. Never use the front shutter.
13. Keep the doors shut while releasing the beam arrest to note the movement of the pointer on the scale.
14. The balance must always be arrested before the objects or weights are placed or taken off the pans.

Titrimetric Analysis II

(Standard Solution and Redox Titrations Involving $KMnO_4$)

A solution of exactly known concentration is called **standard solution**. Any substance which is stable at room temperature and does not react with solvent in which it is dissolved, can be directly weighed to prepare its standard solution.

Standard solution of an acid or base is used to determine the unknown concentration of a solution of bases or acids by volumetric analysis. The strength of standard solution is usually expressed in moles per litre.

Description and preparation of standard solutions are given below:

Primary Standard

A primary standard is a compound of sufficient purity in which total amount of impurities does not exceed 0.01- 0.02%.

The standard solution of these compounds can be prepared by direct weighing of its sample followed by its dissolution in water (or solvent) to obtain a definite volume of solution. This is known as **direct method** of preparing standard solution. Thus, all substances whose standard solutions are prepared by the direct method are known as **primary standards**.

The substance to be used as a primary standard should also satisfy the following requirements:

1. It must be easily available in pure and dry form.
2. It should not undergo any change in air, i.e. it should not be hygroscopic, oxidised by air or affected by gases such as carbon dioxide present in the atmosphere or lose water of crystallisation so that it can be stored safely.
3. It should be easy to detect the impurities present in it.
4. It should have high relative molecular mass so that weighing errors are negligible.
5. Its reaction with another substance should be instantaneous and stoichiometric.
6. The substance should be readily soluble in water.

Note *It is difficult to obtain an ideal primary standard. Therefore, substances having characteristics nearer to the primary standards are usually employed.*

As a rule, unstable hydrated salts should not be used as primary standards. However, sodium carbonate, sodium tetraborate, potassium hydrogen phthalate, oxalic acid, ferrous ammonium sulphate can be used as primary standards because of their sufficient stabilities.

Secondary Standard

The secondary standard solutions are prepared by the **indirect method**. An approximately desired weight of the substance is dissolved in water and the solution is made to a known volume.

The exact strength of the solution is then determined by titrating it with a suitable standard substance. This is called **standardisation**. Thus, a solution of secondary standard is the one which may be used for standardisation after finding out its exact concentration by titrating it against a standard solution of primary standard.

A secondary standard cannot be used for preparing standard solution by weighing. Sodium hydroxide, acetic acid and potassium permanganate are the examples of secondary standard.

Detection of End Point

The point where the reaction between the two solutions is just complete is called **end point**. The end point is detected either by some physical change produced in the reaction mixture itself or by the addition of an auxiliary reagent, known as **indicator**.

At the completion of the reaction, the indicator shows a visible change (e.g. colour change or turbidity) in the solution being titrated. In an ideal titration, the visible end point coincides with the stoichiometric or theoretical end point, but in practice, usually some small difference occurs. This represents **titration error**.

Indicator and the experimental conditions selected should be such that the difference between the visible end point and the theoretical end point is minimum.

Permanganometric Titrations

The titrations involving potassium permanganate as an oxidising agent are called permanganometric titrations.

Potassium permanganate acts as a strong oxidising agent in the presence of dil. H_2SO_4 as it liberates nascent oxygen.

$$2KMnO_4 + 3H_2SO_4 \longrightarrow K_2SO_4 + 2MnSO_4 + 3H_2O + 5[O]$$

or,

$$MnO_4^- + 8H^+ + 5e^- \longrightarrow Mn^{2+} + 4H_2O$$

Potassium permanganate can be used for the estimation of oxalic acid and ferrous salts. It oxidises oxalic acid to CO_2 and ferrous salts to ferric salts in acidic medium.

$$\begin{matrix} COOH \\ | \\ COOH \end{matrix} + [O] \longrightarrow 2CO_2 + H_2O$$

$$2FeSO_4 + H_2SO_4 + [O] \longrightarrow Fe_2(SO_4)_3 + H_2O$$

The oxidation reactions of oxalic acid are accompanied by the evolution of CO_2 gas which is soluble in cold solution. It does not allow the reaction proceed to completion. Therefore, this reaction is carried out at 60-70°C to expel CO_2 gas from the solution. In potassium permanganate titrations, only dilute sulphuric acid is used to acidify the solution. This is because:

(i) dilute sulphuric acid does not react with $KMnO_4$ until a reducing agent is not added.

(ii) if hydrochloric acid is used, it will react with $KMnO_4$ to produce chlorine, which acts as oxidising agent in aqueous solution.

$$2KMnO_4 + 16HCl \longrightarrow 2KCl + 2MnCl_2 + 8H_2O + 5Cl_2$$

More $KMnO_4$ will be consumed in the redox titration.

(iii) if nitric acid is used, it will interfere with the action of $KMnO_4$ as itself an oxidising agent.

(iv) if in alkaline solution, the oxidation is accompanied by the separation of MnO_2 as a dark brown precipitate, the solution which is in process of titration with potassium permanganate must be sufficiently acidic to prevent the formation of MnO_2.

Procedure for Titration

The process of titration is used to find out the volume of one solution required to react completely with a certain known volume of solution of some other substance. Titration is the most important part of volumetric analysis.

It is carried out in the following steps:

1. A glazed tile is placed below the burette and titration flask is placed on it below the burette nozzle. The height of the burette is so adjusted that the nozzle tip just enters the mouth of the titration flask.
2. The initial reading of the burette after filling it with the solution is noted down and solution from the burette (1 mL at a time) is allowed to take out by opening the stopcock with the left hand. The titration flask is kept in the right hand as shown in Fig. 10.14.
3. Swirl the titration flask throughout the titration.
4. Continue to run more of the solution from the burette into the titration flask, keeping it all the time shaking. The solution should fall directly into the solution of titration flask. It should not fall on the walls of the flask.
5. Stop adding the solution when the end point is reached and final reading of the burette is taken. The difference between the final and initial readings gives rough volume of the solution used for the completion of the reaction.
6. The solution from the titration flask is thrown away and the titration flask is washed thoroughly first by keeping it under tap water and then with a little of distilled water. Do not rinse the titration flask.
7. Pour more solution into the burette.
8. Pipette out 15 mL of the solution into the titration flask and add 1-2 drops of the indicator solution.
9. The initial reading of the burette is noted down. Run solution from the burette into the titration flask slowly with constant shaking.

   Continue to add the solution till the volume added is 1 mL less than the rough volume found out in the first titration. Now add the solution dropwise from the burette.
10. Continue to add the solution dropwise from the burette, till by addition of last single drop, the end point is attained.
11. Note down the final reading of the burette. The difference between the final and initial readings of the burette gives the exact volume of the solution required for the completion of the reaction.
12. Check the correctness of the end point by adding one drop of solution (taken in the titration flask) with the help of a pipette. Restoration of original colour confirms the correctness of the end point.
13. Perform 5 to 6 titrations so that at least three concordant readings (difference not more than 0.05 mL) are obtained.

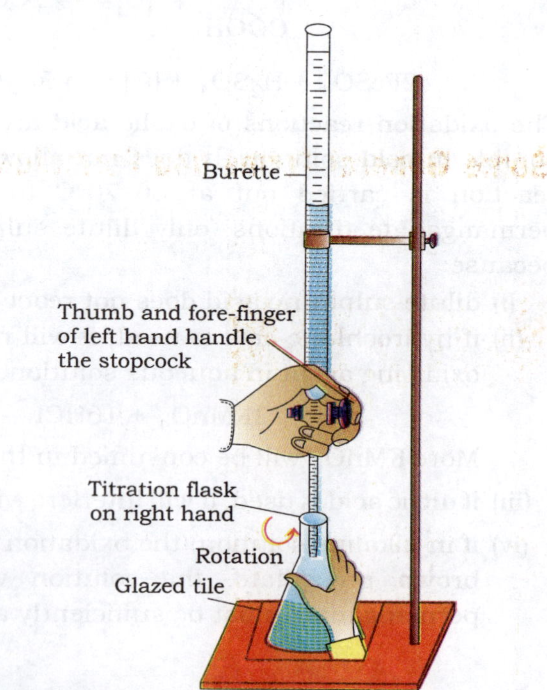

Fig. 10.14 *Handling of a burette in a correct way*

Important Instructions for $KMnO_4$ Titrations

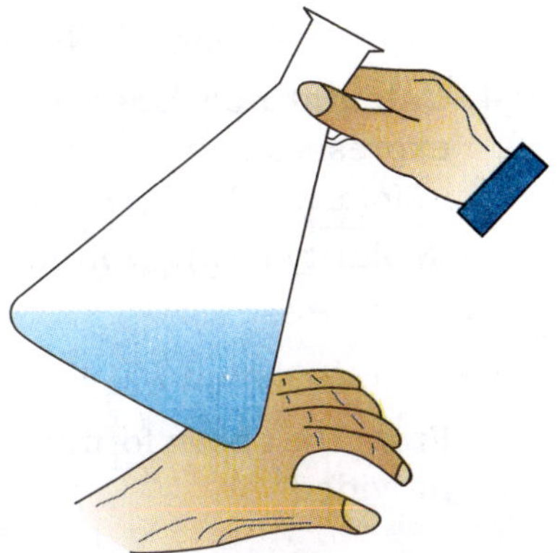

Fig. 10.15 *To observe approximate temperature of the solution*

1. Always take $KMnO_4$ solution in the burette.
2. The use of a burette having a rubber tap should be avoided because $KMnO_4$ attacks rubber.
3. A known volume of the solution to be titrated (like oxalic acid) is taken in a titration flask and an equal volume of dil. H_2SO_4 is added to the flask.
4. If oxalic acid is to be titrated, add required amount of dil. H_2SO_4 and heat the flask at 60-70°C on a wire gauze.
   For getting an idea about the temperature of the solution, touch the flask to the back side of your hand [Fig. 10.15].
   When it becomes just unbearable to touch, the required temperature is reached. The solution is heated so as to increase the rate of reaction which otherwise is slow at room temperature. However, in case of ferrous salts, no heating is required.
5. Read the upper meniscus while taking burette reading with $KMnO_4$ solution.
6. On addition of $KMnO_4$, if a brown precipitate appears, this suggests that either H_2SO_4 has not been added or has been added in insufficient amounts. In such a case, throw away the solution and titrate again.
7. $KMnO_4$ does not dissolve into water readily. It is dissolved by the process of extraction. Transfer the weighed $KMnO_4$ into a beaker and add 20-30 mL of distilled water into it and stir the contents. Transfer the solution into a measuring flask. Add more distilled water (20-30 mL) into the beaker and repeat the operation till the permanganate completely dissolves. Add more distilled water into the measuring flask till the lower meniscus of the solution is in line with the mark on the neck. Stopper the measuring flask and shake to get the solution of uniform strength.
8. The correct end point in potassium permanganate titration is a change of colourless solution to just permanent pink solution.

Some General Terms and Formulae Used in Volumetric Analysis

1. **Molarity** The number of gram moles of solute per litre of the solution is known as molarity of a solution. Mathematically, it may be expressed as:

$$\text{Molarity } (M) = \frac{\text{Gram moles of solute}}{\text{Volume of solution (in litres)}}$$

or

$$M = \frac{\text{Mass of solute (in grams)}}{\text{Gram molar mass of solute} \times \text{Volume of solution (in litres)}}$$

or Gram moles of solute = Molarity (M) × Volume of solution (in litres)

Note *A solution containing one gram mole of solute per litre of the solution is called a* ***molar solution****.*

2. **Normality** The number of gram-equivalents of solute per litre of solution is called normality of a solution. Mathematically, it may be expressed as:

$$\text{Normality } (N) = \frac{\text{Number of gram-equivalents of solute}}{\text{Volume of solution (in litres)}}$$

or

$$N = \frac{\text{Mass of solute (in grams)}}{\text{Gram-equivalent mass of solute} \times \text{Volume of solution (in litres)}}$$

In general, the number of gram-equivalents of solute = Normality (N) × Volume of solution (in litres)

Note *A solution containing one gram-equivalent of solute per litre of the solution is called a* ***normal solution****.*

3. **Strength of solution** The strength of solution is given by

Strength (in g/L) = Molarity × Molar mass

Strength = Normality × Equivalent mass

4. **Calculations Used in Volumetric Analysis** The general formula used in this unit is expressed as:

$$\frac{\text{Molarity } (M_1) \times \text{Volume } (V_1) \text{ of acid}}{\text{Molarity } (M_2) \times \text{Volume } (V_2) \text{ of base}} = \frac{\text{Numerical coefficient of acid in the balanced equation}}{\text{Numerical coefficient of base in the balanced equation}}$$

From the above formula, one can find the molarity of acid (or base) if all the other terms are provided.

Equivalent Mass of Oxidising and Reducing Agents

According to electronic concept, oxidation is the process which results in the loss of one or more electrons by atoms or ions and reduction is the process which results in the gain of one or more electrons by atoms or ions.

The oxidising agent is the substance which gains one or more electrons and gets reduced. The reducing agent is the substance which loses one or more electrons and gets oxidised.

The equivalent mass of an oxidising agent is equal to its molecular mass (or formula mass) divided by the number of the electrons gained by one molecule or ion of the substance in the reaction.

$$\therefore \text{ Eq. mass of an oxidising agent} = \frac{\text{Molecular mass or formula mass}}{\text{No. of electrons gained by one molecule}}$$

$$\text{Eq. mass of a reducing agent} = \frac{\text{Molecular mass or formula mass}}{\text{No. of electrons lost by one molecule}}$$

The equivalent masses of some common substances which we come across during redox titrations at this level are given below in the table.

Molecular and Equivalent Masses of Some Substances

Substance	Molecular mass	Ionic reaction	n	Eq. mass = Mol. mass/n
Potassium permanganate ($KMnO_4$)	158	$MnO_4^- + 8H^+ + 5e^- \longrightarrow Mn^{2+} + 4H_2O$	5	31.6
Mohr's salt [$FeSO_4 \cdot (NH_4)_2SO_4 \cdot 6H_2O$]	392	$Fe^{2+} \longrightarrow Fe^{3+} + e^-$	1	392
Ferrous sulphate anhydrous ($FeSO_4$)	152	$Fe^{2+} \longrightarrow Fe^{3+} + e^-$	1	152
Ferrous sulphate crystals ($FeSO_4 \cdot 7H_2O$)	278	$Fe^{2+} \longrightarrow Fe^{3+} + e^-$	1	278
Oxalic acid anhydrous ($H_2C_2O_4$)	90	$C_2O_4^{2-} \longrightarrow 2CO_2 + 2e^-$	2	45
Oxalic acid crystals ($H_2C_2O_4 \cdot 2H_2O$)	126	$C_2O_4^{2-} \longrightarrow 2CO_2 + 2e^-$	2	63

Experiment 10.1

AIM

To determine the concentration/molarity of $KMnO_4$ solution by titrating it against a 0.1M standard solution of oxalic acid.

Theory/Principle

The equations involved in the titration of oxalic acid against potassium permanganate in the acidic medium are as follows:

1. Molecular Equations

Reduction half-reaction : $2KMnO_4 + 3H_2SO_4 \longrightarrow K_2SO_4 + 2MnSO_4 + 3H_2O + 5[O]$

Oxidation half-reaction : $[H_2C_2O_4 + [O] \xrightarrow{60\,°C} 2CO_2 + H_2O] \times 5$

$$2KMnO_4 + 3H_2SO_4 + 5H_2C_2O_4 \longrightarrow K_2SO_4 + 2MnSO_4 + 8H_2O + 10CO_2$$

2. Ionic Equations

Reduction half-reaction : $[MnO_4^- + 5e^- + 8H^+ \longrightarrow Mn^{2+} + 4H_2O] \times 2$

Oxidation half-reaction : $[C_2O_4^{2-} \longrightarrow 2CO_2 + 2e^-] \times 5$

$$2MnO_4^- + 5C_2O_4^{2-} + 16H^+ \longrightarrow 2Mn^{2+} + 10CO_2 + 8H_2O$$

In this reaction, Mn of $KMnO_4$ reduced from +7 to + 2 oxidation state, i.e. from MnO_4^- to Mn^{2+} and carbon of oxalic acid oxidises from + 3 to + 4 oxidation state, i.e. from $C_2O_4^{2-}$ to CO_2.

Indicator

In these $KMnO_4$ acts as a self indicator.

End Point

Initially, dark purple colour of $KMnO_4$ is discharged when it is added to oxalic acid because of reduction of $KMnO_4$ by oxalic acid. At the end point of titration, the light pink colour persist in the solution because of the presence of a little excess of unreacted $KMnO_4$. This is so because at the end point, no oxalic acid is left in the solution to reduce $KMnO_4$, i.e. oxalate ions are completely consumed. Hence, the light pink colour when persist in the solution shows the completion of titration.

Materials Required

▪ Measuring flask (250 mL)	:	1	▪ Glazed tile (white)	:	1
▪ Burette (50 mL)	:	1	▪ Burner	:	1
▪ Burette stand	:	1	▪ Wire gauze	:	1
▪ Pipette	:	1	▪ Chemical balance	:	1
▪ Conical flask	:	1	▪ Oxalic acid	:	As per need
▪ Funnel	:	1	▪ Potassium permanganate solution	:	As per need
▪ Weighing bottle	:	1	▪ 1.0 M sulphuric acid	:	As per need

Procedure

A. Preparation of 0.1M Standard Solution of Oxalic Acid

1. Weigh an empty, clean, dry weighing bottle on chemical balance.
2. Take oxalic acid to the weighing bottle such that the weight of the weighing bottle increased by 3.150 g.
3. Remove the weighing bottle from chemical balance.
4. Transfer the weighed oxalic acid to the standard measuring flask of 250 mL with the help of funnel.
5. Now, weigh the empty weighing bottle again and find out the weight of oxalic acid transferred to the measuring flask by subtracting this weight from the combined measured weights in step 1 and 2.
6. Then, wash the funnel with distilled water several times to transfer the remaining sticky particles into the measuring flask.
7. Add water in small amounts while washing the funnel.
8. Dissolved all the oxalic acid completely by swirling the measuring flask.
9. Remove the funnel and add more distilled water dropwise to make up the volume to the etched mark.
10. Insert the stopper in the measuring flask and shake it throughly to make uniform solution.

ALERT

- *Oxalic acid is harmful.*
- *Potassium permanganate is harmful, flammable and oxidising.*
- *Conc. sulphuric acid is corrosive and irritant.*

B. Titration of Oxalic Acid Solution against Potassium Permanganate Solution

1. Rinse and fill a clean burette with $KMnO_4$ solution. Remove the air bubble, if any, from the nozzle of the burette by releasing some solution through it. The burette used in the permanganate titration must have a glass stopcock as rubber is attacked by permanganate ions.
2. Pipette out 10 mL of 0.1 M oxalic acid solute to the conical flask and half of the test tube (≈ 5 mL) of 1.0 M H_2SO_4 is added to it in order to prevent the formation of any precipitate of MnO_2 during the course of the titration.
3. Heat the conical flask containing oxalic acid solution on burner by placing the conical flask on wire gauze kept on tripod stand. Heat the contents of conical flask to 50-60°C. This temperature can be checked by touching the conical flask from the back side of your hand. When it becomes unbearable then start the titration.
4. To increase the visibility of the colour change, place the conical flask containing the solution to be titrated over a white glazed tile kept below the nozzle of the vertically fitted burette.
5. Note down the initial reading of the volume of $KMnO_4$ solution in the burette and start adding $KMnO_4$ to the hot oxalic acid solution in small volumes with continuous swirling the solution of conical flask gently. The violet colour of permanganate solution is discharged on reaction with oxalic acid. The end point is indicated by the appearance of permanent light pink colour due to a slight excess of permanganate solution. Note down the final reading of the volume of $KMnO_4$.
6. Repeat the titration to get three concordant readings. Since, the solution of $KMnO_4$ is of dark colour, the upper meniscus should be considered for noting the burette readings.
7. Record the readings in the tabular form and calculate the strength of $KMnO_4$ solution in moles/litre.

Observations

Total volume taken in titration flask = 10 mL of 0.1 M oxalic acid + (≈ 5 mL) of 1 M H_2SO_4

S. No.	Volume of oxalic acid (in mL)	Burette readings		Volume of $KMnO_4$ used $V = (y - x)$ mL
		Initial (x)	Final (y)	
1.				
2.				
3.				

Calculations

1. Amount of oxalic acid to be weighed to prepare 250 mL of 0.1 M solution.

$$\text{Molarity, } M = \frac{\text{Weight}}{\text{Molecular weight}} \times \frac{1000}{\text{Volume (in mL)}}$$

$$0.1 = \frac{\text{Weight}}{126} \times \frac{1000}{250}$$

$$\text{Weight} = 3.150 \text{ g}$$

2. The strength of the unknown solution of $KMnO_4$ in terms of molarity can be evaluated as follows:

$$n_1 M_1 V_1 = n_2 M_2 V_2 \qquad \ldots\text{(i)}$$

where, n_1 is the number of electrons lost per formula unit of oxalic acid in a balanced equation of half-cell reaction. Here, its value is 2.

n_2 is the number of electrons gained per formula unit of potassium permanganate in the balanced equation of half-cell reaction. Here, its value is 5.

M_1 and M_2 are the molarities of oxalic acid and potassium permanganate solutions used in the titration, respectively.

V_1 and V_2 are the volumes used of oxalic acid and potassium permanganate solutions, respectively.

On substituting the value of n_1 and n_2 in Eq. (i), we have

$$(2 M_1 V_1)_{\text{oxalic acid}} = (5 M_2 V_2)_{KMnO_4}$$

$$M_2 = \text{Molarity of } KMnO_4 = \frac{2}{5} \frac{M_1 V_1}{V_2}$$

Strength of $KMnO_4$ can be calculated as follows:

$$\text{Strength} = \text{Molarity} \times \text{Molar mass} = M_2 \times 158 \text{ g/L}$$

Result

1. Molarity of $KMnO_4$ is ....
2. Strength of $KMnO_4$ is .... g/L.

PRECAUTIONS

- *While preparing standard solution, use dropper to add last few drops of water in the standard flask.*
- *Burette used in the permanganate titration must have glass stopcock but not rubber cork because rubber may get attacked by permanganate ions.*
- *While noting the reading, no drop of the solution should hang at the tip of the burette at the end point.*
- *Do not forget to heat the mixture of oxalic acid and H_2SO_4 solutions between 50-60°C while titrating it against potassium permanganate solution.*
- *The calculation of strength of the solution must be upto the fourth decimal place.*

Viva-Voce

Q.1 What is a primary standard?

Ans. Primary standard is a substance whose standard solution of desired concentration can be prepared directly by weighing the exact amount of the substance.

Q.2 What do you mean by standard solution?

Ans. A standard solution of a substance is the solution whose concentration is known accurately. It is prepared by adding known amount of the substance in definite volume of solution.

Q.3 What is the principle of volumetric analysis?

Ans. The principle of volumetric analysis is to calculate the strength of a solution by reacting the known volume of solution with the another solution of which the concentration and volume is known to us.

Q.4 What is an equivalence point?

Ans. When the solution of known concentration (titrant) completely reacts with the solution being titrated (titrand) that point is known as equivalence point.

Q.5 What is an end point?

Ans. After equivalence point, the addition of an extra drop of titrand to the titrant that brings the change in colour of the reaction mixture in the conical flask that point is referred as an end point.

Q.6 Why is it advised to read upper meniscus in $KMnO_4$ titration?

Ans. $KMnO_4$ solution is coloured and therefore, the lower meniscus is not visible accurately.

Q.7 Why is it advised not to blow out the last drop of pipette?

Ans. The last drop in the jet of the pipette is not included to the volume of the pipette.

Q.8 Why are burette and pipette rinsed with the solution with which they are filled?

Ans. In order to remove any water sticking to their sides, which otherwise would decrease the concentration of the solution taken in the burette and pipette.

Q.9 Why do we add dil. H_2SO_4 before doing the titration between $KMnO_4$ and oxalic acid?

Ans. To provide acidic medium for the action of $KMnO_4$. If it is not added then in neutral or basic condition, $KMnO_4$ oxidises to give brown precipitate of MnO_2 which creates problem in visualising the colour change near the end point.

Q.10 While performing the titrations involving $KMnO_4$, sometimes a brown precipitate is obtained. How would you explain the formation of this brown precipitate?

Ans. The brown precipitate is obtained due to the insufficient quantity of dil. sulphuric acid. This brown precipitate is formed due to the incomplete oxidation of $KMnO_4$.

$$4KMnO_4 + 2H_2O \longrightarrow 4KOH + \underset{\text{Brown ppt.}}{4MnO_2} + 2O_2$$

Q.11 Why overheating of oxalic acid solution containing sulphuric acid should be avoided?

Ans. On overheating of oxalic acid solution, it may decompose into CO_2 and CO gas that decreases the concentration of oxalic acid solution.

Q.12 Why does the permanganate solution changes from dark purple to faint pink colour?

Ans. Due to the reduction of purple permanganate ion to colourless Mn^{2+} ion.

Questions From NCERT Lab Manual

Q.1 What specific name is given to the permanganate titrations?

Ans. Permanganometric titrations is the specific name given to the permanganate titrations.

Q.2 Which indicator is used in the permanganate titration?

Ans. Potassium permanganate acts as a self indicator in permanganate titrations. No other indicator is needed in permanganate titration.

Q.3 Why is a burette with pinch-cock regulator not used for the permanganate titration?

Ans. Permanganate ions are powerful oxidising agent so, they must attack the pinch-cock regulator to oxidise it. Therefore, glass stopcock burettes should be used for permanganate titrations.

Q.4 Why do we heat oxalic acid solution containing sulphuric acid upto 50 - 60°C in the permanganate titration?

Ans. The reaction rate between $KMnO_4$ and oxalic acid is very slow at room temperature. Thus, at temperature 50-60° C, they react at considerable rate and after that, Mn^{2+} ions will catalyse the reaction to continuously increase the rate of reaction.

Experiment 10.2

To determine the concentration/molarity of $KMnO_4$ solution by titrating it against standard solution of ferrous ammonium sulphate.

Theory/Principle

Ferrous ammonium sulphate $[FeSO_4(NH_4)_2SO_4 \cdot 6H_2O]$ is a double salt known as **Mohr's salt**. It acts as a reducing agent in the titration against $KMnO_4$ solution by reducing MnO_4^- ions to Mn^{2+}.

The reaction rate between Mohr's salt and $KMnO_4$ solution is very high even at room temperature therefore, during titration, heating of solution is not required.

In fact on heating the Mohr's salt solution, the ferrous ions, Fe(II) ions, may get oxidised to ferric ions, Fe (III) ions, due to the action of oxygen in the air. This oxidation leads to error in the result of volumetric analysis.

Chemical Equations

The reactions involved in the titration of Mohr's salt with $KMnO_4$ are as follows :

1. **Molecular Equations**

Reduction half-reaction: $2KMnO_4 + 3H_2SO_4 \longrightarrow K_2SO_4 + 2MnSO_4 + 3H_2O + 5\,[O]$

Oxidation half-reaction:

$$[2FeSO_4 \cdot (NH_4)_2SO_4 \cdot 6H_2O + H_2SO_4 + [O] \longrightarrow Fe_2(SO_4)_3 + 2(NH_4)_2SO_4 + 13H_2O] \times 5$$

$$2KMnO_4 + 8H_2SO_4 + 10FeSO_4 \cdot (NH_4)_2SO_4 \cdot 6H_2O \longrightarrow K_2SO_4 + 2MnSO_4 + 5Fe_2(SO_4)_3 + 10(NH_4)_2SO_4 + 68H_2O$$

2. **Ionic Equations**

Reduction half-reaction : $MnO_4^- + 5e^- + 8H^+ \longrightarrow Mn^{2+} + 4H_2O$

Oxidation half-reaction : $[Fe^{2+} \longrightarrow Fe^{3+} + e^-] \times 5$

$$MnO_4^- + 5Fe^{2+} + 8H^+ \longrightarrow Mn^{2+} + 5Fe^{3+} + 4H_2O$$

Indicator $KMnO_4$ acts as a self indicator.

End Point Colourless to permanent pink colour ($KMnO_4$ in burette).

Materials Required

- Measuring flask (250 mL) : 1
- Burette (50 mL) : 1
- Burette stand : 1
- Pipette : 1
- Conical flask : 1
- Glazed tile (white) : 1
- Funnel : 1
- Weighing bottle : 1
- Potassium permanganate solution : As per need
- Dilute sulphuric acid : As per need
- Ferrous ammonium sulphate : As per need

Procedure

A. Preparation of 0.05 M Standard Solution of Ferrous Ammonium Sulphate

[Molar mass of $FeSO_4 \cdot (NH_4)_2SO_4 \cdot 6H_2O = 392$ g mol^{-1}]

1. Weigh a clean, dry weighing bottle on chemical balance.
2. Add ferrous ammonium sulphate to the weighing bottle such that the weight of weighing bottle increased by 4.900 g.
3. Remove weighing bottle from chemical balance.
4. Transfer the weighed ferrous ammonium sulphate to the standard 250 mL measuring flask with the help of funnel.
5. Solid sticking to the funnel is transferred into the flask through distilled water and add few drops of dilute H_2SO_4 into the flask to get the clear solution.
6. Shake the flask to dissolve the solid completely and pour the distilled water upto the mark.

⚠ ALERT

- *Potassium permanganate is flammable, oxidising and harmful.*
- *Mohr's salt and dilute sulphuric acid are of low hazard.*
- *Sulphuric acid is highly corrosive.*

B. Titration of Ferrous Ammonium Sulphate Against Potassium Permanganate Solution

1. Rinse and fill the clean burette with $KMnO_4$ solution. Remove the air bubbles, if any, from the nozzle by releasing some solution through it.
2. 10 mL of 0.05 M ferrous ammonium sulphate solution is pipette out to the conical flask and a half test tube (≈ 5 mL) filled with 1.0 M H_2SO_4 is added to it.
3. Note down the initial reading of the volume of $KMnO_4$ and start adding $KMnO_4$ to the conical flask containing ferrous ammonium sulphate solution in small volumes with continuously swirling the solution in conical flask. When the solution becomes permanent pink in colour, this is the end point of titration.
4. Repeat the titration to get three concordant readings.
5. Record the readings in the tabular form and calculate the strength of $KMnO_4$ in moles/litre.

Observations

Total volume taken in titration flask = 10 mL of 0.05 M ferrous ammonium sulphate + (≈ 5 mL) of 1.0 M H_2SO_4 solution.

S. No.	Volume of ferrous ammonium sulphate solution used (in mL)	Burette readings		Volume of $KMnO_4$ used (in mL) $V = (y - x)$
		Initial (x)	Final (y)	
1.				
2.				
3.				

Calculations

1. Amount of ferrous ammonium sulphate to be weighed to prepare 250 mL of 0.05 M solution.

$$\text{Molarity, } M = \frac{\text{Weight}}{\text{Molecular weight}} \times \frac{1000}{\text{Volume (in mL)}}$$

$$0.05 = \frac{\text{Weight}}{392} \times \frac{1000}{250}$$

$$\text{Weight} = \frac{392 \times 0.05}{4} = 4.900 \text{ g}$$

2. The strength of the unknown solution of $KMnO_4$ in terms of molarity can be evaluated as follows:

$$n_1 M_1 V_1 = n_2 M_2 V_2$$

where, n_1 is the number of electrons lost per formula unit of ferrous ammonium sulphate in the half-cell reaction. Here, its value is 1.

n_2 is the number of electrons gained per formula unit of potassium permanganate in a half-cell reaction. Here, its value is 5.

M_1 and M_2 are the molarities of ferrous ammonium sulphate and potassium permanganate solutions used in the titration, respectively and V_1 and V_2 are the volumes of ferrous ammonium sulphate and potassium permanganate solutions, respectively.

$$\therefore \quad (1\, M_1 V_1)_{\text{Ferrous ammonium sulphate}} = (5\, M_2 V_2)_{\text{Potassium permanganate}}$$

$$M_2 = \frac{1}{5}\frac{M_1 V_1}{V_2}$$

Strength of $KMnO_4$ solution = Molarity (M_2) × Molar mass of $KMnO_4$

Result

1. Molarity of given $KMnO_4$ solution is ....
2. Strength of given $KMnO_4$ solution is .... g/L.

PRECAUTIONS

- *Standard solution of ferrous ammonium sulphate should be freshly prepared.*
- *Measuring flask, weighing bottle, funnel and other apparatus used should be clean.*
- *Weighing of ferrous ammonium sulphate should be done accurately.*
- *While preparing a standard solution, use dropper to add last drops of water in standard flask.*
- *While noting the reading, no drop of the solution should hang at the tip of the burette.*
- *For noting the burette reading, always read the upper meniscus for coloured solution.*
- *The last drop of the solution in the pipette should not be blown out.*
- *The pipette and burette with broken nozzle should not be used.*
- *The calculation of strength of the solution must be upto fourth decimal place.*

Viva-Voce

Q. 1 State the principle of volumetric analysis.

Ans. It is based on the fact that the unknown concentration of the known solution can be determined by titrating it with the volume of another solution of known concentration.

Q. 2 Mention the use of a rider and what is its weight?

Ans. A rider is used to weigh chemical samples less than 10 mg. Weight of the rider is 10 mg.

Q.3 **Why $FeSO_4 \cdot 7H_2O$ cannot be considered a primary standard?**

Ans. $FeSO_4 \cdot 7H_2O$ being an efflorescent salt can lose its water of crystallisation and change its composition. Hence, it cannot be used as a primary standard.

Q.4 **Mohr's salt solution is a primary standard. Why?**

Ans. Mohr's salt is a double salt and is available in pure crystalline form. It is not hygroscopic in nature and hence, the concentration of its solution does not change on keeping its solution for long time.

Q.5 **State the difference between molarity and molality.**

Ans. Molarity of the solution is the number of moles of solute dissolved in 1L of solution but the molality is the number of moles of solute dissolved in 1 kg of solvent.

Q.6 **State the relation between molarity and normality.**

Ans. Normality (N) = Molarity $(M) \times n$-factor where, n-factor is the number of electrons gained or lost during reduction or oxidation of 1 mole of the substance respectively.

Q.7 **What is the chemical formula of Mohr's salt?**

Ans. $FeSO_4 \cdot (NH_4)_2SO_4 \cdot 6H_2O$

Q.8 **$KMnO_4$ can oxidise water then why its aqueous solution is used in its volumetric analysis?**

Ans. $KMnO_4$ oxidises water but the rate of reaction is very slow. Thus, if the solution is freshly prepared then this oxidation reaction is not considerable and it can be used accurately to identify the strength of $KMnO_4$.

Q.9 **Why a brown layer is deposited on the glass container in which potassium permanganate solution is stored for a long time?**

Ans. When $KMnO_4$ solution is stored in a glass container for a long time then the light ray falling on it catalyse the oxidation reaction of water by $KMnO_4$ to produce a brown coloured solid, i.e. MnO_2 which is deposited on the glass.

Q.10 **Why is it recommended to remove air bubbles from the nozzle of burette before starting a titration?**

Ans. The air bubbles may escape anytime during the titration of the titrant (which is taken in the burette) and hence, readings obtained may not be accurate.

Q.11 **$KMnO_4$ solution is not filtered through filter paper. Give reason.**

Ans. Filter paper is made up of an organic matter and thus itself gets oxidised and reduces $KMnO_4$.

Q.12 **We generally use Mohr's salt (a double salt) for titration with $KMnO_4$ but not $FeSO_4$. Why?**

Ans. $FeSO_4$ gets readily oxidised by air resulting in the change in composition and concentration of the solution which affects the results of volumetric measurements.

Q.13 **What is meant by the term self-indicator?**

Ans. A self indicator is a substance in any volumetric titration which itself shows the end point of the titration by altering the colour of the reaction mixture.

Q.14 **Explain how $KMnO_4$ acts as self-indicator?**

Ans. $KMnO_4$ reacts with reducing agents like oxalic acid or ferrous sulphate in the presence of dilute sulphuric acid. Even after all the reducing agent has been oxidised, the excess of $KMnO_4$ does not get decomposed and hence imparts pink colour to the solution.

Questions From NCERT Lab Manual

Q.1 What type of titrations are given the name redox titrations? Name some other redox titrations.

Ans. Redox titrations are the titrations in which one substance gets reduced and other substance gets oxidised simultaneously. Example of other redox titration is iodometry in which iodide ion (I^-) is oxidised to iodine molecule (I_2) and other substance like Cu^{2+} ion is reduced to Cu^+ ion.

Q.2 Why is dilute sulphuric acid added while preparing a standard solution of ferrous ammonium sulphate?

Ans. While preparing standard solution of ferrous ammonium sulphate, dil. H_2SO_4 is added to prevent the salt to get hydrolysed by water.

Q.3 Why is ferrous ammonium sulphate solution not heated before titration?

Ans. The rate of reaction between ferrous ammonium sulphate and potassium permanganate is very fast even at room temperature so, there is no need to heat the solution. Also, on heating ferrous ammonium sulphate solution, the ferrous ions may get oxidised into ferric ions by the action of atmospheric oxygen.

Q.4 Why is nitric acid and hydrochloric acid not used in permanganate titration? Explain.

Ans. Nitric acid itself is an oxidising agent thus, it may interfere in the action of permanganate ion in the titration. If hydrochloric acid is added then it gets oxidised by $KMnO_4$ to give chlorine molecule which also acts as an oxidising agent. So, first it consumes some $KMnO_4$ to get oxidised and then chlorine formed from HCl, interfere in the action of permanganate. The reaction of oxidation of HCl with $KMnO_4$ is as follows:

$$2KMnO_4 + 16HCl \longrightarrow 2KCl + 2MnCl_2 + 5Cl_2 + 8H_2O$$

Thus, nitric acid and hydrochloric acid cannot be used.

Q.5 How will you prepare 100 mL of 0.1M standard solution of ferrous ammonium sulphate?

Ans. $$\text{Molarity} = \frac{\text{Weight of solute}}{\text{Molecular mass of solute}} \times \frac{1000}{\text{Volume (in mL)}} \Rightarrow 0.1 = \frac{\text{Weight}}{392} \times \frac{1000}{100}$$

Weight = 3.92 g

Thus, 3.92 g of ferrous ammonium sulphate is taken in standard measuring flask of 100 mL. Then few drops of dilute H_2SO_4 and distilled water are added to it and dissolve the salt completely. After that fill the flask upto the mark with distilled water using dropper for the last drops to reach the markup level. The prepared solution is the desired 0.1 M standard solution of ferrous ammonium sulphate.

Q.6 Why is $KMnO_4$ not regarded as primary standard?

Ans. $KMnO_4$ being a strong oxidising agent, oxidises water into oxygen. However, the reaction rate is small, but light falling on it will catalyse the reaction and produces the Mn (IV) ions. Thus, the concentration of solution is not accurate when it is prepared because of which it is not regarded as primary standard.

Unit 11

Qualitative Analysis

Qualitative analysis of inorganic salts involves the identification of cations and anions present in the salt or mixture of salts. Salts are obtained either by complete or partial neutralisation of an acid and a base. The positive part of the salt, i.e. **cation** is contributed by a base while the negative part, i.e. **anion** is contributed by an acid e.g.

Salt	Cation	Anion
NaCl	Na^+	Cl^-
$CuSO_4$	Cu^{2+}	SO_4^{2-}
$FeCl_3$	Fe^{3+}	Cl^-

Qualitative analysis is accomplished by the reactions which are easily perceptible to our senses such as sight and smell. Such reactions involve formation of a precipitate, change in colour, evolution of gas, etc.

The common procedure for testing any unknown sample is to make its solution and then test this solution for the ions present in it. There are separate procedures for detecting cations and anions, therefore qualitative analysis is studied under cation analysis and anion analysis.

Systematic analysis of an inorganic salt involves the following steps given below.

(i) Preliminary tests (dry tests) of solid salt and its solution.

(ii) Identification of cations and anions by reactions carried out in solution (wet tests) and confirmatory tests.

Preliminary test also known as **dry tests** of a salt gives useful information which simplifies further course of analysis. These tests provides important hints for the presence of certain anions or cations. These involves noting the general appearance and physical characteristics like colour, smell, solubility, etc. of the salt.

Further, gases evolved in the preliminary tests with dil. H_2SO_4 / dil. HCl and conc. H_2SO_4 also give good indication about the presence of acid radicals.

Following are the points which are advised to be noted by the students in order to make the detection of radicals accurate and easy;

(i) Strictly adhere to the systematic scheme of analysis.

(ii) Keep your apparatus clean and do not pour back the reagents into stock bottle, once it is taken out.

(iii) Use distilled water for analysis.

(iv) Use your own glass nozzle for passing H_2S gas and always wash it with water.

(v) Record all observations neatly and accurately during experimentation in a notebook.

Experiment 11.1

AIM

To detect one anion and one cation in a given salt.

Anions CO_3^{2-}, S^{2-}, SO_3^{2-}, SO_4^{2-}, NO_2^-, NO_3^-, Cl^-, Br^-, I^-, PO_4^{3-}, $C_2O_4^{2-}$, CH_3COO^-
(Insoluble salts excluded)

Cations Pb^{2+}, Cu^{2+}, As^{3+}, Al^{3+}, Fe^{3+}, Mn^{2+}, Ni^{2+}, Zn^{2+}, Co^{2+}, Ca^{2+}, Sr^{2+}, Ba^{2+}, Mg^{2+}, NH_4^+

Theory/Principle

Preliminary examination of the salt is based upon the observations obtained by observing the general appearance and physical properties like colour, smell, solubility of the salt (as already discussed). In contrast, the identification of cations and anions is based upon two basic principles:

(i) the solubility product and

(ii) the common ion effect.

When ionic product of a salt exceeds from its solubility product, precipitation takes place. The nature of the ions present in the salt can also be found by its solubility in water and the pH of its aqueous solution.

- If the salt solution is acidic or basic in nature, this suggests that it is being **hydrolysed** in water.
- If the salt solution comes out to basic, the salt may be of **carbonate** or **sulphide**. But, if the solution shows acidic nature, it may be a salt of **weak base** and strong acid, or you can say it is an **acidic salt**. Thus, in case of acidic salt, it is recommended to neutralise the solution with sodium carbonate before carrying out the test for anions.

Hence, the preliminary tests should always be performed before carrying out the confirmatory tests for ions.

ALERT

- *Alcohol, H_2S are inflammable and toxic.*
- *Potassium permanganate is harmful.*
- *Manganese dioxide, lead chromate and oxalate are harmful.*
- *Nitric acid and silver nitrate are corrosive.*
- *Chromyl chloride is oxidising, corrosive, use minimum amount to avoid pollution by Cr^{3+} ions.*
- *Bromine is corrosive, very toxic by inhalation.*
- *Iodine is harmful on inhalation and when comes in contact with skin.*
- *Chlorine, chloroform are toxic by inhalation.*
- *Disposal of iodine is done by adding sodium thiosulphate solution to dissolve the iodine.*

Materials Required

Boiling tubes	: As per need	Test tubes	: As per need
Measuring cylinder	: 1	Test tube stand	: 1
Test tube holder	: 1	Delivery tube	: 1
Corks	: As per need	Filter paper	: As per need
Reagents	: As per need for a particular test	Spatula	: 1
Funnel	: 1	Dropper	: As per need

Systematic Analysis of Anions (or Acidic Radicals)

The acidic radicals are analysed on the basis of preliminary tests which involves the **dry heating** of the salt in a test tube. These tests are based upon the fact that :

- Salts containing CO_3^{2-}, S^{2-}, NO_2^-, SO_3^{2-} and CH_3COO^- ions react with dil. H_2SO_4 to give out CO_2, H_2S, NO_2, SO_2 and CH_3COOH gas or vapours respectively which can be identified by their confirmatory tests.
- Salts containing Cl^-, Br^-, I^-, NO_3^- and $C_2O_4^{2-}$ reacts with conc. H_2SO_4 but not with dil. H_2SO_4 to produce characteristic gases.
- Salts containing SO_4^{2-} and PO_4^{3-} reacts neither with dil. H_2SO_4 nor with conc. H_2SO_4. These are therefore identified by individual tests.

Hence, the acidic radicals may be identified by performing the following tests in the **order given** below :

Step I Preliminary Test with Dilute Sulphuric Acid

In this test, the action of dilute H_2SO_4 on the salt is noted at room temperature and on warming. Carbonate (CO_3^{2-}), sulphide (S^{2-}), sulphite (SO_3^{2-}), nitrite (NO_2^-) and acetate ions (CH_3COO^-) react with dil. H_2SO_4 to evolve different gases. The different characteristics of the gases evolved gives the information about the anions.

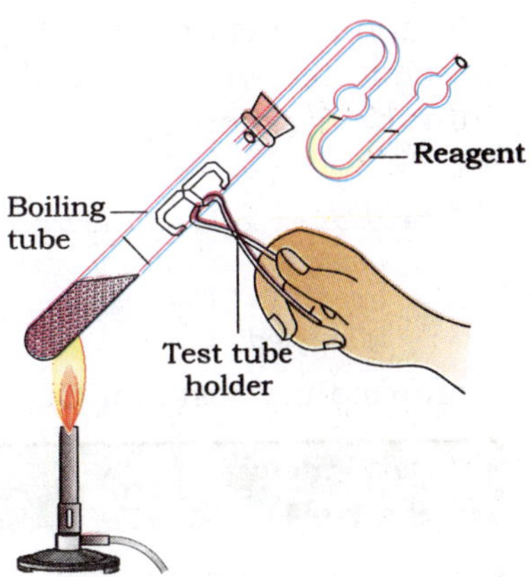

Fig. 11.1 *Testing a gas by heating*

Procedure

1. Take 0.1 g of the salt in a clean and dry test tube and add 1-2 mL of dil. H_2SO_4.
2. Observe the change, if any at room temperature.
3. If no gas is evolved, warm the contents of the test tube.
4. If any gas is evolved, test it by using the apparatus as shown in Fig 6.1.

Observation

Observations of Preliminary test with dilute H_2SO_4

S. No.	Observation	Gas evolved	Possible acidic radicals or anions
1.	Brisk effervescence with the evolution of colourless and odourless gas which turns lime water milky.	CO_2	CO_3^{2-} (carbonate)
2.	Evolution of colourless gas with the smell of rotten eggs (H_2S like smell) which turns lead acetate paper black.	H_2S	S^{2-} (sulphide)
3.	Brown fumes are evolved which turns acidified potassium iodide (KI) solution containing starch solution blue.	NO_2	NO_2^- (nitrite)
4.	Colourless gas with pungent smell of burning sulphur which turns acidified potassium dichromate solution green.	SO_2	SO_3^{2-} (sulphite)
5.	Solution gives colourless vapours with smell of vinegar which turns blue litmus red.	CH_3COOH vapours	CH_3COO^- (acetate)

Note Like CO_2, SO_2 also turns lime water milky but CO_2 is odourless gas and SO_2 has a characteristic smell.

Confirmatory Tests for CO_3^{2-}, S^{2-}, NO_2^-, SO_3^{2-} and CH_3COO^-

Depending upon the solubility of the given salts in water, either water extract (original solution) or sodium carbonate extract is used for performing the confirmatory or wet tests.

1. **Water Extract** It is prepared when salt is completely soluble in water. Dissolve the salt in water taken in a test tube. Shake the test tube to make a clear solution. This aqueous solution is used for confirmatory tests of acid radicals. This water extract is also called original solution of salt.
2. **Sodium Carbonate Extract** It is prepared when salt is insoluble in water.

Preparation of Sodium Carbonate Extract

Take 1g of salt and 3 g of solid carbonate in a boiling tube. Add 15 mL of distilled water to it. Stir and boil the content for about 10 minutes. Cool, filter and collect the filtrate in a test tube and label it as **sodium carbonate extract.**

Theory Behind the Preparation of Sodium Carbonate Extract

When the salts are boiled with sodium carbonate extract, the carbonates of metallic radicals are precipitated while the sodium salts of corresponding acid radicals being soluble in water pass into the solution.

$$ZnS + Na_2CO_3 \longrightarrow ZnCO_3 \downarrow + Na_2S$$

Note *Sodium carbonate extract contains unreacted sodium carbonate in solution, which has to be destroyed before using the extract for various tests. To do this, the extract is acidified with some suitable acid and is boiled to expel CO_2. The selection of acid used for destroying excess Na_2CO_3 depends upon the radical [or anion] to be identified.*

Confirmatory tests for CO_3^{2-} .S^{2-}, NO_2^- ,SO_3^{2-} and CH_3COO^- are listed below :

Confirmatory tests	Procedure	Observation	Inference	Chemistry involved
1 CONFIRMATION OF CO_3^{2-}				
(i) **Dilute acid test**	Add dil. H_2SO_4 [or dil. HCl] to dissolve 0.1 g of salt taken in a test tube.	Brisk effervescence with colourless and odourless CO_2 gas is evolved, which turns lime water milky. But on passing the gas for some more time, through lime water milkiness disappears.	Brisk effervescence of evolution of CO_2 and appearance of milkiness in lime water indicates the presence of CO_3^{2-} ion in the given salt.	$Na_2CO_3 + H_2SO_4 \longrightarrow Na_2SO_4 + H_2O + CO_2\uparrow$ $CO_2 + Ca(OH)_2 \longrightarrow \underset{\text{White ppt.}}{CaCO_3}\downarrow + H_2O$ Milkiness disappears due to the formation of soluble calcium hydrogen carbonate. $CaCO_3 + CO_2 + H_2O \longrightarrow \underset{\text{Soluble}}{Ca(HCO_3)_2}$
(ii) **Barium chloride test**	Add barium chloride or calcium chloride solution to 2 mL of original solution taken in a test tube.	White precipitate of calcium or barium carbonate is formed which is soluble in carbonic acid and mineral acids.	The formation of white precipitate confirms the presence of CO_3^{2-} in the given salt.	$CO_3^{2-} + Ca^{2+} \longrightarrow \underset{\text{White ppt.}}{CaCO_3}\downarrow$ $CO_3^{2-} + Ba^{2+} \longrightarrow \underset{\text{White ppt.}}{BaCO_3}\downarrow$

Confirmatory tests	Procedure	Observation	Inference	Chemistry involved
(iii) **Silver nitrate test**	Add silver nitrate solution to the original solution. Shake the solution and then add excess of $AgNO_3$.	White precipitate of silver carbonate is produced which is soluble in HNO_3 and NH_3. In excess of $AgNO_3$, white precipitate turns yellow.	This change of white precipitate into yellow precipitate in the presence of $AgNO_3$ confirms the presence of CO_3^{2-}.	$CO_3^{2-} + 2Ag^+ \longrightarrow \underset{\text{White ppt.}}{Ag_2CO_3\downarrow}$ This white precipitate turns yellow in the presence of $AgNO_3$ due to the formation of precipitate Ag_2O which is of yellow colour. $\underset{\text{White}}{Ag_2CO_3} \longrightarrow \underset{\text{Yellow}}{Ag_2O\downarrow} + CO_2\uparrow$
2 CONFIRMATION OF S^{2-}				
(i) **Sodium nitroprusside solution test**	Add NH_4OH to 1 mL of water extract or take sodium carbonate extract. Shake it well with dil. H_2SO_4 and then add few drops of sodium nitroprusside solution.	A hydrogen sulphide gas with rotten egg smell is evolved when H_2SO_4 is added to salt solution. On addition of sodium nitroprusside, violet or purple colouration is obtained.	Purple or violet colouration due to the formation of complex compound $Na_4[Fe(CN)_5NOS]$ confirms the presence of S^{2-} ion in the salt.	$Na_2S + H_2SO_4 \longrightarrow Na_2SO_4 + H_2S\uparrow$ $Na_2S + \underset{\text{Sodium nitroprusside}}{Na_2[Fe(CN)_5NO]} \longrightarrow \underset{\text{Violet colour}}{Na_4[Fe(CN)_5NOS]}$
***Note** If salt is insoluble in water use sodium carbonate extract of salt.*				
(ii) **Lead acetate test**	Add dil. H_2SO_4 to 1 mL water extract and warm the solution. Add lead acetate solution to the above solution.	Gas with rotten egg smell is evolved. Black precipitate of PbS is formed which is insoluble in CH_3COOH.	Gas evolved is H_2S, S^{2-} may be present. The black precipitate confirms the presence of S^{2-} ion.	$Na_2S + H_2SO_4 \longrightarrow Na_2SO_4 + H_2S\uparrow$ $(CH_3COO)_2Pb + H_2S \longrightarrow \underset{\substack{\text{Lead sulphide} \\ \text{(Shining black ppt.)}}}{PbS\downarrow} + 2CH_3COOH$
3 CONFIRMATION OF NO_2^-				
(i) **Dilute acid test**	Add dil. H_2SO_4 to a solid nitrite and warm the solution.	Reddish brown fumes are evolved.	Reddish-brown fumes indicate the presence of NO_2^- ion.	Reddish-brown fumes are of NO_2. $2NaNO_2 + H_2SO_4 \longrightarrow Na_2SO_4 + 2HNO_2$ $3HNO_2 \longrightarrow HNO_3 + 2NO + H_2O$ $2NO + O_2 \longrightarrow \underset{\text{Brown gas}}{2NO_2\uparrow}$
(ii) **Starch-iodide test**	Add 1 mL of KI solution to the salt solution or water extract followed by addition of freshly prepared starch solution and acetic acid to acidify the solution. Alternatively, a filter paper moistered with potassium iodide, starch solution and few drops of acetic acid can be exposed to evolved brown gas.	Deep blue colour appears.	The deep blue colouration confirms the presence of NO_2^- ion in the given salt.	$NO_2^- + CH_3COOH \longrightarrow HNO_2 + CH_3COO^-$ $2KI + 2HNO_2 + 2CH_3COOH \longrightarrow 2CH_3COOK + I_2\uparrow + 2NO + 2H_2O$ When liberated iodine interacts with starch, a blue colour solution is formed. $I_2 + \text{starch} \longrightarrow \text{Blue complex}$

Confirmatory tests	Procedure	Observation	Inference	Chemistry involved
(iii) **Silver nitrate test**	Add $AgNO_3$ to water extract of salt.	White crystalline ppt. of $AgNO_2$ is obtained.	The white ppt. confirms the presence of NO_2^- ions.	$NO_2^- + Ag^+ \longrightarrow \underset{\text{White ppt.}}{AgNO_2\downarrow}$
(iv) **Ferrous sulphate test**	Add a few drops of dil. acetic acid and few drops of $FeSO_4$ to a salt solution.	Dark brown or black ppt. is formed.	NO_2^- ions confirmed.	$KNO_2 + CH_3COOH \longrightarrow CH_3COOK + HNO_2$ $3HNO_2 \longrightarrow HNO_3 + 2NO + H_2O$ $FeSO_4 + NO \longrightarrow \underset{\text{Dark brown}}{FeSO_4 \cdot NO}$
(v) **Sulphanilic acid-I 1-naphthyl-amine reagent test (Griss-Ilosvay test)**	Add acetic acid to acidify water extract of salt. Add 2-3 drops of sulphanilic acid solution, followed by 2-3 drops of 1-naphthylamine reagent.	Appearance of red colour.	NO_2^- ion is confirmed.	$NO_2^- + CH_3COOH \longrightarrow HNO_2 + CHCOO^-$ Sulphanilic acid ($NH_3CH_3COO^-$, SO_3H) $+ HNO_2 \longrightarrow$ diazonium compound ($N{=}N{-}OOCCH_3$, SO_3H) $+ 2H_2O$ Diazonium compound ($N{=}N{-}OOCCH_3$, SO_3H) + 1-naphthyl amine (NH_2) $\longrightarrow$ $HO_3S{-}C_6H_4{-}N{=}N{-}C_{10}H_6{-}NH_2$ (Red azo-dye) $+ CH_3COOH$

Note *The test solution should be very dilute. In case of concentrated solutions, reactions does not proceed beyond diazotization.*

4 CONFIRMATION OF SO_3^{2-}

	Procedure	Observation	Inference	Chemistry involved
(i) **Barium chloride, $BaCl_2$ test**	Take 1 mL of water extract or sodium carbonate extract of salt in a test tube and add $BaCl_2$ solution. Further, add dil. HCl to the above solution.	White ppt. of $BaSO_3$ is obtained which is soluble in dil. HCl with the evolution of SO_2 gas.	This confirms the presence of SO_3^{2-} ions.	$Na_2SO_3 + BaCl_2 \longrightarrow 2NaCl + \underset{\text{White ppt.}}{BaSO_3\downarrow}$ $BaSO_3 + 2HCl \longrightarrow \underset{\text{Soluble}}{BaCl_2} + H_2O + SO_2\uparrow$ The precipitate of $BaSO_3$ dissolves due to decomposition of sulphite by dil. HCl.

Note *The white precipitate of sulphite obtained above decolourises acidified potassium permanganate solution.*

$$BaSO_3 + H_2SO_4 \longrightarrow BaSO_4 + H_2O + SO_2$$
$$2KMnO_4 + 3H_2SO_4 \longrightarrow K_2SO_4 + 2MnSO_4 + 3H_2O + 5[O]$$
$$SO_2 + H_2O + [O] \longrightarrow H_2SO_4$$

Confirmatory tests	Procedure	Observation	Inference	Chemistry involved
(ii) **Potassium dichromate, $K_2Cr_2O_7$ test**	Add dil. H_2SO_4 to a water extract of salt. Then, dip acidified $K_2Cr_2O_7$ paper to this solution.	Solution turns green due to the reduction of $K_2Cr_2O_7$ to Cr^{3+} ions.	This confirms the presence of SO_3^{2-} ions.	On treating sulphite with warm dil. H_2SO_4, SO_2 gas with smell of burning sulphur is obtained. $Na_2SO_3 + H_2SO_4 \longrightarrow Na_2SO_4 + H_2O + SO_2$ SO_2 turns $K_2Cr_2O_7$ paper acidified with dil. H_2SO_4 to green. $K_2Cr_2O_7 + H_2SO_4 + 3SO_2 \longrightarrow K_2SO_4 + \underset{\text{Chromium sulphate (green)}}{Cr_2(SO_4)_3} + H_2O$
5 CONFIRMATION OF CH_3COO^-				
(i) **Ethanol test**	Take a salt (0.1 g) in a China dish. Add 1 mL ethanol and 0.2 mL conc. H_2SO_4 and heat.	Fruity odour is observed.	Fruity odour of ethyl acetate indicates the presence of CH_3COO^- ions.	$2CH_3COONa + H_2SO_4 \longrightarrow Na_2SO_4 + 2CH_3COOH$ $CH_3COOH + C_2H_5OH \xrightarrow{H^+} \underset{\text{Ethyl acetate (Fruity odour)}}{CH_3COOC_2H_5} + H_2O$
Note *You can also test the presence of acetate ions by treating it with dil. H_2SO_4. If vinegar smell is obtained, this indicates the presence of acetate ions.*				
(ii) **Neutral ferric chloride, $FeCl_3$ test**	Neutral $FeCl_3$ solution is added to the salt solution taken in a test tube.	Blood red colouration is obtained.	Blood red colour confirms the presence of acetate ion.	Acetate gives deep red colour on reaction with neutral $FeCl_3$ solution due to the formation of complex ion which decomposes on heating to give iron (III) dihydroxyacetate as brown red ppt. $6CH_3COO^- + 3Fe^{3+} + 2H_2O \longrightarrow [Fe_3(OH)_2(CH_3COO)_6]^+ + 2H^+$ $[Fe_3(OH)_2(CH_3COO)_6]^+ + 4H_2O \longrightarrow \underset{\text{Iron (III) dihydroxyacetate (Brown-red ppt.)}}{3[Fe(OH)_2(CH_3COO)]} + 3CH_3COOH + H^+$

Note *Preparation of neutral $FeCl_3$ Add dilute NaOH solution to $FeCl_3$ solution drop by drop along with shaking until a precipitate of $Fe(OH)_3$ is obtained. Filter the precipitate and use the filtrate for analysis.*

Step II Preliminary Test with Concentrated Sulphuric Acid

Procedure

1. If no positive result is obtained from dil. H_2SO_4 test, take 0.1 g of salt in a test tube. Add 3-4 drops of conc. H_2SO_4.
2. Observe the change in the reaction mixture.
3. If no gas is evolved, then warm the mixture.
4. Identify the gas evolved on heating [as given in table below.

Observation with concentrated H_2SO_4

S. No.	Observation	Gas evolved	Possible acidic radical or anions	Reactions involved
1.	Colourless, pungent smelling gas giving dense white fumes when a rod dipped in NH_4OH is brought near the mouth of the test tube.	HCl	Cl^- (Chloride)	$NaCl + H_2SO_4 \longrightarrow \underset{\text{Sodium hydrogen sulphate}}{NaHSO_4} + HCl\uparrow$ (Colourless gas) $HCl + NH_4OH \longrightarrow \underset{\text{(White fumes)}}{NH_4Cl\uparrow} + H_2O$ or $HCl + NH_3(aq) \longrightarrow \underset{\text{Ammonium chloride (White fumes)}}{NH_4Cl\uparrow}$
2.	Reddish brown fumes with a pungent odour. The fumes get intensified on heating the reaction after addition of solid MnO_2 to the reaction mixture. Brown vapours turn starch paper yellow.	Br_2 Vapours	Br^- (Bromide)	$2NaBr + 2H_2SO_4 \longrightarrow \underset{\text{Brown fumes}}{Br_2} + SO_2 + Na_2SO_4 + 2H_2O$ $2NaBr + MnO_2 + 2H_2SO_4 \longrightarrow Na_2SO_4 + MnSO_4 + 2H_2O + Br_2$
3.	Violet pungent vapours which turn starch paper blue and a layer of violet sublimate is formed on the sides of test tube. The violet vapours get intensified on addition of MnO_2 to the reaction mixture.	I_2 Vapours	I^- (Iodide)	$2NaI + 2H_2SO_4 \longrightarrow Na_2SO_4 + SO_2 + 2H_2O + \underset{\text{Violet vapours}}{I_2}$ $I_2 + \text{Starch solution} \longrightarrow \text{Blue colour}$ Some HI, SO_2, H_2S and S are also formed due to the following reactions. $NaI + H_2SO_4 \longrightarrow NaHSO_4 + HI$ $2HI + H_2SO_4 \longrightarrow 2H_2O + I_2 + SO_2$ $6NaI + 4H_2SO_4 \longrightarrow 3I_2 + 4H_2O + S + 3Na_2SO_4$ $8NaI + 5H_2SO_4 \longrightarrow 4I_2 + H_2S + 4Na_2SO_4 + 4H_2O$ On adding MnO_2, the violet vapours become dense. $2NaI + MnO_2 + 2H_2SO_4 \longrightarrow I_2 + MnSO_4 + Na_2SO_4 + 2H_2O$
4.	Brown pungent fumes are evolved on heating salt with conc. H_2SO_4, which gets intensified by the addition of copper turnings and the solution acquires blue colour.	NO_2	NO_3^- (Nitrate)	$NaNO_3 + H_2SO_4 \longrightarrow NaHSO_4 + HNO_3$ $4HNO_3 \longrightarrow \underset{\text{Brown fumes}}{4NO_2} + O_2 + 2H_2O$ $2NaNO_3 + 4H_2SO_4 + 3Cu \longrightarrow \underset{\text{Blue}}{3CuSO_4} + Na_2SO_4 + 4H_2O + 2NO$ The solution turns blue due to the formation of $CuSO_4$. The evolved NO oxidise to give excess of brown fumes. $2NO + O_2 \longrightarrow 2NO_2$ (Dark brown fumes)
5.	Colourless and odourless gas is evolved which turns lime water milky and the gas coming out of lime water if ignited burns with a blue flame.	CO and CO_2	$C_2O_4^{2-}$ (Oxalate)	$(COONa)_2 + H_2SO_4(\text{conc.}) \longrightarrow Na_2SO_4 + H_2O + \underbrace{CO_2\uparrow + CO\uparrow}_{\text{Colourless gases}}$

Confirmatory Tests for Cl^-, Br^-, I^-, NO_3^- and $C_2O_4^{2-}$

Confirmatory tests for Cl^-, Br^-, I^-, NO_3^- and $C_2O_4^{2-}$ which reacts with concentrated sulphuric acid are listed below.

Tests	Procedure	Observation	Inference	Chemistry involved
1 CONFIRMATION OF Cl^-				
(i) **Silver nitrate ($AgNO_3$) test**	To 1-2 mL of sodium carbonate extract of salt and dil. HNO_3 to acidify it or take water extract and add $AgNO_3$ solution.	A curdy white precipitate of AgCl soluble in NH_4OH solution is formed.	This confirms the presence of Cl^- ions in the salt.	$NaCl + AgNO_3 \longrightarrow NaNO_3 + AgCl\downarrow$ (White curdy ppt.) $AgCl + 2NH_4OH \longrightarrow [Ag(NH_3)_2]Cl + 2H_2O$ (Soluble diammine silver (II) chloride)
(ii) **Chromyl chloride test** (a)	Warm the salt with some solid $K_2Cr_2O_7$ taken in a test tube and add conc. H_2SO_4 to it. Heat the test tube and pass the vapours through NaOH, yellow solution is obtained. Divide the solution into two parts. Add few drops of dil. CH_3COOH solution and add lead acetate solution in the first part.	Red vapours of chromyl chloride (CrO_2Cl_2) are formed, which on passing through NaOH forms a yellow solution of Na_2CrO_4. This Na_2CrO_4 produces a yellow precipitate of $PbCrO_4$ when added to lead acetate solution.	Yellow precipitate confirms the presence of Cl^- ions.	$4NaCl + K_2Cr_2O_7 + 6H_2SO_4 \longrightarrow 4NaHSO_4 + 2KHSO_4 + 3H_2O + 2CrO_2Cl_2$ (Chromyl chloride) $CrO_2Cl_2 + 4NaOH \longrightarrow Na_2CrO_4 + 2H_2O + 2NaCl$ Na_2CrO_4 (Sodium chromate) $+ (CH_3COO)_2Pb \longrightarrow PbCrO_4$ (Lead chromate (Yellow precipitate)) $+ 2CH_3COONa$
(b)	In the second part, the yellow solution so obtained above is acidified with dil. H_2SO_4 and small amounts of amyl alcohol and 1 mL of 10% H_2O_2 solution is added to it.	On gentle shaking, the organic layer turns blue due to the formation of CrO_5. CrO_4^{2-} ion formed in the reaction of chromyl chloride with NaOH reacts with H_2O_2 to form CrO_5 which dissolves in amyl alcohol to give blue colour.	This test is also used for detecting Cl^- ions.	$CrO_4^{2-} + 2H^+ + 2H_2O_2 \longrightarrow CrO_5$ (Chromium pentoxide) $+ 3H_2O$
(iii) **Manganese dioxide test**	Take 0.1 g of salt in a test tube, add a pinch of MnO_2 and 3-4 drops of conc. H_2SO_4. Heat the reaction mixture. Bring a moist starch iodide paper near the mouth of test tube.	Greensih-yellow pungent gas of Cl_2 is liberated which turns moist starch iodide paper blue.	Greenish-yellow pungent gas confirms the presence of Cl^- ions.	$MnO_2 + 2H_2SO_4 + 2NaCl \longrightarrow MnSO_4 + Cl_2\uparrow$ (Greenish yellow) $+ Na_2SO_4 + 2H_2O$
2 CONFIRMATION OF Br^-				
(i) **Silver nitrate, $AgNO_3$ test**	To 1-2 mL of sodium carbonate extract of the salt, add dil. HNO_3 (to acidify the extract) and $AgNO_3$ solution. Shake the test tube.	Pale yellow precipitate of AgBr partially soluble in NH_4OH is obtained.	A pale yellow precipitate confirms the presence of Br^- ions.	$NaBr + AgNO_3 \longrightarrow AgBr\downarrow$ (Pale yellow ppt.) $+ NaNO_3$ $AgBr + 2NH_4OH \longrightarrow [Ag(NH_3)_2Br] + 2H_2O$ (Sparingly soluble complex)
(ii) **Carbon disulphide, CS_2 or chlorine water test**	Add freshly prepared Cl_2 water and few drops of carbon disulphide (CS_2) to the salt solution or sodium carbonate extract neutralised with dil. HCl. Shake it well and allow to stand. In place of CS_2, carbon tetrachloride (CCl_4) or chloroform ($CHCl_3$) or dichloromethene can also be used.	An orange-brown coloured layer in CS_2 is obtained due to the liberation of Br_2.	Orange-brown colouration in the organic layer confirms the presence of bromide ions.	$2NaBr + Cl_2 \longrightarrow 2NaCl + Br_2$ $Br_2 + CS_2 \longrightarrow$ Orange-brown layer of Br_2 gas

Tests	Procedure	Observation	Inference	Chemistry involved
		3 CONFIRMATION OF I^-		
(i) **Silver nitrate, $AgNO_3$ test**	Sodium carbonate extract of solution. Take 1 mL of sodium carbonate extract, acidify it with dil. HNO_3 [or simply take water extract]. Add $AgNO_3$ solution to it.]	Yellow precipitate of silver iodide AgI (insoluble in NH_4OH) is obtained.	Appearance of yellow precipitate confirms the presence of iodide ions.	$NaI + AgNO_3 \longrightarrow \underset{\text{Yellow ppt.}}{AgI} \downarrow + NaNO_3$
Note *Water extract can also be used to perform this test.*				
(ii) **Lead acetate test**	To the salt solution [or sodium carbonate extract], add lead acetate solution.	A yellow crystalline ppt. of lead iodide (soluble in hot water) is obtained.	Presence of I^- ions is confirmed.	$2I^- + Pb^{2+} \longrightarrow \underset{\text{Yellow ppt.}}{PbI_2} \downarrow$
(iii) **$CHCl_3$ or Cl_2 water test**	Add 1 mL of $CHCl_3$ (or CCl_4) and chlorine water in excess to the salt solution in water [or sodium carbonate extract] and shake the test tube vigorously.	Violet colouration in organic ($CHCl_3$) layer is observed.	Violet colouration confirms the presence of I^- ions.	$2NaI + Cl_2 \longrightarrow 2NaCl + I_2$, I_2 dissolves in organic solvent and solution becomes violet.
		4 CONFIRMATION OF NO_3^-		
Ring test $FeSO_4$ Dark brown ring	Add 2 mL of conc. H_2SO_4 to 1 mL of an aqueous salt solution and shake well. Cool the test tube under tap water. Now, add freshly prepared ferrous sulphate solution dropwise along the sides of the test tube, so that it forms a layer on the top of the liquid already present in the test tube.	A dark brown ring of nitroso ferrous sulphate, $[Fe(NO)]SO_4$ is formed at the junction of two solutions.	Presence of NO_3^- ion is confirmed.	$NaNO_3 + H_2SO_4 \longrightarrow NaHSO_4 + HNO_3$ $2HNO_3 + 6FeSO_4 + 3H_2SO_4 \longrightarrow 3Fe_2(SO_4)_3 + 2NO + 4H_2O$ $FeSO_4 + NO \longrightarrow [Fe(NO)]SO_4$ Nitroso ferrous sulphate (Brown ring)
		5 CONFIRMATION OF $C_2O_4^{2-}$		
(i) **Calcium chloride test**	1 mL sodium carbonate extract of salt acidified with acetic acid taken in a test tube. Boil off CO_2 and add $CaCl_2$ solution.	A white ppt of calcium oxalate insoluble in ammonium oxalate and oxalic acid solution but soluble in dil. HCl and dil. HNO_3 is obtained.	White ppt confirms the presence of oxalate ions.	$CaCl_2 + Na_2C_2O_4 \longrightarrow CaC_2O_4 \downarrow + 2NaCl$ Calcium oxalate (White ppt.)
(ii) **$KMnO_4$ test**	Filter the white precipitate of calcium oxalate formed in calcium chloride test. The white precipitate is dissolved in dil. H_2SO_4 and then 1 mL of dil. $KMnO_4$ is added and warm the solution.	Pink colour of $KMnO_4$ is discharged. Pass the gas through lime water. It turns milky. White precipitate is formed which dissolves on passing the gas for some more time.	Presence of oxalate ions is confirmed.	$CaC_2O_4 + H_2SO_4 \longrightarrow CaSO_4 + H_2C_2O_4$ $2KMnO_4 + 3H_2SO_4 + 5H_2C_2O_4 \longrightarrow 2MnSO_4 + K_2SO_4 + 8H_2O + 10CO_2$

Step III Test for Sulphate and Phosphate

If no positive test is obtained in steps I and II, then tests for the presence of sulphate and phosphate ions are performed. These tests are listed below:

Confirmatory Tests for SO_4^{2-} and PO_4^{3-}

Tests	Procedure	Observation	Inference	Chemistry involved
1 CONFIRMATION OF SO_4^{2-}				
(i) **Barium chloride test**	Add $BaCl_2$ solution to 1 mL salt solution or sodium carbonate extract followed by the addition of dil. HCl.	White precipitate of $BaSO_4$ is obtained which is insoluble in HCl (conc.) or HNO_3 (conc.).	White precipitate confirms the presence of SO_4^{2-} ions.	$Na_2SO_4 + BaCl_2 \longrightarrow \underset{\text{White ppt.}}{BaSO_4\downarrow} + 2NaCl$
(ii) **Lead acetate test**	Acidify the aqueous solution or sodium carbonate extract with acetic acid and add lead acetate solution.	White precipitate of lead sulphate is formed which is soluble in hot ammonium acetate solution.	Presence of SO_4^{2-} ions is confirmed.	SO_4^{2-} ions give white ppt. of lead sulphate when aqueous solution or sodium carbonate extract neutralised with acetic acid is treated with lead acetate solution. $Na_2SO_4 + (CH_3COO)_2Pb \longrightarrow \underset{\text{White ppt.}}{PbSO_4\downarrow} + 2CH_3COONa$
2 CONFIRMATION OF PO_4^{3-}				
(i) **Ammonium molybdate test**	Acidify the original solution with conc. HNO_3 and add ammonium molybdate solution. Heat to boiling.	A canary yellow precipitate of ammonium-phospho-molybdate is obtained.	A yellow ppt. confirms the presence of PO_4^{3-} ions.	$Na_2HPO_4 + 12(NH_4)_2MoO_4 + 23HNO_3 \longrightarrow \underset{\text{Canary yellow ppt.}}{(NH_4)_3[P(Mo_3O_{10})_4]\downarrow} + 2NaNO_3 + 21NH_4NO_3 + 12H_2O$
(ii) **Magnesia mixture test**	Add magnesia mixture to 1-2 mL of aqueous salt solution and allow to stand.	A white precipitate is obtained.	Presence of PO_4^{3-} ions is confirmed.	$Na_2HPO_4 + MgCl_2 + NH_4OH \longrightarrow \underset{\text{(White ppt.)}}{Mg(NH_4)PO_4\downarrow} + 2NaCl + H_2O$

Systematic Analysis of Cations (Group Analysis for Basic Radicals)

The systematic qualitative analysis of cations can be done with the following steps:

Step I Preliminary Examination of the Salt for the Identification of Cations

Preliminary examination of a salt furnishes important information and it simplifies further course of analysis. Although, these tests are not conclusive yet sometimes, they provide important hints/clues for the presence of certain cations. These tests are also named as **dry tests**.

Dry test involves the following tests :

1. Physical observation of salt or mixture
2. Dry heating test
3. Flame test
4. Charcoal cavity test
5. Cobalt nitrate test
6. Borax bead test

1. Physical Observation of Salt or Mixture

In physical examination, colour, smell and density of a given mixture are observed. To check the smell, take a pinch of the salt between your fingers and rub with a drop of water.

S. No.	Observation	Inference
1.	**Colour of the substance**	
(i)	Blue and if its aqueous solution is also blue.	Salts of cupric (Cu^{2+})
(ii)	Bright Green and if its aqueous solution is also green.	Salts of nickel (Ni^{2+})
(iii)	Dark green and if its aqueous solution is also dark green but becomes light on dilution.	Salts of chromium (Cr^{3+})
(iv)	Violet-pink and if its aqueous solution is pink.	Salts of cobalt (Co^{2+})
(v)	Light pink and if its aqueous solution is colourless.	Salts of manganese (Mn^{2+})
(vi)	Reddish brown	Fe_2O_3
(vii)	Red	HgO, HgI_2, Pb_3O_4, Cu_2O
(viii)	Orange-red	Sb_2S_3
(ix)	Black	CuO, NiO, SnO, FeS, CuS, HgS, PbS, CoS, FeO, Co_3O_4, Ni_2O_3, Cu_2S, $CuBr_2$, NiS, etc.
(x)	Yellow	As_2S_3, CdS, Bi_2O_3, As_2S_5, PbI_2, AgI, Chromates, etc.
(xi)	Yellow-green and if its aqueous solution is light green or almost colourless.	Salts of Fe^{2+}
(xii)	Yellow-brown and if its aqueous solution is yellow.	Salts of Fe^{3+}
(xiii)	Colourless	Transition metals absent except some salts of Mn^{2+}.
(xiv)	Purple	Some Cr^{3+} salts and permanganates.
2.	**Density**	
(i)	Mixture of salts is too light (fluffy powder).	Salts of Zn^{2+}, Bi^{+}, Al^{3+}, Sr^{2+}, Ca^{2+} and Mg^{2+}.
(ii)	Mixture of salts is too heavy.	Salts of Hg^{2+}, Ba^{2+} and Pb^{2+}.
3.	**Deliquescence**	
(i)	Salts absorbs moisture and becomes pasty or like liquid.	If coloured, then $FeCl_3$, $Cu(NO_3)_2$ and $Fe(NO_3)_3$.
		If colourless, then $ZnCl_2$, $MgCl_2$ and $AlCl_3$.

2. Dry Heating Test

Take the given salt around 0.1 g in a clean and dry test tube. Heat the test tube first gently and then strongly. Observe the changes taking place upon heating.

Fig 11.2 *Heat the salt present in the test tube*

It is to be noted that on heating, some salts undergo decomposition, therefore, some characteristic changes in the colour of residue may be obtained.

S. No.	Observation	Inference
1.	**Substance melts**	Salts of alkali metals, chlorides of Hg, Ag and Pb and salts having water of crystallisation.
2.	**Substance cracks**	$Pb(NO_3)_2$, $Ba(NO_3)_2$, NaCl and KI.
3.	**Substance swells**	Alums, salts of phosphate and borate.
4.	**Substance sublimes** on heating and the colour of sublimate is • White • Yellow • Black • Blue, yellow or violet vapours • Grey (having garlic odour)	 $HgCl_2$, As_2O_3, Hg_2Cl_2, $AlCl_3$, Sb_2O_3,halides of NH_4^+. As_2S_3 and HgI_2 Sulphides of Hg, Sb and As Iodides As^{3+}
5.	**Colour of residue** obtained after heating (mainly metallic oxides) • White and non-fusible. • Initially, green but becomes dirty white or yellow on heating. • Yellow-brown when hot, on cooling, it is brown. • Black and infusible. • Dark orange-red in heating state and sublimes. • White infusible and becomes yellow on heating. • Initially, blue or green but becomes white on heating. • Initially, pink but becomes blue on heating.	 Oxides of Ca, Ba, Sr, Mg, Zn and Al. Salts of Fe^{2+} SnO_2 NiO, MnO_2 and CuO HgO Salts of Zn^{2+} Salts of Cu^{2+} Salts of Co^{2+}
	Colourless, odourless gas NH_3, turns red litmus to blue and Nessler's reagent brown.	Ammonium salts (NH_4^+)

Some points to be remembered while performing the heating test :

1. Use a perfectly dry test tube for performing this test. While drying a test tube, keep it in slanting position on the flame with its mouth slightly downwards so that the drops of water which condense on the upper cooler parts, do not fall back on the hot bottom, as this may break the tube.
2. For testing a gas, a filter paper strip dipped in the appropriate reagent is brought near the mouth of the test tube or alternatively, the reagent is taken in a gas detector and the gas is passed through it.
3. Do not heat the tube strongly at one point as it may break, so rotate it continuously to ensure uniform heating.

3. Flame Test

Salt to be analysed is treated with conc. HCl to form metal chlorides which are **volatile** in non-luminous flame and their vapours impart characteristic colour to the flame.

Theory

Metal chlorides formed are thermally ionisable and cations formed absorb heat energy from the flame such that the valence electrons get excited to higher energy levels.

On coming back to their original/stable state, they transmit energy in the form of light of characteristic wavelength. Since, different metal ions emit light of different wavelengths, hence, different colours are imparted by different metal ions.

Procedure

1. To perform flame test, take a platinum wire and make a small circular loop at its one end by winding it around the tapered end of a pencil [Fig. 6.3 (ii)].
2. Clean the platinum loop by dipping it into conc. HCl and then heating it strongly in the non-luminous flame. Repeat this procedure until the wire imparts no colour to the flame.
3. Make a paste of about 0.1-0.2 g of the well powdered sample of the salt with 2-3 drops of conc. HCl on a clean watch glass.
4. Dip the clean loop of the platinum wire in the paste [Fig. 6.3 (iv)]. Introduce the loop into the lower oxidising or non-luminous flame [Fig 6.3 (v)]. First, observe the colour of the flame with the naked eye and then through a blue glass. Salts particularly of group V (Ba^{2+}, Ca^{2+} and Sr^{2+}) are identified by the colours of the flame.

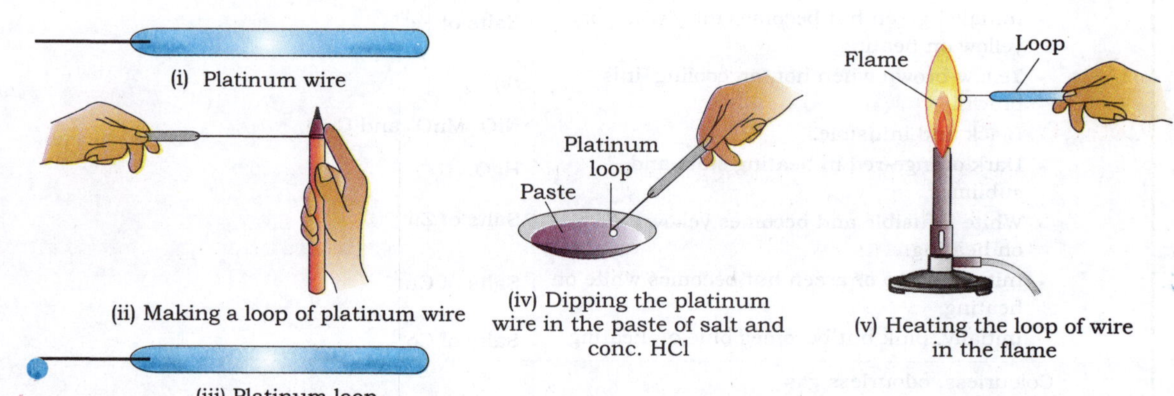

Fig. 11.3 *Performing the flame test*

Observation

S.No.	Colour (with naked eye)	Colour (through blue glass)	Cation (s)
1.	Golden yellow	Invisible	Na^+
2.	Violet	Pink	K^+
3.	Carmine red	Crimson red or pink	Li^+
4.	Brick-red	Light yellowish-green	Ca^{2+}
5.	Apple-green	Bluish-green	Ba^{2+} and Mo^{2+}
6.	Green	Same	Cu^{2+} and Tl^{3+}
7.	Crimson red	Purple	Sr^{2+}
8.	Blue	Same	Cu^{2+}, As^{3+}, Sb^{3+} and Bi^{3+}

Note *Blue colour of Cu^{2+} ion is observed when present with certain complex ions or other elements are present.*

4. Charcoal Cavity Test

Theory

When a salt is fused with anhydrous Na_2CO_3 or oxidising mixture in a cavity on charcoal block in reducing flame, first metallic carbonates and finally, metallic oxides are formed. The metallic oxides so formed appear as coloured residue in the cavity.

(i) $Pb(NO_3)_2 + Na_2CO_3 \xrightarrow{\Delta} PbCO_3 + 2NaNO_3$

$PbCO_3 \xrightarrow{\Delta} \underset{\text{Brown when hot; yellow when cold}}{PbO} + CO_2\uparrow$

(ii) $CuSO_4 + Na_2CO_3 \xrightarrow{\Delta} CuCO_3 + Na_2SO_4$

$CuCO_3 \xrightarrow{\Delta} CuO + CO_2\uparrow$

(iii) $ZnSO_4 + Na_2CO_3 \xrightarrow{\Delta} ZnCO_3 + Na_2SO_4$

$ZnCO_3 \xrightarrow{\Delta} \underset{\text{Yellow when hot; white when cold}}{ZnO} + CO_2\uparrow$

Sometimes, these metallic oxides may be reduced to metals by the action of carbon present in reducing flame. On cooling, these metals form **beads**.

$PbO + C \longrightarrow \underset{\text{Greyish white beads}}{Pb} + CO\uparrow$

$CuO + C \longrightarrow \underset{\text{Reddish beads}}{Cu} + CO\uparrow$

Procedure

1. Make a small cavity in a charcoal block with the help of a knife or a charcoal borer. Do not apply a large pressure, otherwise it will break. [Fig 6.4(i)].
2. Weigh 0.2 g of the given salt and mix it with the 0.5 g of anhydrous sodium carbonate and place this mixture in the cavity.
3. Moisten the mixture in the cavity with few drops of water, otherwise the salt mixture will blow away.
4. With the help of a blowpipe, direct the reducing (luminous) flame of the Bunsen burner towards the cavity [Fig. 6.3 (ii)]. For obtaining reducing flame [Fig 6.4 (iv)], close the air holes of the burner and place the nozzle of the blowpipe just outside the flame and for oxidising flame [Fig 6.3 (iii)]), hold the nozzle of the blowpipe about one-third within the flame.
5. Heat for sometime. Observe the colour of oxide/metallic bead formed in the cavity both when hot and cold [Fig 6.4 (ii)] and draw the inference as per the given table.

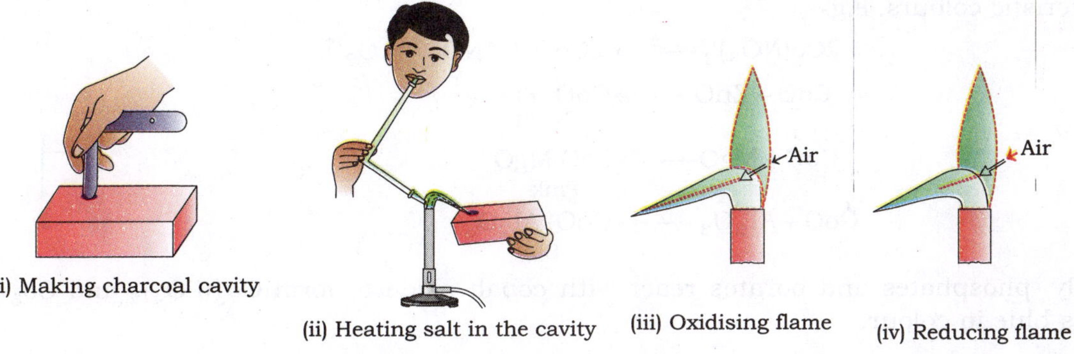

(i) Making charcoal cavity (ii) Heating salt in the cavity (iii) Oxidising flame (iv) Reducing flame

Fig 11.4 *Charcoal cavity test*

Observation

Colour in charcoal cavity test

S. No.	Bead	Crust (Residue)	Inference
1.	Greyish-white soft metallic bead	Brown which turns yellow on cooling.	Pb^{2+}
2.	Lustrous white bead	—	Ag^{+}
3.	White-brown bead	Orange which turns yellow on cooling.	Bi^{3+}
4.		Garlic like smelly fumes with white residue.	As^{3+}
5.	—	Red-brown precipitate which easily turns into vapour.	Cd^{2+}
6.	—	Red crust with smell of ammonia	NH_4^+
7.	—	Black precipitate	Fe^{3+}, Co^{2+} and Mn^{2+}
8.	Red bead	—	Cu^{2+}
9.	—	White residue which glows.	Al^{3+}, Ba^{2+}, Ca^{2+} and Mg^{2+}
10.	—	Yellow when hot, white when cold.	Zn^{2+}

Note *Some points to be remembered while performing charcoal cavity test :*

(i) Always make a fresh cavity for a new test.

(ii) Do not bore a deep cavity.

(iii) Thoroughly clean the mouth of blow pipe before use.

5. Cobalt Nitrate Test

Theory

This test is applied to those salts which leave white residue in the charcoal cavity test. Thus, we can say that this test is performed only when infusible mass (contains metallic oxides like CaO, Al_2O_3, MgO and ZnO) is obtained in charcoal cavity test.

In this test, cobalt nitrate decomposes on heating and form cobalt (II) oxide, CoO, that combines with the metal oxides (white residue of charcoal cavity test) to form double oxides which gives characteristic colours. e.g.

$$2Co(NO_3)_2 \xrightarrow{\Delta} 2CoO + 4NO_2\uparrow + O_2\uparrow$$

$$CoO + ZnO \longrightarrow \underset{\text{Green}}{CoO \cdot ZnO}$$

$$CoO + MgO \longrightarrow \underset{\text{Pink}}{CoO \cdot MgO}$$

$$CoO + Al_2O_3 \longrightarrow \underset{\text{Blue}}{CoO \cdot Al_2O_3}$$

Similarly, phosphates and borates react with cobalt oxide to form $Co_3(PO_4)_2$ and $Co_3(BO_3)_2$ which is blue in colour.

Procedure

1. Add 1-2 drops of cobalt nitrate solution to infusible mass or white residue obtained in charcoal cavity and heat the mixture with the help of blowpipe in oxidising flame (non-luminous flame).
2. Observe the colour of the residue.

Observation

Colour shown in cobalt nitrate test

S.No.	Colour of the residue	Inference
1.	Green	Zn^{2+}
2.	Pink	Mg^{2+}
3.	Bluish-green	Sn^{2+}
4.	Blue	Al^{3+}
5.	Black	Co^{2+}, Fe^{2+}, Mn^{2+}, Ni^{2+}

Note *Cobalt nitrate should not be used in excess otherwise black coloured cobalt oxide* (Co_3O_4) *may be formed and it is difficult to identify other colours in the presence of black colour. Always use dilute solution of cobalt nitrate.*

6. Borax Bead Test

Borax bead test is performed only for coloured salts because borax reacts with metal salts to form metaborates which have characteristic colours.

Theory

On heating borax, $Na_2B_4O_7 \cdot 10H_2O$ on the platinum loop, it loses its water of crystallisation. It swells upto fluffy white porous mass. On further heating, the fluffy mass melts into a colourless liquid which later forms a transparent, colourless, glass like beads of sodium metaborate ($NaBO_2$) and boric anhydride (B_2O_3).

$$Na_2B_4O_7.10H_2O \xrightarrow[-10H_2O]{\Delta} Na_2B_4O_7 \xrightarrow{\Delta} \underset{\text{Sodium metaborate}}{2NaBO_2} + \underset{\text{Boric anhydride}}{B_2O_3}$$

Boric anhydride is non-volatile. When it reacts with coloured metallic salt, a characteristic coloured bead of metal metaborate is formed. Beads of characteristic colours are produced with salts of Cu, Fe Cr, Mn, Co and Ni. The colour of the bead depends upon the flame (luminous or non-luminous) in which it has been heated, e.g, copper forms blue coloured bead in oxidising flame.

$$CuSO_4 + B_2O_3 \longrightarrow \underset{\substack{\text{Cupric (II) metaborate} \\ \text{(green when hot, blue} \\ \text{when cold)}}}{Cu(BO_2)_2} + SO_3 \quad \text{(Oxidising and non-luminous flame)}$$

In reducing flame, two reactions may take place :

(i) The blue $Cu(BO_2)_2$ is reduced to colourless cuprous metaborate.

$$\underset{\text{Blue}}{2Cu(BO_2)_2} + 2NaBO_2 + C \xrightarrow{\text{Luminous flame}} \underset{\substack{\text{Cuprous} \\ \text{metaborate}}}{2CuBO_2} + Na_2B_4O_7 + CO\uparrow$$

(ii) Cupric metaborate may be reduced to metallic copper and the bead appears red and opaque.

$$\underset{\text{Blue}}{2Cu(BO_2)_2} + 4NaBO_2 + 2C \xrightarrow{\text{Luminous flame}} \underset{\substack{\text{Red and} \\ \text{opaque}}}{2Cu\downarrow} + 2Na_2B_4O_7 + 2CO\uparrow$$

Procedure

1. Make a small circular loop at the end of a clean platinum wire. Heat the loop in Bunsen flame until it becomes red hot and then dip it in a heap of powdered borax.
2. Heat it again. The borax will first swell up and then get fused giving a colourless, transparent glass like bead. If the bead is coloured, it means that the platinum wire is not clean. Then, repeat the above procedure till a colourless bead is formed but only after cleaning the wire.
3. Dip the hot bead with a small quantity of dry salt and fuse it in the flame again.
4. Note down the colour of the bead while it is hot and when it is cold in both the flames [Fig 6.5].

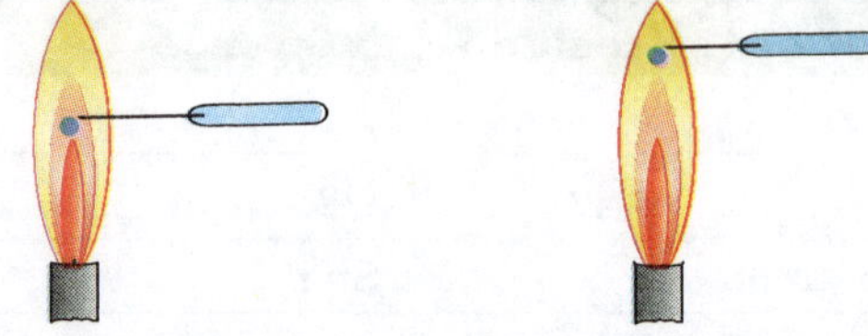

(i) Heating in reducing flame (ii) Heating in oxidising flame

Fig 11.5 *Borax bead test*

5. Now, heat the bead in the reducing (luminous) flame.
6. Note down the colour of the bead observed, once again while it is hot and then cold.
7. To remove the bead from the platinum wire, heat it to redness and tap the platinum wire with your finger [Fig 6.6].

Borax bead

Fig. 11.6 *Removing borax bead from platinum wire*

Observation

Colour in borax bead test

S. No.	Oxidising (non-luminous) flame		Reducing (luminous) flame		Metal
	Hot	**Cold**	**Hot**	**Cold**	
1.	Green	Blue	Colourless	Opaque red	Cu
2.	Yellowish-brown	Yellow	Green	Green	Fe
3.	Yellow	Yellowish green	Green	Green	Cr
4.	Light violet	Light violet	Colourless	Colourless	Mn
5.	Blue	Blue	Blue	Blue	Co
6.	Violet	Reddish brown	Grey	Grey	Ni
7.	Yellow	Colourless	Brown	Brown	Mo
8.	Rose-violet	Rose-violet	Red	Violet	Au
9.	Yellow	Colourless	Yellow	Yellowish-brown	W
10.	Yellow	Pale yellow	Pale green	Pale green to nearly colourless	U
11.	Yellow	Greenish-yellow	Dirty green	Emerald green	V
12.	Yellow	Colourless	Grey	Pale violet	Ti
13.	Orange-red	Yellow	Colourless	Colourless	Ce

Step II Confirmatory/Wet Tests for the Identification of Cations

The basic radicals or cations indicated in the dry or preliminary test are confirmed by the wet tests.

For convenience of the qualitative analysis of cations, these are classified into six groups:

Group	Group reagent	Cation (Basic radical)	Composition of ppt.	Colour of ppt.
Zero	NaOH	NH_4^+	NH_3 gas is evolved	—
I	Dil. HCl	Pb^{2+}	$PbCl_2$	White
II	H_2S in the presence of dil. HCl	Pb^{2+} Cu^{2+} As^{3+}	PbS CuS As_2S_3	Black Black Yellow
III	Conc. HNO_3 and NH_4OH in the presence of excess of NH_4Cl.	Fe^{3+} Al^{3+}	$Fe(OH)_3$ $Al(OH)_3$	Brown white gelatinous ppt.
IV	H_2S in the presence of NH_4OH.	Co^{2+} Ni^{2+} Zn^{2+} Mn^{2+}	CoS NiS ZnS MnS	Black Black Bluish-white Flesh colour
V	$(NH_4)_2CO_3$ in the presence of NH_4OH.	Ba^{2+} Ca^{2+} Sr^{2+}	$BaCO_3$ $CaCO_3$ $SrCO_3$	White White White
VI	Na_2HPO_4	Mg^{2+}	$Mg(NH_4)PO_4$	White

Preparation of Original Solution

The first essential step for the identification of cations is to prepare a clear and transparent solution of the salt. This is called **original solution.**

To prepare the original solution, following solvents are tried one after the other in the systematic order, i.e. if the salt does not dissolve in a particular solvent, even on heating, try the next one. The solution must be transparent and should not have any suspended particles. List of the solvents is given below:

1. **Distilled water** (cold, hot) Take a little amount of the salt in a clean boiling tube and add a few mL of distilled water and shake it. If the salt does not dissolve, heat the content of the boiling tube till the salt completely dissolves.
2. **Dilute HCl** If salt is insoluble in water, take fresh salt in a clean boiling tube and add a few mL of dil. HCl to it. If the salt is insoluble in cold, heat the boiling tube till the salt is completely dissolved.
3. **Concentrated HCl** If the salt does not dissolve either in water or dilute HCl even on heating try to dissolve it in few mL of conc. HCl by heating.

Note Dil. HNO_3 *or* H_2SO_4 *cannot be used in place of HCl because* H_2SO_4 *causes the precipitation of* Pb^{2+}, Ba^{2+}, Sr^{2+} and Ca^{2+} *as insoluble sulphates while* HNO_3 *is an oxidising agent and can bring about the oxidation of* H_2S *to give yellow precipitate of S in the second group.*

Group Analysis

Analysis of Zero Group Cation, NH_4^+

Experiment and Procedure	Observation	Inference	Chemistry involved
The given salt around 0.1 g is heated with 1-2 mL of conc. NaOH solution.	A pungent smell of ammonia is obtained.	NH_4^+ cations may be present.	Ammonia gas is evolved by the action of sodium hydroxide on ammonium salts like NH_4Cl, $(NH_4)_2SO_4$, etc. $(NH_4)_2SO_4 + 2NaOH \longrightarrow Na_2SO_4 + 2NH_3 + 2H_2O$
Bring a glass rod dipped in HCl near the mouth of the test tube.	White dense fumes are observed.	NH_4^+ cations are present.	The evolved gas reacts with HCl to give visible white fumes of NH_4Cl. $NH_3 + HCl \longrightarrow \underset{\text{White fumes}}{NH_4Cl} \uparrow$
Pass the gas through Nessler's reagent.	Brown precipitate is obtained.	Presence of NH_4^+ ions is confirmed.	On passing the gas through Nessler's reagent, a brown colouration or a precipitate of basic mercury (II) amido-iodine is formed. $\underset{\text{Nessler's reagent}}{2K_2HgI_4} + NH_3 + 3KOH \longrightarrow \underset{\text{Basic mercury(II)amido-iodine (brown ppt.)}}{HgO \cdot Hg(NH_2)I} + 7KI + 2H_2O$

Analysis of Cations Belonging to Group I-VI

For the detection of cations belonging to groups I to VI, the cations are precipitated from the original solution by using the group reagents according to the scheme given below :

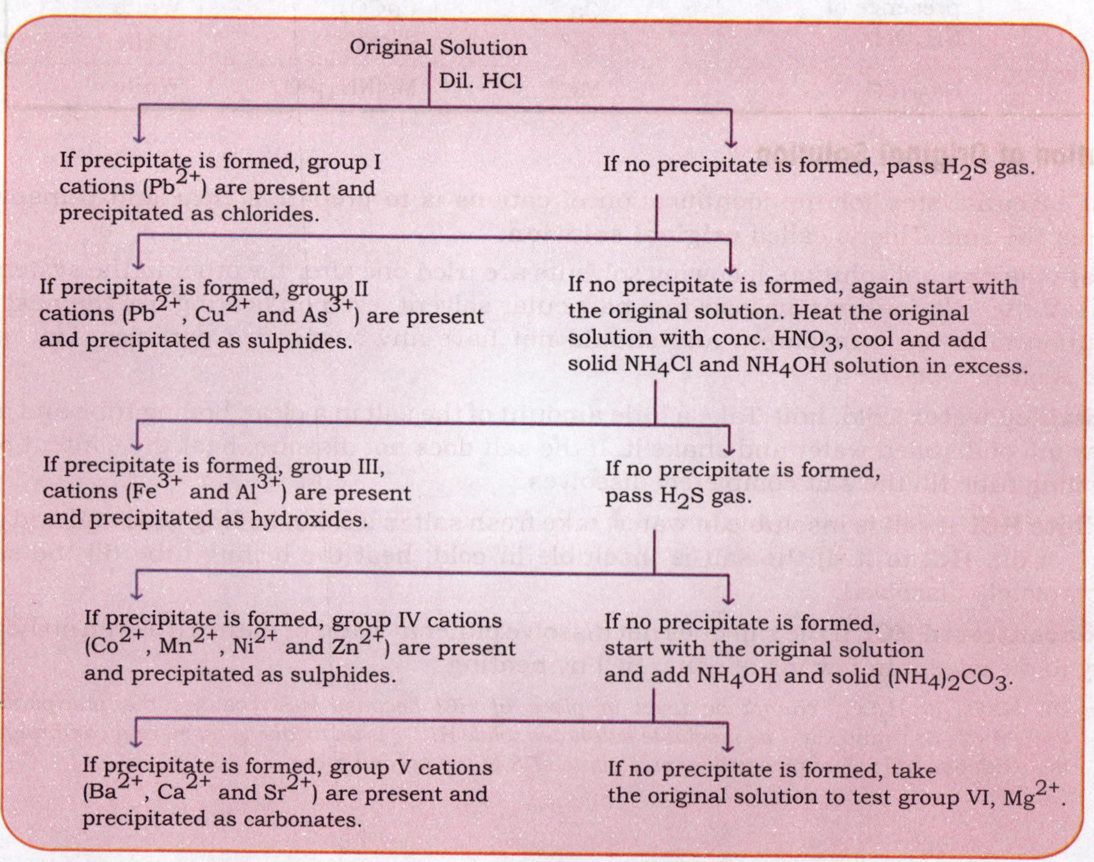

Various tests are used to analyse and confirm the basic radicals or cations belonging to a particular group. These are listed below :

Experiment and Procedure	Observation	Inference	Chemistry involved
1 ANALYSIS OF GROUP I CATIONS			
To the original solution prepared in water, add dil. HCl.	A white precipitate is formed.	Group I, Pb^{2+} may be present.	Lead is precipitated as lead chloride. $\underset{\text{Present in a given salt}}{Pb^{2+}} + 2Cl^- \longrightarrow \underset{\text{White ppt.}}{PbCl_2 \downarrow}$
Note *In case the original solution is prepared in conc. HCl, dilute the solution with cold water and cool the test tube under tap water.*			
Confirmatory Tests for Pb^{2+} Dissolve the white precipitate in hot water and divide the solution into three parts			
(i) **Potassium iodide test** Add KI (potassium iodide) solution to the first part of the hot solution.	A yellow precipitate of lead iodide is formed which is soluble in boiling water and on cooling, shiny crystals are formed.	Presence of Pb^{2+} ions is confirmed.	$\underset{\text{(Hot solution)}}{PbCl_2 + 2KI} \longrightarrow \underset{\text{Yellow ppt.}}{PbI_2 \downarrow} + 2KCl$
(ii) **Potassium chromate test** Add potassium chromate (K_2CrO_4) solution to the second part of the solution.	A yellow precipitate of lead chromate is formed which is soluble in hot NaOH solution but insoluble in ammonium acetate solution.	This confirms the presence of Pb^{2+} ions.	$\underset{\text{Hot solution}}{PbCl_2} + K_2CrO_4 \longrightarrow \underset{\text{Lead chromate (Yellow precipitate)}}{PbCrO_4 \downarrow} + 2KCl$ $PbCrO_4 + 4NaOH \rightleftharpoons \underset{\text{Sodium tetra hydroxo-plumbate (III)}}{Na_2[Pb(OH)_4]} + Na_2CrO_4$
(iii) **Dilute sulphuric acid test** To the third part of the hot solution, add few drops of alcohol and dil. H_2SO_4.	A white precipitate of lead sulphate is formed which is soluble in ammonium acetate solution due to the formation of tetraaceto plumbate (II) ions.	This confirms the presence of Pb^{2+} ions.	$PbCl_2 + H_2SO_4 \longrightarrow \underset{\text{White ppt.}}{PbSO_4 \downarrow} + 2HCl$ $PbSO_4 + 4CH_3COONH_4 \longrightarrow \underset{\text{Ammonium tetraaceto\_ plumbate (II)}}{(NH_4)_2[Pb(CH_3COO)_4]} + (NH_4)_2SO_4$ The above reaction is promoted by the addition of few drops of acetic acid.
2 ANALYSIS OF GROUP II CATIONS			
If group I is absent, add excess of water to the same test tube, shake and warm the solution, pass H_2S gas for 1-2 minutes.	Appearance of precipitate is observed.	It indicates the presence of group II cations.	
Pass more H_2S gas through the solution to ensure complete precipitation. Filter and collect the precipitate.	Black or yellow coloured ppt. is formed.	Black ppt. indicates the presence of Cu^{2+} or Pb^{2+} ions. Yellow ppt. indicates the presence of As^{3+} ions.	

Experiment and Procedure	Observation	Inference	Chemistry involved
Dissolve the collected precipitate in excess of yellow ammonium sulphide solution and shake the test tube.	Precipitate may be soluble or insoluble in ammonium sulphide solution.	If black precipitate is insoluble, **group II A** (copper or lead group) is present and if yellow precipitate is soluble, **group II B** (arsenic group) is present.	
Confirmatory Tests for Group II A Cations (Pb^{2+} and Cu^{2+} ions) Boil the black precipitate with (1-2 mL) dilute nitric acid and add few drops of alcohol and dil. H_2SO_4.	Either white ppt. or no ppt. is formed.	White ppt. indicates the presence of Pb^{2+} ions and no ppt. indicates the presence of Cu^{2+} ions.	**For Pb^{2+} ions** Lead sulphide precipitate dissolves in dilute HNO_3. On adding dilute H_2SO_4 and few drops of alcohol to this solution, a white precipitate of lead sulphate appears. $\underset{\text{Black ppt. (Soluble in } HNO_3)}{3PbS} + 8HNO_3 \longrightarrow 3Pb(NO_3)_2 + 4H_2O + 2NO + 3S$ $Pb(NO_3)_2 + H_2SO_4 \longrightarrow 2HNO_3 + \underset{\text{White ppt.}}{PbSO_4 \downarrow}$ **For Cu^{2+} ions** Copper sulphide dissolves in nitric acid due to the formation of copper nitrate. $\underset{\text{Black ppt.}}{3CuS} + 8HNO_3 \longrightarrow 3Cu(NO_3)_2 + 4H_2O + 2NO + 3S$
Tests for Pb^{2+} ions Dissolve the white ppt in ammonium acetate solution and acidify it with acetic acid. Divide the solution into two parts: **Tests for Cu^{2+} ions** If no ppt is formed, then add NH_4OH solution in excess.	**For Pb^{2+}** No colouration or ppt is formed in case of Pb^{2+} ions. **For Cu^{2+}** Blue colouration is observed.	**For Cu^{2+}** Blue colouration indicates the presence of Cu^{2+} ions.	**For Pb^{2+} ions** $\underset{\text{White ppt.}}{PbSO_4} + 4CH_3COONH_4 \longrightarrow (NH_4)_2[Pb(CH_3COO)_4] + (NH_4)_2SO_4$ **For Cu^{2+} ions** A small amount of NH_4OH precipitates basic $CuSO_4$ which is soluble in excess of NH_4OH due to the formation of tetra amminocopper (II) complex. $S + 2HNO_3 \longrightarrow H_2SO_4 + 2NO$ $2Cu^{2+} + SO_4^{2-} + 2NH_3 + 2H_2O \longrightarrow Cu(OH)_2 \cdot CuSO_4 + 2NH_4^+$ $Cu(OH)_2 \cdot CuSO_4 + 8NH_3 \longrightarrow \underset{\text{Tetra ammine coper (II)}}{2[Cu(NH_3)_4]} \underset{\text{Sulphate (Deep blue)}}{SO_4} + 2OH^- + SO_4^{2-}$

Experiment and Procedure		Observation	Inference	Chemistry involved	
For Pb^{2+} ions	**For Cu^{2+} ions**				
(i) **Potassium chromate, K_2CrO_4 test** To the first part, add K_2CrO_4 solution.	(i) **Potassium ferrocyanide test** Add acetic acid (to acidify the solution) and potassium ferrocyanide solution.	**For Pb^{2+} ions** A yellow ppt. is observed in potassium chromate test. **For Cu^{2+} ions** A chocolate brown ppt. is observed in potassium ferrocyanide test.	**For Pb^{2+} ions** A yellow ppt. confirms Pb^{2+} ions. **For Cu^{2+} ions** A brown ppt. confirms the presence of Cu^{2+} ions.	**Potassium chromate test** $(NH_4)_2[Pb(CH_3COO)_4] + K_2CrO_4 \longrightarrow \underset{\text{Yellow ppt.}}{PbCrO_4\downarrow} + 2CH_3COOK + 2(NH_4)_2SO_4$	**Potassium ferrocyanide test** $[Cu(NH_3)_4]SO_4 + 4CH_3COOH \longrightarrow CuSO_4 + 4CH_3COONH_4$ $2CuSO_4 + \underset{\text{Potassium hexacyano ferrate (II)}}{K_4[Fe(CN)_6]} \longrightarrow \underset{\text{Copper hexacyano ferrate (II) (Chocolate brown colour)}}{Cu_2[Fe(CN)_6]\downarrow} + 2K_2SO_4$
(ii) **Potassium iodide test** To the second part, add KI solution.	(ii) **Potassium iodide test** To second part, add acetic acid and KI solution.	**For Pb^{2+} ions** A yellow ppt. is formed in KI test **For Cu^{2+}** A white ppt. is formed in KI test.	**For Pb^{2+} ions** Yellow ppt. confirms the presence of Pb^{2+} ions. **For Cu^{2+} ions** A white ppt. confirms the presence of Cu^{2+} ions.	**Potassium iodide test** $Pb^{2+} + 2I^- \longrightarrow PbI_2$	**Potassium iodide test** White precipitate is due to formation of Cu_2I_2 and the brown colour is due to liberated of I_2. $2CuSO_4 + 4KI \longrightarrow \underset{\text{White ppt.}}{Cu_2I_2\downarrow} + \underset{\text{Brown colouration}}{I_2} + 2SO_2$
Confirmatory tests **For Group II B Cations** [As^{3+} ions] Dissolve the yellow precipitate in yellow ammonium sulphide solution and acidify the solution with dilute HCl.		A yellow precipitate is formed.	As^{3+} ions are present.	Ammonium thioarsenides formed on dissolution of As_2S_3 decomposes with dilute HCl and a yellow precipitate of As_2S_5 is formed. $As_2S_3 + 3(NH_4)_2S_2 \longrightarrow 2(NH_4)_3AsS_4 + S$ $2(NH_4)_3AsS_4 + 6HCl \longrightarrow As_2S_5\downarrow + 3H_2S + 6NH_4Cl$	
Heat the yellow precipitate with conc. HNO_3 and add ammonium molybdate solution.		A canary yellow precipitate is formed.	Presence of As^{3+} ions is confirmed.	As_2S_5 dissolves in conc. HNO_3 on heating due to arsenic acid formation which gives a canary yellow precipitate on addition of ammonium molybdate solution. $\underset{\text{(Yellow ppt.)}}{As_2S_5} + 10HNO_3 \xrightarrow{+4H_2O} \underset{\text{Arsenic acid (Soluble)}}{6H_3AsO_4} + 10NO + 15S$ $\underset{\text{Arsenic acid}}{H_3AsO_4} + 12(NH_4)_2MoO_4 + 21HNO_3 \longrightarrow \underset{\text{Yellow ppt. of ammonium arsinomolybdate}}{(NH_4)_3[As(Mo_3O_{10})]_4\downarrow} + 21NH_4NO_3 + 12H_2O$	

Experiment and Procedure	Observation	Inference	Chemistry involved
3 ANALYSIS FOR GROUP III CATIONS			
If group II is absent, take the original solution and add 2-3 drops of conc. HNO_3 to oxidise Fe^{2+} to Fe^{3+}, ions. Boil the solution for few minutes and cool it. Add 2 g of NH_4Cl and boil again, cool the solution under tap water. Add excess of NH_4OH solution till it smells of NH_3 and shake the test tube.	Either brown or white precipitate is formed.	Brown precipitate indicates the presence of Fe^{3+} ions while white gelatinous precipitate indicates the presence of Al^{3+} ions.	Original solution when heated with nitric acid, ferrous ions are oxidised to ferric ions. $2FeCl_2 + 2HCl + [O] \longrightarrow 2FeCl_3 + H_2O$ The group III cations are precipitated as hydroxides on the addition of excess of ammonium hydroxide, NH_4OH. $FeCl_3 + 3NH_4OH \longrightarrow 3NH_4Cl + Fe(OH)_3\downarrow$ (Reddish brown ppt.) $AlCl_3 + 3NH_4OH \longrightarrow 3NH_4Cl + Al(OH)_3\downarrow$ White ppt. These precipitates dissolve in dilute HCl due to the formation of corresponding chlorides.
Note *Add sufficient quantity of* NH_4Cl*, otherwise the hydroxides of higher group may be precipitated alongwith the radicals of third group. Sometimes, the addition of conc.* HNO_3 *in the analysis of group III serves to oxidise* Fe^{2+} *to* Fe^{3+} *ions. Thus, before confirming* Fe^{3+} *ions, first confirm* Fe^{2+} *ions.*			
Confirmatory Test for Fe^{2+} ions Add conc. HNO_3 to the original solution and few drops of potassium ferricyanide solution.	A deep blue colouration is obtained.	This deep blue colouration confirms Fe^{2+} ions.	Turnbull's blue precipitate is formed. $3Fe^{2+} + 2K_3[Fe(CN)_6] \longrightarrow Fe_3[Fe(CN)_6]_2 + 6K^+$
Confirmatory Tests for Fe^{3+} and Al^{3+} ions			
Brown Precipitate Fe^{3+}			
Dissolve the brown precipitate in dil. HCl and divide into two parts :			Reddish brown precipitate of $Fe(OH)_3$ dissolves in HCl and $FeCl_3$ is formed. $Fe(OH)_3 + 3HCl \longrightarrow FeCl_3 + 3H_2O$
(i) **Potassium ferrocyanide test**			
Add potassium ferrocyanide solution to the first part.	A blue colour precipitate appears when solution containing $FeCl_3$ is treated with potassium ferrocyanide solution.	Prussian blue colouration confirms the presence of Fe^{3+} ions.	Prussian blue precipitate is due to ferric ferrocyanide. $4FeCl_3 + 3K_4[Fe(CN)_6] \longrightarrow Fe_4[Fe(CN)_6]_3\downarrow + 12KCl$ ($K_4[Fe(CN)_6]$: Potassium ferrocyanide; $Fe_4[Fe(CN)_6]_3$: Prussian blue ppt.) If potassium hexacyanoferrate (II) is added in excess then $KFe[Fe(CN)_6]$ is formed which tends to form a colloidal solution and cannot be filtered. $FeCl_3 + K_4[Fe(CN)_6] \longrightarrow KFe[Fe(CN)_6] + 3KCl$ (Soluble prussian blue)

Experiment and Procedure	Observation	Inference	Chemistry involved
(ii) **Potassium thiocyanate test** To the second part, add potassium thiocyanate (potassium sulphocyanide) solution.	A blood red colouration appears.	Blood red colouration confirms the presence of Fe^{3+} ions.	$\underset{}{FeCl_3} + \underset{\text{Potassium thiocyanate}}{3KSCN} \longrightarrow 3KCl + \underset{\text{Blood red colour}}{[Fe(SCN)_3]}$
White Precipitate Al^{3+} Dissolve the white precipitate in dilute HCl and divide it into two parts :			$Al(OH)_3 + 3HCl \longrightarrow AlCl_3 + 3H_2O$
(i) **Lake test** Add blue litmus solution to the first part and add ammonium hydroxide solution drop by drop along the sides of the test tube till blue colour develops.	A blue mass floating in the colourless solution appears.	Blue mass formation confirms the presence of Al^{3+} ions.	When blue litmus is added to the solution, a red colouration is obtained due to acidic nature of the solution. On addition of NH_4OH solution drop by drop, the solution becomes alkaline and $Al(OH)_3$ is precipitated which adsorbs blue colour from the solution and forms insoluble adsorption complex named lake. $AlCl_3 + 3NH_4OH \longrightarrow 3NH_4Cl + \underset{\text{Blue colour adsorbs by this ppt.}}{Al(OH)_3\downarrow}$
(ii) To the second part, add NaOH solution and warm.	A gelatinous white precipitate is obtained soluble in excess NaOH.	A white precipitate confirms the presence of Al^{3+} ions.	When the solution containing $AlCl_3$ is treated with NaOH, a white gelatinous precipitate of $Al(OH)_3$ is formed which is soluble in excess of NaOH due to the formation of sodium aluminate. $AlCl_3 + 3NaOH \longrightarrow Al(OH)_3\downarrow + 3NaCl$ $\underset{\text{White ppt.}}{Al(OH)_3} + NaOH \longrightarrow \underset{\text{Sodium aluminate}}{NaAlO_2} + 2H_2O$

4 ANALYSIS OF GROUP IV CATIONS

If group III cations are absent, pass H_2S gas in the solution taken for group III for a few minutes.	Either white, black or flesh coloured precipitate appears.	Group IV cations Zn^{2+}, Mn^{2+}, Ni^{2+} or Co^{2+} may be present.	On passing H_2S gas through group III solution, cations Zn^{2+}, Mn^{2+}, Ni^{2+} and Co^{2+} precipitates as their sulphides. $Zn(OH)_2 + H_2S \longrightarrow 2H_2O + \underset{\text{White ppt.}}{ZnS\downarrow}$ $Mn(OH)_2 + H_2S \longrightarrow 2H_2O + \underset{\text{Buff or flesh coloured ppt.}}{MnS\downarrow}$ $Ni(OH)_2 + H_2S \longrightarrow 2H_2O + \underset{\text{Black ppt.}}{NiS\downarrow}$ $Co(OH)_2 + H_2S \longrightarrow 2H_2O + \underset{\text{Black ppt.}}{CoS\downarrow}$

Confirmatory Test for Zn^{2+} ions Dissolve the precipitate in dil. HCl. Boil off H_2S and divide the solution into two parts:	ZnS dissolves in HCl to form $ZnCl_2$. $ZnS + 2HCl \longrightarrow ZnCl_2 + H_2S\uparrow$

Experiment and Procedure	Observation	Inference	Chemistry involved
(i) **Sodium hydroxide test** To the first part, add NaOH solution.	A white precipitate is obtained soluble in excess of NaOH solution.	This confirms the presence of Zn^{2+} ions.	On addition of NaOH, white precipitate of $Zn(OH)_2$ is formed which is soluble in excess of NaOH solution on heating. $ZnCl_2 + 2NaOH \longrightarrow \underset{\text{White ppt.}}{Zn(OH)_2} \downarrow + 2NaCl$ $Zn(OH)_2 + 2NaOH \longrightarrow \underset{\text{Sodium zincate}}{Na_2ZnO_2} + 2H_2O$
(ii) **Potassium ferrocyanide test** Neutralise the second part with NH_4OH and add potassium ferrocyanide solution.	A bluish-white ppt. appears.	This confirms the presence of Zn^{2+} ions.	When potassium ferrocyanide $K_4[Fe(CN)_6]$ solution is added to the solution after neutralisation by NH_4OH, a bluish-white precipitate of zinc ferrocyanide appears. $2ZnCl_2 + K_4[Fe(CN)_6] \longrightarrow \underset{\text{Bluish - white}}{Zn_2[Fe(CN)_6]} \downarrow + 4KCl$
Confirmatory test for Mn^{2+} ions Dissolve the precipitate in dil. HCl by boiling off H_2S gas. Then, add NaOH solution in excess.	A white precipitate is formed which turns brown on keeping.	The presence of Mn^{2+} ions is confirmed.	MnS precipitate dissolves in dil. HCl by boiling and forms a white precipitate of $Mn(OH)_2$ with NaOH solution when added in excess. $MnS + 2HCl \longrightarrow MnCl_2 + H_2S\uparrow$ $MnCl_2 + 2NaOH \longrightarrow \underset{\text{White ppt.}}{Mn(OH)_2} \downarrow + 2NaCl$ $Mn(OH)_2$ turns brown due to atmospheric oxidation into hydrated manganese dioxide. $Mn(OH)_2 + [O] \longrightarrow \underset{\text{(Brown colour)}}{MnO(OH)_2}$
Confirmatory Test for Ni^{2+} and Co^{2+} ions Dissolve the precipitate in aqua-regio. Now, evaporate the solution to dryness and cool. Dissolve the residue in water and divide the solution in two parts.			$3NiS + 2HNO_3 + 6HCl \longrightarrow 3NiCl_2 + 2NO + 3S + 4H_2O$ $2CoS + HNO_3 + 3HCl \longrightarrow CoCl_2 + NOCl + S + 2H_2O$
For Ni^{2+} ions **Dimethyl glyoxime test** Add NH_4OH solution to the to the first part and then few drops of dimethyl glyoxime are added and shake the test tube.	A bright red precipitate is obtained.	The red precipitate confirms the presence of Ni^{2+} ions.	When dimethyl glyoxime is added to the aqueous solution of nickel chloride and made alkaline by adding NH_4OH solution, a brilliant red precipitate is obtained. $NiCl_2 + 2NH_4OH + 2\underset{\text{Dimethyl glyoxime}}{\begin{matrix}CH_3-C=NOH \\ \vert \\ CH_3-C=NOH\end{matrix}} \longrightarrow$ [Ni(dimethylglyoximate)$_2$ complex: $CH_3-C=N$ / $CH_3-C=N$ and $N=C-CH_3$ / $N=C-CH_3$ coordinated to Ni, with $OH \cdots O$ and $O \cdots HO$ bridges] Bright red ppt. $+ 2NH_4Cl + 2H_2O$

Experiment and Procedure	Observation	Inference	Chemistry involved
For Co^{2+} ions **Potassium nitrite test** Add NH_4OH solution to the second part and then add acetic acid and a crystal of potassium nitrite.	A yellow coloured complex or precipitate is obtained.	A yellow precipitate confirms the presence of Co^{2+} ions.	When potassium nitrite is added to an aqueous solution of salt containing cobalt and the solution is neutralised with dil. CH_3COOH, a yellow precipitate of cobalt complex named potassium hexanitritocobaltate (III) is formed. $CoCl_2 + 7KNO_2 + 2CH_3COOH \longrightarrow \underset{\text{Potassium hexanitritocobaltate (III) (Yellow precipitate)}}{K_3[Co(NO_2)_6]} + 2KCl + 2CH_3COOK + H_2O + NO$
Note *Pass H_2S gas only through a test portion. If no precipitate results, reject the test portion and proceed for group V with the remaining solution. In case a dirty white precipitate results, then test for Mn^{2+} or Zn^{2+}. Also note the colour of the original salt.*			
5 ANALYSIS OF GROUP V CATIONS			
If group IV cations are absent, then proceed for detection of group V cations. For this, add 2-3 g of solid NH_4Cl to the original solution. Boil and cool the contents. Add an excess of NH_4OH solution till it smells of ammonia and then add solid $(NH_4)_2CO_3$.	A white precipitate is observed.	The appearance of white precipitate indicates the presence of group V cations.	When $(NH_4)_2CO_3$ is added to the salt solution containing NH_4Cl and NH_4OH, the carbonates of Ba^{2+}, Sr^{2+} and Ca^{2+} are precipitated. $BaCl_2 + (NH_4)_2CO_3 \longrightarrow \underset{\text{White ppt.}}{BaCO_3\downarrow} + 2NH_4Cl$ $SrCl_2 + (NH_4)_2CO_3 \longrightarrow SrCO_3\downarrow + 2NH_4Cl$ $CaCl_2 + (NH_4)_2CO_3 \longrightarrow CaCO_3\downarrow + 2NH_4Cl$
Preserve the small amount of precipitate for flame test. Then, dissolve the remaining white precipitate by boiling with dilute acetic acid and divide the solution into three parts one each for Ba^{2+}, Sr^{2+} and Ca^{2+} ions.	White precipitate dissolves.	The insoluble carbonates of Ba, Sr and Ca dissolves in acetic acid due to the formation of soluble acetate.	$BaCO_3 + 2CH_3COOH \longrightarrow (CH_3COO)_2Ba + H_2O + CO_2\uparrow$ $SrCO_3 + 2CH_3COOH \longrightarrow (CH_3COO)_2Sr + H_2O + CO_2\uparrow$ $CaCO_3 + 2CH_3COOH \longrightarrow (CH_3COO)_2Ca + H_2O + CO_2\uparrow$
Confirmatory Tests for Ba^{2+} ions			
(i) **Potassium chromate test** To the first part, add potassium chromate solution.	A yellow precipitate is obtained.	The yellow precipitate indicates the presence of Ba^{2+} in the salt.	K_2CrO_4 gives yellow precipitate of $BaCrO_4$ with barium acetate, $(CH_3COO)_2Ba$. $(CH_3COO)_2Ba + K_2CrO_4 \longrightarrow \underset{\text{Yellow ppt.}}{BaCrO_4\downarrow} + 2CH_3COOK$
(ii) **Flame test** Heat the preserved precipitate in the non-luminous flame of Bunsen burner taken on a platinum wire which is dipped in conc. HCl to observe the colour of the flame produced.	A grassy green flame is obtained which is visible through blue glass.	A grassy green colour of the flame confirms the presence of Ba^{2+} ions.	—

Experiment and Procedure	Observation	Inference	Chemistry involved
Confirmatory tests for Sr^{2+} ions			
(i) **Ammonium sulphate test** To the second part of the solution, add ammonium sulphate solution. Heat and scratch the sides of the test tube with a glass rod and cool.	A white precipitate is obtained.	The white precipitate indicates the presence of Sr^{2+} ions.	Ammonium sulphate gives a white precipitate of strontium sulphate with strontium acetate. $(CH_3COO)_2Sr + (NH_4)_2SO_4 \longrightarrow \underset{\text{White ppt.}}{SrSO_4 \downarrow} + 2CH_3COONH_4$
(ii) **Flame test** Heat the precipitate taken on the platinum wire directly on the non-luminous flame.	A crimson red flame is produced.	A crimson red flame confirms the presence of Sr^{2+} ions.	
Confirmatory tests for Ca^{2+} ions			
(i) **Ammonium oxalate test** To the third part of the solution, add ammonium oxalate solution and shake well.	A white precipitate of calcium oxalate is obtained.	The white precipitate indicates the presence of Ca^{2+} ions.	Ammonium oxalate gives a white precipitate with calcium acetate. $(CH_3COO)_2Ca + (NH_4)_2C_2O_4 \longrightarrow \underset{\text{White ppt.}}{(COO)_2Ca \downarrow} + 2CH_3COONH_4$
(ii) **Flame test** Heat the precipitate taken on the platinum wire directly on the non-luminous flame.	A brick red flame which looks greenish-yellow through blue glass.	A brick red flame confirms the presence of Ca^{2+} ions.	

Note *The radicals of group V should be tested in the order* Ba^{2+}, Sr^{2+}, Ca^{2+} *[Easy to remember as Bata shoe company]. If* Ba^{2+} *is confirmed, do not proceed to test for* Sr^{2+} *and* Ca^{2+}. *Similarly, if* Sr^{2+} *is confirmed do not test for* Ca^{2+} *ions.*

6 ANALYSIS OF GROUP VI CATION, Mg^{2+}

Experiment and Procedure	Observation	Inference	Chemistry involved
If group V is absent, test for the group VI cation. To a part of the original solution, add 2-3 g of solid NH_4Cl and NH_4OH solution in excess. Warm and cool the solution and then add solution of disodium hydrogen phosphate till white crust formation takes place in the inner walls of the test tube.	A white crystalline precipitate is obtained on the inner walls of the test tube which is scratched with a glass rod.	A white precipitate indicates the presence of Mg^{2+} ions.	$Mg^{2+} + 2NH_4Cl \longrightarrow MgCl_2 + 2NH_4^+$ $MgCl_2 + NH_4OH + Na_2HPO_4 \longrightarrow \underset{\text{White ppt.}}{Mg(NH_4)PO_4 \downarrow} + 2NaCl + H_2O$

Note *Sometimes precipitate of magnesium ammonium phosphate appears after sometime. So warm the solution and scratch the sides of test tube after adding sodium hydrogen phosphate solution.*

Result

(i) The cation(s) present in the salt/salt mixture is/are ...

(ii) The anion(s) present in the salt/salt mixture is/are ...

PRECAUTIONS

- *Always use an apron, eye protector and hand gloves while working in the chemistry laboratory.*
- *Before using any reagent or chemicals, read the labels on the bottles carefully. Do not use unlabelled reagent.*
- *Never mix chemicals and reagents unnecessarily. Never taste any chemical.*
- *Be careful in smelling chemicals or vapours. Fan the vapours gently towards your nose. Do not put your nose directly above the test tube or beakers for smelling.*
- *Wash your hands immediately after touching any salt as it may be corrosive.*
- *Do not add sodium metal to water or do not throw it in the sink or dustbin.*
- *Be careful while heating the test tube. The test tube should never point towards a person while heating or adding a reagent.*
- *Always use the reagents in minimum quantity. Use of reagents in excess, not only leads to wastage of chemicals but also causes damage to the environment.*
- *Always pour acid into water for dilution. Never add water to acid.*
- *Be very careful while dealing with the explosive compounds, inflammable substances, poisonous gases, electric appliances, glass wares, flame and the hot substances.*
- *Always wash your hands after the completion of the laboratory work.*
- *Keep your working surrounding clean. Never throw papers and glass in the sink. Always use dustbin for this purpose.*

Viva-Voce

Q.1 What is meant by the term qualitative analysis?

Ans. Qualitative analysis is a type of analysis which deals with the methods that are used to determine the constituents of a compound.

Q.2 Inorganic salts ionise when dissolved in water. Explain why?

Ans. Because of high dielectric constant of water, the force of attraction between the two ions get separated. These ions are further stablized by solvation.

Q.3 How is water extract prepared?

Ans. The given salt or mixture is shaken with distilled water in a test tube to make a clear solution. The solution is then filtered and the filterate is known as water extract.

Q.4 Mention a gas other than carbon dioxide (CO_2) which turns lime water milky.

Ans. Sulphur dioxide (SO_2)

Q.5 Explain why organic layer becomes more dark coloured than the aqueous layer in the test of Br^- and I^- ions.

Ans. Br_2 and I_2 are more soluble in organic compound than water and therefore, organic layer gets more dark coloured than the aqueous layer.

Q.6 Can we use water instead of NaOH in chromyl chloride test? If yes, then explain your answer with reactions.

Ans. Yes, water can be used instead of NaOH in chromyl chloride test as chromyl chloride dissolves in water giving chromic acid which gives yellow precipitate with lead acetate solution. Following reactions takes place.

$$CrO_2Cl_2 + 2H_2O \longrightarrow H_2CrO_4 + 2HCl$$

$$\underset{\text{Chromic acid}}{H_2CrO_4} + \underset{\text{Lead acetate}}{Pb(COOCH_3)_2} \longrightarrow \underset{\substack{\text{Lead Chromate} \\ \text{(Yellow ppt.)}}}{PbCrO_4} + 2CH_3COOH$$

Q.7 A dark brown ring is formed at the junction of two layers while performing ring test. Explain.

Ans. Since, sulphuric acid being heavier forms the lower layer and reacts only with a small amount of nitrate, whereas, $FeSO_4$ forms a layer at its surface. Therefore, a brown ring is formed only at the junction of the two layers.

Q.8 Explain how dry heating test is performed and what information you get if blue or green residue becomes white on heating?

Ans. In dry heating test, the clean and dry test tube containing 0.1g of salt is heated over a flame. Blue or green residue becoming white on heating shows the presence of Cu^{2+} ions.

Q.9 What is the colour of the salt when zinc salt is heated?

Ans. A yellow residue when it is hot and a white residue when it is cold.

Q.10 Why does conc. HCl should be used in preparing a paste of the salt for flame test?

Ans. Salts to be analysed by flame test is treated with conc. HCl to form metal chlorides which are more volatile than other salts.

Q.11 Borax bead tests is not applicable for white salts. Why?

Ans. Because white salts do not form coloured metaborates.

Q.12 Why should only one or two particles of the given salt should be touched with the bead in borax bead test?

Ans. An opaque bead is formed if salt is used in excess.

Q.13 Why Pb^{2+} is included in both the groups. i.e., group I and group II?

Ans. In case of group I, lead is precipitated as $PbCl_2$. Since, $PbCl_2$ is slightly soluble in water and therefore, Pb^{2+} is not completely precipitated in group I. Thus, to remove Pb^{2+} ions completely, it is included in group II, where it is precipitated as PbS.

Q.14 Why is it compulsory to confirm the presence of phosphate group in the filtrate of group II if As^{3+} is present in the mixture?

Ans. As both As^{3+} and PO_4^{3-} gives yellow precipitate with ammonium molybdate and therefore presence of phosphate group is confirmed in the filtrate of group II, if As^{3+} is present in the mixture.

Q.15 Why a salt containing lead turns black in colour, if kept in laboratory for long time?

Ans. It happens because of the formation of black lead sulphide by the action of H_2S in the atmosphere.

Q.16 What is colour of nickel and manganese salts?

Ans. Nickel salts are bluish green or green in colour. On the other hand, manganese salts are light pink or flesh in colour.

Q.17 Which group reagent is used for the analysis of group v radicals?

Ans. Group reagent for group V radicals is $(NH_4)_2CO_3$ in the presence of NH_4Cl and NH_4OH.

Questions From NCERT Lab Manual

Q.1 What is the difference between a qualitative and a quantitative analysis?

Ans. Qualitative analysis deals with the identification of the constituents, i.e. acidic or basic radicals of a compound. On the other hand, quantitative analysis helps to estimate the concentration/amount/ percentage of these elements present.

Q.2 Name the anions detected with the help of dilute H_2SO_4.

Ans. NO_2^-, S^{2-}, SO_3^{2-}, CO_3^{2-} and CH_3COO^-.

Q.3 Why is dilute H_2SO_4 preferred over dilute HCl while testing anions?

Ans. On treating the salt with HCl, along with the gas evolved by the salt, HCl gas is also evolved. This can cause interference and the actual gas cannot be identified, whereas with H_2SO_4, no such problem arises.

Q.4 How can sodium carbonate extract be prepared?

Ans. The salt is mixed with double the amount of solid Na_2CO_3 and about 20 mL of distilled water is added. It is then boiled till its volume is reduced to one-third and then filtered. The filtrate is sodium carbonate extract.

Q.5 How will you test the presence of carbonate ion?

Ans. On treating the mixture with dil. HCl , CO_2 gas is evolved. When the gas is passed through lime water, it turns milky due to the formation of insoluble precipitate of calcium carbonate.

$$Na_2CO_3 + 2HCl \longrightarrow 2NaCl + H_2O + CO_2\uparrow$$

$$\underset{\text{Lime water}}{CO_2(g) + Ca(OH)_2(aq)} \longrightarrow \underset{\text{Milkiness}}{CaCO_3(s)\downarrow} + H_2O(s)$$

Q.6 What is lime water and what happens on passing carbon dioxide gas through it?

Ans. Lime water is a solution of calcium hydroxide [$Ca(OH)_2$]. It turns milky on passing CO_2 gas through it due to the formation of white precipitate of insoluble calcium carbonate.

Q.7 Carbon dioxide gas and sulphur dioxide gas both turn lime water milky. How will you distinguish between the two?

Ans. On passing through acidified $K_2Cr_2O_7$ solution, SO_2 turns $K_2Cr_2O_7$ green while CO_2 shows no effect .

Q.8 Name the radical confirmed by sodium nitroprusside test.

Ans. Sulphide (S^{2-}).

Q.9 How do you test the presence of sulphide ion?

Ans. Add ammoniacal sodium nitroprusside to the aqueous salt solution, a violet colouration occurs which confirms the presence of S^{2-} ion.

$$\underset{\text{Sodium sulphide}}{Na_2S} + \underset{\text{Sodium nitroprusside}}{Na_2[Fe(CN)_5NO]} \longrightarrow \underset{\text{Violet colour}}{Na_4[Fe(CN)_5NOS]}$$

Q.10 Why does iodine give a blue colour with starch solution?

Ans. The blue colour is due to the formation of inclusive complex between iodine and amylose unit of starch.

Q.11 Name the anions detected by conc. H_2SO_4.

Ans. Cl^-, Br^-, I^-, $C_2O_4^{2-}$ and NO_3^-.

Q.12 Describe the layer test for bromide and iodide ions.

Ans. To the salt solution, dil. HCl and 1-2 mL of CS_2 is added and mixed well. Then, add chlorine water and shake it well.

Orange and violet colour in CS_2 layer appears in case of bromide and iodide ions, respectively.

$$2KBr + Cl_2 \longrightarrow 2KCl + Br_2 \qquad 2KI + Cl_2 \longrightarrow 2KCl + I_2$$

$$Br_2 + CS_2 \longrightarrow \text{Yellow or orange colour} \qquad I_2 + CS_2 \longrightarrow \text{Violet coloured layer}$$

Q.13 What is the composition of dark brown ring which is formed at the junction of two layers in the ring test for nitrates?

Ans. $[Fe(NO)]SO_4$ (nitroso ferrous sulphate)-brown ring

Q.14 Can we use glass rod instead of platinum wire for performing the flame test? Explain your answer.

Ans. No, we cannot use glass rod because glass contains sodium silicate which imparts its own golden yellow colour to the flame and hence, it will not give any accurate result.

Q.15 Why is platinum metal preferred to other metals for the flame test?

Ans. Platinum does not react with acids and also does not impart any characteristic colour to the flame. Thus, it is preferred for the flame test.

Q.16 What is Nessler's reagent?

Ans. Nessler's reagent is $K_2[HgI_4]$, potassium tetraiodomercurate (II).

Q.17 Why is original solution for cations not prepared in conc. HNO_3 or H_2SO_4?

Ans. Conc. H_2SO_4 would lead to the precipitation of cations of group V as sulphate and conc. HNO_3 is an oxidising agent which on decomposition gives oxygen. When H_2S is passed, in the presence of HNO_3, a yellow precipitate of sulphur is obtained.

$$H_2S + 2HNO_3 \longrightarrow 2NO_2 + 2H_2O + \underset{\text{Yellow ppt.}}{S\downarrow}$$

Q.18 Why is silver nitrate solution stored in dark coloured bottles?

Ans. If $AgNO_3$ is kept in light coloured/transparent bottles, it breaks down to give black/brown silver oxide and nitric acid.

$$2AgNO_3(aq) + H_2O(l) \longrightarrow Ag_2O(s) + 2HNO_3(aq)$$

If stored in dark bottles, this reaction is minimised and the reagent can be kept for quite a long time.

Q.19 Why does conc. HNO_3 kept in a bottle turn yellow in colour?

Ans. Due to the decomposition of HNO_3, NO is formed which is further oxidised to NO_2. The yellow colour is due to the dissolved NO_2.

$$4HNO_3 \longrightarrow 4NO_2 + 2H_2O + O_2$$

Q.20 Why is the reagent bottle containing sodium hydroxide solution never stoppered?

Ans. NaOH reacts with CO_2 from air to form $NaHCO_3$ and Na_2CO_3. Hence, NaOH bottles containing solution should not be stoppered as opening of them may become very hard and eventually becomes impossible with carbonate crust.

Q.21 Name a cation, which is not obtained from a metal.

Ans. Ammonium ion (NH_4^+).

Q.22 How can you test the presence of ammonium ion?

Ans. Add NaOH to the salt and heat it. If NH_3 gas evolves, NH_4^+ ion is present. Pass this gas through Nessler's reagent, a brownish precipitate or colouration is observed.

Q.23 Why cannot conc. HCl be used as a group reagent in place of dil. HCl for the precipitation of 1st group cations?

Ans. The reason is that using conc. HCl would cause interference of $PbCl_2$ into the solution due to the formation of chloroplumbous complex by conc. HCl .

$$PbCl_2 + 2HCl \longrightarrow [PbCl_4]^{2-} + 2H^+$$

Q.24 Why is it essential to boil off H_2S gas before precipitation of radicals of group III?

Ans. If H_2S would not be boiled off, group IV cations will also get precipitated along with the group III radicals.

Q.25 Why is heating with conc. HNO_3 done before precipitation of group III?

Ans. It is done to oxidise ferrous salts to ferric salts and also helps in the removal of H_2S gas.

Q.26 Can we use ammonium sulphate instead of ammonium chloride in group III?

Ans. No, ammonium sulphate cannot be used in place of NH_4Cl in group III because it would cause precipitation of group V radicals as their sulphates in group III.

Q.27 How can one prevent the precipitation of group IV radicals with the second group radicals?

Ans. HCl is added to the solution in group II before passing H_2S gas to avoid the precipitation of group IV radicals.

Q.28 Why is NH_4OH added before $(NH_4)_2CO_3$ solution while precipitating group V cations?

Ans. $(NH_4)_2CO_3$ contains some NH_4HCO_3 in it. NH_4OH is added to convert NH_4HCO_3 to $(NH_4)_2CO_3$ so that Ba^{2+}, Sr^{2+} and Ca^{2+} can be completely precipitated.

Q.29 Why should the solution be concentrated before proceeding to group V?

Ans. If solution is not concentrated, then the precipitation of the cations of group V will not occur completely with the group reagent $(NH_4)_2CO_3$.

Q.30 Why are the group V radicals tested in the order Ba^{2+}, Sr^{2+} and Ca^{2+}?

Ans. Tests of Sr^{2+} and Ca^{2+} are also given by Ba^{2+}. Similarly, Sr^{2+} also gives the test of Ca^{2+}. Thus, before confirming Sr^{2+}, we have to confirm the absence of Ba^{2+} and before confirming Ca^{2+}, we have to show the absence of both the ions of Ba^{2+} and Sr^{2+}.

Q.31 Why do we sometimes get a white precipitate in group VI even if the salt does not contain Mg^{2+} radical?

Ans. The salt may contain Na^+ radical which may form white precipitate even if Mg^{2+} radical is absent.

Q.32 Why do bromides and iodides not give tests similar to chromyl chloride test?

Ans. Because instead of the formation of chromyl bromide and chromyl iodide, Br_2 and I_2 gases are evolved.

$$K_2Cr_2O_7 + 6KBr + 7H_2SO_4 \longrightarrow 3Br_2\uparrow + Cr_2(SO_4)_3 + 4K_2SO_4 + 7H_2O$$

$$K_2Cr_2O_7 + 6KI + 7H_2SO_4 \longrightarrow 3I_2\uparrow + Cr_2(SO_4)_3 + 4K_2SO_4 + 7H_2O$$

Q.33 What do you understand by the term common ion effect?

Ans. Common ion effect is the suppression of dissociation of weak electrolyte in the presence of a strong electrolyte having a common ion. For example, in the presence of a strong electrolyte NH_4Cl, a weak electrolyte NH_4OH is less dissociated due to the presence of NH_4^+, a common ion between them. This fact is based on Le-Chatelier's principle.

$$NH_4Cl \longrightarrow NH_4^+ + Cl^- \quad \text{...(i)}$$

$$NH_4OH \rightleftharpoons NH_4^+ + OH^- \quad \text{...(ii)}$$

More NH_4^+ will shift the equilibrium backwards in reaction (ii) leading to the formation of more NH_4OH and hence, dissociation of NH_4OH is suppressed.

Suggested Experiments for Specimen Record of Salt Analysis

To analyse the provided salt for one anion and one cation present in it.

Materials Required

Boiling tubes, test tubes, test tube holder, test tube stand, delivery tube, corks, filter papers and reagents as per requirement.

Procedure

S.No.	Experiment	Observation	Inference
1.	**Physical examination** (i) Noted the colour of the given salt. (ii) Observed the smell of the salt.	(i) White (ii) No specific odour	Cu^{2+}, Fe^{2+}, Fe^{3+}, Ni^{2+}, Mn^{2+} and Co^{2+} may be absent. NH_4^+, S^{2-}, SO_3^{2-} and CH_3COO^- may be absent.
2.	**Effect of heating** Heated a pinch of the salt in a dry test tube and noted the colour of the gas evolved and change in the colour of the residue on heating and cooling.	(i) A reddish brown gas evolved which turns $FeSO_4$ solution black. (ii) Colourless and odourless gas (CO_2) which turns lime water milky. (iii) The sublimate is formed on the upper cooler parts of the test tube and colour of the sublimate is white	NO_3^- may be present CO_3^{2-} may be present NH_4 + may be present
3.	**Charcoal cavity test** Mixed a pinch of the salt with double the quantity of Na_2CO_3 and heated the mixture on a charcoal cavity in the reducing flame.	White residue	Zn^{2+}, Pb^{2+}, Mg^{2+}, etc., may be absent.
4.	**Cobalt nitrate test** To the above white residue, added a drop of cobalt nitrate solution. Heated it again in oxidising flame.	No characteristic colour.	Zn^{2+}, Mg^{2+} and PO_4^{3-} may be absent.
5.	**Borax bead test** Did not perform this test since, the given salt was white.		Cu^{2+}, Mn^{2+}, Co^{2+}, Ni^{2+} and Fe^{3+} may be absent.
6.	**Flame test** Prepared a paste of the salt with conc. HCl and performed flame test.	Persistent grassy green flame on prolonged heating.	Ba^{2+} may be present.
7.	**Dil. sulphuric acid test** Treated a pinch of the salt with dil. H_2SO_4 and warmed.	No gas is evolved.	S^{2-}, CO_3^{2-}, NO_2^-, CH_3COO^- and SO_3^{2-} are absent.
8.	**Conc. sulphuric acid test** Heated a pinch of the salt with conc. sulphuric acid and then added it to a paper pellet.	A reddish-brown gas is evolved and it turns $FeSO_4$ solution black.	NO_3^- may be present.

S.No.	Experiment	Observation	Inference
9.	**Confirmatory test for NO_3^-** (Nitrate) (i) **Ring test** To 2-3 mL of the salt solution, add conc. H_2SO_4 (2 mL) and shake. Add freshly prepared $FeSO_4$ solution along the sides of the test tube carefully. (ii) **Copper chips test** Heated a pinch of the salt with conc. sulphuric acid and a few copper turnings.	A dark brown ring formed at the junction of the two liquids. Reddish-brown gas evolved.	NO_3^- is confirmed. NO_3^- is confirmed.
10.	Heated a pinch of salt with conc. NaOH solution.	No evolution of ammonia gas.	NH_4^+ absent.
11.	**Preparation of original solution** (OS) Shake a pinch of the salt with water. To a part of the original solution, added 1-2 mL of dilute hydrochloric acid.	Clear solution obtained. No ppt. formed.	Labelled it as original solution (OS) Group I absent (Pb^{2+} absent).
12.	Through a part of the above solution, passed H_2S gas.	No ppt. formed.	Group II absent Cu^{2+}, Cd^{2+}, As^{3+}
13.	To the remaining solution, added a pinch of solid ammonium chloride. Boiled the solution, cooled it and added excess of ammonium hydroxide solution.	No precipitation seen.	Group III absent (Fe^{3+} and Al^{3+} are absent).
14.	Through a part of this solution, passed H_2S gas.	No precipitation was seen.	Group IV absent (Zn^{2+}, Mn^{2+}, Ni^{2+} and Co^{2+} are absent)
15.	To the remaining ammoniacal solution, add ammonium carbonate solution.	White ppt. formed.	Group V present. (Ca^{2+}, Ba^{2+} and Sr^{2+} are present)
16.	**Confirmatory test for barium (Ba^{2+}) ions** Filtered the above white ppt. and dissolved the ppt. in hot dilute acetic acid. (i) **Potassium chromate test** To one part of the above solution, add few drops of potassium chromate solution. (ii) **Flame test** Performed flame test with the salt.	Yellow ppt. Persistent grassy green flame on prolonged heating.	Ba^{2+} is confirmed. Ba^{2+} is confirmed.

Result

The given salt contains : Acidic radical (anion) - NO_3^- (nitrate ion)

Basic radical (cation) - Ba^{2+} (barium ion)

Project 1

AIM

To study the presence of oxalate ions in guava fruit at different stages of ripening.

Theory/Principle

Guava is a common tropical fruit found in India and many other places around the world. It is sweet, juicy and light or dark green coloured fruit. It has a green colour but acquires yellow colour on ripening and has a specific smell. It is a rich source of **oxalate ions** and its concentration varies during different stages of ripening. It contains maximum amount of **vitamin C** after 'Amla'. Oxalate ions present in the guava fruit are made to go into the solution by boiling its pulp with distilled water. The oxalate ions present in solution can be titrated against $KMnO_4$ solution in acidic medium.

Materials Required

- Mortar and pestle : 1
- Beakers (250 mL) : As per need
- Funnel : 1
- Pipette (50 mL) : 1
- Burette (250 mL) : 1
- Conical flask (150 mL) : 1
- Iron stand : 1
- Weight box : 1
- 0.05 N $KMnO_4$ solution : As per need
- Measuring flask : 100 mL
- Dil. H_2SO_4 : As per need
- Distilled water : As per need
- Burette stand : 1
- Guava (from unripe to full ripe variety) : As per need
- Knife : 1

Procedure

1. Take different samples of guava fruit (green, pale-green, yellowish-white and yellowish, i.e. from unripe to fully ripe variety).
2. Now, take 100 g of one of the sample of guava fruit, crush it into a mortar and transfer the paste in 100 mL of water in a beaker.
3. Boil the contents for 10-15 mins. After that, cool the contents and filter them.
4. Pipette out filterate (i.e. 20 mL of gauva juice) in a conical flask, add about 20 mL of dilute sulphuric acid to it. Heat the mixture to about 60°C and titrate it against 0.05 N $KMnO_4$ solution taken in the burette. The end point is detected by the appearance of permanent light pink colour.
5. Repeat the procedure with other samples of guava and make observations.

⚠ ALERT

$KMnO_4$ solution is flammable and harmful to skin.

Observations

Guava extract (solution)	Burette readings		Volume of $KMnO_4$ (0.05 N) used in mL	Concordant reading
	Initial	Final		
Ripe guava				x mL
Semi-riped guava				x_1 mL
Raw-guava				x_2 mL

End point = Colourless to pink

Calculation

For ripe guava,

$$\underset{\text{(Guava solution)}}{N_1V_1} = \underset{\text{(}KMnO_4\text{ solution)}}{N_2V_2}$$

$$N_1 \times 20 = 0.05\text{N} \times x \qquad (\because \text{ volume of } KMnO_4 \text{ used} = x\,\text{mL})$$

Normality of oxalate, $N_1 = \dfrac{0.05\text{N}}{20} \times x$

Strength of oxalate in ripe guava solution = N_1 × Eq. wt. of oxalate ion

Similarly, calculate the strength of oxalate in semi-riped and raw-guava solution and interpret the result.

Result

The strength of oxalate ion in

1. ripe guava is .... g L^{-1}.
2. semi-riped guava is .... g L^{-1}.
3. raw-guava is .... g L^{-1}.

Conclusion

The strength of oxalate ions increases with ripening.

PRECAUTIONS

- *Make separate solution of three fruits, do not mix them.*
- *Boil the fruit pulp with equal amount of water and for the same length of time in case of all the three fruits.*
- *Wash properly the pestle and mortar before starting with other semi-ripe or raw-guava.*

Viva-Voce

Q.1 What is the colour of ripe guava?

Ans. Yellow colour.

Q.2 Name one vitamin present in guava fruit.

Ans. Vitamin C.

Q.3 Is oxalate ion present in guava fruit? If yes then how will you detect its presence?

Ans. Yes, guava contains oxalate ion. Its presence can be detected from its pulp by boiling the pulp with distilled water and then the test of oxalate ion is carried out. Its amount can be tested quantitatively by titrating it against standard solution of $KMnO_4$ in the presence of dilute H_2SO_4.

Q.4 Write the structure of oxalate ion.

Ans. The structure of oxalate ion:

$$\left[\begin{matrix} O \\ O^- \end{matrix} \!\!>\! C - C \!<\!\! \begin{matrix} O \\ O^- \end{matrix} \right]^{2-}$$

Q.5 Write the reaction when oxalate ion is treated with $KMnO_4$ solution.

Ans.

$$5 \begin{matrix} COO^- \\ | \\ COO^- \end{matrix} + 16H^+ + \underset{\text{Pink}}{2MnO_4^-} \longrightarrow \underset{\text{Colourless}}{2Mn^{2+}} + 8H_2O + 10CO_2$$

Q.6 Doctor's suggest to take low oxalate food, why?

Ans. Because high oxalate food is harmful for human body. High oxalate level can trigger or worsen kidney stones.

Q.7 How does the concentration of oxalate ions vary in guava with its ripening?

Ans. The concentration of oxalate ions increases with ripening.

Q.8 Name the indicator used in redox titration of $KMnO_4$.

Ans. In redox titration of $KMnO_4$, indicator is not used because $KMnO_4$ itself acts as an indicator.

Q.9 What is the relation between oxalate and vitamin C in a ripe guava?

Ans. Vitamin C gets converted into oxalate with ripening of the fruit. Hence, amount of oxalate may be a reflection of amount of vitamin C in fruit.

Q.10 What is the colour of the pulp of guava fruit?

Ans. Cream coloured.

Project 2

AIM

To study the quantity of casein present in different samples of milk.

Theory/Principle

Milk as a whole contains water, minerals (Ca, K, Na and trace metals), vitamins (A, D, E and K), carbohydrates, proteins and fats.

The lactose (milk sugar) and the major milk protein, i.e. casein is found only in milk.

Casein is the protein which is present in milk in the form of calcium salt, **calcium phosphocaseinate**. This salt has a complex structure and forms micelles. The outer surface of this micelle is negatively charged. Therefore, when dilute acids like acetic acid, HCl, etc., is added to milk, the negative charges are neutralised and the neutral protein precipitates out. Thus, addition of 1% aqueous solution of acetic acid to milk causes precipitation of casein.

$$Ca^{2+}\text{-Caseinate} + 2CH_3COOH(aq) \longrightarrow \text{Casein}(s) + (CH_3COO)_2Ca(aq)$$

Casein has an isoelectric pH of 4.7 and it can be separated easily around this pH.
It readily dissolves in dilute acids and alkalies.

Materials Required

- Conical flask : 1
- Beakers (500 mL) : As per need
- Funnel : 1
- Measuring cylinder (100 mL) : 1
- Watch glass : 1
- Filter paper : 1
- 1% acetic acid/1% HCl : As per need
- Different samples of milk : As per need
- Glass rod : 1
- Weight box : 1
- Physical balance : 1

Procedure

1. Take 200 mL of each sample of milk in separate 500 mL beakers.
2. Heat the beakers containing milk sample upto 50-60°C.
3. Now, add few drops of 1% acetic acid solution (or 1% HCl solution) slowly with constant stirring with a glass rod for 5-10 mins.
4. After adding acetic acid, casein coagulates as an amorphous substance.
5. Filter the precipitate with the help of funnel and wash the precipitates several times with tap water.
6. Remove the fat by using a suitable organic solvent like alcohol. Now, again wash the casein with water and dry it. Weigh a dried casein in a watch glass.

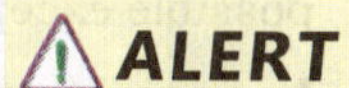

Acetic acid is corrosive, irritant and pungent smelling.

Observations

Volume of the milk sample taken is 200 mL.

Sample No.	Weight of casein isolated (in g)	Percentage (%) of casein
1.	W_1	$\frac{W_1}{200} \times 100 =$
2.	—	—
3.	—	—
4.	—	—

Result

Different samples of milk contains different percentage of casein.

PRECAUTIONS

- *During filtration, press the casein with saptula.*
- *Use only required amount of acid for complete precipitation.*
- *Use fresh milk.*
- *Use same amount of each sample for the experiment.*

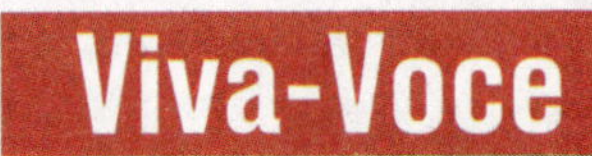

Q.1 What is casein?

Ans. Casein is the main protein present in milk and in cheese (in coagulated form).

Q.2 Write some uses of casein.

Ans. Casein is used in processed foods and in adhesives, paints and other industrial products.

Q.3 Why casein is called highly nutritious protein?

Ans. All the amino acids that are essential to man are present in casein in high proportions with the possible exception of cysteine. Thus, casein may be considered as a highly nutritious protein.

Q.4 Is casein present in soluble form in milk?

Ans. Casein exists in milk in complex groups of molecules (calcium phosphocaseinate) that are called micelles. The casein micelles may be considered to exist in milk as a very stable colloidal dispersion.

Q.5 What type of protein is casein-fibrous or globular?

Ans. Casein is a globular protein.

Q.6 Name the vitamins present in milk.

Ans. Vitamin A, D, E and K.

Q.7 Which compound is responsible for the white colour of milk?

Ans. Casein is responsible for the white opaque appearance of milk in which it is combined with calcium and phosphorus as clusters of casein molecules, called micelles.

Q.8 Name the major constituents of milk.

Ans. The major constituents of milk are water, proteins, fats, carbohydrates and minerals.

Project 3

AIM

Preparation of soyabean milk and its comparison with the natural milk with respect to curd formation, effect of temperature, etc.

Theory/Principle

Milk is considered to be a complete food as it contains all necessary nutrients (proteins, carbohydrates, fats, minerals, vitamins and water) required for body growth.

In summers, milk is stored at low temperature in refrigerators. This happens due to the bacterial activity of ***Lactobacillus* bacteria,** which turns lactose sugar into lactic acid. In acidic conditions, casein of milk starts separating out as a precipitate. When the acidity in milk is sufficient, it forms a semisolid mass which is called curd. The curd formation may be studied by keeping the milk at different temperatures.

Soyabean milk, on the other hand, is obtained from a plant source, soyabeans. The beans of soyabean plant is served as a food for animals and human beings.

Materials Required

- Beaker (500 mL) : As per need
- Glass rod : 1
- Thermometer : 1
- Tripod stand : 1
- Buffalo milk : As per need
- Curd : As per need
- Pestle and mortar : 1
- Measuring cylinder (250 mL) : 1
- Burner : 1
- Muslin cloth : 1
- Soyabeans : As per need
- Distilled water : As per need

Procedure

1. Take about 100 g of soyabean seeds in a 500 mL beaker and dip them completely in sufficient amount of water. Left the seeds soaked till next day.

All the materials are of low hazard.

2. Next day, take these seeds out and grind them to a fine paste using pestle and mortar.
3. Add about 200 mL of distilled water taken in a measuring cylinder to the paste and mix it well using glass rod.
4. Pour the contents through a piece of muslin cloth to filter it.
5. The clear white filtrate is soyabean milk. Compare its taste with that of buffalo milk.
6. Now, take 100 mL of each, the buffalo milk and the soyabean milk in four separate beakers [2 beakers contain buffalo milk and 2 beakers contain soyabean milk].
7. Heat the two beakers containing buffalo milk at 30°C and 40°C respectively. Similarly, heat the two beaker containing soyabean milk at 30°C and 40°C respectively.
8. Add about 10 g of curd in these four beakers and leave the beakers undisturbed.
9. Note down the time for the formation of curd in each beaker.
10. Compare the thickness and taste of the curd formed in four beakers.

Observations

Type of milk	Beaker No.	Temperature	Time taken for curd formation	Thickness of curd	Taste of curd
Buffalo milk	1	30°			
	2	40°			
Soyabean milk	3	30°			
	4	40°			

Result

1. Curd from the buffalo milk is found to be .... (thicker/thinner) than the curd from the soyabean milk.
2. The best temperature for the formation of good quality curd for buffalo milk is .... °C and for soyabean milk is ....°C.

Conclusions

1. Natural milk is sweet in taste while soyabean milk is not.
2. Curd formed from natural milk at higher temperature is more sour.
3. The rate of formation of curd in natural milk and soyabean milk increases with increase in temperature.

PRECAUTIONS

- *Do not overheat the milk as it may kill the curd forming bacteria Lactobacillus.*
- *Take equal quantity of both milk. Unequal quantity of milk may give altered result in respect of firmness and taste of curd formed.*

Viva-Voce

Q.1 Why milk is considered as complete food?

Ans. Because milk contains almost all types of essential nutrients (viz. proteins, fats, carbohydrates, minerals and vitamins).

Q.2 Name the bacteria responsible for the formation of curd from milk.

Ans. Lactobacillus.

Q.3 What is the botanical name of soyabean?

Ans. Glycine max.

Q.4 Why is it suggested to heat the milk at a temperature of around 35°C in order to make curd from it?

Ans. Because bacterial activities are at peak at a temperature around 35°C.

Q.5 Which type of milk taste sweeter, buffalo milk or soyabean milk and why?

Ans. Buffalo milk because it has higher content of lactose sugar.

Q.6 Which type of milk is much better for health, buffalo milk or soyabean milk and why?

Ans. Soyabean milk as it does not contain carbohydrates and fats and therefore, it is given to diabetic patients and also to those who are on slim diet plan.

Project 4

AIM

Study the effect of potassium metabisulphite as a food preservative under various conditions (temperature, concentration, time, etc.)

Theory/Principle

Food when left at an optimum temperature (~ 35°C) for longer period of time, it spoils due to the fermentation by microbes (usually bacteria and fungi). To prevent foods from being spoiled, certain chemical substances are added to them, which are called **food preservatives.** The condition for a food preservative to be used is that it should not be harmful for human body.

The commercially used food preservatives in India are sodium benzoate, potassium metabisulphite and potassium bisulphate.

Materials Required

- Boiling tubes : 6
- Peeler/Knife : 1
- Amla fruits : As per need
- Spices : As per need
- Glass bottles : As per need
- Mustard oil : As per need
- Distilled water : As per need
- Glass rod : 1
- Physical balance : 1
- Salt : As per need
- Potassium *meta*-bisulphite : As per need
- Pestle and mortar : 1

Procedure

Potassium metabisulphite causes respiratory and skin irritation so should be handled with care.

1. Collect amla fruits and wash these with water.
2. Cut these amla fruits into small pieces with a knife.
3. Mix the salt and spices to these pieces.
4. Weigh and pour 25 g of amla pieces into each of the six boiling tubes labelled as *A*, *B*, *C*, *D*, *E* and *F*.
5. Weigh 500 mg of potassium metabisulphite and dissolve it in 20 mL of distilled water.
6. Keep boiling tube '*A*' without mixing preservative and oil.
7. In boiling tubes *B* and *C*, add 1 mL of the preservative solution and 2 mL of oil and mix the mixture with glass rod. Keep the boiling tube *B* at the room temperature (25-35°C) and the boiling tube *C* at a temperature of 40°C.
8. In boiling tubes *D*, *E* and *F* add 2 mL, 4 mL and 8 mL of the preservative solution respectively and 2 mL of mustard oil. Keep these tubes at the room temperature.
9. Prepare again the fresh mixtures (25 g amla + 2 mL preservative + 2 mL oil) in boiling tubes *A'*, *B'* and *C'*. Keep them at 40°C temperature.
10. Keep these boiling tubes for 3 to 5 days.
11. Check the growth of any microbe like fungi in these test tubes after each day.

Observations

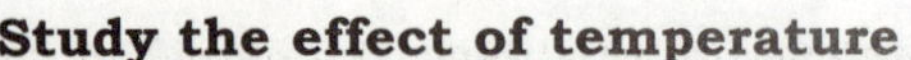

Study the effect of temperature

Boiling tubes	Amount of amla + potassium *meta*-bisulphite + oil	Temperature of storage	Growth of microorganisms
B	25 g + 1 mL + 2 mL	25 - 35°C	
C	25 g + 1 mL + 2 mL	40°C	

Study the effect of concentration at room temperature

Boiling tubes	Amount of amla	Amount of potassium *meta*-bisulphite + oil	Growth of microorganisms
D	25 g	2 mL + 2 mL	
E	25 g	4 mL + 2 mL	
F	25 g	8 mL + 2 mL	

Study the effect of time at 40°C

Boiling tubes	Amount of amla + potassium *meta*-bisulphite + oil	No. of days	Growth of microorganisms
A′	25 g + 2 mL + 2 mL	3	
B′	25 g + 2 mL + 2 mL	4	
C′	25 g + 2 mL + 2 mL	5	

Result

1. Growth of microorganisms was observed highest, when the temperature maintained was ....(25°C/40°C).
2. Growth of microorganisms was observed highest, when the concentration of the potassium metabisulphite and oil was .... (2 mL + 2 mL/4 mL + 2 mL/8 mL + 2 mL).
3. Growth of microorganisms was observed highest, when the amla along with preservative was stored for .... (3 days/4 days/5 days).

Conclusions

1. The growth of the microorganisms is maximum at room temperature, i.e. 25-35°C .
2. The growth of the microorganisms is lowest when the concentration of preservative is highest.

PRECAUTIONS

- *Boiling tube should be clean and dry to observe the growth of fungi.*
- *Mix the preservative thoroughly.*
- *Once the amla solution is kept for observation, do not disturb or shake it as it may cause hindrance to the growth of microbes.*

Viva-Voce

Q.1 Define food preservatives. Give two examples.

Ans. Food preservatives are the chemicals which save foods from being spoiled by the microbial activity.

e.g. 1. Sodium benzoate; 2. Potassium metabisulphite

Q.2 Name any two types of microbes responsible for food spoilage.

Ans. Bacteria and fungus.

Q.3 Name any two types of food that can be preserved by using potassium bisulphate.

Ans. Fruit juices and jams.

Q.4 What is the effect of heating and freezing temperature on microbial activities?

Ans. Heating at or above 60°C kills many of the microbes while freezing temperature (~0°C) inhibits the microbial growth.

Note *In the above project, potassium bisulphate ($KHSO_4$) cannot be used. This is because it is not regarded as safe for direct food preservation purposes. Rather, it is primarily used in wine making and other industrial applications like pH adjustment and as a cleaning agent.*

Project 5

AIM

To study the digestion of starch by salivary amylase and the effect of pH and temperature on it.

Theory/Principle

Salivary amylase is secreted by salivary glands of animals. The enzyme ***ptyalin*** or **amylase** is present in human saliva. This enzyme acts particularly on starch and break it down it into simpler molecules, like **glucose**, **maltose** and **proteins** into amino acids and fats into fatty acids and glycerol, which are further absorbed in intestine.

$$\text{Starch} + H_2O \xrightarrow{\text{Amylase}} \text{Maltose} + \text{Glucose}$$

Amylase is also secreted by **pancreas** in small intestine to ensure complete breakdown of starch. The hydrolysis of starch is an exothermic reaction. The rate of hydrolysis of starch vary under different conditions like pH and temperature. It may be studied by treatment with iodine solution. Starch gives deep blue colour with iodine solution but the products of hydrolysis do not impart any colour.

Materials Required

- Iodine solution : As per need
- Test tube : As per need
- Stopwatch : 1
- NaCl solution : As per need
- Dil. NaOH : As per need
- Beaker (100 mL) : As per need
- Boiling tube : As per need
- Water bath : 1
- dil. HCl : As per need
- Starch solution : As per need

Procedure

Collection of Saliva

1. Take about 25 mL of warm distilled water in the mouth. Mix saliva to the water by gargling. Collect this saliva solution in a beaker.

Preparation of 1% Starch Solution

2. Take 6 g of starch in a beaker and add 60.0 mL of distilled water. Boil for 2-3 mins and filter.

> **ALERT**
> *Iodine solution is irritant and harmful to skin.*

Study of Digestion of Starch

3. Now, take 10 mL of freshly prepared starch solution in a boiling tube and add 2-3 mL of 1%NaCl solution to the tube. Keep the boiling tube on a water bath at around 35°C for 15 mins.
4. After taking out the boiling tube from the water bath, pour 2-3 mL of the saliva solution into it and start the stopwatch immediately.
5. After 1 min, take 2-3 drops of the content from the boiling tube and pour it into a test tube containing iodine solution. Shake the test tube well and note down the change in colour, if any.
6. Repeat the step 5 at an interval of every 1 min until there is no change in colour is observed. Record the readings in a tabular form.

Study the Effect of Temperature

7. To study the effect of temperature, take three clean test tubes and add 10 mL of freshly prepared 1% starch solution [prepared in steps 2 and 3] to each test tube and pour 2-3 mL of saliva into the test tubes.
8. Place these test tubes in water baths maintained at 30°C, 40°C and 50°C.
9. After 1 min, take 2-3 drops of the content from each test tube and pour it into three different test tubes containing iodine solution. Shake each test tube well and note down the change in colour, if any.
10. Repeat step 9, at an interval of every minute until there is no change in colour is observed. Record the readings in a tabular form.

Study the Effect of pH

11. Take three test tubes and add 1% freshly prepared starch solution [prepared in steps 2 and 3] to each test tube and pour 2-3 mL saliva into each test tube.
12. To each test tube, add distilled water, dil. HCl and dil. NaOH [each 5 mL], respectively.
13. Place all these test tubes in the water bath kept at 35-40°C. Start the stopwatch immediately.
14. After 1 min, take 2-3 drops of the content from each test tube and pour it into three different test tube containing iodine solution. Shake each test tube well and note down the change in colour, if any.
15. Repeat step 14 after an interval of every minute until there is no change in colour is observed. Record the readings in a tabular form.

Observations

S. No.	Procedure	Observation	Inference
	A. DIGESTION OF STARCH BY AMYLASE		
1.	Starch + I_2 solution (at 1 min)	.... (colour of the mixture observed)	.... (starch hydrolysed or not)
2.	Starch + I_2 solution (at 2 min)	.... (colour of the mixture observed)	.... (starch hydrolysed or not)
3.	Starch + I_2 solution (at 3 min)	.... (colour of the mixture observed)	.... (starch hydrolysed or not)
	and so on	.... (colour of the mixture observed)	.... (starch hydrolysed or not)

B. EFFECT OF TEMPERATURE ON STARCH HYDROLYSIS

No. of minutes	Colour intensity of solution [starch + I_2] in test tube 1.	Colour intensity of solution [starch+ I_2] in test tube 2	Colour intensity of solution [starch + I_2] in test tube 3	Hydrolysis of starch or not
1	—	—	—	—
2	—	—	—	—
3	—	—	—	—
and so on	—	—	—	—

C. EFFECT OF CHANGE IN pH ON STARCH HYDROLYSIS				
No. of minutes	**Colour intensity of solution [starch + I_2] in test tube 1**	**Colour intensity of solution [starch + I_2] in test tube 2**	**Colour intensity of solution [starch + I_2] in test tube 3**	**Hydrolysis of starch or not**
1	—	—	—	—
2	—	—	—	—
3	—	—	—	—
and so on	—	—	—	—

Result

1. Digestion (hydrolysis) of starch by amylase is found to be completed in .... mins.
2. Hydrolysis of starch is maximum at .... °C.
3. Hydrolysis of starch is maximum in .... (acidic, basic or neutral medium).

Conclusions

1. In case of digestion of starch by amylase, the intensity of the blue colour goes on decreasing with time and finally no colour is obtained. This indicates the complete digestion of starch into maltose and glucose by the action of salivary amylase.
2. The rate of hydrolysis of starch is maximum at 30°C.
3. The rate of hydrolysis of starch is maximum at pH value equals to 7. Thus, it does not occur in acidic as well as basic medium.

PRECAUTIONS

- *Keep an eye on stopwatch to avoid any misobservation.*
- *Conduct the hydrolysis of starch in acidic medium and basic medium separately. As on adding both dil.HCl and dil.NaOH together will bring the pH around neutral value (i.e. pH~7).*

Q.1 Name an enzyme responsible for the digestion of starch in our digestive system.
Ans. Amylase.

Q.2 Why digestion of starch is necessary in our digestive system?
Ans. Because simpler products of digestion (like glucose and fructose) can be easily absorbed in our alimentary canal.

Q.3 Which test is used to detect the presence of starch in a food item?
Ans. Iodine test.

Q.4 Which gland(s) in human body secrete the enzyme amylase?
Ans. Salivary gland and pancreas.

Q.5 At what pH digestion of starch best takes place?
Ans. At pH equal to 7, i.e. in neutral medium digestion of starch best takes place.

Q.6 What happen when Benedict's reagent is added to the hydrolysed starch?
Ans. Brick red precipitate is obtained because glucose being a reducing sugar reduces the Benedict's reagent.

Project 6

AIM

A comparative study of the rate of fermentation of following materials : Wheat flour, gram flour, potato juice, carrot juice, apple juice, etc.

Theory/Principle

Fermentation is a biochemical process which is carried out with the help of enzymes (biological molecules that acts as catalysts). Basically, fermentation is the slow decomposition of complex organic compounds into simpler compounds by the action of enzymes.

Foods like wheat flour, gram flour are the rich sources of starch which undergo fermentation by the enzyme diastase to give maltose.

$$\text{Starch} \xrightarrow{\text{Diastase}} \text{Maltose}$$

The fruit and vegetable juices contains sugars like sucrose, glucose and fructose. These sugars when fermented in the presence of yeast cells are converted to ethyl alcohol.

$$\text{Sucrose} + H_2O \xrightarrow{\text{Invertase}} \text{Glucose} + \text{Fructose}$$

$$\text{Glucose} \xrightarrow{\text{Zymase}} CO_2 + \text{Ethyl alcohol}$$

The rate of fermentation depends upon the temperature, pH and concentration of carbohydrates. Different source materials contain different amounts of carbohydrates, hence, they have different rates of fermentation.

Materials Required

- Conical flasks : As per need
- Glass tube : As per need
- Wheat flour : As per need
- Apple juice : As per need
- Sugar cane juice : As per need
- Glass rod : 1
- Balloon : As per need
- Potato juice : As per need
- Carrot juice : As per need
- Distilled water : As per need

Procedure

A. Comparison of Rate of Fermentation of Different Substances

1. Take about 10 g of wheat flour in a conical flask (100 mL) and add about 80 mL of distilled water into it.
2. Stir the contents of the flask well and then add 2 g of yeast to the flask. Stir the contents again and place a cork fitted with glass tube and a balloon on the flask (as shown in the given figure).

3. As the fermentation proceeds CO_2 gas is evolved and the balloon inflates. The extent to which the balloon inflates in the given time is the measure of the rate of reaction.
4. Repeat the above steps for potato juice, carrot juice, apple juice and sugar cane juice and record the observations.

Determination of the rate of fermentation

B. Effect of Concentration of Yeast

1. Take 10g of wheat flour each in three conical flasks and add 80 mL of distilled water to each. Stir them well and mark them as *A*, *B* and *C*.
2. Add 1 g, 3 g and 5 g of yeast in flasks *A*, *B* and *C* respectively. Stir the contents well and fit the flask with cork, glass tube and balloon.
3. Observe the extent of inflation of balloon of each set up after 5 mins.

C. Effect of Time

1. Take 10 g of wheat flour in a conical flask and add 80 mL of distilled water and 2g of yeast to it.
2. Fit the flask with cork, glass tube and balloon. Stir it well.
3. Observe the extent of inflation at 5 mins, 10 mins and 15 mins.
4. Repeat the steps 1-3 with other given food substances also.

D. Effect of Temperature

1. Take three conical flasks and add 10 g of wheat flour and 80 mL of distilled water and 2 g of yeast into each flask. Stir them well and mark them as *A′*, *B′* and *C′*.
2. Keep the flasks *A′*, *B′* and *C′* at a temperature of 25°C, 30°C and 35°C respectively for 5 mins.
3. Observe the extent of inflation of balloon of each set up after 5 mins.
4. Repeat the steps 1-3 with other given food substances also.

Observations

A. Rate of Fermentation of Different Substances

Note down the extent of inflation of balloon in case of each substance. Highest inflated balloon suggests that the higher amount of carbon dioxide gas released, hence, higher the rate of fermentation.

1. Highest inflated balloon in 5 mins was noticed for ....
2. Lowest inflated balloon in 5 mins was noticed for ....

B. Effect of Concentration of Yeast

Higher the concentration of yeast added, higher will be the rate of reaction, hence, higher inflation of balloon will be observed.

1. Highest inflated balloon is noticed for a concentration of yeast =........ g
2. Lowest inflated balloon is noticed for a concentration of yeast = ... g

C. Effect of Time

1. Highest inflated balloon was noticed in .... mins.
2. Lowest inflated balloon was noticed in .... mins.

D. Effect of Temperature

1. Highest inflated balloon was noticed at .... °C.
2. Lowest inflated balloon was noticed at .... °C.

Extent of inflation of balloon	Samples in different conditions
A. **When different substances are used**	
High	....
Low	....
B. **When concentration of yeast changed**	
High	Concentration of yeast =
Moderate	Concentration of yeast =
Low	Concentration of yeast =
C. **When time period of fermentation varied**	
High	Time allowed for fermentation = ...
Moderate	Time allowed for fermentation = ...
Low	Time allowed for fermentation = ...
D. **Effect of temperature**	
High	Temperature allowed for fermentation = ...
Moderate	Temperature allowed for fermentation = ...
Low	Temperature allowed for fermentation = ...

Result

1. The highest rate of fermentation was found to be in case of .... (name of the substance).
2. The highest rate of fermentation was observed when the concentration of yeast was .... g.
3. The highest extent of CO_2 released was observed when the fermentation was allowed for .... min.
4. The highest rate of fermentation was observed when fermentation was carried at a temperature of .... °C.

PRECAUTIONS

- *Fit the cork and glass tube to the conical flask properly and tie the balloon (using a thread) to the glass tube tightly.*
- *Do not overheat or freeze any sample as it may cease the fermentation process.*

Viva-Voce

Q.1 Define fermentation.

Ans. Fermentation is breaking down of complex molecules (like starch, sucrose, etc.) into simpler molecules (like ethyl alcohol, lactic acid and carbon dioxide) in the presence of enzymes.

Q.2 Name two enzymes involved in the fermentation of sucrose.

Ans. Invertase and zymase.

Q.3 Give an example of fermentation by other than microbes.

Ans. Muscle cell of animals also perform fermentation during physical work. Where oxygen supply becomes limited, resulting in the creation of lactic acid.

Q.4 Name a fermentation process done by bacteria.

Ans. Making of curd with the help of Lactobacillus bacteria.

Project 7

AIM

Extraction of essential oils present in saunf (aniseed), ajwain (carom) and elaichi (cardamom)

Theory/Principle

The term essential oils literally means "oils derived from the essence of plants". The essence or aroma of plants is due to volatile oils present in them. Thus, the volatile oils which impart characteristic odour or aroma to spices or flowers are called **essential oils**. These oils are used in perfumes, flavouring agents, medicines and even as insect repellants. Essential oils are complex mixtures of esters, alcohols, aldehydes, ketones and other organic compounds. They are generally non-polar compounds and thus are soluble in non-polar solvents like petroleum, ether and benzene.

Essential oils may occur in all parts of the plant, but they are often concentrated in the seeds or flowers. They are obtained from respective plants through the process of steam distillation and extraction. The technique of steam distillation permits the separation of volatile components from non-volatile materials without raising the temperature of distillation above 100°C. Thus, steam distillation reduces the risk of decomposition of essential oils.

Materials Required

▪ Round bottom flask	:	As per need	▪ Iron stand	:	2
▪ Conical flask	:	As per need	▪ Sand bath	:	1
▪ Steam generating copper vessel	:	1	▪ Separating funnel	:	1
			▪ Tripod stand	:	1
▪ Condenser	:	1	▪ Glass tubes	:	As per need
▪ Burner	:	1	▪ Petroleum ether	:	As per need
▪ Aniseeds, carum and cardamom	:	As per need			

Procedure

1. Take 100 g of crushed aniseed in a conical flask and add 100mL of petroleum ether (of boiling range 60°- 80°C). Close the mouth of the flask with a rubber cork and shake the content well for 5 mins.
2. Leave the content undisturbed for a day. Filter the solution and collect it in a round bottom flask fitted with a condenser. The condenser is attached to a receiver while the round bottom flask is attached to a steam generating vessel as shown below:

Petroleum ether is volatile and highly flammable so, keep it away from flames.

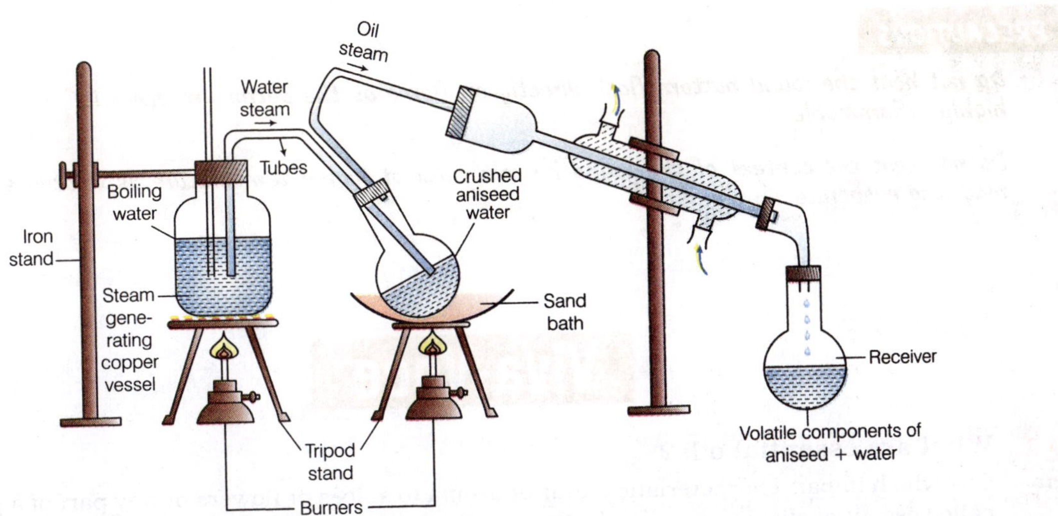

Extraction of essential oil by steam distillation

3. A current of steam generated by the steam generating copper vessel as shown above is passed through delivery tubes into round bottom flask where steam volatile components of aniseed pass through the condenser along with the steam. These contents after condensation are collected in a receiver.
4. This process is continued for half an hour.
5. Transfer the distilled liquid from receiver to a separating funnel of 250 mL and extract with 10 mL portions of petroleum ether in three times.
6. Collect the petroleum ether extract in a conical flask and dry it with the help of anhydrous sodium sulphate.
7. Distil off the solvent by carrying out distillation on a water bath leaving behind the essential oil.
8. Note the colour, odour and weight of the essential oil.
9. Repeat this experiment with carom and cardamom seeds also.

Note *To prevent excessive condensation of steam, the content that is present in round bottom flask may be heated by a Bunsen burner.*

Observations

Weight of the flask in which extract of oil is taken = x g

Weight of the flask in which only oil is left behind = y g

$$\text{Weight of oil} = (x - y)\text{g}$$

S. No.	Essential oil of	Colour	Odour	Weight $(x-y)$ g
1.	Aniseed			
2.	Carom			
3.	Cardamom			

Result

1. 100 g of crushed aniseed yielded .... mL of its essential oil.
2. 100 g of crushed carom yielded .... mL of its essential oil.
3. 100 g of crushed cardamom yielded .... mL of its essential oil.

PRECAUTIONS

- *Do not heat the round bottom flask directly on flame as the petroleum ether is highly inflammable.*
- *Do not heat the content of the round bottom flask at higher temperature as volatile essential oil may also evaporate.*

Viva-Voce

Q.1 What are essential oils?

Ans. Oils which impart characteristic odour or aroma to spices or flowers or any part of a plant is called essential oils.

Q.2 Give example of any two essential oils and write their uses.

Ans. (i) Agar oil is used for fragrance.

(ii) Eucalyptus oil is used as a germicide.

Q.3 Mixture *A* contains two components having boiling points 75°C and 110°C and mixture *B* contains two components both having boiling points nearly 90°C. Which of these two mixtures can be separated by fractional distillation process and why?

Ans. Mixture *A* because of significant difference in boiling point of the two components.

Q.4 Why is petroleum ether used for the extraction of essential oils?

Ans. Essential oils are more soluble in petroleum ether than water so, oils can be easily extracted from petroleum ether.

Project 8

AIM

To study the common food adulterants in fat, oil, butter, sugar, turmeric powder, chilli powder and pepper.

Theory/Principle

Food product sellers sometime mix cheaper but having similar appearance substances to a foodstuff partially with a motive to earn more profits. This substituted substance not only lowers the quality of taste and nutrition but also causes serious health hazard to people consuming it. This practice of mixing is called **adulteration**. Sometimes, seeds, barks, leaves and other matter are dressed upto look like genuine foodstuffs and are used to adulterate pure ones.

Adulteration in Spices

Like powdered bran and sawdust may be present in ground spices. e.g. Sawdust is added to the turmeric powder, artificial colours are added to the chilli powder. Easily obtainable seeds are substituted for cumin, cardamom, black pepper, mustard seeds, etc.

Adulteration in Oils

Edible oils and fats are adulterated with cheap edible and non-edible oils. Seeds of Argemone Mexicana resemble mustard and are used to mix with mustard seeds and oil extracted from seeds is used to adultrate oils such as coconut, mustard, sesame and groundnut. Argemone oil is poisonous and its use results in epidermic dropsy in human beings. Oils and fats are also adulterated with petroleum products which cause gastrointestinal disorders.

Adulteration in Flours

Talc and chalk powder are used to adulterate wheat flour, arrowroot powder and confectionary. Starch is used as a filler in milk and milk products.

Coaltar dyes and mineral pigments like lead chromate and red or yellow earth are common food adulterants used for colouring milk products, confectionary, soft drinks, beverages, tea, spices, bakery products, fruits and vegetables to give better look. Although, the adulterants food substitutes look visibly indifferent but they can be detected easily by chemical methods.

Table. Some common food products and their adulterants

S. No.	Foodstuff	Adulterants
1.	Tea	Exhausted tea leaves, coloured sawdust
2.	Oil and fats	Cheap, non-edible oils
3.	Wheat flour	Talc and chalk powder
4.	Sugar	Chalk, washing soda
5.	Black pepper	Dried Papaya seeds
6.	Butter and Desi ghee	Vanaspati, paraffin wax, starch materials
7.	Milk	Water, fatless milk, starch
8.	Salt	Chalk powder
9.	Red chilli powder	Brick powder or injurious colours
10.	Rice	Stone chips, resembling rice
11.	Masoor bengal gram dal, red gram dal, black gram and channa	Khesari dal

Note *Consumption of khesari dal causes paralysis of lower limbs.*

Materials Required

- Test tubes : As per need
- Burner : 1
- Glass tumbler : 1
- Black pepper : As per need
- Sugar : As per need
- Turmeric powder : As per need
- Chilli powder : As per need
- Potassium iodide : As per need
- Conc. HCl : As per need
- Dilute and Conc. H_2SO_4 : As per need
- Glacial CH_3COOH : As per need
- Butter : As per need
- Red chilli powder : As per need
- Fats/Oil : As per need
- Dilute HNO_3 : As per need
- Distilled water : As per need

Procedure

A. To Test Vanaspati Ghee in Butter

1. Take about 1 g of butter sample in a test tube and heat it gently to melt it.
2. Add about 0.5 g of sugar and 4-5 drops of HCl. Shake the mixture for 5-6 mins.
3. Note down the change in colour of the mixture, if any.

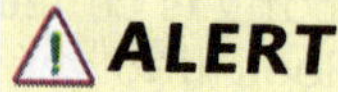

ALERT

Conc. H_2SO_4 and conc. HCl are highly corrosive and skin irritant.

B. To Test Dyes in Fats and Oils

1. Take about 1 mL of the given fat or oil in a test tube. Add 1 mL of the mixture of conc. H_2SO_4 and glacial acetic acid in the ratio 1:4.
2. Shake the content gently and heat it moderately.
3. Note down the change of colour, if any.

C. To Test Chalk in Sugar

1. Take about 1g of sugar in a test tube and add 2 mL of dilute H_2SO_4 in it.
2. Observe the effervescence evolved, if any.

D. To Test Papaya Seeds in Black Pepper

1. Take beaker half-filled with water and add about 5 g of black pepper in it.
2. Observe if any seed floats on water surface or not.

E. To Test Artificial Colour in Chilli Powder

1. Take a glass tumbler filled with distilled water and add about 5 g of red chilli powder in it.
2. Stir the mixture well using a glass rod and allow it to stand for 8-10 mins.
3. Note down if brick red colour is appeared in water or not.

F. To Test Red Lead Salts in Chilli Powder

1. In a beaker add 1g chilli powder and dil. HNO_3.
2. Filter the solution, to filtrate add 2 drops of potassium iodide solution.
3. Observe if any change occur.

G. To Test Coloured Sawdust with Coaltar Dye in Turmeric Powder

1. Take about 2 g of turmeric powder in a test tube and add 5-6 drops of conc. HCl into it .
2. Observe the change in colour, if any.

H. To Test Coloured Chalk Powder in Turmeric Powder

1. Take about 0.5 g of turmeric powder in a test tube and add 1 mL of dilute H_2SO_4.
2. Observe the effervescence evolved, if any.

Observations

S.No.	Tested foodstuff	Procedure	Observation	Inference
1.	Butter	Sample + sugar + HCl	Colour of mixture changes to pink.	Vanaspati ghee is present.
2.	Fats and oils	Sample + H_2SO_4 + CH_3COOH + heat	Appearance of pink colour.	Non-edible dyes are present.
3.	Sugar	Sample + H_2SO_4	Evolution of effervescence.	Chalk is present.
4.	Black pepper	Sample + water	Floatation of some seeds.	Papaya seeds are present.
5.	Chilli powder	Sample + distilled water	Brick red colour appeared in water.	Artificial colour is present.
6.	Chilli powder	Sample + $HNO_3 \longrightarrow$ filtrate + KI solution	Yellow ppt. formed.	Lead salt present in chilli powder.
7.	Turmeric powder	Sample + conc. HCl	Violet colour appears which persists on dilution with distilled water.	Coloured sawdust is present.
8.	Turmeric powder	Sample + dil. H_2SO_4	Evolution of effervescence	Coloured chalk powder is present.

Result

Adulteration found in the following foodstuffs:

1. Butter : .... (Yes/No)
2. Fats/oils : .... (Yes/No)
3. Sugar : .... (Yes/No)
4. Black pepper : .... (Yes/No)
5. Chilli powder : .... (Yes/No)
6. Turmeric powder : .... (Yes/No)

PRECAUTIONS

- *Handle the HCl and H_2SO_4 carefully.*
- *Avoid overheating of any sample mixture as it may alter the test result.*

Viva-Voce

Q.1 Define adulterants.

Ans. Adulterants are the cheaper and usually harmful substances mixed in foods with a motive to earn more profit by the sellers.

Q.2 Give examples of any two types of adulteration.

Ans. (i) Mixing of chalk in sugar.

(ii) Mixing of coloured sawdust in turmeric powder.

Q.3 Why sugar adulterate with chalk evolve effervescence on reaction with H_2SO_4?

Ans. Because H_2SO_4 reacts with calcium carbonate (of chalk) and evolve CO_2 as effervescence.

$$CaCO_3 + H_2SO_4 \longrightarrow CaSO_4 + H_2O + CO_2\uparrow$$

Q.4 Why adulterated butter gives pink colour on treatment with HCl?

Ans. Because butter is adulterated with vanaspati ghee which contains sesame oil. The sesame oil on reaction with HCl gives pink colour.

Q.5 Which is the most useful reagent to test adulterated food?

Ans. Hydrochloric acid.

Q.6 What are the common adulterants in desi ghee?

Ans. Vanaspati ghee or paraffin wax.

Q.7 How will you detect the presence of lead salts in turmeric powder?

Ans. Dissolve 0.1 g of turmeric powder in 2-3 mL of dilute HNO_3 and filter the solution. Add KI solution to the filtrate, appearance of yellow precipitate indicates the presence of lead salts.

Some Important Laboratory Reagents

A. Strengths of Concentrated Acid Solutions

S.No.	Acid	Specific gravity	Percentage by mass	Approximate strength
1.	Glacial acetic acid (CH_3COOH)	1.05	99.5	17 M
2.	Hydrochloric acid (HCl)	1.18	37	12 M
3.	Nitric acid (HNO_3)	1.41	70	16 M
4.	Sulphuric acid (H_2SO_4)	1.84	96	18 M
5.	Phosphoric acid (H_3PO_4)	1.69	85	14.8 M

Note *Concentrated acids are directly used as supplied.*

B. Preparation of Commonly used Dilute Solutions of Acids

S.No.	Name of acid	Concentration	Method of preparation
1.	Dil. sulphuric acid (H_2SO_4)	1.25 M (2.5 N)	Add 111 mL of conc. H_2SO_4 slowly and with constant stirring in 500 mL of distilled water. Cool and make up the volume to 1L.
2.	Dil. hydrochloric acid (HCl)	2.5 M (2.5 N)	Add dropwise 333.3 mL of conc. HCl in the distilled water and make up the volume to 1L.
3.	Dil. acetic acid (CH_3COOH)	2.5 M (2.5 N)	Add 147 mL of glacial acetic acid slowly and with constant stirring in distilled water. Cool and make up the volume to 1L.
4.	Dil. nitric acid (HNO_3)	2.5 M (2.5 N)	Add 156.2 mL of conc. HNO_3 to distilled water and make up the volume to 1L.

C. Preparation of Commonly used Dilute Solutions of Bases

S.No.	Name of base	Concentration	Method of preparation
1.	Dil. sodium hydroxide (NaOH)	2.5 M (2.5 N)	Dissolve 100 g of NaOH pellets in 1L of distilled water.
2.	Dil. potassium hydroxide (KOH)	2 M (2N)	Dissolve 125 g KOH pellets in 1L of distilled water.
3.	Lime water, $Ca(OH)_2$	0.02M (0.04 N)	Shake 2-3 g of calcium hydroxide [$Ca(OH)_2$] with 1 L distilled water filter the solution after sometime and keep in a reagent bottle.
4.	Dil. ammonium hydroxide solution, NH_4OH	2 M (2 N)	Pour 133.3 mL of conc. ammonia solution in distilled water and make up the volume to 1L.
5.	Dil. ammonia solution	15 M (15 N)	Used as directly supplied.

D. Preparation of Salt Solutions

S.No.	Name of the salt	Concentration	Method of preparation
1.	Ammonium acetate (CH_3COONH_4)	2M (2N)	Dissolve 154 g of the ammonium acetate salt in the distilled water and dilute to 1L.
2.	Ammonium carbonate [$(NH_4)_2CO_3$]	1.7 M (3.5 N)	Dissolve 160 g of ammonium carbonate in 140 mL liquor ammonia and make up the solution to 1 L with distilled water.
3.	Ammonium chloride, (NH_4Cl)	5 M (5N)	Dissolve 267.5 g of the salt in distilled water and dilute to 1L.
4.	Ammonium molybdate [$(NH_4)_6Mo_7O_{24}\cdot 4H_2O$]	0.5 M	Dissolve 88 g of molybdate salt in a mixture of liquor ammonia solution 120 mL conc. ammonia solution + 80 mL distilled water) and add 240 g of ammonium nitrate and dilute to 1L with distilled water.
5.	Ammonium oxalate $(COONH_4)_2$	0.5 M (1 N)	Dissolve 71 g of ammonium oxalate salt in distilled water and dilute to 1L.
6.	Ammonium sulphate $(NH_4)_2SO_4$	1 M(2 N)	Dissolve 132 g of the salt in distilled water and dilute to 1L.
7.	Ammonium thiocyanate (NH_4CNS)	0.25 M (0.5 N)	Dissolve 38 g of the salt in 1L water.
8.	Calcium chloride ($CaCl_2$)	0.5 M (0.5 N)	Dissolve 55 g of the salt in distilled water and dilute to 1L.
9.	Copper sulphate ($CuSO_4 \cdot 5H_2O$)	0.5 M (0.5 N)	Dissolve 125 g of crystalline salt in 500 mL water, add 3 mL concentrated sulphuric acid and dilute to 1L.
10.	Cobalt nitrate [$Co(NO_3) \cdot 6H_2O$]	0.15 M (0.3 N)	Dissolve 44 g of the salt in distilled water and make up the volume to 1L.
11.	Disodium hydrogen phosphate ($Na_2HPO_4 \cdot 12H_2O$)	0.3 M	Dissolve 107.4 g of the salt in distilled water and make up the volume to 1L.
12.	Ferric chloride ($FeCl_3 \cdot 6H_2O$)	0.33 M	Dissolve 90 g of the salt in distilled water containing 10 mL of conc. HCl and make up the volume to 1L.
13.	Ferrous sulphate ($FeSO_4 \cdot 7H_2O$)	0.5 M	Dissolve 140 g of the salt in about 500 mL water, add 7 mL of conc. H_2SO_4 and dilute to 1L.
14.	Lead acetate [$(CH_3COO)_2Pb \cdot 3H_2O$]	0.5 M	Dissolve 189.7 g of lead acetate salt in 500 mL of distilled water containing 15 mL acetic acid and make up the volume to 1L with distilled water.
15.	Magnesium sulphate ($MgSO_4 \cdot 7H_2O$)	0.25 M	Dissolve 61.6 g of the salt in 1L water.
16.	Mercuric chloride ($HgCl_2$)	0.25 M (0.5 N)	Dissolve 67.9 g of the salt in small amount of distilled water and make up the volume to 1L.
17.	Potassium chromate (K_2CrO_4)	0.25 M (0.5 N)	Dissolve 49 g of the salt in distilled water and dilute to 1L.
18.	Potassium dichromate ($K_2Cr_2O_7$)	0.1 M (0.6 N)	Dissolve 29.4 g of the salt in distilled water and make up the volume to 1L.
19.	Potassium ferrocyanide $K_4[Fe(CN)_6] \cdot 3H_2O$	0.1 M	Dissolve 42.2 g of the salt in distilled water and dilute to 1L.
20.	Potassium ferricyanide $K_3[Fe(CN)_6]$	0.2 M	Dissolve 65.8 g of the salt in distilled water and dilute to 1L.

E. Preparation of Common Lab Reagents

S.No.	Name of the Reagents	Concentration	Method of Preparation
1.	Bromine water (Br_2)	0.5 N	Prepare saturated solution by shaking 11 mL of liquid bromine with water keep it in a dark bottle.
2.	Chlorine water (Cl_2)	3 N	Prepare chlorine gas by treating solid $KMnO_4$ with conc. HCl. Saturate one litre of distilled water with chlorine gas and keep the solution in a dark coloured bottle.
3.	Dimethyl glyoxime ($C_4H_8O_2N_2$)	1 %	Dissolve 10 g of the white needle shaped solid dimethyl glyoxime in 1L ethyl alcohol.
4.	Diphenyl amine $(C_6H_5)_2NH$	0.5 N	Dissolve 0.5 g of the solid diphenyl amine in 85 mL of conc. H_2SO_4 and dilute it with distilled water to 100 mL.
5.	Hydrogen peroxide (H_2O_2)	—	Used as 3 % commercial solution
6.	Iodine solution (I_2)	0.1 N	Dissolve 12.7 g of iodine in a solution of 20 g of pure KI in 30 mL of water and dilute to 1L with water.
7.	Magnesia mixture	—	Dissolve 55 g hydrated magnesium chloride and 70 g ammonium chloride in 650 mL water and add 350 mL conc. ammonia.
8.	Nessler's reagent ($K_2[HgI_4]$)	—	Dissolves 3.5 g potassium iodide in 10 mL water. Add 1.7 g mercuric chloride solution slowly to the prepared KI solution until a permanent precipitate occurs. Dilute the precipitate to 100 mL with 10% diluted NaOH NaOH solution.
9.	Alkaline solution of Nessler's reagent (K_2HgI_4)	—	Dissolve 10 g of KI solution in 10 mL of ammonia free water. Add saturated $HgCl_2$ solution 160 g per litre in small quantities at a time and shake the solution until a slight permanent precipitate forms. Then add 80 mL of 9 N NaOH solution and dilute to 200 mL. Allow to stand overnight and decant off the clear liquid.
10.	Sodium nitroprusside $Na_2[Fe(CN)_5NO]$	—	Dissolve 4 g of the solid in 100 mL of distilled water.
11.	Yellow ammonium sulphide $[(NH_4)_2S_x]$	—	Take about 200 mL of conc. ammonia solution in a bottle and saturate it with H_2S gas. Add 10g of sulphur and 200 mL of conc. NH_4OH. Warm gently and shake well until sulphur is completely dissolved. Dilute the solution to 1L with distilled water.
12.	Buffer solution in non-aqueous media [for EDTA titration]	—	Dissolve 67.5 g of ammonium chloride in 570 mL of conc. NH_3 solution and dilute of 1L.
13.	Eriochrome black-T (EBT) in non-aqueous media (indicator for EDTA titration)	—	Dissolve 0.5 g of solid eriochrome black-T in methanol and make up the volume to 100 mL.

APPENDIX 2

Preparation of Special Reagents Used for Organic Analysis

S.No.	Name of the reagent	Method of preparation
1.	Alcohol [1:1]	Mix equal volumes of rectified spirit and distilled water.
2.	Alcoholic (KOH)	Dissolve 12g of KOH in 100 mL ethanol by boiling for 30 minutes.
3.	Alkaline β-naphthol	Dissolve 10g of β-naphthol in 100 mL of 10% NaOH solution.
4.	Bromine in carbon tetrachloride	Shake 4 mL of liquid bromine with 100 mL of CCl_4 and stopper the bottle.
5.	Barfoed's reagent	Dissolve 13g of copper acetate in 200 mL of 1% acetic acid.
6.	Benedict's solution	Dissolve 17.3g of crystalline copper sulphate in 100 mL of water. Separately dissolve 173g of sodium citrate and 100 g of anhydrous sodium carbonate in 800 mL of water. Mix both the solutions and dilute to 1L.
7.	Ceric ammonium nitrate solution	Dissolve 40 g of the reagent in 100 mL of 2N nitric acid.
8.	2, 4-dinitrophenylhydrazine reagent	
	(i) For water soluble compounds	Add 0.5 g solid in a mixture of 42 mL conc. HCl and 54 mL water and dissolve by warming on water bath. Add water to make up the volume to 250 mL.
	(ii) For compounds not soluble in water	Dissolve 1 g of reagent in 7.5 mL conc. sulphuric acid. Add this solution gradually to 7.5 mL rectified spirit. Make up the volume to 250 mL by adding water.
9.	*Fehling's solution *A*	Dissolve 69.28 g of copper sulphate crystals in 1L of water.
10.	*Fehling's solution *B*	Dissolve 350 g of Rochelle's salt and 100 g sodium hydroxide in 1L of water.
11.	Hydroxylamine hydrochloride	Dissolve 69.5 g of dry solid in 1L of methyl alcohol.
12.	Molisch's reagent	Dissolve 10 g of 1-naphthol in 100 mL of rectified spirit.
13.	Ninhydrin reagent	Prepare 0.25% aqueous solution.
14.	Potassium permanganate	Prepare 1% aqueous solution.
15.	Schiff's reagent	Dissolve 1 g of rosaniline in 50 mL water with gentle warming, cool, saturate with sulphur dioxide gas. Dilute the solution upto 1L with water. If pink colour reappears on standing add few drops of saturated aqueous solution of SO_2 with stirring until the colour just disappears.
16.	Seliwanoff's reagent	Dissolve 1 g of resorcinol in 100 mL of 20% hydrochloric acid.
17.	Sodium hypochlorite (2M)	Dissolve 100 g of NaOH in 20 mL of water in a large beaker. Cool the solution and add about 500 g of crushed ice. Weigh the beaker on a rough balance and pass chlorine gas until the weight increases by 72 g. Dilute the solution to 1L with water. The solution must be kept in a cool dark place. Even then it slowly decomposes.
18.	Tollen's reagent	To 1 mL of 2% solution of silver nitrate add 1 mL of 10% sodium hydroxide till the precipitate just appears. Add solution of ammonium hydroxide with stirring till the solution becomes clear. Ammonium hydroxide should not be added in excess. Always use fresh Tollen's reagent.

APPENDIX 3

Indicators and their Preparation

A. Preparation of Some Important Indicators

S. No.	Name of indicator	Preparation	Strength
1.	Phenolphthalein	In 100 mL ethyl alcohol dissolve 1g of phenolphthalein.	1%
2.	Methyl orange	In 1L of distilled water dissolve 1g of the solid.	0.1%
3.	Methyl red	Dissolve 1g of the solid in 600 mL of ethyl alcohol and dilute with 400 mL of water.	0.1%
4.	Litmus solution (blue)	Add 1g of solid blue litmus in 1L of distilled water.	1%
5.	Litmus solution (red)	Add 100 g drops of dil. HCl to the prepared blue litmus solution until it changes to red.	1%

B. Preparation of Test Papers

S. No.	Name of the test papers	Method of preparation
1.	Dichromate paper	Dissolve a crystal of solid potassium dichromate ($K_2Cr_2O_7$) in a test tube containing water. Soak the filter paper sheet in it and dry in air and cut into small strips.
2.	Lead acetate paper	Dissolve 10 g of lead acetate in 100 mL water in a beaker or China dish soak the filter paper sheet in it, dry it away from H_2S and cut into small strips.
3.	Litmus paper	Soak a filter paper sheet in litmus solution dry in shade and cut into small strips.
4.	Starch paper	Soak filter paper sheet in starch solution, dry and cut into small strips.
5.	Starch iodide paper	Mix equal quantities of starch solution and potassium iodide in a beaker or China dish. Soak a filter paper sheet in it and dry in air and cut into small pieces.

APPENDIX 4

Equivalent Weights of Common Chemicals

A. Equivalent Weights of Common Acids

S. No.	Acids	Chemical formulae	Molecular weight (*MW*)	Equivalent weight (*MW*/Basicity)
	Monobasic			
1.	Hydrochloric acid	HCl	36.5	$\frac{36.5}{1} = 36.5$
2.	Acetic acid	CH_3COOH	60	60 / 1 = 60
	Dibasic			
3.	Anhydrous oxalic acid	COOH | COOH	90	90 / 2 = 45
4.	Hydrated oxalic acid	COOH | $\cdot 2H_2O$ COOH	126	126 / 2 = 63
5.	Sulphuric acid	H_2SO_4	98	98 / 2 = 49
	Tribasic			
6.	Phosphoric acid	H_3PO_4	98	98 / 3 = 32.67

Experiment No.________ Date ________ Page No. ________

Teacher Signature________________

Experiment No.________ Date ________ Page No. ________

Teacher Signature________________

Experiment No.________ Date ________ Page No. ________

Teacher Signature ________________

Experiment No.________ Date ________ Page No. ________

Teacher Signature________________

Experiment No.________ Date ________ Page No. ________

Teacher Signature____________________

Experiment No.________ Date ________ Page No. ________

Teacher Signature ________________

Experiment No.________ Date ________ Page No. ________

Teacher Signature ________________

Experiment No.________ Date ________ Page No. ________

Teacher Signature________________

Experiment No.________ Date ________ Page No. ________

Teacher Signature________________

Experiment No.________ Date ________ Page No. ________

Teacher Signature________________

Experiment No.________ Date ________ Page No. ________

Teacher Signature________________

Experiment No.________ Date ________ Page No. ________

Teacher Signature________________

Experiment No.________ Date ________ Page No. ________

Teacher Signature________________

Experiment No.________ Date ________ Page No. ________

Teacher Signature________________

Experiment No.________ Date ________ Page No. ________

Teacher Signature________________

Experiment No.________ Date ________ Page No. ________

Teacher Signature________________

Experiment No.________ Date ________ Page No. ________

Teacher Signature________________

Experiment No.________ Date ________ Page No. ________

Teacher Signature________________

Experiment No.________ Date ________ Page No. ________

Teacher Signature ________________

Experiment No.________ Date ________ Page No. ________

Teacher Signature________________

Experiment No.________ Date ________ Page No. ________

Teacher Signature________________

Experiment No.________ Date ________ Page No. ________

Teacher Signature ________________

Experiment No.______ Date ______ Page No. ______

Teacher Signature ______

Experiment No.________ Date ________ Page No. ________

Teacher Signature ________________

Experiment No.________ Date ________ Page No. ________

Teacher Signature________________

Experiment No.________ Date ________ Page No. ________

Teacher Signature________________

Experiment No.________ Date ________ Page No. ________

Teacher Signature________________

Experiment No.________ Date ________ Page No. ________

Teacher Signature________________

Experiment No.________ Date ________ Page No. ________

Teacher Signature________________

Experiment No.________ Date ________ Page No. ________

Teacher Signature________________

Experiment No.________ Date ________ Page No. ________

Teacher Signature________________

Experiment No.________ Date ________ Page No. ________

Teacher Signature________________

Experiment No.________ Date ________ Page No. ________

Teacher Signature________________

Experiment No.________ Date ________ Page No. ________

Teacher Signature________________

Experiment No.________ Date ________ Page No. ________

Teacher Signature________________

Experiment No.________ Date ________ Page No. ________

Teacher Signature ________

Experiment No.________ Date ________ Page No. ________

Teacher Signature________________

Experiment No.________ Date ________ Page No. ________

Teacher Signature________________

Experiment No.________ Date ________ Page No. ________

Teacher Signature ________________

Experiment No.________ Date ________ Page No. ________

Teacher Signature________________

Experiment No.________ Date ________ Page No. ________

Teacher Signature________________

Experiment No.________ Date ________ Page No. ________

Teacher Signature________________

Experiment No.________ Date ________ Page No. ________

Teacher Signature________________

Experiment No.________ Date ________ Page No. ________

Teacher Signature____________________

Experiment No.________ Date ________ Page No. ________

Teacher Signature________________

Experiment No.________ Date ________ Page No. ________

Teacher Signature________________

Experiment No.________ Date ________ **Page No.** ________

Teacher Signature________________

Experiment No.________ Date ________ Page No. ________

Teacher Signature________________

Experiment No.________ Date ________ Page No. ________

Teacher Signature________________

Experiment No.________ Date ________ Page No. ________

Teacher Signature________________

Experiment No.________ Date ________ Page No. ________

Teacher Signature________________

Experiment No.________ Date ________ Page No. ________

Teacher Signature________________

Experiment No.________ Date ________ Page No. ________

Teacher Signature________________

Experiment No.________ Date ________ Page No. ________

Teacher Signature________________

Experiment No.________ Date ________ Page No. ________

Teacher Signature________________

Experiment No.________ Date ________ Page No. ________

Teacher Signature________________

Experiment No.________ Date ________ Page No. ________

Teacher Signature________________

Experiment No.________ Date ________ Page No. ________

Teacher Signature________________

Experiment No.________ Date ________ Page No. ________

Teacher Signature________________

Experiment No.________ Date ________ Page No. ________

Teacher Signature________________

Experiment No.________ Date ________ Page No. ________

Teacher Signature________________

Experiment No.________ Date ________ Page No. ________

Teacher Signature________________

Experiment No.________ Date ________ **Page No.** ________

Teacher **Signature**________________

Experiment No.________ Date ________ Page No. ________

Teacher Signature____________________

Experiment No.________ Date ________ Page No. ________

Teacher Signature________________

Experiment No.________ Date ________ Page No. ________

Teacher Signature________________

Experiment No.________ Date ________ Page No. ________

Teacher Signature________________

Experiment No.________ Date ________ Page No. ________

Teacher Signature________________

Experiment No.________ Date ________ Page No. ________

Teacher Signature ________________

Experiment No.________ Date ________ Page No. ________

Teacher Signature________________

Experiment No.________ Date ________ Page No. ________

Teacher Signature________________

Experiment No.________ Date ________ Page No. ________

Teacher Signature ________________

Experiment No.________ Date ________ Page No. ________

Teacher Signature ________________

Experiment No.________ Date ________ Page No. ________

Teacher Signature ________________

Experiment No.________ Date ________ Page No. ________

Teacher Signature________________

Experiment No.________ Date ________ Page No. ________

Teacher Signature________________

Experiment No.________ Date ________ Page No. ________

Teacher Signature________________

Experiment No.________ Date ________ Page No. ________

Teacher Signature________________

Experiment No.________ Date ________ Page No. ________

Teacher Signature________________

Experiment No.________ Date ________ Page No. ________

Teacher Signature________________